CITIZEN
TEACHER

Margaret Haley, 1920s (Courtesy Chicago Historical Society)

I believe thoroughly that the public school must become a more potent, conscious, and recognized factor in the civic life of the large communities, and this work can go along with the work of securing better conditions for teachers; indeed, it is an essential part of it.

—Margaret Haley, 1903

Cautious, careful people, always casting about to preserve their reputation and social standing, never can bring about a reform. Those who are really in earnest must be willing to be anything or nothing in the world's estimation.

—Susan B. Anthony, 1860

CITIZEN

TEACHER

*The Life and Leadership
of Margaret Haley*

KATE ROUSMANIERE

STATE UNIVERSITY OF NEW YORK PRESS

Published by
STATE UNIVERSITY OF NEW YORK PRESS, ALBANY

© 2005 State University of New York

Printed in the United States of America

For information, address State University of New York Press,
194 Washington Avenue, Suite 305, Albany, NY 12210-2365

Production, Laurie Searl
Marketing, Susan Petrie

Library of Congress Cataloging-in-Publication Data

Rousmaniere, Kate, 1958–
    Citizen teacher : the life and leadership of Margaret Haley / Kate Rousmaniere.
        p. cm.
    Includes bibliographical references and index.
    ISBN 0-7914-6487-3 (alk. paper) — ISBN 0-7914-6488-1 (pbk. alk. paper)
    1. Haley, Margaret A. 2. Teachers—United States—Biography. 3. Women teachers—United States—Biography. 4. Labor unions—United States—Officials and employees—Biography. 5. Teachers' unions—United States—History. I. Title.

LA2317.H26R68 2005
371.1'0092—dc22   200406585

10 9 8 7 6 5 4 3 2 1

CONTENTS

ACKNOWLEDGMENTS

I am indebted to my colleagues in the Department of Educational Leadership at Miami University, Ohio, citizen teachers one and all.

The Spencer Foundation supported me with two grants to further this work, and the Newberry Library in Chicago gave me one year of peace to write. I am also grateful to the American Federation of Teachers' Albert Shanker Fellowship for Research in Education, administered through the Walter P. Reuther Library, Wayne State University.

Many thanks are due to a number of libraries and their stewards, especially the late, great Archie Motley at the Chicago Historical Society, and Piriya Metcalfe of the CHS photography division, Dan Golodner at the Walter Reuther Library, Debby Steffers of the Morris Public Library, and Ed Via of Miami University's Interlibrary Loan Office. Permissions for reproduction of photographs and printed material are from the Jane Addams Memorial Collection and the Chicago Historical Society.

Other scholars have helped me to conceptualize the themes of Margaret Haley's life and to articulate her vision to a contemporary audience. Wayne Urban paved the way for this biography with his scholarship in the history of teachers, and his friendship and counsel has guided much of my thinking in this venture. Long conversations with Jackie Blount about women in educational leadership, past and present, helped to resurrect Margaret Haley's spirit. The Teachers' Work/Teachers' Union Special Interest Group of AERA has provided good companionship, and I am especially thankful to Joe Newman, Harry Smaller, Chris Murray, Lois Weiner, and Kathleen Murphey for their support. The Biography and Archives SIG of AERA has supported this and other creative ventures into biography. Sharon Lane conducted some critical early research. Elliott Gorn helped in countless ways. Other colleagues who have advised, accompanied, and supported my work on this project are: Nancy Beadie, Cathy Burke, Mary Kupiec Cayton, Geraldine Clifford, Kari Dehli, Linda Eisenmann, Barry Franklin, Connie Goddard, Joyce Goodman, Jim Grossman, Ian Grosvenor, Kathleen Knight

Abowitz, Martin Lawn, Valinda Littlefield, John Lyons, Jane Martin, Yoon Pak, Stephen Provasnik, Sally Schwaeger, Frank Simon, Marjorie Theobald, Alan Wieder, Kathleen Weiler, Ruth Watts, and Roberta Wollons. John Bercaw helped Margaret Haley to become more human.

This book is dedicated to my mother and the memory of my father—two civic hearts.

INTRODUCTION

CITIZEN TEACHER

MARGARET HALEY BELIEVED that the public school was the heart of democracy and that teachers were its life blood. For the first forty years of the twentieth century, this Chicago elementary school teacher took to the national stage, arguing that public education was the primary civic and economic responsibility of the state. As the dynamic leader of the first American teachers' union, she inspired thousands of the nation's women elementary teachers to conceive of themselves as political beings, and she initiated a nationwide struggle for democratic management and fiscal equity in public education.

Margaret Haley's life goal was to educate American citizens about the political economy of schooling. She did this through popular campaigns in which she instructed the public about school finance while exposing corporate tax deductions that drained school budgets, arguing that such practices not only undercut the quality education of a majority of the nation's children, but also perverted democracy. Her legal suit demanding that some of the leading Chicago corporations pay their required taxes to support public schooling remains one of the great battles in American educational history, and it designates Margaret Haley as the first watchdog for equitable school funding.

Haley also argued for democracy in the content and character of educational practice. She objected to the increasing rigidity and standardization that she saw developing in early-twentieth-century schools, calling it "factoryizing education," where the teacher became "an automaton, a mere factory hand" who was required to mechanically carry out the orders of distant school administrators.[1] She proposed an alternative model of schools as democratic workplaces where teachers' professional authority and children's natural interest drove the school day. If the school could not "bring joy to the work of the world," she argued, then "joy must go out of its own life, and work in the school as in the factory will become drudgery."[2] Out of her belief that public education was an integral component of civic improvement, Haley inspired other women teachers to build professional associations, and she led what became America's first teachers' union—the Chicago Teachers' Federation—and encouraged teachers' participation in city, state, and national politics. Haley's commitment to the nurturance of civic activism in a democracy marks her defining characteristic as a "citizen teacher."

The driving force behind all of Haley's activities was her vision of citizenship— that teachers, parents, and children had the right and responsibility to be involved in the democratic process. In the years before women could vote, and before most Americans even earned a high school diploma, Margaret Haley asserted that women public school teachers were citizens who were obligated not only to teach citizenship but to engage in public policy decisions. This was an audacious claim, and she electrified the public as she built a nationwide labor movement for women teachers. Charismatic, ambitious, and fearless, Haley fought for economic and political equity for the disenfranchised, leading the media to call her the Joan of Arc of classroom teachers, a feminine social warrior, who was a "modern knight in a gown."[3] She herself described her life's work as a populist "battleground" in which she had beaten her fists "against stone walls of power and privilege."[4] She saw her struggle for equitable school funding and democratic education as nothing less than a war over the soul of American democracy.

Most American teachers do not know of Margaret Haley. I never heard her name while teaching high school, although I worked with an activist group of teachers who would have been energized by her vision. Only in graduate school did I learn about Haley when I read the few published historical studies that heralded her as a radical school reformer, labor activist, and feminist leader who boldly challenged common stereotypes of the demure lady schoolteacher. I was inspired by Haley's outright advocacy of teachers' participation in school management and her charismatic leadership style that drew women elementary teachers out of their classroom into an assertive political unit. And I was intrigued by the way she twisted her identity as a female school teacher into a belligerent public activist, designing into her own version of public leadership a feminist deviation of President Theodore Roosevelt's dictum, "speak softly and carry a big stick." "I didn't have a big stick," she quipped in her aptly titled autobiography *Battleground*, "but I had a little one with nails in it."[5] For all teachers, but especially women teachers who work for school improvement and social justice, Haley is a powerful role model.

As I engaged in more in-depth research on Margaret Haley, I began to understand some of what was behind this dynamic image. More than a firebrand troublemaker on the political margins, Haley was also an advocate for comprehensive structural change in public school systems. Throughout her long public career, she saw equitable economics as the key to equitable education, and she persistently argued that case before local and state legislatures. Long before researchers began to link the poverty level of school communities with unequal educational opportunities, Haley argued that all schools needed more funding, and that the absence of sufficient school funding indicated the failure of civic responsibility. The wealthy held a greater burden of responsibility than the poor, but all citizens were responsible for upholding their end of the social contract by supporting public education. To Haley, taxes reminded citizens of their common commitment to their common nation.

Haley's vision of economic equity and civic responsibility has not survived in contemporary education, and the effects of that loss have been devastating. As her biographer, I have often imagined how furious she would be if she saw the state of contemporary education. Systematic finance inequities plague the nation's school systems; tax resistance is upheld by political leaders as a civic right; and modern national culture promotes mistrust between citizens and their publicly funded agencies. In my own state, Ohio, for more than a dozen years the legislature has ignored the State Supreme Court order that the school funding system is unconstitutional because it relies too heavily on local property taxes. Less notable, but central to the state's school funding problem, is that income from the corporate franchise tax has lessened from 16 percent of Ohio's revenue to 5 percent.[6] Corporate tax abatements have shifted the burden of property tax onto individuals, yet, as Haley prophesized one hundred years ago, this corporate privilege is excluded from conversations about tax inequity. As I wrote this biography, balancing Haley's vision on one hand and the state of contemporary public education on the other, I often wondered what happened to the mantle of civic responsibility that Margaret Haley handed down, and how it was that such an ethic could be absent from today's public schools.

I share with Margaret Haley the vision that schools need to be central to the social and political calculus of the country, and that teachers need to be protected, rewarded, and respected for their work. Like Haley, I believe that school taxes are a civic investment in the future. This biography is written to reintroduce Haley's vision into the public conversation about schooling, and to offer a historical perspective to the battle for school finance reform. It is also written to inspire contemporary educators with the dynamic story of the teacher leader Margaret Haley who, one hundred years ago, led the first battle for equitable school funding and teachers' professional rights.

CHAPTER ONE

THE EDUCATION OF A TEACHER

MARGARET HALEY WAS THE CHILD of Irish Americans, and in this she was both lucky and unlucky. Among Irish immigrants in nineteenth-century America, her parents were among the most fortunate. The Haleys and the Tiernans left Ireland before the great potato famine killed more than a million Irish and left their survivors destitute. Arriving in the New World in the years before the Civil War, the two families moved west to frontier Illinois where they were able to take advantage of ready jobs and cheap land. Both families scrambled up from poverty to become stable, landowning citizens, so that by the time Margaret Haley was born in 1861, her parents had the economic security to raise a large family with the comforts of many native-born white American families. Haley described her childhood as universally happy, marked by loving parents, a comfortable home, formal education, and the simple pleasures of rural life. But the family also suffered its share of personal tragedies and financial instability, and as working-class Irish Catholics, Margaret Haley's family was socially and economically marginalized. Like other Irish Catholic immigrants, the Haleys responded to such systematic bigotry by unifying among their own and developing dynamic political beliefs about justice and opportunity in American society. They turned to unions and to radical economic politics, even as they maintained a strong belief in the American system through which they had gained their measures of success. This interweaving of fortune and misfortune taught young Margaret Haley about both the great promises and the barriers for working people in America. As a young girl, she learned that life could be good, but that there were also battles to be fought in order to make it better.

Margaret Haley identified strongly with her Irish Catholic roots, particularly in terms of the legacy of political rebellion and "independence of mind."[1] She wrote very little about her parents as individuals, but her few references highlighted their political and cultural identity. Haley's mother, Elizabeth Tiernan, was born in Ireland in 1825, one of Thomas and Bridget Tiernan's thirteen children. As Irish Catholics, Thomas and Bridget were

1

certainly not well-off people. Their granddaughter Margaret thought the family was from Dublin, although it is more likely they were rural people who only came to Dublin on their way out of the country.[2] Regardless, the Tiernans were probably poor, although not destitute; they had enough means to be able to immigrate to the United States in 1827 with their large family and wend their way to the Midwest where they bought land and taught their children to read and write.

The most famous Irish immigration wave to the United States happened as a result of the potato famine of 1845–49, when more than one million Irish perished from starvation and related disease and just as many fled the county. In fact, the Irish had been coming to the United States and Canada before the famine due to smaller incidences of crop failure and disease. Between 1815 and 1845, before the worst of the potato famine even began, more than a million Irish, most of them Catholic, entered the United States escaping both poverty and political repression. Margaret Haley's maternal grandparents, Thomas and Bridget Tiernan, who were born in the late 1770s, would have considered their country occupied by an enemy force. The English had ruled Ireland for centuries, and by 1700, English Protestants controlled three-fourths of Irish land, and were increasingly repressive of Catholic religion and Gaelic culture. The famous Irish Penal Laws, first instituted by the British in the sixteenth century, relegated the majority Irish Catholic population to sub-citizen status, denying them the right to vote, sit in Parliament, practice law, possess weapons, purchase property, or establish schools or teach or speak their native Gaelic language. English control reduced most Catholics to illiterate, poverty–stricken laborers or tenant farmers, but it also energized the Irish Catholic religion, sense of identity, and political outrage. Irish Catholic political activists formed secret societies to lobby, intimidate, and harass English Protestant landowners, and through the eighteenth and nineteenth centuries, guerrilla war raged in parts of rural Ireland. Both Thomas and Bridget would have watched the failed Irish Rebellion of 1798 and the resulting British policy that in 1801 changed Ireland from an embattled colonial entity to an official part of the United Kingdom, an act that, the British hoped, would quell Irish nationalism but which in fact did the reverse.

In the first two decades of the 1800s, Irish nationalist leaders such as Robert Emmett and Daniel O'Connell institutionalized the politics of Irish resistance. Thomas and Bridget would have heard of the squelched rebellion of 1803, which turned into a riot on the streets of Dublin and ended with the execution and martyrdom of Robert Emmett, calling for Irish independence from the gallows. Thomas and Bridget may have finally considered emigration in 1827 for a variety of reasons. Both in their late forties, they may have finally gathered together enough resources for the move. Furthermore, by 1827 an American economic depression had ended and prospects in the New World were vitalized. Also in 1827, the British repealed all restrictions on emigration; passage fares decreased, and more working-class Irish were able to emigrate. All of these conditions led the Tiernans to pack up at least seven of their children and abandon Ireland.

Like most pre-famine Irish immigrants, the Tiernans came to the United States out of a desire for economic independence, and some kind of upward mobility that was not allowed them in Ireland. For a growing number of Irish Catholics, Ireland was a strangled and economically restricted feudal economy; inheritance laws limited land ownership to the eldest son, and the Penal Laws limited economic and professional initiative. For those Irish who were able to consider an alternative, moving to America meant the opportunity for economic self-sufficiency. Political frustration welded with economic frustration, which mixed also with deep ambivalence about leaving the homeland; thus, for pre-famine Irish like the Tiernans, emigration meant both a move toward economic self-sufficiency and a continued connection to Ireland's politics. They were upwardly mobile, but still political radicals.[3]

The Tiernans' upward mobility was not immediate. After leaving Ireland in 1827, they landed in a North American port and moved to a local Irish immigrant community where they lived for up to eight years, gradually gathering their resources. In 1835, when Elizabeth was ten, the family moved to Waukegan, Illinois, just north of the new town of Chicago, where they were among the first settlers in the community. There, the Tiernans fared well. By 1840, sons John and Hugh each bought eighty acres of land and another son, Bartholomew, was elected ward alderman.[4] Landowners and citizens on the American frontier, the Tiernans had reached their goal of economic and social security. When she met her future husband, Elizabeth would have been considered somewhat of a catch—a literate, healthy, young Irish woman from a solid, landowning country family.

Margaret Haley's father was born in the New World. As an adult, Michael Haley alternately reported that he was born in Canada or New York, but with each tale, he highlighted some aspect of his Irish identity and the injustices suffered by the Irish. At one point he reported that as a child he watched the burning of the Ursuline Convent in Charlestown, Massachusetts, by a mob of anti-Catholic Know-Nothings—a secret society of Anglo-Protestant nativists who focused their violent hatred on Catholics.[5] It was this experience, he told his daughter, that brought him west to a place where he hoped to find more opportunity and less bigotry against the Irish. But later in his life, Michael Haley reported that he had been in Ireland during the famine and seen "the poor people of Ireland die of hunger while the land was monopolized by the rich."[6] Yet this story could only be true if Haley had visited Ireland as a young man in the 1840s, the height of the famine—something that seems highly unlikely for a working-class man, especially since, of all American immigrant groups, the Irish were the *least* likely to return to their homeland.[7] Furthermore, by the late 1830s Michael Haley had moved west, not east, to work on the construction of the Illinois and Michigan Canal.

The construction of the Illinois and Michigan Canal between in the 1830s and '40s changed the shape of northern Illinois forever. By linking Lake Michigan, at Chicago, with the Des Plaines and Illinois Rivers, the canal created an uninterrupted navigable waterway between the Great Lakes and St. Louis on the Mississippi River. Stretching one hundred miles, the canal was a massive construction project that required laborers to literally dig an enormous trench through the plains of northern Illinois. The Illinois-Michigan canal builders advertised for working men in Ireland and in the cities on the American east coast. The high population of Irish workers became part of local lore and reinforced a common ethnic stereotype that to dig a canal at least four things were necessary: "a shovel, a pick, a wheelbarrow, and an Irishman."[8] In 1837 ten-year-old Michael Haley joined thousands of Irish Catholic laborers digging out the canal. The project immediately ran into financial difficulties and workers' wages were cut. Short on cash, contractors paid their workers in canal scrip, which the state agreed to accept as payment for state land. Many Irish contractors and laborers, including Michael Haley, used this opportunity to buy their first farm land along the canal so that, by 1850 more than one-third of all the new farmers and landowners in Northern Illinois were Irish.[9]

Working on the canal, men were paid to blast, shovel, and grade ditches in the unprotected, unshaded heat and humidity of the prairie summer and frigid winters. Workers lived in temporary wooden shacks in laborers' shantytowns and were plagued by disease. In 1838 well over five hundred laborers died in a malaria epidemic, spread in part by the mosquitoes that swarmed around the muddy canal ditches.[10] Poverty and exhaustion led to workers' riots and petty jealousy culminating in what the press called "Irish Wars." In 1847, workers organized a two-week-long strike for improved working conditions—a shorter workday, a wage increase, and more humane management. The striking workers described workdays that lasted from 4:30 a.m. to 7:45 p.m. under harsh foremen for $1 a day.[11]

Michael Haley grew up in this hardscrabble and politically charged culture. At ten, he was a "jigger carrier," a job usually assigned to boys who carried the daily allotment of a jigger of whiskey to each worker, an experience that he later said contributed to his life-long abstention from alcohol.[12] After spending some years as a common laborer, he gradually moved into stonecutting, and ultimately construction and engineering.

By 1850, the twenty-three-year old Michael Haley had moved to Lockport, a small Irish Catholic working-class town with a few stores and taverns on the Des Plaines River just north of Joliet. There he perfected his skills as a stonecutter, carving the stone masonry that lined the canal and the blocks that became the base of the Joliet bridge over the Des Plaines. He lodged with a family who introduced him to their relative, Elizabeth Tiernan. The two married in the late 1850s and settled in Lockport where, in 1860, they had their first child, Thomas, and a year later, on November 15, 1861,

Margaret Angela, named after Elizabeth's younger
lowed rapidly: Jenny in 1863; Eliza in 1864; James
Dennis in 1868; and Mary four years later.[13]

It was significant to Margaret Haley that she wa
War and in the home state of Abraham Lincoln and El
murdered in 1837 by a mob while defending his ab
others of her generation, she believed that no child b
prairies in the twenty years after Appomattox grew up with
"that men lived in causes and for causes."[14] The social reform
who was born a year before Haley in another northern Illino
bered the day that Lincoln died, finding the gateposts wreath
her father in tears. At four and a half years old, the image
Addams's mind and became her "initiation, my baptism as it were, int
thrilling and solemn interests of a world lying quite outside the two white
gateposts."[15] Margaret Haley recorded no such memories, although she may
well have experienced the emotional demonstrations of public mourning on
May 2, 1865, when President Lincoln's funeral train passed through Lockport
and Joliet on its way to the state capitol of Springfield.[16]

The legacy of the Civil War shaped Haley's consciousness more than
the war itself. The end of the war caused a severe economic depression that
was intensified by the return of soldiers to the labor market. Because the war
decimated a generation of young men for marriage and work, it led to radical
changes in the economic and social experiences of northern white women.
A spirit of Irish nationalism also characterized the war around Chicago,
where an Irish Brigade of more than one thousand volunteers, including
many from Joliet, had organized in 1861. The regiment's success in battle
further bolstered Irish pride, even as relations between the Irish and African
Americans (whose freedom they were officially fighting for) deteriorated in
job competition in the aftermath of the war.[17] Haley would live out these
cultural politics in her own life: although an eloquent advocate of libratory
causes and human rights, she was profoundly ambivalent about African American political and economic rights, and she championed the cause of working-
class whites—especially the Irish Catholics—over any other group. For Haley,
it was the selective symbolism of the Civil War, more than the actual causes
or results of the war, that held meaning. War carried a powerful metaphor that
she drew on throughout her life, titling her own autobiography *Battleground*
and often referring to the "unending war" between the disempowered against
the powerful and "the frontier of the war for human rights."[18]

RURAL CHILDHOOD

Soon after Margaret's birth, the family moved to the country three miles
outside of Joliet to the land that Michael Haley had obtained with his canal
workers' scrip. They lived on a farm, but Michael Haley was not a farmer;

ʍr to tend what were probably cornfields with some cows,
ʍontinued work on the canals.[19] The family was economically
ʍ Michael reported that his real estate was worth $10,000 and
ʍestate $2,500. With seven children aged one to nine, they hired
ʍd the fourteen-year-old daughter of Irish immigrants as a domestic
ʍ and two laborers who worked the fields.[20]
ʍMargaret Haley recalled her family as caring and friendly: parents and
ʍngs grew up together in harmony, "with no one of us imposed upon or
ʍposing on another."[21] The children played games, rode the farm horses,
and took trips to town for market day and church. They watched the natural
rhythms of the seasons and the working rhythms of farmers sowing and
harvesting. Her first memory was of the vivid blue sky above golden wheat
fields, an image that haunted her the rest of her life when she thought of
children raised in cramped and dirty cities. The open spaces also taught the
value of freedom: As an older woman, Haley believed that the "vast dome
of the midland sky and the great sweep of the midland prairies" imbued "a
stirring sense of the freedom of life," and of the great possibilities available
to young children.[22]

In 1872, a series of disasters struck the family. Michael Haley lost the
lease on the farmland, the first of many strange economic crises that would
checker his career. The family moved to the tiny village of Channahon, a
few miles away, where, almost upon their arrival, the entire village was
struck by malaria, and Haley's newborn sister Mary died. The family's sorrow
was compounded when within a few months, twelve-year-old Thomas Haley
drowned, thereby fulfilling a dark family tradition running back two generations that the eldest son of the family would drown. Barely eleven years old,
Margaret Haley saw death twice and was suddenly thrust into the role of
eldest child.[23]

Michael Haley had moved to Channahon to join in a new sandstone
quarry business along the shores of the Des Plaines River. The great Chicago
fire in 1871, which had leveled more than eighteen thousand buildings and
incinerated the downtown business district, increased the demand for fire
resistant sandstone and furthered the growth of stone quarry and construction enterprises. Within a year after entering the business in 1872, Haley's
firm employed 160 workers to cut and prepare sandstone for Chicago's rebuilt
buildings and bridges.[24]

The village of Channahon was built along the river bluffs of the junction of the Illinois-Michigan canal and the Des Plaines River. With only a
few hundred residents, in 1878 the town had only one grocery store, two
blacksmith's shops, one wagon shop, and a hardware store. To the Haley
children the tiny town was "a world in miniature." The Channahon quarry
offered unending interest to the children on a variety of levels. The road to
the quarry crossed a canal lock, which the children enjoyed watching in
operation. Interesting to young Margaret Haley, too, was that Michael Haley

had to pay a one-cent toll on the road to the quarry and his objections to this furthered his involvement in local politics.[25]

Throughout Haley's youth, her father embodied and articulated the key radical labor politics of the day. Haley remembered him as a passionate student of economics, populist politics, and Irish nationalism. He seemed to identify as a universal laborer—both farmer and stoneworker—and his political affiliations reflected his breadth, eclecticism, and energy.[26] Michael Haley was a member of the Knights of Labor, the first national labor union in the country, and he supported the platform of utopian socialism and antimonopolism that characterized the Knights of the 1870s and '80s. In these early years, the Knights also challenged the racist structure of American society by welcoming African American workers and promoting the unification of black and white workers.[27]

Michael Haley was also strongly identified with Irish nationalist politics. His sense of Irish Catholic identity might have been furthered in these years as he watched the local growth of the anti-Catholic Know-Nothing Party, the same group that had arsoned the Catholic church in Boston that Haley said that he witnessed as a boy.[28] Michael Haley also supported the Irish National Land League, an Irish American lobbying group organized to support economic and political reform in Ireland. The Land League was wildly popular among the Irish American working class, and served to solidify Irish American identity by aligning the injustices of England with those of American monopolists.[29]

In Margaret Haley's few documented recollections about her childhood, her father played a central and powerful role. Her memory of her father was as a dynamic man, a larger than life figure who brought the issues of the outside world into the home by inviting farmers, laborers, and political activists to the house to discuss contemporary politics and labor issues in America and Ireland. The children were allowed to sit in on these debates and by listening, young Margaret Haley learned early on that even though she lived in a peaceful rural environment, there was "a world of events outside."[30] As an older woman, she recalled that a defining moment in her childhood was at age twelve when her father received a pamphlet on finance from Alexander Campbell, a Joliet politician who was part of the Greenback-Labor alliance that blamed the ongoing depression of the 1870s on bankers and that promoted currency reform to benefit labor. Young Margaret Haley read the pamphlet with intense interest and later credited that experience with her recognition "of the association between a governmental currency system and the daily lives of the people of the country."[31] Raised on the image of the Knights of Labor as an inclusive force for all laborers, and educated in the economic politics of farmers, canal workers, and Irish nationalism, Michael Haley's children learned about both the potential of liberal capitalism and its dangers, especially in a world where the interests of monopoly were not controlled.

Margaret Haley left almost no description of her childhood, and no photographs or original writings from her youth survive. All that we know about her, we know from her own words as an adult, and they offer a unique perspective on her personality development. The older Margaret Haley's memories of her childhood present a double-sided image that would become her characteristic self-definition. On the one hand, she described herself as a small and sickly young girl who spent much of her youth as an unobtrusive observer of the world, learning to read at her mother's knee, and eavesdropping on her elders' political discussions. But Haley's recorded reminiscences also reflect her interest in a stronger, more forceful character. She said that she betrayed early signs of a strong will and temper: Once she became impatient with her baby sister Eliza and hit her with a metal urn, inflicting a mark that Eliza carried for the rest of her life.[32] And her description of her precocious interest in politics and "the world of events outside" highlight an early commitment to political interests outside of the domestic sphere. Whether any of Haley's memories accurately portray her actual childhood is to some extent beside the point. The way in which the elder Haley framed her childhood memories reveals much about her own self-conception. Her depiction of herself as an innocent and feminine girl, and simultaneously as a politically oriented character was a trope that she would use to describe herself throughout her life, as she learned to defend her aggressive political activism by asserting her self-deprecating identity as a humble lady schoolteacher.

RURAL SCHOOLING

As an older woman, Margaret Haley recalled her experience as a student in the little village school in Channahon as one of the great experiences of her life. Even in a small rural community such as Channahon, there was a vast difference between country and village schooling. To accommodate the demands of agricultural work, rural district schools were closed during planting and harvest times. These schools were characteristically bleak and drab institutions, according to the Will County superintendent who visited the five rural Channahon schools in January 1872. The buildings were old and crowded one-room structures in various states of disrepair. The classrooms housed no globes, maps, or charts, and only an eclectic assortment of textbooks. In some buildings there were broken desks and crumbling plaster; in others the problems lay in the teacher. Two male teachers struck the superintendent as particularly aberrant: One elderly and experienced male teacher used "ancient habits" of both pronunciation and methods of teaching, while the other was eccentric in his dress and nervous manner.[33]

The county school superintendent was particularly gloomy about the qualifications of teachers in his district. Only a tiny fraction of Will County teachers had any formal preparation and none had graduated from teacher training school or university. In fact, most rural teachers across the state had poor preparation and little access to new educational ideas. The licensure of teachers involved little more than filling out a form, and teachers' licenses were renewed in a perfunctory manner with little or no test of scholarship or pedagogical science. Without even a high school in the county, students could become teachers after finishing barely an elementary school education. Some teachers attended teacher institutes that ran during the summer for a few days. But in Will County in 1871, less than half of the county's four hundred teachers attended any institute. On the bright side, Will County seemed in little worse condition than many of her sister counties across the state.[34]

In comparison to the rural district schools, the graded village school in Channahon that Margaret Haley attended offered a far superior education. For one thing, the school was large and students were organized according to grade or age, so that there was some attention to the specific needs of children at different learning stages. The school ran on a consistent, nine-month schedule and was housed in a two-story wood frame building with three classrooms—one for each primary, intermediate, and secondary grade. The school was also well stocked with supplies, including a piano.[35] In the 1870s, this village school was ranked among the best in the county.

To Margaret Haley, the most memorable part of the Channahon school was her teacher, Cyrus Brown, a Civil War veteran in his early thirties. Born in New York State, Brown joined the Union Army as a teenager, and took part in the recapture of Charleston, South Carolina. At one point he was an officer for the Third United States Colored Troops, the Corps de Afrique, and led 150 African American men to the front along the South Carolina sand dunes, dodging rockets and sea storms for a number of weeks. Like many men teachers, Brown now taught school while he studied to become a lawyer.

Haley described Cyrus Brown as a unique teacher in part because he did not rely on textbooks, preferring instead to teach a more flexible class from his own knowledge. Brown's attitude toward teaching may have been a reaction to his own examination experience to qualify as an officer for the Union Army. At that examination, Brown later remembered, a major in full uniform sat at the head of an expansive table, surrounded by an intimidating crowd of other officers. "The victim was placed at the foot of this table and made a target for all the eyes belonging to these be-laced and be-shoulder-strapped men of war, whilst a rapid fire question-gun was trained directly upon the bulls eye of the dazed understanding. That gun, aimed now by [the major] and now by one of the lesser dignitaries, ranged up and down every vital part of the body of one's knowledge." The candidate was thus "riddled like a target from circumference to center."[36] Given that Brown probably had no formal teacher training, his own experiences as a cadet might well have taught him the benefits of engaged teaching and the rejection of formalized structures that silenced students' voices.[37] He was, as Haley herself might word it in her later years, a "wide awake" teacher in his practice.

SMALL TOWN LIFE

Three years after the Haleys moved to Channahon, the stone quarry gave out, and Michael Haley moved his family to the nearby town of Morris. There he joined a quarry mining firm where he made a local name for himself when he devised a method for making flexible cement mortar. The cement was both highly adhesive and resistant to even more heat than stone at a fraction of the cost. Michael Haley earned a patent in 1877 and marketed his cement as a replacement for firebrick for the lining of furnaces.[38]

Margaret Haley remembered Morris as the least interesting of all the places she lived in as a child. Morris was a good-sized town, the county seat, and situated between the Illinois-Michigan canal and the Chicago, Rock Island, and Pacific Railroad line. In the mid-1870s when the Haleys lived there, the town had well over one hundred commercial and professional businesses, the county courthouse, and a railway station.[39] In many ways, it seemed an idyllic mid-century country town. And in many ways, Michael Haley seemed to be following an idyllic path of upward mobility. He moved his family into a group of houses on the east side of town, across the street from the largest Catholic icon in town—the newly built Church of the Immaculate Conception.[40] Michael Haley was earning enough money to send his eldest daughter to the local Catholic academy, which cost $85 a term. In many ways, he may have felt that he had reached the comfortable middle class.

But like other typical country towns, Morris was marked by ethnic and class divisions. In rural midwestern communities throughout the nineteenth century, Irish Catholics remained a segregated underclass, despised and isolated by native-born Protestants only somewhat less than African Americans.[41] In Morris, the wealthy Protestant town fathers lived on the west side of the town center, while the east side was the Irish and working-class community, an area that had been marked as such since the town was founded decades earlier.[42] Although Irish and Scottish laborers were only 25 percent of the town's total workforce in 1860, they comprised three-fourths of the town's unskilled labor force, working on the canal, trains, sandstone quarries, and in coal mines on the edge of the town.[43] These workers all lived on the east side of town, neighboring other Irish Catholic laborers, masons, plasterers, and clerks.

That Haley could afford to send his daughter to St. Angela's Catholic Academy for girls indicated his wealth, but it in no way indicated his acceptance into the upper echelon of Morris society. Like many Catholic families climbing into the middle class, attendance at a convent school revealed both a commitment to Irish Catholic identity and hopes for upward mobility. Nineteenth-century Irish American Catholics developed a profound suspicion, if not hatred, of the emerging public school system, objecting to the nondenominational Protestantism of the curriculum, the nativist assumptions of the schoolbooks, and the bigotry of Protestant public school teach-ers. In nearby Chicago, Catholic leaders labeled the public schools as noth-ing less than "atheistical, godless, and pernicious— prolific hotbeds of prostitution, indecency, blasphemy, naivery and crime."[44] But the educa-tional options for Catholic children were limited. Throughout most of the nineteenth century, only private convent academies existed for the educa-tion of Catholic girls. St. Angela's Academy in Morris, founded in 1857 by the Sisters of Holy Cross, was just such a school.[45]

Margaret Haley rarely referred to her two years of Catholic education and did not even mention St. Angela's in her autobiography. But she wrote her autobiography as a public document, intended to further her life-long campaign to support public education. Acknowledging her own attendance at a private Catholic school would hardly have furthered her political cause. It is also possible that Haley herself was unimpressed by her education in the convent, and that she devoted her life to making such schools unnecessary.

Certainly the type of education that Haley probably received at St. Angela's seems antithetical to all of her later beliefs about democratic school-ing and progressive teaching. By definition an elitist institution, St. Angela's three-story mansion and ten acres of private grounds was a monument to upward mobility and traditional gender roles.[46] Haley's education there was designed to prepare her for either middle-class motherhood or the convent. Religion formed the core of the curriculum, and since the nuns' own educa-tional training was limited, academic instruction was weak. In her two years at St. Angela's, Haley might have studied Bible, religious philosophy, litera-ture, and history in a curriculum designed to reinforce religious beliefs. The teachers emphasized traditional gender roles in their instruction of music, art, and embroidery, sewing, and needlework. Courses were taught with tra-ditional pedagogy of memorization and recitation, written quizzes and exams, and public oral exams by visiting priests.[47] Haley's only documented com-ment about the school was in reference to a very meticulous and demanding English teacher and an elderly French sister, who stood out because she was "a humanitarian, who taught art and, incidentally, the art of living."[48] This linking of education with humanity was the crux of Haley's life-long political work, but except for that one teacher, the convent school did not seem to provide any examples of it. Indeed, she spent the remainder of her life fighting against the kind of hierarchy and rigidity that characterized a con-vent school such as St. Angela's.

CATAPULTED

In 1878 Margaret Haley's family and schooling influences intersected in the experience that she later said "catapulted" her into teaching. Her under-standing of the cause was that in June, the courts closed Michael Haley's quarry outside of Morris because Haley refused to join his partners in a bribe for a contract. The family's financial situation "folded up like a concertina," which forced a catastrophic change in Margaret Haley's life plans.[49] She had been enjoying school and hoped to continue, but the family's financial crisis pushed her, the eldest child, into the work force.

On the day that her father's business was closed, Margaret Haley was in the St. Angela's auditorium, taking part in the school's closing exercises. Her father walked in to the hall and as soon as she saw his face, she immediately knew that he had lost his business and that she, the eldest child, would have to get a job, to "dig for myself and for the rest of them." If she lived a hundred years, she remembered almost sixty years later, "I'll never forget my father's face and all it conveyed of defeat and the consequences. It meant for me the end of school and I had to prepare to do something else."[50]

Haley's interpretation was double-sided. On one hand, she saw her own loss. She knew her comfortable life was over, that she would not be able to continue school. "I had been singing. I didn't sing anymore," she recalled.[51] Simultaneously, the experience reaffirmed her ongoing political education: seeing her father's face and all it conveyed of defeat furthered her commitment to preventing that kind of tragedy from happening to other honest working people. What Haley apparently never saw, or never believed, were her father's own weaknesses or failures. Whether Michael Haley's economic problems were caused by the unstable economy of the 1870s, the corruption of an unregulated market, or his own incompetence, the lesson that his eldest daughter took was a deep suspicion of economic greed, and this became the driving force behind her own political vision. From her father, too, she learned about the double-edged sword of stubbornness. Her father's commitment to what he saw as right had led to economic catastophy for the family, and the elder Margaret Haley speculated on his wisdom in upholding such principles at such a cost. But ironically, such stubbornness over principles proved to be her own Achilles' heel; like her father before her, Haley would often see political compromise as the relinquishment of correct principles, and thus not worth consideration, whatever the cost.

At the core of Margaret Haley's early education was her experience of class and ethnic identity. The Haley family was part of the rising working-class Irish immigrant community, what some historians have described as "labor aristocracy" or "lace curtain Irish."[52] In many ways, the family was lucky, and this luck taught their children about the possibilities and opportunities available to them. By watching the world around her, young Margaret Haley learned about her family's position in society—about what they were due as hardworking citizens, and about what they deserved but would not get as a result of their class and ethnicity.

Reinforcing the Haley family identity as Irish Catholic working-class immigrants was the identification of a group from which they believed they had to distinguish themselves in order to achieve upward mobility —African Americans. For nineteenth-century Irish Catholic immigrants, the goal of becoming a solidified class with working rights and privileges would come only with the creation of a subclass over which they could be superior. Deeply held and evolving notions of race were class specific, and used by the white working class to create African Americans as "other," as the despised race and the inferior worker. Until that moment when the Irish "became white," working-class Irish Catholic families were themselves burdened by their own racialized identity.[53]

Race played a small but significant role in Haley's childhood. Joliet, Illinois, the town of her birth and the largest metropolitan center in the county, was a predominantly white town, but it was also a locale on the Underground Railroad, and a place where, after the Civil War, southern African Americans passed through on their way to Chicago.[54] Yet Margaret Haley grew up in essentially a white world, seeing black people as unfortunate strangers who wandered nearby, but rarely into her own life. In Channahon, the little village outside Joliet where she spent her early childhood, there were only two black residents, and some elderly whites in the village recalled "Nigger Dick," whom they paternalistically called an "honorary early resident."[55] A more powerful memory for Haley was the day that she looked out the window of the family farmhouse and saw African American workers carting away the annual corn harvest. Hired by the man to whom Michael Haley lost his lease, the older Margaret Haley's memory of these underpaid African American laborers was not one of empathy for a class of people whose occupational options were restricted, but anger and resentment at the personal loss for her family.[56] Thus, like many working-class Irish Americans, her emerging political consciousness was racially defined, and she would never learn how to include African Americans into her political theory of economic rights.

In the shadows of Margaret Haley's account of her early life, we can see that gender, too, shaped her emerging view of the world. Haley was eleven when her older brother drowned, leaving her to be the eldest in a family of seven children. At age sixteen, her father's business loss forced her into the workforce to support her family. For all the pain of these events, these incidences also legitimated Haley's move into the public world. It was the death of one male and the financial catastrophe of another that offered Haley some sense of purpose and responsibility, and the opportunity to escape from a traditional nineteenth-century woman's life.

By the time she was a teenager, Margaret Haley had lived a classic American life. Born in the rural heartland, influenced by national and economic phenomena, and cared for and supported by an emotionally close family, she had a relatively fortunate, if economically unsteady, childhood. Like the children of other immigrants, she would find her cultural identity to be both a barrier and an asset; like other women who moved into the public world of work, she would find that her gender both restricted her and provided her specific opportunities. The restrictions of both also presented her with unique opportunities: the vibrant and passionate politics of the labor aristocracy, and the ironic advantages presented to educated women by the feminized occupation of teaching. By the time she was sixteen, Margaret Haley was moving both inside and outside the American norm.

SCHOOLTEACHER

Margaret Haley became a professional teacher in September 1878. She was sixteen years old and was still wearing pigtails and a girl's short skirt. Small for her age, she looked so young that on the first day of school, a six-year-old mistook her for another pupil.[57] Although inexperienced, she was not unusually young for rural schoolteachers at the time, nor was her career choice unusual. Haley's mother urged her eldest daughter to go into teaching in order to help the family, but also because teaching offered the best alternative for young Irish Catholic women. By the 1880s, first and second generation Irish American women with some education saw a career in teaching as almost part of the natural life line. Local parishes and dioceses supported female education as a counter to the Protestant-based public school system, and Irish American women who suffered ethnic discrimination in other white-collar jobs benefited from the job patronage system in Irish-dominated civil service and governmental structures, including the feminized occupation of teaching. Teaching offered a young rural immigrant's daughter a life of unprecedented independence.

Furthermore, for someone with the relatively advanced education that Haley had, it was easy to become a teacher. In July 1878, barely a month after she graduated from St. Angela's under the cloud of her father's financial crisis, she sat for the county exam for elementary teaching certification.[58] There, with a group of other prospective teachers, she gave written responses to the oral questioning of Grundy County Superintendent John Higby. A former teacher and professor at Illinois State Normal School, Higby was known for his precision and clarity, asking questions that the local newspaper approved of as "direct and pointed, without ambiguity, and not of that spongy kind" that could result in a half-dozen partially correct answers.[59] Higby was also an affable man who was committed to the further education of teachers, and his exam was not as terrifying an experience as qualifying exams were often said to be. Nor was it difficult. Of the 132 applicants for the elementary teaching certificate in Grundy County in 1877–78, only five were rejected. Haley earned what was called a "second grade certificate" which qualified her to teach the equivalent of what is now elementary school.[60]

Margaret Haley then joined the flood of teachers called to the rapidly expanding public school system. In the years after the Civil War, state officials across the country designed a legal and financial framework for a standardized public school system. Accompanying the growth in school classrooms and enrolments in this period was the increase in regulations for the preparation of teachers. Educators argued that a state public school system could work only if it was accompanied by systematized teacher training programs, and they rallied legislative support for the establishment of state-funded teacher education schools along the model of the Prussian teacher seminary and the French *école normale*. The first state normal school was established in Lexington, Massachusetts, in 1839; by 1870 forty normal schools existed across the country, preparing elementary and secondary teachers as well as school administrators. Normal schools were coeducational, two and three-year programs that offered students education in general subjects as well as classroom instruction and management. Because of the dearth of secondary and university education through the nineteenth century, normal schools often acted as a combination of both. Particularly in small rural communities, a normal school often served as a general educational experience for students with a variety of backgrounds and professional interests.[61]

In Morris, Illinois, a small normal school opened up during the summer that Margaret Haley prepared for her first job. The Morris Normal School offered a number of programs for students with particular interests, including studies in advanced elementary education, a "scientific course," which prepared students for business and public work, college preparatory studies, and teacher training.[62] The Morris program was immensely popular: in its first year, it enrolled about one hundred regular students, fifty evening students, and nine teachers.[63] Normal schools often supplemented their program with summer or weekend teacher institutes for people who were already working in schools and who, like Margaret Haley, had moved immediately from the role of student to one of teacher. The summer before she became a teacher, Haley attended summer classes at the new Normal School, and every weekend during her first year of teaching, she returned to Morris to continue her studies.

Haley enjoyed her education at Morris, and she greatly admired her teachers there. The men who ran the Normal School in Morris were particularly well prepared in the new field of teacher training. The school's founder, John W. Cook, was later president of Illinois State and Northern Illinois State Normal School and was a leading advocate of the normal school movement in Illinois.[64] Cook's co-director of the school, Orrin Carter, was an experienced educator who was studying to be a lawyer and later became chief justice of the Illinois Supreme Court.[65] The teachers at Morris Normal emphasized the practicality of the subjects taught and the active involvement of the student in the educational process. The program rejected old-fashioned rote memory learning and instead promoted problem solving and close analytical work. Science classes took frequent field trips to study nature; in mathematics class students explored the structure of mathematical problems; history classes studied the nature of law and citizenship as well as historical events; and students studied debating and composition to encourage active participation in society as citizens.[66] Haley was inspired by the teaching, recalling that "if you had any sense of responsibility to children, it would awaken it. If you had any conscience, it would arouse it."[67] John Cook and Orrin Carter, she recalled, "were very enthusiastic young men and live wires and they did a lot for young teachers just when they needed it."[68]

Haley's first teaching job was in a little country school with forty students near Dresden Heights, a small community about ten miles from Morris. She taught at the school for eight months, earning about $30 a month, an average wage for a female teacher in Illinois at the time.[69] From her first day, she loved teaching, and she gloried in a new sense of responsibility. She found the work easy, in part because the expectations of the poor community were so low—one member of the school board was illiterate and barely understood what a teacher was supposed to do. Her first success was with a five-year-old boy named Jimmie, whom she taught to read by using a new method of phonics that she learned at the Morris Normal School. Traditional teaching practice was that children should learn to read by spelling out each letter of a word—the alphabet method. Under the new phonics method, children were taught to focus on the sounds, and simultaneously on the whole concept or symbol of the word. Under her tutelage, Jimmie quickly surpassed his classmates in reading. The boy's nine-year-old uncle was also in her school and young Jimmie's success caused such conflict between the boys that the family invited the young teacher to their house for supper to try to understand what had made Jimmie so advanced.[70] Haley also received help from her county superintendent, John Higby, who visited almost every school in the county once a year for about two hours. Higby's gentle supervision furthered Haley's understanding that teaching was a skilled craft deserving of constant study and professional advisement.[71]

At the end of her first year of teaching, Haley's family moved back to Joliet. Michael Haley had secured a job as an inspector of material for the construction of Chicago's City Hall and Joliet was a preferable base for his work. For the next two years, Margaret Haley taught in a one-room country school, just outside of town.[72] In Joliet, she met other people who were studying new educational movements and here she caught what she called "the spirit of the system."[73] In August 1882, she made a further commitment to her education by registering for four weeks of summer school at Illinois State Normal University.[74] Illinois Normal in the 1880s was an exciting place to study teaching because leading proponents of the Herbartian theory worked there. Herbartians, named after the German educator Johann Friedrich Herbart, explored early psychological concepts of learning in which curriculum was developed in stages that paralleled the stages of development of the child. Their emphasis was on how children learned instead of the scientific training of skills.[75] Haley's experience at Illinois Normal was cathartic, both in terms of what she learned and because it marked her first time living away from home and devoting herself to her professional education. Normal was seventy-five miles downstate from Joliet, and Haley probably lodged in one of the many boarding houses set up for visiting students. There she met teachers from all over Illinois, most of whom, like Haley, had a few years teaching experience.[76]

For many Illinois teachers, summer school was a jolting and not altogether pleasant experience. Some described the initial shock of living away from home, the huge size of the institution, and the rigorous demands of the program. Many rural teachers, used to their small town communities and their one and two room schools, were unnerved to enter an assembly room that fit hundreds of students, and in front of which stood a man "with a pencil, as a sword or scepter" who would "threaten them, or scold them" to complete their studies and occasionally to report their knowledge publicly at the blackboard. One contemporary of Haley's remarked that there was "little of the milk of human kindness" wasted upon students by faculty at Illinois Normal, and that the entire setup of the institution was so large and anonymous that it seemed designed to threaten students with "total annihilation."[77] To combine this experience with that of boarding away from home may have made for an intimidating experience that only the most brave would undertake.

Haley's experiences at Normal revolved around her studies with Edmund Janes James, the principal of the Model High School department, and a scholar of education and economics whose research interests included the labor movement, tax reform, and school reform. A former student of and friend to John W. Cook, James was twenty-seven years old in 1882, and the co-editor with the progressive educator Charles DeGarmo of the *Illinois School Journal* where James wrote about taxation, finance, compulsory education, immigration, and classroom pedagogy. [78] He was also a notoriously stimulating teacher who made a point of connecting theory with practice. In James's economics class, Haley read Henry George's recently published *Progress and Poverty*, a book that was revolutionizing liberal American economic theory with its proposal for a single tax system that would allow a more egalitarian operation of the capitalist system. George's theory, Haley recalled, opened up to her "a wide world" of economic restructuring for social improvement.[79]

After her experience at Normal, Haley returned to her school in Joliet "with a greatly increased idea of my own importance." Her narrative of this time in her life suggests some self-aggrandizement at the expense of detail. In a dramatic tale that she would retell many times in her later life, Haley asked her superintendent for a raise of five dollars a month—from $35 to $40—to which he agreed, but then he postponed the actual raise. Haley sent him an ultimatum: If he did not pay her a higher salary by noon of the first day of the fall term, she would resign. The raise was not offered and she took the next train to Chicago.[80]

It is more likely that Haley was headed to Chicago anyway. Her father had been working there for some years and her younger siblings were now of age to look for work. Furthermore, Chicago was the goal of thousands of aspiring young people in the late nineteenth century because it offered economic promise, adventure, and culture. To young Theodore Dreiser some years later, Chicago promised romance and excitement, even with its dreary neighborhoods, clattering railways, and filthy industries. Dreiser described Chicago as "a city which had no traditions but was making them, and this was the very thing that every one seemed to understand and rejoice in."[81] Chicago was also the logical place for an Irish Catholic teacher to go. By the late nineteenth century, Chicago housed the fourth largest Irish population in the United States, and Irish Catholic women flocked to teaching as quickly as their brothers rushed to civil service jobs of police and fire protection. When Margaret Haley moved to Chicago, anywhere from one-quarter to one-third of all the city's public school teachers were women of Irish Catholic descent, and this community provided both job connections and social acceptance.[82] As Haley herself admitted, the city was the lodestar for many ambitious young Midwestern women. In one of her later memoirs, Haley downplayed the salary incident and instead described the move to Chicago as an inevitable step into her own destiny: "It wasn't courage" that took her there, she recalled, "it was just that I never had any doubt."[83]

Newly moved to Chicago, Haley took a job as a substitute teacher at a school in Lemont, a community just south of the city, from Fall 1882 to Spring 1883.[84] In Fall 1883, she taught at Lewis Champlin School in the Englewood community on the southern edge of Chicago. At one of these two schools she had her first experience with a poor principal, one who Haley believed had little more than a primary education. Haley called her a "fraud" who was so ignorant that her teachers essentially ran the schools themselves. This situation worked to Haley's advantage because it allowed her to freely practice the new methods that she had learned in teacher education classes.[85]

In the spring of 1884, waiting to find a permanent job, Haley enrolled at the Cook County Normal School which was gaining fame under its dynamic new principal, Francis Wayland Parker. A former school superintendent in Massachusetts, Parker's educational philosophy was a microcosm of progressive educational thought at the time. He was particularly influenced by Friedrich Froebel, the German originator of the kindergarten, who promoted respect for even the youngest children's activities, ideas, and expressions of individuality. For both Froebel and Parker, the growth of the child was the purpose of the entire educational enterprise, and both rejected the traditional structure of schooling where the schoolmaster imposed his will on the child. Froebel also promoted an appreciation for the group within which the child lived and learned. The notion—later to be picked up by John Dewey—was that the school was itself a small society, and that children could learn social rules and values accordingly.[86]

Parker had a simple educational credo: The child should be the center and inspiration of the school's activities and the school should pursue two objectives—character development and a democratic social order. He argued that traditional teaching methods ignored the child's natural curiosity of the world and squelched the natural interest in experimentation and observation. Parker introduced drawing and music as a central part of the child's curriculum, as well as nature studies and field trips, and he opposed the system of rewards and punishments, competitive emulation, recitation, word cramming, and memorization. The ideal school should be an embryonic democracy, a community that would in and of itself educate children for good citizenship in a democracy. Traditional education produced passive citizens, but the new education created "free people." For Parker, politics and pedagogy were inseparable: Child-centered pedagogy was an integral piece of democratic society.[87]

Parker's ideas about the role of the teacher were as revolutionary as his ideas about the role of children in schools. Given the educational importance of classroom relations, the teacher was elevated to the role of the shaper of children's values and ethics. Parker believed that the individual classroom teacher needed to have the authority of a policymaker, a novel role for female elementary schoolteachers.[88] In addition, a normal school should have a much broader scope than the simple training of teachers; it should be a "laboratory and educational experiment station, whose influence penetrates, permeates, and improves all education and educational thinking."[89] Parker designed his teacher training sessions to force candidates to evaluate each other and encourage each other's progress. What was important to Parker was "constant change, elimination, innovation, experiment, tentative conclusions—this was the manner of progress."[90]

Haley spent only a few months at Cook County, but she was profoundly influenced by Parker's personality and teachings. She later described him as someone who broke old traditions of education, freeing women teachers to use their minds in the same way that modern fashions had freed women's bodies from the corset. She was particularly inspired by Parker's lectures on the school as a social community, his insistence on academic freedom, and his promotion of principles of self-discovery in interdisciplinary and interactive classes.[91] Parker's education, she recalled "shook educational practices loose from the old foundations."[92]

Stylistically, Parker was an attractive role model for Haley: he was a rule breaker, an iconoclast, and an evangelist. His warm and engaging personality could also be bombastic. As teachers told him their teaching ideas, he would push them to think more deeply. His voice would boom out, "Why?" and, "Yes, but will it work again?" and, "Does it benefit the children?"[93] Haley recalled that Parker believed so thoroughly in his own ideas, that he was willing to fight for them, and he was "a sturdy fighter. He enjoyed nothing so much as a lively round with an opponent of his teaching ideas, and his method of refuting their contentions left no ground beneath their feet."[94] He was, she recalled, "a prince of enthusiasts" who was "by no means pacific in his quest for sweetness and light. He roared, he growled, he stormed, he banged, . . . he shook the dry bones in things and in people. He scared the wits out of students, and he terrified teachers. He sent for parents and shamed them into aiding their children. He was Reform Rampant—and I watched him with unterrified glee." Parker apparently never scared Haley, who saw his direct approach as a practical and effective method of exacting change. "More sure than anyone else," she recalled, "he taught me that a straight line is the shortest distance between two points." To Haley, Francis Parker was "a great light shining on the barren fields of education in the United States."[95]

From this great light, Haley went to teach in one of the darkest educational environments in Chicago.

SIXTEEN YEARS IN A CLASSROOM

Margaret Haley began teaching at the Hendricks School in September 1884. She was hardly a nervous and insecure first-year teacher. She was twenty-three years old with more than five years' teaching experience under her belt. She had worked in a number of barren school buildings, under one incompetent principal, and with many poor students, and she had a few semesters of teacher training in two of the best teacher education institutes in the state. But none of this could have prepared her for the enormity of the challenges of the Chicago public school system in the early 1880s.

The Hendricks School was a public grammar school housing grades 3 to 6, located on the edge of what was known as Packingtown, the residential community of workers hired to slaughter cows and pigs and pack their meat in the infamous Chicago stockyards. This was the world of industrial poverty that Upton Sinclair wrote about in his 1906 muckraking novel *The Jungle*, a community where in 1889 fifty-seven slaughtering houses and meat packing plants employed twenty thousand workers, primarily first and second-generation European immigrants.[96]

Contemporary observers described Packingtown as a dreary urban community of "gray streets, gray houses, and smoke-laden air," marked by devastating squalor and the ubiquitous odors of the packing houses.[97] It was an expansive industrial neighborhood of factories, animal yards, slaughterhouses, grain elevators, iron mills, slag heaps, and coal piles, bordered by huge clay holes which the city used for garbage dumps, vacant lots used to dry the hair and skin of slaughtered hogs and cattle, which attracted hoards of bluebottle flies, and the notorious Bubbly Creek, a noxious cesspool for the sewage of the packing houses. The entire area was crisscrossed by forty-three train lines that rattled and roared through the neighborhood on street level, clogging intersections and terrorizing pedestrians. Through the turn of the century, only a few main streets in Packingtown were paved, and the sewage and city water system were so backward that stagnant water created a dark leathery slime that appeared so solid that sometimes small animals and children tried to walk on it and were sucked under and drowned.[98]

But according to contemporaries, the most distinctive aspect of Packingtown was not the sights but the smells of the neighborhood industry built on the slaughter and packing of animal flesh. The famous Chicago winds blew a variety of odors out of the stockyards—the choking smell of fresh meat, the stench of sour garbage, and the reek of thousands of hogs and cows.[99] Haley herself described the Stockyards district as a "sprawling, malodorous neighborhood."[100]

The Hendricks School was located on a major commercial street that led directly into the Stockyards eight blocks west. It was close enough to the plants so that even the slightest western breeze would blow the infamous aromas into open school windows, and the unpaved 43rd St. was busy with commercial traffic, the almost continual construction of new buildings, tourists en route to view the infamous Stockyards, and workers going to and from work or to the hundreds of saloons that surrounded the yards. A few blocks away from the school was Chicago's largest and most popular gambling house, owned by the son of the notorious Mrs. O'Leary whose cow was blamed for starting the great Chicago Fire of 1871. Adding to the bustle from the street was the clatter of three major railway lines that passed within five blocks of the school, carrying passengers to and from Chicago or doomed animals to slaughter. Church bells clanged from the Methodist church two blocks west and from the 160-foot bell tower of St. Gabriel's Catholic church two blocks south. And in the distance, the noise of the Stockyards itself infiltrated the school windows: "Thousands of cattle bellowing . . . hogs squealing, and so many men roaring."[101]

As the odors and noises from the street poured through the school windows, so too did the culture and politics of a working-class community. Haley's first students at Hendricks were primarily German and Irish, the children of skilled butchers and packing house workers with full-time employment in the Stockyards. But even though she later remembered these children as "alert and eager to learn," they were hardly privileged children.[102] Families in Packingtown were crowded into wood frame tenements, the men eking out lives of ten hour workdays in the packing houses, women taking on piecework and boarders in already cramped apartments, and children leaving school early to find work. Tuberculosis, consumption, diphtheria, and other infectious diseases ravaged the people of Packingtown, and Upton Sinclair described how the notorious Chicago winters swept through the fragile frame houses with "icy, death dealing fingers."[103] Children's lives worsened through the 1880s as the stockyards expanded. By the turn of the century, the Packingtown population included an increasing number of unskilled Bohemians, Poles, and Lithuanians, whose cultural and language differences led Haley to refer to them unsympathetically as the "Huns and the Vandals."[104] A medical inspector in the 1890s found almost 20 percent of students at one Packingtown school below their grade level. They were poorly dressed, thin, anemic, "and apparently neglected."[105] Through the

1890s, Packingtown workers were the object of vigorous labor organizing campaigns, and the main Knights of Labor organizer held meetings for his local in the Buckley School, a few blocks from Hendricks. The community was enlivened by regular mass rallies, literature distribution campaigns, and street skirmishes between strikers, scabs, and militia hired by the industries.[106]

Although a series of compulsory education acts and child labor laws in the 1880s required Chicago children aged seven to fourteen to attend public school, through the turn of the century about one-half of Chicago's children who entered primary school left before the required age. Thus, Margaret Haley's sixth grade classroom was the last schooling that many of the Hendricks children would see before they entered the factories or the streets.[107]

Margaret Haley started teaching in a school that was so new that for its first two years it was referred to officially only as the Forty-Third Street School. It was built in 1884 as one of four new schools designed to accommodate the children of the growing population of Stockyards' workers. Located on a corner lot, it was a three-story brick building that in its style resembled a nearby factory more than a rural country schoolhouse. It was probably the largest building on the block, located in an area of residential tenements, working-class cottages, and small commercial buildings. On the first floor of many Chicago school buildings, a hall ran through the center of the building, connecting to four or five classrooms, the principal's office, and an area where teachers picked up their classroom keys in the morning. A stairway led upstairs to more classrooms and one large room with a piano that doubled as a recitation room and assembly hall. The fifteen classrooms were rectangular, with walls painted a light tinted color and blackboards around at least two sides, cabinets to hold books and supplies, and rows of connected desks bolted to the floor with seating for forty-eight students. Each room had a separate closet with seats where students could take off their coats and boots. There was a girls' and boys' playroom and outside playground, reflecting a popular social belief that coeducation was acceptable as long as the genders were separated for playtime.[108]

This was how the Hendricks School looked on its first day of school in September 1884, but over time the building expanded with the community and aged with daily use. [109] Hendricks was designed to seat 715 students, but within a few years enrollment increased to more than one thousand, so three rooms in the attic were rebuilt into classrooms, and new bookcases, desks, ink wells, and blackboards were ordered. But even these rooms did not provide adequate space, so in many classrooms students doubled or tripled up at desks designed to fit only one. Over the sixteen years of Haley's tenure, physical facilities were damaged or wore out, so that throughout the school year, the building janitor and engineer were in the basement banging away at steam pipes and plumbing, on the roof repairing the shingles, in the hallways fixing floorboards, or on the grounds painting the picket fence, repaving the sidewalk, and spreading black earth on the playground. Walls needed replastering, drafty windows needed to be caulked, and window shades needed to be mended. Minor disasters occurred, including a small fire in the building and a storm that damaged the flagpole. At one point, the principal began to worry about vandalization of the building after hours, so he requested locks for the rear hall door and for the outside gates. A building filled with young people strained under their energetic romping that teachers could not completely control: Stairwell banisters were bent from children leaning on them, window sashes were broken from too much yanking on them, drains were clogged with children's dirt, classroom desks were broken from some childhood fracas. The flagpole rope had to be replaced after ten years, indicating the strain of children tugging on it day after day. Exhausted from their long days at work, busy teachers lost their classroom keys and needed replacements.

Over the years, modern facilities were also added to the building; probably the most significant one for teachers and students was the replacement of an old pan closet toilet with siphon toilets in the teachers', students', and principals' lavatories, thereby vastly improving the environment in and around those rooms. A new ventilating apparatus helped teachers keep the air in their rooms moving, and presumably addressed the problem of the dust and odors that infiltrated from the street. But even this new mechanism needed mending, because some grates rattled when the heat was turned on, or possibly when the ground shook from a nearby train passing.

This was the place that Margaret Haley headed to for sixteen years of school mornings, from September to May, with a Thanksgiving holiday in late November and Christmas holiday in late December. She arrived at the building at 8:45, fifteen minutes before some eight hundred to one thousand students gathered on the playground and crammed their way into the building, forty-eight of them filing into each classroom. In her own crowded room, the sixth grade teacher whom students called Miss Haley began class at 9 a.m. with a half-hour opening exercise that included some singing. Through the morning, she taught fractions and introduction to geometry, political and physical geography, the history of the United States through the War of Independence, lessons in city and county government, reading, composition, music, and drawing, and a course in physiology and hygiene with special references to the effects of alcohol and narcotics. To help her teach, her classroom was supplied with arithmetic and writing charts, a historical atlas, some Webster's dictionaries, an eight-inch globe, and maps of the world, the United States, and Illinois.[110]

For ten minutes each day, Miss Haley supervised organized physical activities in the crowded classrooms, leading arm, leg, and breathing exercises while students stood at their seats. While supervising her classroom, Miss Haley kept an eye on the classroom thermometers to keep the room between sixty-five and seventy degrees, whether the air outside the windows registered below freezing or steaming hot. She was prohibited from using corporal punishment with her forty-eight ten, and eleven-year-old boys and girls, and was urged instead to maintain a stern, but still caring approach of "moral suasion" to maintain order. She supervised a fifteen-minute mid-morning recess and monitored students as they left the building at noon for lunch. Because she and many of her colleagues lived far from school, they probably stayed in the building for lunch, eating at their desks or in a make-shift teachers' lounge. At 1:30, the children were back at class until 3:30, and by 4 p.m. Miss Haley had closed her classroom, placing her room key in the proper position on the key board in the principal's office.[111]

Was Haley able to make her own classroom at Hendricks the active and social place that her teachers John W. Cook, Edmund James, and Francis Parker had trained her to do? Since she never described her own teaching style, we can only guess how she developed her own educational theories. Given the required curriculum, the crowded classroom, and the problems raised by students' poverty and linguistic diversity, it is hard to imagine how any Chicago teacher devised anything but the most mechanical rote lessons for her students, and at least one observer described exactly that. In his scathing 1892 survey of American city schools, muckraker Joseph Rice found Chicago classrooms full of students glued to their desks, monotonously reading, writing, ciphering, and reciting from textbooks all day long.[112]

But progressive pedagogy may have been more prevalent in Chicago schools than Rice saw, since less than a year after his observations, the Chicago Board of Education erupted in controversy over a charge that the city curriculum was driven by too many progressive "fads," including too many courses in art, music, and physical culture.[113] Margaret Haley herself believed that even at their worst, Chicago schools were less restrictive than those in many eastern cities because they were lacking "the melancholy attitude of Puritanism."[114] Indeed, the years that Margaret Haley was a teacher were the years that some of the most innovative educators worked in the Chicago public school system.

Notable among these was Albert G. Lane, the superintendent of Chicago schools from 1891 to 1898. A graduate of the first class of the Chicago High School teacher-training program, and a former school principal and superintendent of Cook County, Lane promoted particularly progressive programs. He oversaw the expansion of manual training classes, kindergartens, classes for students with special needs, night school for working people and immigrants, and a residential parental school. Lane also welcomed the contributions of outside groups—be it the Women's Christian Temperance Union's introduction of a temperance unit to the curriculum; an essay contest sponsored by the *Daily News*; the Public School Art Society's contributions of pictures for the bare walls of classrooms; or the School Children's Aid Society's donations of clothing for poor children.[115]

The joint influence of Francis Wayland Parker at the Normal School and Lane in the superintendency led to the hiring and nurturing of some remarkable assistant officers in the school system. Josephine C. Locke was head of the art department of the Chicago Public Schools between 1890 and 1900. A former teacher under Parker at the Cook County Normal School, Locke advocated the integration of art into urban schools where the lives of city children were otherwise bereft of creative influence.[116] According to Locke, a main motive of art instruction was to restore the life of nature to city dwellers, and she believed that the problems of public schools were due to an overemphasis on mechanical and "business" methods, and the "failure to appreciate imagination."[117] Haley called Locke "a bubbling fountain of joy" who came to Chicago "to teach the art of life as well as of technic."[118]

Another progressive leader was District Superintendent William W. Speer. Speer was a former superintendent of schools in Marshall County, Iowa, where he had introduced modern methods of teaching writing, science, and arithmetic. He was most famous for developing a new method of teaching arithmetic that emphasized the "visualization" of the entire concept of the mathematical problem. Speer had also worked with Parker, originally at a Summer School in Martha's Vineyard and later as vice-principal in the department of mathematics at Cook County Normal School.[119] Between 1896 and 1902 Speer was district superintendent in one of the poorer districts of Chicago. Common to both Speer's and Locke's work was lessening the influence on textbooks and increasing students' use of their own skills in inventive exercises.

But the most inspiring school administrator to Chicago's women teachers was District Superintendent Ella Flagg Young. Young had passed her teachers' examination at the precocious age of fifteen, but because she was too young to teach, she studied in a two-year teacher-training course. After teaching for a few years, she was promoted to head assistant at the Brown School, and in 1865, at age twenty, she was appointed principal of the model elementary school of the Chicago Normal School. In 1868, she married a merchant, William Young, who died within the year, and the young widow returned to her work in schools. For the next eighteen years, Young rose through the ranks of Chicago school administration until 1887 when she was appointed district superintendent, in one of the poorest districts in the city—the district adjoining Haley's and sharing a similar population of poor and immigrant children. In her twelve years in that office, Young won the respect of Chicago teachers because of her commitment to teacher education and her belief that teachers should be more involved in school administrative decisions. For Margaret Haley and other young teachers in Chicago's schools, the presence of Ella Flagg Young, William Speer, and Josephine Locke in the higher levels of the city school administration showed a commitment to progressive educational principles. To Haley, they "stood for color in education," and promised to "leaven the lump" of the city's school system.[120]

In her own school, too, Haley received inspiration. For the entirety of her career at Hendricks, she worked under a liberally minded principal, John

W. McCarthy, who kept his teachers abreast of school politics. To his teachers, he often quoted the famous Irish nationalist poet and journalist John
Boyle O'Reilly, now in political exile in the United States and promoting
Irish Home Rule and labor rights for Irish American workers through the
pages of the popular Boston *Pilot*.[121] He presented to Haley a model of administrative leadership that was interwoven with Irish Catholic identity and
labor politics.

Yet even with such inspiration, Haley must have been limited in her
ability to teach creative lessons by her crowded classroom, her exhausted and
hungry students, the absence of supplies and space, and the lack of parks or
a safe neighborhood in which to take field trips. Her later pronouncements
that teachers should have the right to shape the classroom into a caring and
supportive environment for children may suggest that she herself did not
have much of that opportunity. Indeed, part of her own politicization process
may have been the contrast between her own progressive teacher training
and the restrictive working conditions in her school.

Another political lesson came from the changes that Haley saw over
her sixteen years of employment at Hendricks. In the 1880s, Chicago schools
were locally run community institutions. Given the minimal teacher training
available, hiring was an informal process based as much on connections as on
objective qualifications. Haley recalled that her own job was promised to her
through her cousin, and she herself probably played a role in securing a job at
Hendricks for her sister Jenny, and after Jenny transferred to another school,
the third Haley sister, Eliza. For much of Haley's tenure at the school, two
other pairs of sisters worked there as well. Such hiring practices reflected the
informal community-based practices of late-nineteenth-century schooling.[122]

But if Hendricks was originally a stable, community-based staff, as time
went on, it became increasingly less so. Two years after it opened, one-half of
the staff had been transferred, mostly to other schools in the same overcrowded
district. So transitory was the staff at Hendricks that in 1889, Margaret Haley
was the only original teacher left at a school that had been in existence only
five years. By her eleventh year of teaching at Hendricks, more than one-half
the staff had been at the school for fewer than five years. The mobile staff at
Hendricks may have had two effects on Haley. First, because most teacher
transfers were not voluntary, their increase in number suggests that the demands of an expanding city school system may have taken precedence over the
priorities of teachers and the community, presenting Haley with an early lesson in school board politics. Secondly, transfers undercut any sense of community and collective history among the adults in the building.[123]

Over sixteen years, the staff changed in other ways too. Through the
turn of the century, Chicago school teaching was an attractive job for young
white ethnic women from working-class families. The civil service character
of urban public school teaching offered the stability of a standard salary scale
and job security. The traditional hiring practices that relied on patronage

meant that teachers were likely to find a job in the community in which they and their families lived. The minimal preparation for teaching furthered working-class women's access to the profession. Many teachers, like the Haley sisters, were from the rising working-class or labor aristocracy, from families who sacrificed a few months of family income to keep a daughter in school so she could become a teacher. When Haley first entered Chicago schools, aspiring elementary teachers needed only the equivalent of a high school education through scattered normal school and other teacher training classes.[124] As late as 1897, more than three thousand of the city's four thousand elementary and grammar school teachers had gone directly from high school to the teacher's desk.[125] Only the three hundred secondary teachers in Chicago's few high schools were required to have a college degree.

But during the 1890s, the opportunities to enter teaching became more restrictive. The heart of the great school reform movements of the late nineteenth century was to "professionalize" teaching by requiring more preparatory schooling. In Chicago, the professionalization movement in education was instigated by a survey of the schools, published in 1892, that asserted that the city's schools lagged behind those of other major American cities primarily because of its underdeveloped teacher education, minimal qualification standards, and a weak apprenticeship and appointment system.[126] In 1893, the City of Chicago instituted a one-year training requirement and expanded the elementary teacher exam to include a section on pedagogical theory as well as general knowledge. By 1898, reformers promoted a requirement of at least one year of postsecondary schooling for elementary teachers. One effect of these changes was the gradual discouragement of working-class women from entering elementary teaching and an increased number of teachers from the middle class who could afford the extra schooling. In 1880, four years before Margaret Haley began teaching, almost one-half of all Chicago teachers came from working-class backgrounds, while by 1900 barely one-third did. The proportion of teachers from immigrant families also decreased during that time. [127] New elementary teachers in the 1890s were more likely to come from a different, higher class background than Haley and her cohort. This new group also had a more systematic experience of preparation for teaching, which emphasized a set body of scientific theories in education. This experience differed radically from Haley's own education as a community teacher hired through community networks, and a student of progressive, child-centered pedagogy. As younger teachers entered the Hendricks School through the 1890s, Haley may have observed both the class difference and a different attitude about the occupation of teaching.

In later years, Haley would try to articulate her ambivalence about these changes. She regarded teaching as a highly skilled profession that demanded advanced education and extensive preparation. Indeed, she applauded the message of her teacher education instructors—that skilled teaching was not merely the culmination of multiple experiences, but the result of purposeful, knowledgeable, and creative preparation. Teaching was a science that demanded close study. Yet Haley simultaneously objected to the ways in which increased education requirements excluded working-class women and introduced competition to the hiring process. She believed that teachers should be part of the community in which they worked, both physically and by class and ethnic identity. But these beliefs clashed with new professional standards that required an elite, highly trained teaching corps that was ready and able to teach any students anywhere. Haley's inability to compromise her ideas about these aspects of professionalism would haunt her leadership of teachers throughout her career. Her ambivalence stemmed from her own experience as a working-class teacher in a community school who had exceptional, but irregular training. For the rest of her life, she would have difficulty understanding why her experience could not be universalized for all teachers.

In 1895, at age thirty four, Margaret Haley was the most senior, and possibly also the eldest teacher at Hendricks. The only people who shared her memories of the original Forty-Third Street School were her principal and assistant principal. At least one of her original colleagues from her first years teaching at Hendricks had died, and this may have added to her sense of loss in a rapidly changing and increasingly youthful system. Over the years, her classroom had become crowded with more poor children from more foreign backgrounds, and school politics seemed to be working against progressive education and the notion of a stable community-based school. By 1895, Margaret Haley may have believed that her classroom at Hendricks was an increasingly lonely and isolated place.

CHAPTER TWO

THE EDUCATION OF AN ACTIVIST

WHEN MARGARET HALEY DESCRIBED her introduction to political activism, she talked about entering a movement. Politics was not just an interest or an activity, but a way of being that changed the way she looked at the world and the way she organized her life. Her entry to political work was not so much a cathartic experience as it was a gradual awakening that took place over a four-year period when, as a single woman in her thirties, she began to step out into the world. Until then, she was a daughter, sister, and teacher. Certainly she had political values instilled in her from her Irish Catholic laborite father, work experience from her years as a classroom teacher, and progressive ideas about educational practice from her early teacher training. But her life, as she described it, revolved primarily around family concerns and activities. In contrast, the character that evolved from her first political encounters in the late 1890s is a striking figure of great energy and passions, a charismatic public speaker, and an opinionated, aggressive, and often belligerent political activist. How did this coming to consciousness and change of character happen?

In her autobiography, written when she was in her sixties, Haley titled the chapter that covers this period "I Find the Battleground," and it chronicles her first involvement in political activities: her gradual introduction to women's organizations, followed immediately by her assertive seizing of leadership in those organizations. Typical of her autobiographical writing, Haley offered little personal insight into the experience, and almost no clue as to how she felt in her first political encounters. Nor does she explain how she changed, almost overnight, from a private daughter, sister, and teacher, into a public political activist.

Of course, Haley never intended her autobiography to be a personal story, but rather the story of a political institution—the Chicago Teachers' Federation, the organization with which her identity became almost totally merged. Following the model of male labor union leaders' autobiographies, she divided her life story between her years of family life and teaching—

about which she recorded very little—and her later years of public work for teachers—what she would later refer to as "Forty Fighting Years." In her writing, it was the public political work of the organization that she emphasized, not her own development. Haley was never a particularly self-reflective person anyway, and in one ironic moment of personal insight in her memoirs, she noted that in her early years she was "even less introspective" than she was as an older woman.[1]

Indeed, Haley persistently denied *any* personal motivation for her political activism, repeatedly asserting that she backed into politics by accident, that she was the kind of woman who was more interested in shopping for a new dress than in taking on any cause. "I had a habit of getting into all the fights that were going on," she wrote in 1935 about this period of her life, "and I always fell into them—I never went into one deliberately; they were ready made."[2] Whether intentional or not, this posture worked to her benefit as a woman public leader. By presenting herself as almost an innocent bystander, Haley minimized her own agency as an activist. This allowed her to continue to present a self-effacing feminine façade to the world even as simultaneously she became a domineering and energetic public figure. By denying her own initiative, Haley could appear to be merely the passive recipient of a powerful force for justice that swept her up inevitably into the movement. As the older Haley mused: "Without conscious intention I had, I can see now, been moving toward what must have been my vocation: a fighting future."[3]

LEAVING HOME

About the time that Margaret Haley began teaching at Hendricks School, Michael Haley bought a roomy two-story wood frame house on a large plot of land on West 63rd St. in Englewood, a new village on the southern edge of Chicago that was attracting upwardly mobile working-class Irish. For ten years the Haley parents and adult children lived together in this family home as the younger sisters also became teachers and the younger brothers took on their own skilled labor and civil service jobs. There, Haley remembered, they lived together as "quiet citizens in a quiet community."[4]

The closeness of Jackson Park and the Midway—wide swaths of unsettled land that later became part of the World's Fair and the University of Chicago—gave the family the opportunity to enjoy nature again. But Haley was also thrilled by urban life; she and her brother Dennis took the streetcar into Chicago to see theater, and the next night Dennis would act out the show for the rest of the family. On other nights they gathered to read Dickens out loud and sing, and occasionally they would discuss the political events of the day. Like many Irish Catholic families, the Haleys were intensely dependent on each other for entertainment, and there was a strong and lifelong bond between the siblings that Haley experienced as a kind of mystical connection.[5] She also liked her parents, and they seemed to like each other. For many years, there was no reason for Haley to leave the house on 63rd St.; her family was the core of her social and personal life.

In January 1888, the sixty-two-year-old Haley matriarch, Elizabeth, died. What little Haley wrote of her mother portrayed her as a supportive and nonjudgmental figure who encouraged her eldest daughter to go into teaching. Compared to her dynamic and erratic husband, Elizabeth played the role of the family moderator and caregiver.[6] For Margaret Haley, the loss of this calm and stabilizing force may have been sharpened by the fact that it made her, at twenty-six, the senior female member of the household.

Margaret Haley never married, and it is instructive to hypothesize why, and to consider the effect that her singleness had on her life and work in these years. Legally, she could have married and kept her job at Hendricks School. Unlike smaller rural districts and other cities, Chicago had no marriage bar for women teachers, so Haley did not have to choose between a classroom and a wedding. And Margaret Haley was not too old to marry; Irish American women tended to marry late (her sister Jenny married in 1892 when she was thirty, and their own mother had married when she was in her mid-thirties), in order to postpone childbearing and to extend their working years.[7]

But even if it was legal to marry and teach school, married women teachers were subtly discouraged from the job by custom and practice. A woman teacher was almost by definition a single woman: at the turn of the century, 70 percent of all American teachers were women, and 95 percent of these were single, widowed, or divorced.[8] Women teachers with children were especially discouraged from continuing their work in schools, and if Irish Catholic marriage meant anything, it meant the promise of children. So for all intents and purposes, it would have been almost impossible for Haley to stay at work if she married. And Margaret Haley may have wanted to keep teaching for more reasons than a steady income. She had been teaching since she was sixteen, and the work may have reinforced her role as an integral part of her family, a provider and role model for her two younger sisters, who became teachers, and her three younger brothers. Teaching gave Haley a place in the world, an identity and an occupation that she may not have been willing to abandon.

Probably a more helpful question than why Haley did not marry is what she gained from staying single. Singleness was hardly an unusual state in the late nineteenth century, particularly in Irish Catholic families. Haley's brother James and her sister Eliza never married, and the children had at least two unmarried aunts on their mother's side.[9] Singleness offered some clear advantages for working women, including the opportunity to take an active role in public life while retaining contacts with family. For many women, this understanding of singleness often corresponded with an emerging feminist consciousness. Although Haley herself never articulated it as such, her Federation colleague Catherine Goggin once explained that the high number of single woman teachers was due to their inherent independence. A woman teacher, Goggin argued, "learns to govern, not to be governed . . . she cannot be molded to suit any man. Her individuality has become too strongly developed." About her own refusal to marry, Goggin added that she simply could not face a man calling her a pet name such as "Ducky" when he came home from work expecting dinner on the table.[10]

Of course, Haley also may not have married because, simply, she didn't want to. We know that she remained single in the legal sense, but we know much less about her personal life. It could be that when Margaret Haley moved away from her family home around 1895 it was to develop or continue a relationship with a particular man or woman. Between 1900 and 1904 Haley did live with another woman, Carolyn Lynch, who was a teacher and Federation member, but the two lived in a rooming house with Lynch's two sisters. In 1907 Haley moved in with her Federation colleague Catherine Goggin, but she moved out in 1911, then back in for a year in 1914. In the two decades after 1895, Haley lived a peripatetic life in no fewer than nine different residences, including the homes of a brother and sister, an apartment up the street from her downtown office, and in a house on Chicago's near north side. If any of these living arrangements were connected to romantic relationships, no evidence to that effect has survived. Certainly Haley developed intense collegial relationships, spending full days and nights with women teachers and activists in meetings, writing petitions, lobbying politicians, and on the road in publicity and organizing campaigns. Whether or not Haley had primary sexual or emotional relationships with these or other women or men, we do know that she received emotional support from her family and from selected colleagues and friends within the Teachers' Federation.[11]

Around 1895, when Haley was in her mid-thirties, she moved out of her family home. It was not particularly unusual for an unmarried, steadily employed schoolteacher to live apart from family. Although most single women in the nineteenth century spent the entirety of their lives living with their families, by the late nineteenth century it was increasingly common for urban single working women to live on their own. In turn-of-the-century Chicago, about one-fifth of adult working women lived in boarding homes or as lodgers; up to a quarter of these were single women over the age of thirty-five.[12] In a teaching population that was predominately single women, probably up to one-quarter of them lived away from their families. Of all working women, teachers were probably the most financially able to live independently. For one thing, teachers were among the best paid of all working women: Chicago teachers' starting annual income at this time was at least $100 more than women who worked in the needle trades or manufacturing—the vast majority of all working women. Furthermore, teachers had job security and the promise of wage increases for the first few years of work. In 1895, the board of education salary schedule provided for annual increases in salary—from a starting annual wage of $500 to a cap of $800 in the eighth year.[13] Between 1894 and 1897, when the nation was wracked with a terrible economic depression, up to one-third of all Chicago workers were unemployed, and many of those working suffered wage cuts. But teachers' salaries remained stable, and the number of teachers hired by the city school system *increased* in these years by an average of 370 positions per year.[14]

Physical independence was one benefit of this job security. Some teachers rented a room in a boarding house or lodged with families, or sometimes with other women teachers. Such experiences offered women teachers their own social and psychological space and freedom from the daily housekeeping chores that an unmarried daughter would shoulder in the family home. It also offered them a broader social life in the city with other single women and men.

But the effects of moving out on one's own were not just personal; the move could also bring increased political awareness about work. Single working women who lived apart from their families might have been more likely to be aware of economics because they were more conscious of the immediate value of their own wage.[15] White-collar women workers were already in a position to think about the value of their wages in comparison to men's wages because they tended to work in closer proximity to men than did women who worked in factories or domestic service. Although teaching as an occupation was highly feminized, the school system as a whole was not, and while occupational divisions within the system were sharply gendered, men and women still worked together in the same buildings and departments. Women teachers worked under school principals, supervisors, and assistant superintendents—most of whom were men—who earned at least three times their salary, although they were required to have only a little more education than were teachers. High school teachers, half of whom were men and had college degrees, started at double the salary of elementary school teachers, almost all of whom were women. And school engineers, or janitors, all of whom were men, and who had no educational requirement, earned at least as much as an elementary teacher.[16] Women teachers also saw their brothers in other civil service positions in the police and fire departments who had fewer educational requirements than teachers but earned more than they did. Women teachers who lived together compared notes about these issues and gradually began to see the educational organization as systemically prejudiced against women.

If moving out of the family home offered Margaret Haley personal independence and a new insight into the Chicago public school system, the move may also have furthered the creation of her own distinct political identity. For all that Haley admired her father—the opinionated and committed supporter of labor and the Irish Land League—he also appears to have been a stubborn and energetic man who wanted to be in control of his world.[17] Michael Haley's politics were the masculine politics of the building

trades and the Knights of Labor. And while Margaret Haley's politics had
roots in those issues, she was increasingly identifying as a woman teacher in
a city public school system. As Margaret Haley aged, still admiring her father
and agreeing with him on many political issues, she may also have wanted
to step out of his strong and masculine shadow and pick up her own gauntlet.

TEACHER POLITICS: THE PENSION

The political world into which Haley stepped in 1895 was deeply gendered.
From her Irish Catholic laborite father and brothers, she was aware of a wide
and pervasive political network in the city of Chicago, but that network was
primarily a masculine one. Beginning in the late nineteenth century, Irish
American men held a powerful sway on ward and city politics in Chicago: Irish
men were the foundation of civil service, transportation, and construction
workers in the city, and by the turn of the century they were the heart of the
city's labor movement.[18] This was a hard-driving masculine ethnic politics, one
that took place in work sites, labor halls, clubs, lodges, and saloons and that
dealt with the delivery of jobs, services and favors between men.

Irish Catholic women were not excluded from the benefits of Irish
politics—by 1900, up to one-third of Chicago's teachers were of Irish heritage and many of these earned their jobs in community schools through the
local connections of Irish friends or family.[19] And certainly Irish American
women lived within the communities, read the newspapers, and supported
the causes of Irish nationalism and labor identity handed down from their
fathers. But male and female spheres were sharply divided in Irish American
labor and politics. The work of women differed radically from that of their
men, centering in feminized factory work and domestic work and in white-
collar jobs of teaching, nursing, and clerical work. Irish Catholic women's
political work also took place in gendered locales, including women's auxiliaries to unions and separate female units in mutual aid societies. The reluc-
tance of male Irish American political leaders to support woman suffrage
epitomized their adherence to gender segregation.[20]

Some labor organizations were more inclusive of white women from all
backgrounds, but still may not have been attractive to teachers, either because of the emphasis on industrial work or the radical ties to socialism. The
Irish-dominated Knights of Labor included women in their assemblies as
early as 1879, and some teachers joined, but most women members were
either factory workers or had ties with industrial labor.[21] It is more likely that
Irish American teachers such as Haley would have been attracted to the
Illinois Women's Alliance, which was active between 1888 and 1894 and
was a broad-based coalition of women's organizations, including church groups,
professional organizations, settlement houses, labor activists, and suffragists,
that promoted reforms in Chicago's schools and factories. Leading the Alliance fight against child labor and for compulsory schooling was Corinne

Brown, a single-taxer turned socialist, a former Chicago schoolteacher for thirteen years and principal for six years. Brown promoted the construction of new school buildings, the introduction of kindergartens, free textbooks, and the expansion and enforcement of compulsory education laws. But even though Brown was herself a former teacher, the Alliance attracted few teachers to its ranks, and Haley herself never mentioned it.[22] There was also a Teachers' Club in Chicago in the 1890s that was affiliated with the Illinois Federation of Women's Clubs, but it was a relatively apolitical organization that was more concerned with broad educational issues than with teachers' rights as workers.[23]

In fact, teachers were largely absent from both the radical and progressive reform movements of the 1890s and labor and feminist organizations. Why? One reason is that the occupation of teaching was ambiguous in both its class and gender status. In 1880, almost one-half of all Chicago's women teachers came from working-class backgrounds, but many of these women, including Margaret Haley, might be better identified as members of a labor aristocracy who promoted a liberal platform of equal rights republicanism, improved material welfare, and job autonomy, and not radical political change. Because of women teachers' slim hold on something resembling middle-class status, they may have been particularly disinclined to join radical groups. But neither were women teachers intrinsically attracted to middle-class women's reform organizations. Teaching was a feminized occupation associated with middle-class notions of maternal nurture and self-sacrifice, but it was also a civil service job that did not earn women either the comfort or the status of the middle class. Furthermore, social barriers existed between Protestant middle-class women's groups that dominated the social reform agenda of Chicago, and Roman Catholic middle-class women's groups. What all of this meant in terms of politics was that teachers could identify both with working-class wage laborers and with middle-class professionals because they were, in a sense, both. It also meant that they felt excluded from both the class-based and masculinized industrial labor movement and the women's middle-class reform movements.[24] Politically, women teachers were strangers in two worlds.

Teachers' working conditions reflected this ambiguity. Compared to most women's paid labor, teaching was among the best-paid jobs, with job security and comfortable working conditions. But this privilege was mitigated by a number of factors. Teachers' working conditions were not always as refined as the public would like to think. The city struggled to accommodate the flood of new students through the 1890s, housing 10 percent of students in rented rooms that were not equipped as classrooms, and another 10 percent in half-day classes. Many other schools in rapidly growing poor districts were not officially overcrowded but were in fact overflowing; for example, through the 1890s the Hendricks School functioned at 140 percent capacity with makeshift rooms and jammed classrooms. At least fifty of the city's three hundred school buildings were very old and in disrepair, lacking adequate lighting, ventilation, sanitary facilities, and fire escapes. Many older schools were surrounded by new city buildings that blocked light from their windows, and few buildings of any age had adequate playground facilities.[25]

Through the late nineteenth century, urban teachers raised an increasingly loud chorus of concerns about their work, many of which reflected Margaret Haley's own concerns about the Hendricks School. New compulsory education laws brought huge increases in school enrollments, particularly immigrant and poor students, thereby intensifying the work of teachers. The simultaneous centralization and professionalization of city school administrations led to a loss of teachers' authority in their classroom and school building, as traditional practices of locally designed curriculum and informal local hiring networks gave way to more distant and strict regulatory systems. And while teachers' salaries were high compared to most other paid work for women, women elementary teachers' salaries through the 1880s and 1890s were stagnant compared to the rising salaries of new administrators and high school teachers, most of whom were men. The women elementary teachers who had the greatest complaints were those teachers with many years of experience who worked in a system structured under the belief that teaching was a short-term job for young woman until they married. For these older, experienced, and independent women, the managerial practices and assumptions in city schools were becoming increasingly oppressive. Women teachers' labor concerns, then, were complicated, and not easy to match with those of their sisters and brothers who worked in factories and sweat shops.

Clearly, what teachers needed was to develop their own political movement that could articulate the particular interests of the occupational group itself. But this in and of itself was a challenge because of the enormous pressure for women teachers to *not* be self-interested. The very ideology and structure of the occupation of teaching as developed through the nineteenth century was organized around women teachers sacrificing themselves to nurture other people's children. Horace Mann, Henry Barnard, Catherine Beecher, and other engineers of nineteenth-century common schools placed as the cornerstone of educational progress women teachers' ability to "naturally" care for children, to be subservient to men administrators and, above all, to selflessly work for minimal pay.[26] This ethos of self-sacrifice was one of the major barriers to women teachers' political development. According to Catherine Goggin, a founding member of the Chicago Teachers' Federation, teachers would never become political forces until they got beyond "the very general feeling that anything savoring so strongly of material interests was almost sinful."[27] Teachers could not begin to think about reform and political activism until they felt empowered to think about themselves. Self-interest, then, was the spark for progressive political consciousness, but it was also anathema to teachers' professional identity.

Given the taboo against women teachers organizing for self-protection, it follows that their first attempts at organization were for protection only *after* they left the classroom. Across the country in the 1890s, women teachers' first moments of political activism were around securing their own pension. In this, teachers were not alone: Protective legislation issues such as the pension were among other American women's first major forays into governmental reform in the nineteenth century. Middle-class women organized around securing Civil War pension programs and later child labor laws, eight-hour workday laws, and health insurance to improve the lot of working women. Volunteer reform groups such as the National Federation of Women's Clubs and the National Congress of Mothers argued that protective legislation was necessary not only for women workers but also for their children, thus spinning their cause as broad social reform and minimizing the damaging implications of unfeminine selfishness in their quest for financial remuneration.[28]

For women teachers, the pension was a particularly high priority. Because women teachers were for all practical purposes barred from marriage and motherhood, longtime teachers would leave the occupation with little savings and no children who could support them in their old age. The first teachers' pension legislation was passed in Brooklyn, New York, in 1879, and by the New York State legislature in 1895. New Jersey and other states followed suit, recognizing that the promise of a pension for older teachers worked as a positive recruitment device for younger teachers. The pension was designed for all teachers, female and male, elementary and secondary (and in some cities, administrators and school staffs), but women teachers conceived of the pension as a direct response to gender inequity in both schools and society at large. Women teachers observed that male civil service workers including firemen and policemen had pension coverage and they did not. In systems such as Chicago's, which had hired entire cohorts of teachers in the 1870s and '80s, there were large numbers of women teachers with more than twenty years' teaching experience who were on the edge of retirement in the 1890s with virtually no support system under them.[29]

In one of the few historical moments of agreement between activist teachers and school administrators, late-nineteenth-century city school boards did not oppose the adoption of teachers' pensions, although their thinking about the purpose of the pension differed radically from teachers'. By the 1890s, new city school systems faced a great employment problem. As women teachers aged without any retirement plan, many of them stayed in the system, continuing their outdated methods of instruction and drawing their relatively high salaries. In Chicago in 1894, out of a teaching force of almost four thousand teachers, 227 had twenty years or more experience, including twenty-six who had taught more than thirty years.[30] School systems also had problems hiring new teachers: Low salaries, and the opening up of other white-collar work that required less educational training than teaching, were siphoning a lot of prospective women teachers away from the occupation. More troubling to some school administrators was the "type" of woman teacher who was drawn to the occupation—as more first and second-generation immigrant women entered teaching, school administrators and politicians alike worried publicly about the cultural, personal, and political "character" of women teachers from working-class and Irish Catholic backgrounds.[31] Equally troubling was the absence of men who entered teaching, a trend which threatened to create a veritable masculinity crisis in both schools and society. In 1895, barely 5 percent of all Chicago teachers were men, and more than half of those were employed in high schools only.[32]

School administrators saw the pension as a way to achieve both economic efficiency and some social control over the shaping of the teaching force. The pension, along with tenure and higher salaries, was urban school administrators' attempt to flush out superannuated teachers and to attract more young teachers, more male teachers, and more highly educated teachers. The pension was also attractive to school boards because, as it was originally constructed as a deferred wage, they could justify postponing raising teachers salaries with an unpopular tax increase.[33]

But although school boards might support pensions, it was teachers who initiated the fight for them. The campaign for the teachers' pension in Chicago was initiated in 1892 by a solitary teacher, Arvilla C. DeLuce, who had a lifelong interest in pensions. As a young teacher, she had a memorable conversation with a group of older women teachers who asked her how long she intended to teach. DeLuce replied prophetically, "I shall teach until we all get a pension," to which her older colleagues laughed in disbelief. More recently, DeLuce's husband and father had encouraged her to start a campaign for the pension. Like many women teachers, DeLuce had reason to worry about her future. In 1892, she was a teacher with twenty-eight years' experience in the Chicago schools, married and in her late forties. Her husband of twenty-five years had alternately worked as a school janitor, druggist, and self-employed baker, and almost certainly had no pension of his own.[34]

DeLuce methodically planned her campaign over a two-year period. First she requested a transfer from teaching seventh and eighth grade to a primary grade so she would have more free time after school. On her own, she drafted a plan of action and a preliminary form of the law to be presented to the legislature. Next she wrote a personal note to all thirty teachers in her own school, asking if each teacher would be willing to support a legal case for a pension. All the teachers in the school except one agreed. Then she prepared a questionnaire for teachers in each school in the city, and a majority of teachers responded in favor of a pension. By 1894, DeLuce had attracted a core of newly activist teachers including Catherine Goggin, a thirty-nine-year-old elementary teacher with twenty years of teaching experience. Goggin and DeLuce identified a single teacher in each Chicago school who they felt had the savvy to get signatures for a petition supporting a pension. Although Margaret Haley had met neither women, and was as of yet uninvolved in the movement, she was pegged to organize the teachers at Hendricks. Like DeLuce, Haley recalled resistance and disbelief from some of the teachers to whom she circulated the petition whose experiences led them to disbelieve that politicians would ever listen to women.[35]

The teachers took their petitions to the state capitol in Springfield to lobby Governor Altgeld who not only supported the proposal, but added a civil service clause that provided teachers with tenure and guaranteed that any eligible teacher who was fired would receive her contributed pension money back. Recipients were entitled to one half of the amount of their salary received at the time of retirement up to $600.[36] Women teachers were eligible five years before men, reflecting the popular belief that women were not strong enough to work for as many years as men. Catherine Goggin criticized the board of education for this gender bias, but acknowledged that it was not a surprise given that the bill was written in a state that still classed women among "the seven unrepresented species of citizens, namely aliens, criminals, insane, idiots, paupers, minors, and—women."[37]

The pension law passed the state legislature in February 1895. Arvilla DeLuce promptly resigned the following year and was one of the first Chicago teachers to collect her pension.[38]

THE PROGRESSIVE EDUCATION OF AN EDUCATOR

Meanwhile, Margaret Haley was going back to school to study what was commonly referred to as "the new education," or what later became known as progressive education—the range of innovative curricular and pedagogical movements at the turn of the century that linked schooling to progressive social change. Central to these movements was the reconceptualization of schooling from a rigid course of study based on intellectual ideas to a social program that began with the needs and interests of children. The roots of progressive education went as far back as eighteenth-century European theorists Jean-Jacques Rousseau, Johann Pestalozzi, and Friedrich Froebel, and had been seen in America in the work of the Herbartians at Illinois Normal School and Francis Parker at Cook County Normal School. But it was the philosophical writings of John Dewey, based on his observations of children at the Laboratory School at the University of Chicago in the 1890s, that crystallized progressive education in America. Central to Dewey's thinking was the notion of the classroom as a small, child-centered society, where children's spontaneous and natural instincts and interests could be integrated into the cultural objectives of the curriculum.[39] Haley had heard theories to this effect from the untrained but inspired instruction of Cyrus Brown and from her normal school instructors at Illinois Normal and Cook County. Later, she would see the way in which progressive educational ideas blended imperceptibly into the political and economic vision presented by her first hero, Henry George, but for the moment her interests were focused solely on questions of classroom practice.

In 1896, Haley went to a two-week Summer Institute for Teachers at the School of Pedagogy at the University of Buffalo. Opened in 1895 under the direction of Frank McMurry, a former faculty member from Illinois Normal, the program was designed for advanced study by current teachers and school administrators. There she heard the pragmatic philosopher William James deliver one of his "Talks to Teachers on Psychology," which Haley praised as a "mighty wind whirling through dark corridors, clearing out cluttered corners of the mind." Because of James, she left Buffalo "thrilled with the pride" of her profession.[40]

The following summer, Haley went to a Catholic summer school in Madison, Wisconsin, led by the Dominican Sisters from Sinsinawa, Wisconsin.[41] Catholic summer schools were part of the liberal social movement of the American Catholic church designed to expose parochial and public school teachers to contemporary social problems and secular intellectual debates.[42] The summer school in Madison was the brainchild of the Sinsinawa Mother Superior and Thomas Edward Shields, one of the leading Catholic educators of the day. Their joint goal was to promote reconciliation between the study of science and the practice of faith in education. Although Shields critiqued the philosophy of John Dewey as being "materialistic," he promoted Deweyan principles. The elementary school classroom, Shields later wrote, should not be "a quiet, sad place, where little children fear to move lest they should disturb a nervous teacher," but it should be an active and social place where children learned "from each other more than they learn from the teacher and where they learn by doing rather than by hearing."[43] Teachers needed appropriate training in pedagogical techniques and psychology to create such an educational environment. It was from Shields's visiting lectures and other courses in literature, psychology, political science, and pedagogy at the Sinsinawa summer school that Haley recalled she learned the "widening view" about "the fundamental issue in the unending war for academic freedom: the right of the teacher to call his soul his own."[44]

But perhaps as powerful as the content of the curriculum was the experience of Sinsinawa itself. The Dominican sisters at Sinsinawa had been renowned since the 1860s for their pioneering education programs and for their self-sufficient community of women on the northern prairies. Sinsinawa sisters had designed their own teaching mission in a local convent academy, developed education programs for their congregation and community, and instituted an ongoing program of teacher preparation institutes for teaching sisters. This was a distinct community of women with power and intellect that exemplified not only a model for communal life, but also one of creative initiative in educational reform. Their commitments to intellectual development, as well as social reform, provided Haley with role models of dynamic leadership by other Catholic women.[45]

Haley's first notions of the school as an agency of social reform were developed at these summer schools for teachers where she learned more about progressive child-centered pedagogy and about the importance of intellectual clarity and social activism. Combined with her earlier readings in Henry George, and her familiarity with labor politics, her summer school studies in the mid-1890s helped her develop a vision of the school as the center of a progressive welfare state.

In the winter of 1898, a few months after Haley's return from the Sinsinawa summer school, she began her political life.

THE FORESTERS FIGHT

In 1898, Haley's sister Jenny's husband was diagnosed with cancer soon after the birth of their first child. Concerned about their financial future, the two sisters joined the Women's Catholic Order of Foresters, an organization devoted to the distribution of insurance, pensions, and death benefits to Catholic women.[46] In the years before the establishment of civil service pensions, it was fraternal insurance organizations such as the Foresters that offered the only form of life insurance for working families. Like many fraternal organizations, male and female, the Foresters was both a benefit society and a cultural organization for its members. The Women's Catholic Order of Foresters offered women the opportunity to become involved in public life and to practice organization on their own. This certainly was the case for Haley who used the Foresters as a testing ground for her own political muscle. Haley joined the organization and almost immediately became involved in a battle to make it more democratic. She played the role of a populist gadfly, organizing to unseat a woman who Haley claimed was an autocratic leader. Haley's tactics were belligerent and aggressive; she used her expertise in parliamentary procedure to push and bend meetings to her benefit, and these tactics eventually exhausted her enemies' patience. Her actions created hysteria and confusion in the organization, and earned her lifelong admirers and enemies. It was a flamboyant if somewhat bizarre entry onto the public stage.

Originally, however, Haley had little interest in the group. When she first joined the Foresters she was a "dimly obscure and entirely uninterested member" of one of the local districts. But within a few months of joining, she was struck by the realization that the leader of the group, Mrs. Elizabeth Rodgers, had secured her own election for a lifetime term. Haley was appalled: Life terms smacked of the royalty that Irish nationalists and American democrats were taught to eschew. Furthermore, the Foresters' highly ritualistic organizational culture already veered toward a monarchal style: District groupings were called "courts," each of which had a supervisory priest from the local parish and passwords for district members. The president was called the "High Chief Ranger." Haley thought these traditions silly and dangerous for the democratic process, since leaders seemed to become swept

up in the rituals and acted "as if they belonged to the nobility."[47] This was
the problem she saw with Elizabeth Rodgers and her adoring membership.

Ironically, given her father's affiliation with the Knights of Labor, Haley's
enemy here was one of the most beloved women officials in that organization. In 1898, Elizabeth Rodgers was a fifty-one-year-old Irish-born mother
of ten, and the grande dame of the Knights of Labor with over two decades
of leadership in women's labor auxiliaries. She was an Irish Catholic women
labor activist—a potential role model for Haley.[48] But to Haley, Elizabeth
Rodgers was a reprehensible leader who acted like a queen.

Haley convinced her district court to join her in objecting to the life
clause and in early spring 1898, she was elected a delegate to the upcoming
convention. Typically, in her autobiography she downplayed her own initiative—"I didn't know why I was chosen to lead the fight"—even as she
charged headfirst into it.[49] In preparation for the battle, she joined with a
group of other Foresters' women to study parliamentary law.

The study of parliamentary law through Robert's Rules of Order was
enormously popular in late-nineteenth-century women's volunteer groups.
First published in 1876, Robert's Rules fed a growing demand for procedural
technique in local clubs and organizations. The 1880s and '90s saw a growth
of drill classes and study groups in parliamentary law, wall charts that outlined the precedents of motions, and manuals to educate people in the skills
they saw as necessary for American citizenship. Robert's Rules was particularly popular with the newly formed women's groups of the Progressive Era—
from the Women's Christian Temperance Union, to suffrage organizations,
to a constellation of literary groups and women's clubs. One of the assets of
Robert's Rules for women was the way in which the procedure formalized
relationships, prohibiting personalization and promoting cool order. Robert's
Rules helped to replace the popular image of emotional and chatty matrons
sipping tea with that of a purposeful, democratically run organization. The
procedures allowed women not only to claim authority in a public space, but
also to command respect. Another useful aspect for a new Foresters member
such as Haley was that under Robert's Rules, new members were allowed as
much voice as long-term members.[50]

Margaret Haley's priest later told her that given the nature of her
opposition in the Foresters, she might have been wiser to bring to the convention not a manual of parliamentary law but a shotgun.[51] On the convention floor in April 1898, Haley and her colleagues tried in vain to challenge
the legality of Elizabeth Rodgers's life clause. Following Robert's Rules, they
asked how the provision for the life term was written into the Foresters'
constitution without an amendment, and they questioned the legality of
electing a president for one year and subsequently extending that term to
life. But the High Chief Ranger consistently called them out of order, refused
their motions, and denied voice votes. On the second day of this, Haley had
had enough, and she exploded, calling the chair "an autocrat." She charged:

"Your rule is gag rule. Your convention is a mob. I'v\
mob before, and I won't be one now."[52] Her charge inst\
in the hall. Elizabeth Rodgers tried to expel Haley from b\
and the order, and women on both sides of the debate we\
were appalled that Haley challenged the chair in such a rude w\
were furious at Rodgers for refusing to hear the challenge. Tempe\
room swirled with "terrible passions," Haley recalled. "Women\
sobbed, shouted. Through it all Mrs. Rodgers pounded the gavel. W\
came rushing toward me, hands upraised, eyes gleaming with hatred." Ro\
charged that Haley had "vilified and abused" her, and she implied that Haley\
was mentally unstable. One delegate said that Haley called Rodgers a "fiend\
incarnate." Another delegate claimed that Haley slanderously called Mrs.\
Rodgers an "acrobat," apparently misunderstanding Haley's public accusation\
that she was an "autocrat."[53]

By convention vote, Haley was expelled from the order, but the body
also voted to withdraw Rodgers's life term clause. The priest of Haley's district court then advised her to challenge the expulsion and to sue for libel—
not an unprecedented act since in the previous year another expelled member had sued the Foresters for $10,000.[54] Haley took the case to a lawyer and
filed an injunction to prevent the Foresters from sending the announcements
of her expulsion to the members.[55] The judge who granted the injunction
was Edward F. Dunne, who later became mayor and governor of Illinois, and
a strong supporter of the Teachers' Federation. Haley's lawyer and parish
priest spoke to the convention advising them to reinstate Haley before she
filed suit. The delegates agreed to reinstatement on the condition that Haley
promise not to sue and make a public apology to Elizabeth Rodgers. Haley
came to the meeting to find the membership in a frenzied state, pleading
Haley to apologize. Haley refused, at which point Elizabeth Rodgers went
down on her knees, and began to pray. The shouting started again, but the
priest managed to quell it.[56] Haley finally agreed to apologize, but she did so
in her soon to be characteristic manner saying: "I'm sorry I offended anybody. *Even if* what I said was true, I should not have said it." This statement
set off another tumult: Elizabeth Rodgers was furious, the priest scolded
Haley, and the whole convention was set into hysterical motion again. Haley
had made her point, and she left the organization.

Two years after the battle, the Foresters were still trying to rid themselves of the divisiveness of Haley's legacy as they argued over deleting or
retaining her name from the official minutes. The very mention of her name
caused Foresters members to fall into a rampage of detailed recollections of
the trouble that she had caused. Many delegates must have sighed with relief
at the resolution that passed at the convention in 1900, that the name of
Margaret Haley not be mentioned in the hall again.[57]

Haley herself never mentioned the Foresters again either, but she acknowledged that in many ways the battle prepared her for her later work

the Federation.[58] Certainly, the encounter honed her new skills with
ïamentary procedure, gave her experience in public speaking, creating
ꜣlitions within large groups, and challenging authority. It may also have
ꜣarked her interest in confrontational politics.

Although a seemingly isolated and obscure bit of political drama, Haley's
incident with the Foresters was a portentous entry onto the public stage. In
Haley's retelling, her transformation from the innocent teacher interested in
pedagogical improvement into a combative, irascible firebrand was an abrupt
one, with no explanatory transition. It is likely that Haley had already taken
opinionated stands in her work and private life, and that her moxie had been
developing for some time. But Haley's decision to take on the Foresters fight
and soon thereafter become active in the Chicago Teachers' Federation at
this time in her life is also significant. In 1898, Haley was thirty-seven years
old, single, and no longer a dependent of her parents. She had traveled to
distant cities on her own, was attending to her own retirement and life
insurance plans, and had begun to study principles of political organization.
She had also spent considerable time examining the strengths and weaknesses of the occupation on which she had been engaged for over twenty
years, and she had the personal and political maturity to consider taking risks
and fighting for change.[59]

THE CHICAGO TEACHERS' FEDERATION

In the heat of the Foresters fight, Haley was elected a vice president of the
newly founded Chicago Teachers' Federation. The Federation was organized
in 1897 as a direct result of political threats to the newly established teachers' pension law. One problem with the pension law was that it did not
provide enough money to the system. Individuals did not have to contribute
a fixed amount before receiving a benefit, so that a teacher with twenty years
of tenure was entitled to retire in 1897 with an annual pension of $600 a
year, even though she would have contributed only a few dollars since the
pension system began two years earlier. When a lot of older women elementary teachers began to retire, the pension fund was almost depleted.

Furthermore, male high school teachers and principals complained that
the gender bias of the pension law meant that they had to stay in the system
five years longer than women before they could draw their pension, and
higher paid male educators contributed more money on a percentage basis
than elementary teachers.[60] Not that there was any love lost between elementary and high school teachers, who were already divided by gender
(one-half of all high school teachers were men), training (a college degree
was required to teach high school compared to the equivalent of a high
school degree to teach in the lower grades), salaries, and perceived professional status and authority. "There are but few things in common between
high school and grade teachers," remarked one male high school teacher,

adding that the political activities of some elementary teachers further proved their inferiority as they were "politicians first and then teachers."[61] Such critiques by male educators confirmed a growing feeling among women elementary teachers that nobody would be making any effort to improve their material conditions without regular pressure.

A small number of women elementary teachers met in the spring of 1897 and planned an organization of teachers that would not only defend the pension but also would take up other issues of interest to classroom teachers, and, in preparation for further work, study parliamentary law. Intentionally, they restricted membership to those "actually engaged in the work of teaching" in the elementary schools, thereby excluding even sympathetic high school teachers or principals.[62] The Federation was not closed to men—for many years a male elementary teacher was the Federation secretary—but for all intents and purposes, it was a female organization. The teachers held two mass meetings and appointed Catherine Goggin and two other women as leaders. Within three months, the young organization had reached a membership of 250, and six months later, more than 2,500—well over half of all elementary teachers. The first work of the Federation was to defend the pension and to raise salaries for experienced teachers, who had in the past twenty years received an increase of less than 7 percent, although supervisory and administrative salaries had in the same time increased in amounts varying from 14 percent to 100 percent. This meant that in 1897 about four thousand elementary teachers were working under practically the same salary schedule that had been in force in 1877.[63]

In June, the Federation requested improved salaries and the board of education ignored them. Six months later, the Federation returned with a petition signed by 3,567 teachers, and they advised the board that if it did not have the money to run the schools, it might as well close them. The board acquiesced by adopting a new salary scale that gave each teacher of more than seven years experience a $75 raise, and promising all teachers a raise of $50 in 1899 and again in 1900.[64]

The teachers had won their first battle.

CATHERINE GOGGIN

By all accounts, Catherine Goggin was the driving force behind the establishment of the Chicago Teachers' Federation, and she quickly became its guiding light. A powerful and self-confident leader in her own right, part of Goggin's effectiveness in the new Federation would come from the way that she balanced off the very different strength of Margaret Haley. Although also the daughter of Irish Catholic immigrants, Goggin was strikingly different from Haley in both temperament and political style.

Catherine Goggin was born in 1855 in Adirondack, New York, the daughter of Irish immigrants. Goggin's father Patrick and his first wife had

Catherine Goggin, 1901 (Courtesy Chicago Historical Society)

two sons and a daughter, but one son died in infancy, the other at age ten, and his wife some time later. The widowed Patrick remarried, but the family troubles continued. The second Mrs. Goggin had a son who died as an infant, and two daughters—Catherine and two years later Margaret. Sometime later the family moved to Chicago, possibly to live near the family of Patrick's brother John. In Chicago, young Catherine Goggin attended the Franklin School where Albert G. Lane, who later became superintendent of schools, was principal. She went on to Central High School, one of the two high schools in the city. In early October 1871, just as she was beginning her last year of high school, the Chicago Fire destroyed ten schools; all the city's classes were suspended for two weeks and 135 teachers were thrown out of work. The school system responded by doubling up teachers and students in classrooms.[65] Goggin graduated in 1872 in a class of about forty students, with an elementary teaching certificate.

Goggin began teaching the city's poorest children at the Clarke School in the middle of the Stockyards district. Her first years of teaching elementary school were trial by a different kind of fire. Chicago schools in the 1870s were crippled by severe underfunding as the city poured most of its public resources into rebuilding its charred infrastructure. An economic depression lasting from 1873 to 1879 further damaged the city, and the impact on schools was devastating. In 1875, only Goggin's third year as a teacher, less than one-fifth of Chicago children attended school regularly, and even these children sat in overcrowded classrooms. In 1878, school appropriations were cut 20 percent and teachers were paid in scrip with an average 18 percent loss in pay.[66] During these years, Goggin's mother and father died, and in 1880, her twenty-three-year-old sister Margaret died of consumption. Catherine Goggin was twenty-five years old.[67]

Goggin did have one surviving family member nearby who proved to be a defining influence on her life. Her cousin James Goggin, seven years her senior, was a Chicago lawyer and judge of some prominence. Born in Northern Ireland, he was raised and educated in the Illinois capitol of Springfield, and was admitted to the Chicago bar in 1866. In 1871, he was appointed to the Chicago Board of Education and four years later he was elected attorney for the board. He was appointed superior court judge in 1892. By the time of his death in 1898, he was a widely admired local judge with a liberal reputation. The relationship between the bachelor judge and his teacher cousin was close. As board member and attorney, James Goggin occasionally called on his cousin to help out a teacher in trouble or to advise him on teacher matters, an experience that taught her about principles and theory of law. The two were also personally close: Catherine Goggin was with her cousin at his death bed, and she buried him in the family gravesite next to her sister.[68]

In 1881 Goggin moved to the Jones School where she taught for the next nineteen years. Located on the south side of the Chicago Loop, Jones was one of the oldest schools in the city, although its original building was one of the ten school buildings destroyed by the 1871 fire. The building was rebuilt but then destroyed by another fire in July 1874. By 1890, it had lost most of its prestige as an original school, in part because of its location in the First Ward which had a larger enrollment of African American and Chinese children than any other ward. Indeed, the conditions of the Jones School were among the most desperate in the city: It was an elementary

school, although most students did not make it past the primary grades, and it
suffered the lowest daily attendance rate of all schools in the district.[69] Goggin's
working conditions were also unique in that she worked both with and for
people of color, and she had at least one African American colleague, Mollie
Hudson, a graduate of Jones who worked at the school from 1887 to 1919.[70]

By 1897, Catherine Goggin had experienced a full cross section of the
Chicago public school system: As a student in a well-supported elementary
and grammar school and as a high school student in the elite Central High
School she saw the best that city schooling could offer, including the community response to the disaster of the 1871 fire. As a teacher, however, she
must have been disappointed. Working in schools with the city's poorest
children, she saw the school system cut back on its support of education,
including teachers' basic pay. And by observing and working with her cousin,
she may have begun to understand how to improve public schools through
the legal system.

Goggin's political talents were based in her perceptive social skills. Teachers and political colleagues testified that Goggin exuded a warm personality
and a sense of humor that could ease tension. She was, one *Chicago Tribune*
reporter attested, "one of the least obtrusive of women," although her strength
of character was also very apparent.[71] In one particularly contentious fight
early in the Federation's existence, as teachers were clamoring for attention in
a large meeting hall, Goggin stepped up to the stage. "It was like magic," her
friend Margaret Haley recalled, as "the moment Miss Goggin stepped to the
platform and put out her hand, order was restored. . . . The hush that fell over
that house was positively solemn." With calm achieved, Goggin stepped off
the platform and came down the aisle. When a teacher started to compliment
her, she dramatically took off her hat and bowed, which set the whole hall
laughing. "She had not only restored order but good nature."[72]

Haley saw Goggin's style as being slower and more deliberate than her
own highly energetic approach, and she admired Goggin for it. Rather than
being forceful and proactive, Goggin "watched things as they were moving,"
confirming her support and measuring up her opposition. Goggin also used her
social skills to further her political work. She had "the power to attract others,
to get others talking and thinking about the question," Haley recalled.[73] "Her
wisdom was uncanny. . . . She never said she wanted you to do anything and
she would never lay down the law. She threw it out as a hint or a suggestion,
and in such an interesting way, serious at times and funny at other times. And
always there was in it that idea of—do what you please, yourself. She never
superimposed it on you. That put the responsibility on you." Catherine Goggin,
Haley remembered, "could have taught you the world." [74]

From the time Goggin and Haley began to work together in the 1898
Federation election campaign, they created a symbiotic duo of different speeds
and tactics that they would continue through the next eighteen years of
work together. Goggin was as quiet and measured as Haley was outgoing and

impetuous; where Goggin used her social skills and style to win hearts, Haley used her charismatic energy to win points. Goggin took on managerial roles at meetings and in the Federation; Haley took on the public fighting roles that pushed the Federation agenda. Haley came off as David fighting Goliath, and Goggin as wise King Solomon. By late 1898, these two mythic characters were ready for battle.

HARPER

In December 1898, Haley's principal, John McCarthy, showed her a copy of a newly released board of education report that he believed the new Teachers' Federation needed to take very seriously. This was not the first time that Haley's principal had nudged her toward political work; he often brought in news clippings about the board of education, urging his teachers to keep up to date on school politics. This new report, he said, was something completely different and quite dangerous. If its recommendations were implemented into school law, it would radically change the Chicago school system for the worse. He urged Haley to take the report to the Federation and organize a response.

The dangers of the report—commonly called the Harper Report after the chair of the commission, William Rainey Harper, who wrote it—were not immediately obvious to Haley or most other Federation members. Written by a commission appointed by the mayor to reform the city school structure, the report was a mixed bag of progressive curricular additions and administrative adjustments. It called for the establishment of advisory teacher councils, kindergartens throughout the city, more playgrounds, and the creation of one central commercial high school and two manual training high schools. The report also recommended against a salary increase for teachers, and for a provision that teachers be fired or retained on the basis of their teaching efficiency as judged by the building principal—a proposal that undermined the recently achieved tenure law. The report also recommended that a college degree be a requisite for entering teaching, that a system of merit pay be introduced, and that male teachers earn higher salaries than women. A final, significant recommendation was to consolidate local ward-based systems of schooling under a powerful superintendent appointed by the city mayor and monitored by a smaller board of education that would also be appointed by the mayor.[75]

The identity of the author of the report should have cued the teachers to the problem. William Rainey Harper, president of the private University of Chicago, was appointed to the Chicago Board of Education in 1897 where he was one of the most vociferous opponents of salary raises for teachers. Teachers' opposition to Harper led Mayor Carter Harrison to reappoint him from the board of education to the chair of the Education Commission, which was authorized to propose a reform agenda to the city school system.

In the meantime, Harper had pressured the mayor to replace Superintendent Albert G. Lane, who was respected by teachers, with Benjamin Andrews, the president of Brown University and former president of Denison University, whose only professional experience had been in higher education. Almost immediately, Superintendent Andrews gained the reputation of being so bureaucratic that the teachers derisively nicknamed him "Bulletin Ben." Harper was also legendary for his public arrogance about teachers who he believed should not complain about their salaries because they were getting as much pay as his wife's maid.[76] Haley felt that Harper was ultimately a man intrinsically opposed to the democratic process and that he had been personally threatened by the mobilization of women teachers for the pension. She described Harper as an elitist reactionary, woman-hating mossback and the mouthpiece of John D. Rockefeller who had founded the elitist University of Chicago in 1892.[77]

But Haley still had not grasped the real danger of Harper's report until it was finally made clear to her by Frances Temple, a high school math teacher who had come to the Teachers' Federation to argue that the main impact of the Harper Report was the proposal to reorganize the school administrative structure from a local community-based organization to a smaller and more centralized body. Accompanying this administrative centralization was the adoption of business principles to the management of schools with the goal of a streamlined system emphasizing financial efficiency over educational principles. Frances Temple pressed the Federation to consider the grave implications of such changes on teachers' autonomy: Threatened was teachers' right to express themselves in school management matters from textbook selection to the development of courses of study to the organization of local schools. Haley eventually saw Frances Temple as the switch that finally turned on the light bulb of her understanding about school politics. Haley had known about the tendency toward centralization that was sweeping over the country, but she had not fully understood the potential impact on teachers. Until Temple made sense of the matter to Haley, "it was all chaos" in her mind.[78]

Finally Haley got it: School organization meant power, and teachers were going to be locked out of power by the Harper proposal. Gradually, Haley would come to see the fight over the Harper Report as part of a long continuum of political battles between organized business interests and educational interest, and ultimately between men and women over access to political voice. When she finally read the report, she saw "a deeply laid conspiracy to establish an autocratic system of administration in the Chicago schools" and she believed that "this was the scheme of big business to get control of the public schools." But the battle was not only with Harper and his minions but also with the sitting president of the Federation, Elizabeth Burdick, and her supporters who were generally in agreement with the Harper Report.[79] The debate over the Harper proposal became as much a battle over the political perspective of the Federation as a fight with the city administration. Haley and Goggin found that their battleground had two fronts.

Barely a month after it was written, the recommendations from the Harper Report were worked into a bill for the state legislature by the Chicago Civic Federation, an organization founded by middle-class social reformers and business leaders to improve the city's civic and welfare structures. Haley and Goggin met to organize against the bill, which set them on a collision course with the objectives of President Burdick. When at a Federation meeting Haley was nominated as representative of her district to go to Springfield to lobby against the Harper Bill, Burdick abruptly adjourned the meeting before the vote could be taken. Undaunted, Haley's district formed a makeshift group on their own and nominated Haley anyway. Then they wrote a resolution and petition that they distributed widely. Recognizing that most citizens had not heard of the Harper Bill, Haley shrewdly wrote the petition to ask not for approval or disapproval of the bill, but simply to ask the legislature to postpone consideration of the bill until people had time to read about it. The Federation then sponsored scores of community meetings where Haley explained the dangers of the bill, and sent teachers out to the streets with petitions for citizens to sign in opposition to it.[80] Haley crowed that these meetings showed teachers how democratic their organization could be when managed by a presiding officer and representative board that was "fair and just."[81]

Goggin and Haley may have been fair and just in their leadership, but they were also astute tacticians who developed a popular practice of allowing the opposition to speak at a Federation meeting, thereby presenting the enemy in full view of the membership. During one Federation meeting, a member of the city legislature who backed the Harper Bill asked if he could speak on behalf of it. Goggin asked the hundreds of Federation members—almost all women—if they wanted to hear him, which they did. The result was only humiliation to the man, who Haley said "looked like a turkey in the stubbles. He would first stand on one foot and then on the other foot. He began by saying that he had introduced the bill. Then a sigh went over the house and a groan." But then he said that this didn't necessarily mean he would support the bill, and that when he introduced it, he didn't realize how much the teachers would oppose it. Clearly underestimating the political tenor of the group, he said that he thought that any bill that the president of the University of Chicago introduced would be a good bill, at which point somebody in the audience yelled out that the University of Chicago was "Rockefeller's oil tank."[82] The man left the hall in humiliation. Sometimes, Haley reflected, "the enemies of a cause do it far more good than do its friends."[83]

The theme of opposing business interests in schools quickly became the driving force in the campaign to defeat the Harper Bill. By highlighting Harper's link to the millionaire Rockefeller and to moneyed interests, the debate over restructuring the city public school system was deflected to a debate about power and class interests in a democratic society. This broadened the relevance of the issue from specific school politics to social and economic reform—a topic that garnered enthusiastic response. Former governor John Altgeld derided the Harper Bill as a proposal to turn the school system "over to the domination of the Standard Oil Trust," the powerful corporation that Rockefeller owned.[84] Then the Chicago Central Labor Council critiqued the proposed college education requirement as a strategy to exclude working-class women from the occupation, and called Superintendent Andrews a "moral leper" whose purpose was "to promote Rockefeller's ideas." When the elite Chicago Women's Club backed off from its original support for the Harper Bill after meeting with the Federation, the teachers' cause had turned a corner.[85]

In Springfield, Haley attended the state legislature's education committee meeting where she showed the representatives the petitions, and argued that the Harper Bill gave the superintendent of the Chicago schools autocratic power unknown even to the Czar of Russia. In her soon to be characteristic use of hyperbole, Haley argued that the bill provided for a superintendent with so many powers that he "would need to be omnipotent as well as omni-present in all parts of the system at all times and capable of perfect justice, and that the only instance in history where there had been such a visitor to the earth was nineteen hundred years ago and that he was crucified." The teachers of Chicago, she could testify, did not believe that if Jesus returned to this earth, he would come via the University of Chicago.[86] Humiliated by the public presence of the teachers, the legislature voted down the Harper Bill in the spring of 1899.

THE FIGHT FOR LEADERSHIP

Having identified business interests at the core of Harper's proposal for school reform, Haley and Goggin now saw them hibernating in the leadership of the Teachers' Federation.[87] The problem was President Elizabeth Burdick, who had been one of the founding members of the Federation and president for the previous two years. Burdick and her supporters backed the Harper Bill and Superintendent Andrews. Most troubling to Haley and Goggin was Burdick's support of the firing of Josephine Locke, the head of the city's school art department. Haley believed that Locke was dismissed because she had objected to the board's requirement that art teachers use a certain set of drawing books. Locke's theories of art relied on children's natural creativity, and not on the use of textbooks, and she was supported in her ideas by the Chicago Art Institute. But the school board had already contracted with a textbook publisher, and Locke's position was a direct challenge to that deal. To Haley, the firing of Josephine Locke was an example of the alliance of the board of education with economic interests—in this case, powerful textbook companies against the wisdom of an experienced and progressively minded educator.[88]

There were other reasons to dislike Burdick. Catherine Goggin had challenged Burdick for the presidency in the spring of 1898 and had lost by only a few votes, and a rumor spread amongst the teachers that the election had been rigged. There were significant differences between the two candidates' camps: Burdick and her vice president, Mary Bratten, both taught in the wealthier schools on the north side of the city while Goggin and Haley and their supporters taught in poorer schools of the south side.[89] To further inflame the contest, Haley spread scurrilous gossip about the married Burdick corresponding inappropriately with another man. This would not be the last time that the shrewd Haley would color her opposition with innuendo. But nor were her tactics unique: As Haley spread titillating gossip, her opponents sent out mass mailings that Catholic Goggin was part of a global conspiracy by the pope to take over the school system.[90]

As opposition to the president mounted in the Federation after the 1898 election, Burdick tried to postpone the installation of newly elected officers in order to extend her authority. Her extension proposal was defeated at the monthly Federation membership after heavy lobbying from the floor by Haley and Goggin.[91] At the next meeting, Haley levied a parliamentary barrage on President Burdick, challenging her for not documenting her expenditures, for allowing an unauthorized member to make a report to the group, and for other administrative problems. Haley insisted that her voice be heard and that her protests be duly recorded. At this point, Burdick had enough and she submitted a dramatic resignation letter that claimed that since her election the previous spring, she had been hounded out of office by parliamentary exceptions, objections, and repeated efforts "to block and obstruct every move. I have felt that the meetings have been contests for individual supremacy, in which I have barely held my own. I feel the burden no longer to be borne, and I lay it down. I am not able to *endure* longer." Typically, the gracious and politically apt Goggin refused her resignation, while Haley remained silent. [92] Burdick appointed the vice president of her district, Mary Bratten, as acting president. Haley uncharitably referred to Bratten as "Napoleon."[93]

Goggin declared her candidacy for the spring 1899 election and the Burdick forces began to lobby for a third candidate to split the vote and defeat Goggin. So contentious was the climate that Ella Flagg Young was called in to mediate. Young was district superintendent in Catherine Goggin's district and clearly showed her affinity for Goggin's cause. Haley and Goggin met at Young's house one evening to sketch out the problem and eventually to orchestrate their own power play. The three women invited to their meeting the teacher who had been identified by the Bratten camp to nominate a third party candidate. Blanche Loveridge, who was a young teacher with barely five years' experience, may not have known what she was walking into. Haley immediately pounced on the young woman and asked her what she thought she was doing by promoting a third party candidate. Loveridge argued that the teachers were embarrassed by the divisive struggles within the organization and that they just wanted to find a way to make peace, to which Haley drilled her on whether she had ever taken the time to find out what the struggles were about in the first place. Haley continued lecturing the teacher, telling Loveridge that if she had lived during the American Revolution she would be a Tory and that "any teacher who did not take her part on the right side of a struggle that was going on in the Federation was unfit to teach children either American History or American citizenship." Ella Flagg Young played off of Haley's vituperative energy, walking to the end of the room where she would "smile her characteristic smile" and then come back and call Haley off before she overwhelmed Loveridge with her volley.[94] Their lobbying was successful: At the meeting where Loveridge was supposed to nominate her candidate, she remained silent.

Catherine Goggin and Mary Bratten began their campaigns for the presidency of the Federation in a heightened political drama. As acting president, Bratten tried to undermine the election process by renting a meeting hall that could accommodate only half the number of teachers who were eligible to vote and that would be available for only a two-hour period. Then Bratten declared that she had the authority to appoint clerks and judges of the election. In an executive meeting, Haley challenged these revised electoral plans and the two women started yelling at one another, with Haley shaking her fist in Bratten's face. When Bratten got up to leave the fray, Haley grabbed hold of her skirt and held her, physically, in the room, until another member seized the chair and proposed Haley's motion.[95]

Bratten tried another tactic. She went to a judge to confirm the legality of her decisions about the election, although unfortunately for her, the judge she consulted was Orrin Carter, Margaret Haley's old teacher from the Morris Normal School who was now on the state court. Upon hearing about Bratten's move, Haley also went to Judge Carter to complain, and when the judge agreed to review the case, he started off the hearing in his packed courtroom by welcoming his old friend Margaret Haley. He then proceeded to affirm all of Haley's points.[96]

Election day was Saturday, March 25, and teachers flocked to the voting booths. Teachers from District 5, the Stockyards district in which Haley taught and in which she was running for vice president, turned out the largest numbers. Catherine Goggin received 1,700 votes and her opponent 500. In a style that would become characteristic of Goggin's leadership, she salved the bitter feelings within the Federation with her charm and humor. Called to the podium at the first meeting after the election, she received the teachers' applause and, referring to her simple outfit, she told the teachers that they had successfully persuaded her to buy a new hat.[97]

Goggin became president just in time for a new crisis with School Superintendent Andrews. In June, Bulletin Ben fired a music teacher, Agnes Heath, and replaced her with a man without going through the regular hiring process. The next week he perfunctorily issued a memorandum requiring applicants for the principalship to have a college degree.[98] In protest of Andrews's actions, District Superintendent Ella Flagg Young submitted her resignation. This sent a shock wave through the teachers. Goggin wrote Young that teachers in her district felt "utter desolation" about this news. The last few months' problems with the Harper Bill and the contentious election had been difficult, she wrote, but "with you in the office we felt that there was always a friend as well as an official."[99] The teachers mobilized and issued a statement that linked the firing of Josephine Locke and the music teacher Agnes Heath, the Harper Bill, and Young's resignation all as direct consequences of a strategy to wrest control of the public schools from citizens and put it in the hands of an elite few. This, the Federation acknowledged, was not particular to Chicago, but was part of an emerging trend to put public schooling under the influence of universities and private business interests.[100]

Continuing his barrage on the teachers when school started in the fall, "Bulletin Ben" announced that all principals were to make reports on teachers, noting their "fidelity and consecration," ability to govern, books they had read, and personal inquisitiveness. Then he pressed his luck by proposing to reorganize the board of education, and giving himself a salary raise. As his board resisted, the press and the teachers intensified their criticism of Andrews as an arrogant autocrat. In early November 1899, the board of education announced they would accept Andrews's resignation. Andrews resigned and returned to higher education, taking on the position of chancellor of the University of Nebraska, where he had an enormously popular nine-year career. Ironically, among his achievements at Nebraska was his support and hiring of faculty who were fired from other institutions for their controversial ideas.[101]

BATTLE LESSONS

Ultimately, Haley saw all these early Federation fights as educative for the teachers because they learned not only to identify inequities in the school system but also to exercise their political voice. The presidential battle marked the shaping of the Federation from a relatively passive association that affirmed the city school administration, to a more aggressive, activist, organization that had the muscle to stand up for teachers' interests.[102] For women who were prohibited from voting, such activism taught them valuable lessons. Indeed, Haley believed that groups such as the Foresters and the Federation were more effective than the vote in getting women involved in public life, arguing later in her life that "voting women today owe more than they know to William Rainey Harper." [103] Haley also sharpened her political skills in these early battles. She learned that the petition offered power to disenfranchised women who had unique access to a large body of citizens, and she learned to trust her own dynamic political speaking skills which drew people together for mass education and signature gathering under the eager eyes of newspaper reporters. Haley learned other tricks of the political trade. By getting herself elected to the Committee on Printing in the Federation, she took charge over the printing of election ballots. Knowing that the first column on a ballot received more votes by undecided voters, she placed her own candidate in that slot, thereby assuring the success of her own platform. Her knowledge of Robert's Rules of Order also gave her the upper hand as she maneuvered meetings, and sometimes people, to achieve the votes she wanted. [104]

Haley wrote in her autobiography that in the late 1890s she "found the battleground." In these few years she began to see how the battle over education was as much a fight over political power and financial interests as it was over classroom practice. Late-nineteenth-century school reformers argued that a centralized administrative authority would address the problems raised by an expanding school system. Haley joined other critics by asserting that this model created a hierarchy that gave more authority to bureaucratic officials at the top than to teachers, parents, and local communities at the bottom, all in the name of saving money. What she called the "mercenary ideal" reversed the democratic order and made schools look more like factories than like educational environments. [105] School administrators and their allies in government and business claimed that these new management models were designed to improve educational efficiency. Haley saw this argument as merely a ruse for depriving teachers of professional authority, while allowing the wealthy to save their own money by paying less in taxes. In this new political economy of education, the school administrator became the equivalent of the wealthy industrialist "and the thousands below him the mere tools to carry out his directions." [106]

But the battle lines of Haley's war were not as clearly drawn as she might have imagined. The reorganization of city school administrations into a centralized body of management was a cause promoted by many progressive educators who saw the local control of schools as the breeding ground for political graft and inefficient teacher education and supervision. These reformers argued that the creation of a streamlined, seemingly egalitarian and objective "system" of schooling would provide equity in public services to all students. Many reformers also welcomed the inclusion of business into school management, arguing that business would provide more funding to strained school budgets and more direction to school curricula, which were disconnected from the needs of modern society. Thus, although Haley positioned herself as an opponent of the powerful rich, many reformers saw her as the opponent of a new creative collaboration between private citizens and the state. Her single-minded vision on this matter would prove to haunt her in her later relationships with social and educational reformers.

Haley's commitment to her ideals drove her into political work, but the thrill of inventing a public life for herself may also have been a powerful lure for her. Using the tools of the trade—women's self-protective organizations, Robert's Rules of Order, and her own knowledge of labor politics—she recreated herself from a classroom teacher to a scrappy and dynamic organizational leader. She was nudged along by colleagues who saw her potential for public work, but she also unabashedly enjoyed the vigor and conflict of political work.

This was the firebrand Haley: an energetic political activist whom friends and foes alike described with respect and awe. In her autobiography, Haley emphasized this political style, often by retelling some of her activities in a highly individualized, heroic fashion that may not always have been true. She tended to make herself the dramatic solo figure, charging ahead with few supporters and little preparation. In fact, Haley was rarely alone in this work; she was usually supported by a mass of teachers who did much of the footwork and office labor of this grassroots political organization. Haley did not so much deny this history, as she underplayed it and highlighted her own leadership role.

Where did Margaret Haley learn this egocentric and powerful political style? Certainly she did not see it in her female colleagues. Arvilla DeLuce, the teacher who single-handedly organized teachers to support a pension, led a taciturn and careful lobbying campaign. Her friends Ella Flagg Young and Catherine Goggin led restrained political campaigns of negotiation and compromise. Haley's political style was more closely modeled on that of male labor leaders, including her own dynamic father. This makes sense because the Federation, newly shaped by Goggin and Haley, was structured as a self-protective trade union. The Federation was not a reform or social welfare organization designed to help others, but a self-protective agency for women workers, and Haley modeled her role as leader on other trade union leaders.

But unlike male trade union leaders, Haley also had to negotiate her identity as a woman and as a teacher—both identities that were socially defined as passive and self-sacrificing. So even as she touted her leadership on the "battleground," she also took pains to explain her political work in a more traditionally feminine way. In her autobiography, she recalled when her newly widowed sister Jenny's only daughter, Margaret Haley's own namesake, was struck gravely ill. Haley prayed for her life, and in her prayer she struck a bargain with the Almighty that if He spared her niece, she would devote her life to improving the lives of all children. At first she did not know what that work would be, but on the last day of the old century, she committed the rest of her life to the service of working for teachers, by which she would be working for children, because "only through the freedom of their teachers could the children remain free."[107]

In fact, Jenny's husband did not die until 1902, so the prophetic incident with the newly fatherless niece could not have happened until Haley was already a full-time leader of the Federation. But Haley's re-told tale of divine inspiration leading her to political work was a useful way for her to publicly justify her very unfeminine public life. She continually claimed that she "never wanted to fight"—the opening lines in her autobiography. "I knew something of the theory of politics but nothing of its practice," she recalled about her entry into the Foresters battle, and adding for emphasis, "I weighed less than a hundred pounds. I was far more interested in a new blue silk dress than I was in any cause."[108] By denying that she was looking for trouble, Haley could place the weight of the trouble on the offending party. If it was not her intention to create a problem, then the problem must have existed there in the first place, whether it was undemocratic processes or unqualified leaders. Haley could thereby excuse her otherwise shockingly assertive and highly unfeminine behavior. She never *chose* to act this way; she was forced to out of a commitment to justice and democracy. By claiming that she tried to avoid conflict, even as she spent her professional life as the figurehead of conflict, she legitimated her behavior, both to the outside world and to herself.

It is a complicated and contradictory figure that Margaret Haley presented in her written sources, at once a solitary feminine character who was forced into politics by the raving injustices of the world, yet also one who hurled herself head first into controversy. The diminutive woman who claimed that she preferred shopping to politics was the same woman who incited chaos in public meetings, who yelled out objections, lectured, drilled, shook her fists, and grabbed at her enemy's skirts. For good reason was her identity fractured, because as a woman teacher activist, Haley was a walking contradiction. She was a unionist, with a radical tradition of Irish Catholic labor behind her, but she was also a white-collar worker in the feminized job of teaching. She claimed to be working to improve the lives of children, but she was also working to improve the material conditions of her own occupational group. To maintain public support and develop allies, Haley had to carefully walk the line between radical unionism and social welfare, between the self-preservation that was allowed for masculine and working-class workers, and the concern for others that was expected of women and white-collar workers. Essentially, she had to tell two stories and invent two selves. This was the conundrum that was the occupation of the teacher activist.

Regardless of her self-perception, Haley knew that her life had changed. On December 31, 1899, Haley went to a New Years Eve party where bells rang and whistles blew and everybody laughed and shouted and sang. "But just as the first gun of Nineteen Hundred roared into the night, I looked backward for a moment, and said goodbye to youth." [109]

CHAPTER THREE

BATTLEGROUND

HALEY'S LIFE REALLY DID CHANGE at the New Year. On Christmas Eve, 1899, the Chicago Board of Education announced that it would not be giving teachers the $50 salary increase promised two years earlier because the board had run out of money. A few days later, Haley heard from a fellow teacher that a number of large Chicago public utility corporations were not paying taxes on property that was valued at millions of dollars. The Pullman Company alone had one million dollars' worth of property that escaped taxation, and the People's Gas Company more than fifty million. The teachers thought that the board of equalization—the elected state agency authorized to assess corporate taxation monies—was allowing this to happen. Haley was intrigued by the striking coincidence that the school board ran out of money at the same time that corporations were illegally discounting their taxes in a system where 90 percent of school income derived from property taxes. She began to investigate.[1]

The key to the very complicated tax problem that Haley faced was part of a larger challenge that faced late-nineteenth-century tax collectors: How to measure the value of corporate entities such as railway, gas, and electric utility companies, whose value rested less in actual tangible goods—such as buildings and machinery—and more in the *intangible* value of stocks, bonds, and in particular, the franchise, or the public gift of land for corporate usage. The intangible franchise value alone comprised the largest single value of a public utility, worth about eight times more than any property, and economists around the nation struggled with ways to assess and tax this growing, but seemingly immeasurable value.[2] This problem was particularly troubling to farmers, on whom traditional property taxes weighed most heavily, and to liberal antimonopolists who saw corporation value increase as a result of public gifts of land with no corresponding increase in taxation. In 1872, as a result of pressure from organized farmers, the state of Illinois settled on a solution: Local assessors would assess the value of corporations' tangible property, and each corporation would report the value of its intangible property,

Margaret Haley, 1910 (Courtesy of Chicago Historical Society)

after which an elected board of equalization would confirm and assess taxation accordingly through an established equation.[3]

   This was the stated law, upheld by the State Supreme Court as a fair
method of assessment, but corporations were reluctant to follow. In the years
after 1872, the amount of the assessment money of intangible values of

corporations in Illinois declined steadily, so that in 1900 the total assessed value of 334 corporations in the state was about $5 million—the same amount assessed twenty-five years earlier with only one hundred corporations.[4] Corporations were simply not declaring their intangible value, and the board of equalization was allowing this to happen as a result of bribery and kickback deals, or what late-nineteenth-century reformers referred to generically as "boodling."[5] In Chicago in 1900, for example, five major public utility corporations were not being assessed for millions of dollars of intangible value and the city was losing millions of tax dollars every year. The victims of this alliance were the city's public services, including schools, which depended on tax dollars.

In consultation with lawyers, the Chicago Teachers' Federation filed a legal mandamus proceeding in court against the board of equalization, demanding that it do its job. The case was filed in the name of Catherine Goggin, in part because she was then president of the Federation, but also for tactical reasons because of the name recognition of her uncle, James Goggin, the popular city judge who had recently died.[6] The case was limited to the assessment of five public utility companies—another tactical move because unlike private industries, utility companies could not leave town, and because these companies had valuable franchises in the public streets of the city to which all Chicagoans paid money. That the companies that supplied public services for transportation, water, electricity, telephone, and gas were not paying their taxes back to the public carried special political weight.[7] Haley took a personal leave from teaching and spent the first ten months of 1900 researching and preparing the case. The Federation hired Isaiah Greenacre, an experienced Chicago tax attorney; throughout the case Haley also solicited advice and support from the state's attorney and friendly judges, lawyers, and political officials.

In November 1900, a state judge agreed to hear the case, but it was postponed until March 1901. On May 1, 1901, a judge declared that the board of equalization's assessment of the five corporations was illegal and that the corporations owed the city $1,800,000, but after various appeals which lasted well into the following year, the corporations were required to pay only about one-half of the original amount. Furthermore, when the board of education received its share of the money, it voted to use the money to pay for cleaning schools and paying coal bills, not for teachers' salaries. Haley then led another suit against the board of education which was decided for them in August 1904, and 2,300 teachers were awarded back salary increases ranging from $14 to $150.[8]

The tax fight became the defining cause of the newly founded Federation. It also became the base of Haley's political platform about democracy, economic equity, and the civic responsibility of the state.

THE SINGLE TAX AND SCHOOL FINANCE REFORM

Margaret Haley's thinking about economic reform was based on a theory of civic responsibility and economic equity that inspired other progressive activists in this period—Henry George's single tax theory. Haley first read

George's statement on single taxes, *Progress and Poverty*, in the early 1880s at Illinois Normal School in the class led by the economist Edmund Janes James. Haley's father had been reading Henry George as well.[9] But even without the tutelage of her father and Professor James, Haley's interest in and enthusiasm for Henry George would not have been unusual. With the publication of *Progress and Poverty* in 1879, George was immensely popular with progressive thinkers and especially Irish Americans, in part because of George's adoption of the land issue in Ireland. For both Haleys, George's message of both the symbolic and the material primacy of land, and the role of taxation as reform was particularly attractive.

Henry George was only one of a number of late-nineteenth-century Progressive Era reformers who saw the reorganization of the American economic system as the keystone to social reform. Central to their plan was their faith in taxation as the best way to equalize economic disparities and to redistribute wealth.[10] George in particular believed that the Industrial Revolution had brought alienation from the land, the growth of complicated government systems, the privilege and corruption of monopoly, and increasing divisions between rich and poor. But George's solution was far from the radical rejection of liberal capitalism proposed by Marxists; rather, he advocated a more benign way of controlling monopoly through taxation.

George's key concept was that the land was the source of all real wealth because it was land that produced wealth. A single tax on land would shift the burden of taxation from workers on the land to those who owned the land; from wealth created by labor to wealth created by the community. Thus, land that was highly productive, for example, land that held industry, would be taxed more than land that produced less wealth, for example, farmland. According to George and his followers, this simplified taxation system would abolish all graft and prioritize the needs of the community, it would promote the more efficient use of land with fewer discrepancies in wealth in both rural and urban America, it would lead to increased wages and decreased unemployment for workers, and it would create more public revenue available to spend on the public good. The single tax would thus effectively destroy monopoly and revive economic opportunity by removing the robber baron's privilege. Also attractive to reformers was the notion that the single tax and its benefits could be achieved without violent overthrow of a government. All that was needed for a single tax was good legislation.

In cities around the country, political figures tried to apply George's theory of single tax to the urban condition.[11] To these urban political reformers the single tax was particularly appropriate because of the increasing value of urban property with the consequential increase in need for public revenue to be spent on civic improvements. The movement for single tax tended to take on a larger symbolic quality of "civic revival" through broad municipal reform issues. The gist of the movement was that the institution that controlled the apportionment of taxation was a powerful agency of class rule, and if that institution was guided by a vision of equity, reapportioned taxes could be used as mechanism of social readjustment. To these municipal reformers, taxes were the key to eradicating economic injustice.[12]

In the years that she fought the tax battle, Haley brushed shoulders with some of the leading lights of this movement. One of her more influential allies was Tom Johnson, mayor of Cleveland, Ohio, from 1901 to 1909, whose colorful life story included years as a wealthy steel magnate until the day he read *Progress and Poverty*, when his "whole outlook on the universe" changed.[13] To commit himself to the single tax cause, Johnson sold all his assets and ran for mayor of Cleveland. One of Johnson's emphases as mayor was public education about municipal finance, and he promoted citizens' economic education in tax schools. To Johnson, taxation was nothing less than the lynchpin of social inequality. In 1901 he wrote Haley and Goggin in passionate prose that unequal taxation "subjugated" the masses, and kept them in the "grip of monopoly."[14]

Haley also admired the work of Samuel "Golden Rule" Jones, mayor of Toledo, Ohio, between 1897 and 1904. A Welsh immigrant, Jones had spent years working as a laborer in oil fields until he invented a revolutionary device called a sucker rod which eased the drawing of oil from the ground. He became a wealthy manufacturer in Toledo with his invention, but the social effects of the economic depression of the 1890s wore on him, and he gradually developed a political theory based on Christian Socialist principles. To Jones, poverty was the result of a flawed system, not a flawed individual. If society followed the tenets of Jesus' basic teachings about the Golden Rule of equanimity and caring for all, then economic inequality would disappear. Jones reformed his own factories, establishing health plans for workers, paid vacations, profit sharing, higher pay, and a shorter work week, and he sponsored picnics and other family events for his workers and their families. Convinced to run for mayor by labor and social welfare groups, Jones expanded his Golden Rule philosophy to civic management by developing community and social services and expanding political representation to include the working class under the theory that the only justification for government taxation was "to make conditions of life easier and better for the people than they could possibly be without it."[15]

However much she admired these men, Haley was never as strong a single tax activist as they were, in part because she saw single taxers as somewhat "cloudy" thinkers who refused to develop practical plans of implementation.[16] Furthermore, even if single taxers *had* developed a political plan, as a woman she was limited in her ability to participate in those plans. As a woman, Margaret Haley could not become mayor of Chicago, or even alderman because, until 1913 she could not even vote in any state election except school board. But she could lobby, educate, and use the law to uphold already established laws. For Haley, the ultimate power of the single tax movement was as a motivating and educative force. Years after she first read

Henry George as a young teacher, Haley saw the power of *Progress and Poverty* not so much in the specific single tax theory as in its effect enlightening people about the relationship between taxation and social justice.[17]

As a teacher activist, too, single tax theory held limited appeal because it was specifically opposed to special interests, including the special interests of particular civil servants such as teachers. For all her admiration of the broad vision of single taxers, Haley's primary interest was the legal requisition of tax money for public school teachers. This telescoping of broad political theory to address the specific needs of teachers was something that Haley would learn how to do well throughout her career as a teacher activist. Whether it was single tax, municipal reform, or women's suffrage, Haley found a way to take the vision of a larger issue and focus it to support teachers' specific needs.

There was a cost, however, to Haley's single-focused cause. Like her opposition to reformers' attempt to professionalize teaching by increasing certification requirements and her objection to reformers' proposals to centralize school administration, Haley's critique of the single tax cause rested solely on her interpretation of what she believed was best for teachers. Her relentless focus on teachers opened her up to the charge that she was not really interested in broad social change as she claimed, but only in her occupation. Although she consistently argued that economic and social equity was her goal, her uncompromising attention to teachers' economic advancement made her appear more like a self-interested labor power broker than a visionary social reformer. Haley's own reading of her goals is less clear: To some extent, she believed that what was best for teachers *was* best for society. At other times, she was more defensive, mistrustful that other reform movements would adequately address the needs of teachers.

One incident during the tax struggle epitomized the way in which Haley's reading of the single tax movement was modified by her goals as a teacher activist. In 1901, in the middle of the teachers' law suit against the board of equalization, the Illinois state legislature passed a law that reversed many of the benefits of the pension that the Federation had won for the teachers four years previously. Haley was convinced that the legislature was punishing the teachers for their ongoing lawsuit, and she was unforgiving of public figures who claimed that they supported the tax fight while also supporting the hated pension revision. One of these disappointments was Hiram B. Loomis, a single taxer and former physics professor who had just published an article praising the teachers' tax challenge (although significantly, his article only barely recognized the role of the Federation in the case). Loomis supported the bill that limited the teachers' pension, and his justification to Haley was that as a single taxer, his principles would not permit him to continue paying into a pension. In the ideal world, apparently, the single tax would provide all retired citizens with support. Haley would have none of this argument, and she suspected Loomis of being self-serving. Later, when

Loomis was appointed principal of one of the most prestigious high schools in Chicago, her suspicions were confirmed.[18] To Haley, this single tax promoter, however visionary his principles, was still able to undercut teacher reforms and reap his own personal privileges.

WOMEN'S POPULAR CAUSE

For all that Haley emphasized that the goal of the tax case was the security of economic benefits due to teachers, she realized that an equally important impact of the case was the symbolic and physical entry of women teachers into the exclusive halls of male-dominated government. Both Haley and Goggin liked to remind the public that the Federation was not asking for any specific privileges, nor making any radical demands. Rather, they were merely asking for the enforcement of law. Although as women they could not vote, they paid taxes, and according to some arguments, that allowed them rights as citizens.[19] And, as shaped by Haley and Goggin, their social purpose as teachers was intricately connected to the wider world of citizenship. Indeed, this nexus of teacher empowerment and citizenship was one of the founding principles of the Federation. As Catherine Goggin told the new members in her first inaugural address as Federation president in 1899:

> [A]ny force or influence which tends to exalt or enhance the position of the teacher tends equally to the development of broader citizenship and higher aims of the people, and conversely, any project under whatever specious or high-sounding name it may appear, which tends to the deterioration of our public schools, conduces to bad citizenship and low ideals.[20]

Part of Haley and Goggin's tactic was to convince women teachers of their very identity as citizens, and of their right to fight for their rights, even in the face of severe opposition. As Mary Herrick, the historian of the Chicago schools, wrote, the Federation leaders understood "that the machinery of government could be used by ordinary people for what they thought was just, if they were willing to stick it out."[21]

Haley thus balanced her specific demands for teachers' rights with the rhetoric of the broader women's reform movement that women's responsibility was to keep male politicians in line. Denied a formal political voice through suffrage, Progressive-Era women took part in a broad network of political lobbies. The political culture of Chicago's middle class-women reformers at the turn of the century centered around the notion of "municipal housekeeping"—a citywide agenda that implied not just social betterment, but also the institutionalization of a publicly financed welfare structure, modeled on the ideal caring home and community. Municipal housekeeping placed the interests of the family and community as central to the interests of the state, and the school was included in the social equation of the state as a large home. As one prominent proponent of municipal housekeeping expressed it: "Woman's place is Home. . . . But Home is not contained within the four walls of the individual house. Home is the community. The city full of people is the Family. The public school is the real Nursery. And badly do the Home and Family need the mother."[22] School issues as they related to poor urban children—compulsory enrollment, curriculum, school building maintenance, and school health—were a critical part of Chicago women reformers' programs.[23]

Similarly, Haley promoted the tax fight as one that would serve both teachers' needs specifically and the broader interests of the city at large. The tax struggle was "the people's victory," as much as it was the teachers' victory.[24] And indeed, much of the nation did see the teachers' tax struggle this way. The topic of tax reform for schools hit a powerful double chord that attracted both economically minded business men and social reformers concerned with women and children. To many Chicagoans, the Federation campaign against "tax dodging" was much more than interest group politics, but rather an agenda that cut a wide path across a number of political interests.[25]

In the popular press, teachers' claim for their promised salary increase was transformed into a flamboyant battle between the sexes where prim and proper schoolmarms took on cigar smoking bureaucrats. In these popular images, teachers' labor claims were downplayed and their gender identity highlighted. A popular Chicago daily encapsulated this vision, portraying the teachers' cause as a dramatic battle between right and wrong, justice and evil:

> Mandamus Proceedings were brought by the teachers
> Against the incorporate Tax-dodging Creatures
> "No, no," say the ladies, "you can not flim flam us,
> We'll keep up the fighting, though every man damn us."[26]

Federation teachers furthered the image of valiant female public servants fighting for justice. In the Federation *Bulletin*, a teacher wrote an epic poem about women and civic duty in "The Tax War," which began:

> The Teachers' Federation
> When it sought to right a wrong
> Was well aware 'twould have to fight
> A battle 'gainst the strong.
>
> With patriotic fervor
> For the good of all concerned
> It studied civic method
> And why funds were short, soon learned.

The poem concluded with a call for women's unity:

> As ever, 'tis the women
> Who must suffer in the fray;
> They can not vote, and therefore
> We'll cut their meager pay.
>
> Brave hearts, be not discouraged,
> For when the fight is done,
> The world and you will reap the fruit
> Of victories you have won.[27]

The specificity of the teachers' cause was often subsumed under a broader reform agenda, as Federation supporters saw the image of women elementary teachers monitoring the government as far more engaging a rallying point than the specific cause of teachers' low pay. A male lawyer wrote to the Federation leadership:

> How cheerful it is to know that we men have such efficient women in the public service to prod us to the full limit of our duty. I would have given three dollars and sixteen cents to have seen those fellows squirm when that meek (!) and quiet Haley got wound up and shotting [sic] off her hot shot at the many million dollar corporations. It must have been fun.[28]

Other reports of the tax fight simply ignored the teachers' primary objective of a salary increase and focused solely on the issue of municipal waste and corruption. This emphasis on government watchdogging reinforced the popular belief that the teachers had no self-interest, and that this was a cause larger than themselves. Like the traditional view that women taught school because they loved children and not for money, some supporters of the Federation saw Haley's group as self-sacrificing angels for civic reform. The Catholic Archdiocese of Chicago approvingly described the teachers' campaign as a moral one and not one of self-interested teachers or suffragists.[29] The Bishop of Peoria wrote that the Federation had successfully avoided partisan politics while still inspiring teachers with "new courage, a higher moral earnestness and a nobler pride in their vocation."[30] According to this view, the importance of the tax fight was not that the teachers had fought for an improvement in their working conditions, but that they had forced city officials to do their civic duty correctly. The Federation tax fight was thus divested of its specificity and became merely an agency of tax reform—albeit an unusual one because it was led by women.

Women's reform groups also approved of the Teachers' Federation tax struggle, and they also deviated away from teachers' interests into the more amorphous areas of social reform. As the Chicago tax fight gained national notoriety, Haley became wildly popular among women's groups who admired her as an icon of women's social reform. A mother of six in Wisconsin invited Haley to speak to the County Fair where she had recently founded an Educational Department. Wouldn't Haley come speak "on taxation and on schools and on teaching? . . . I think our young people need more enlightenment of these subjects and we can get along with less horse racing."[31]

Haley herself sometimes suspected the way that the tax fight was broadened to leave teachers' interests behind. When the Cleveland chapter of the Women's Christian Temperance Union invited Haley to speak to their group, claiming that their city too, "needs this lesson," Haley refused the invitation after she discovered that the group was not particularly popular among teachers. Instead, she sought an audience with the Cleveland Board of Education and a teachers' institute.[32] Certainly Haley was not above mixing causes to promote her own. When the suffrage leader Susan B. Anthony argued that the Federation was supporting all women's best interest, Haley made sure to publicize the support of this nationally known figure.[33] Haley's struggle was to maintain the popular image of broad social reform while still addressing the specific needs of women teachers.

FIGHTING THE FIGHT

Haley's experience of the tax case was four years of exhausting, time-consuming work. She had to independently learn corporate tax codes and revenue laws for the state of Illinois, and then learn how corporations and government officials were avoiding those codes. She consulted with innumerable lawyers, judges, government clerks, secretarial staff, and fellow teachers. She lobbied and cajoled legislators and fed information to reporters. She spent thousands of hours in government offices, court rooms, and hearing halls—usually as the only woman in the room—trying to gather information from committees that met irregularly, and from men who ignored or sneered at her. She traveled extensively to Springfield, the capital of the state and at that time a few hours' train ride from the central station in Chicago, and when the case was under review in the state court she stayed there for weeks at a time. She recalled her life then as one of "vibrating between the legislative halls in Springfield and the judicial chamber where the suit was pending."[34] In Chicago she traveled across the city speaking at community gatherings both large and small to educate teachers, parents, and citizens about the case and to raise money for the Federation's campaign. Toward the end of the case, she went on speaking tours across the country to drum up support and popularize the case.

Having taken a leave from teaching, Haley spent most of the winter of 1900 reading up on tax law, consulting with lawyers and local judges,

Federation promotional flyer, 1903 (Courtesy Chicago Historical Society)

lobbying teachers and communities for support, and preparing what would become the legal case. At a very basic level, she was trying to understand the law, in which she had no formal training, and the workings of corporate finance, in which she also had no training. She sent to Springfield for tax reports for the previous twenty-five years and made an exhaustive study of them. She mastered the reports of the state auditor, and the annual reports of the five public utility corporations identified as the subjects of the case. She learned about and followed the stock market, and studied every relevant state and federal Supreme Court decision on taxation. Then she tried to find out in what ways the legally defined procedures of tax assessment were being followed, or more likely, not being followed.

Day and night, wrote a praising reporter, "she lived in these studies until she had wormed out every item of importance."[35] When not deciphering tax codes, she visited government offices to investigate the required forms, accounting sheets, and lists that were supposed to be completed and sent out, but that never were. Clerks caught in a maze of bureaucracy and graft would disappear into other rooms in response to Haley's questions, return with negative responses, and then sometimes admit to the fact that in all their years in that office, none of the legal procedures that she was describing were ever followed.[36] For a number of weeks in Springfield, she tried to track down meetings of the board of equalization and found that although it met every Tuesday morning, it promptly adjourned and the men talked casually in small groups, and then mysteriously disappeared out of different doorways to places that Haley could never find. Sometimes she would enter a room only to see a single board member leaving the room announcing that the meeting had just adjourned.[37]

Haley and Goggin, who together constituted the investigating committee of the Teachers' Federation, were constantly reminded that they were invading a sacred space where they as women and as teachers did not belong. One Chicago representative lectured Haley about the loss of protection that the teachers were risking by taking on the tax case: "When you teachers stayed in your school rooms, we men took care of you; but when you go out of your schoolrooms, as you have done, and attack these great powerful corporations, you must expect that they will hit back."[38] Haley, of course, objected both to the implication that teachers *had* been taken care of in the past, and to the notion of punishment for behavior that was perfectly legal. The Chicago *Tribune* sharply disapproved of the teachers' tax case, too, arguing that the problem of taxes was "outside the teachers' province," while the Chicago *Chronicle* criticized the Federation because it was "impertinent for public employees to lobby to get more pay for themselves."[39]

The teachers had to almost literally break down doors to even begin the investigation. The initial inquisition into the tax case led Haley and Goggin into the Cook County Courthouse in central Chicago in search of the board of equalization reports, an experience that made them feel like invaders into a foreign territory. They were led by a boy assistant into both the literal and metaphorical halls of masculine bureaucracy—as Haley later described it: "through circuitous passages, where we wound in and out among bookracks, long tables from which men, seated on high stools, peered curiously at us from under green eye shades, on through gateways, locked on the inside, but opening to the touch of our guide." In the office of Archie Cameron, the acting county clerk for Cook County for the past forty years, the women were told to sit on two stools from which they were then ignored while Cameron conversed with lawyers. Haley grew impatient, and got off her stool to listen in on the conversations which were about tax issues. As she listened, three men drew their chairs closer together, so that she could hear only part of the conversations, "only the crumbs that fell."[40]

When Haley approached Cameron and requested the board of equalization report, he refused to show it to her and said that there was nothing illegal in the board's work. Haley replied, "I will not take any man's word for it," and stated that she had a right as a citizen to see the report. Cameron ignored her, but she persisted, and he eventually handed her the requested document.[41]

This was the first of many cases in which Haley shrewdly played off on her feminine identity to gain access to information. Because male public officials regarded women as so politically harmless, they inadvertently handed her information. She later recalled that her "apparent innocence and real ignorance" were tactical assets. "Public officials looked upon me as a curious and pestiferous infant, and finding that I could not be put off, told me what I wanted to know in the superior assurance that I was incapable of making any trouble." Plodding through offices and official reports, she gathered the facts of the case, and learned the power that those facts could have, even to powerless women: "I learned that a voteless woman with the facts could accomplish more than an enfranchised male contented to be ignorant."[42]

She was less successful with the lawyers and assessors for the corporations and their legislative friends, many of whom responded to this female invasion of their sphere with violent fury. On one train trip to Springfield, Haley sat in a car with seemingly every politician from Chicago, men who symbolized, to Haley, "the alliance between entrenched capital and purchasable politicians."[43] One of them "hurdled onto the train in a high drunken state, yelling at the top of his lungs about those damn school teachers," until the porter and brakeman dragged him through the coach where Haley sat and dumped him on the floor of the baggage car while he continued to yell at the women who were threatening his old-line political power.[44] At one meeting held in the state house in Springfield, a corporation lawyer shouted across the room at Haley and Goggin that they were "taxeaters" who should be thrown out the window.[45]

Powerful members of the board of equalization leered at Haley and made sexual innuendos about her. The teachers' lawyer, Isaiah Greenacre reported attending a meeting where a sexual bargain was offered in order to silence the "two damned women nuisances." An elected member of the board of equalization said to him: "I'm a bachelor and Louis Hershimer here is a widower. I'll let Louis have his choice of these two teachers and I'll take what's left . . . anything to get rid of them!"[46]

Haley made no record of any fears she had about the violent and sexualized nature of this behavior. Rather, in her public speeches and writings, she mocked and belittled the enemy, thereby reinforcing her larger portrait of corporate greed and governmental corruption with the image of immoral and uncivilized men. Given that many of her opponents were already notorious "boodlers" who boasted colorful names such as "Fire Escape Gus" Nohe, "Tobacco Hank" Evans, and "Billy Goat" Cadwallader, it was easy for Haley to rhetorically create an image of hordes of greedy and arrogant politicians and "oily" lawyers who "bared fangs" at her.[47] With characteristic theatrics, she regaled the teachers with the story of one particular Chicago lawyer who had a facial expression that illustrated "all the latent feelings that Darwin says has come down to us from remote ancestors."[48]

At times, she described the enemy as pathetic and incompetent men who needed women to keep them in order. When Haley wrote out a guide for the tax assessors to complete their job properly, they whined that they were "forced to do the work of a ten dollar a week clerk" and that they had to do it at the "demand of those women."[49] Haley also mocked her enemy by highlighting the bizarre and almost slapstick aspects of the case, emphasizing the great lengths to which the captains of industry would go to avoid facing the small citizen calling for justice. She hired a man to track down key witnesses who were so fearful of testifying against their bosses that Haley's man literally had to chase them down in barrooms and back stairwells.[50] She told stories of corporate lawyers stepping into closets and never reappearing and of grown men who turned pale at the sight of the diminutive Haley. She also learned how to use her observations to the benefit of the teachers' case. When one member of the board of equalization told Haley that she should not waste her time looking for a legally appointed committee that was supposed to determine tax rates, because the committee actually never met, Haley noted the conversation and used it in her testimony before the court, charging the board with dereliction of its duty.[51] And at every board meeting, she hired a stenographer to coolly record everything that was said, including the curses.[52]

But behind Haley's valiant and self-confident narrative were moments of concern, self-doubt, and grave anxiety. Haley and Goggin were terribly anxious each time the case moved on to a new judge, and in the middle of the case they were sideswiped by public charges in the newspapers that they were paying more attention to the case than to teachers.[53] The case also took an enormous toll on her health. Always energetic and passionate, in the first early weeks of the case as she came upon the initial evidence, Haley barely ate or slept. She finally collapsed and had to be cared for by her sister at home for a few days. Other mysterious ailments haunted her: an aching tooth, a hurt foot, and innumerable colds, all of which suggest either Haley's own physical fragility or that she unconsciously used her physical health to force herself to slow down.[54]

Life in Springfield was especially frustrating for Haley. "I despise this place," she wrote in no uncertain terms to Goggin. It was boring and lonely and the town itself was "devilishly pokey."[55] Her friends worried about the propriety of Haley being the only woman in state house meetings or court-rooms, so if Goggin could not be with her, she made sure to hire women stenographers, but they offered her little comfort: She alternately described them as being "Miss Busy Body" or as "having vacant space in the steno-graphic corner of her cranium."[56] The work in Springfield was also hampered by the lack of office space, supplies, and regular secretarial help. Haley once organized an important meeting in her lodging house for the Federation lawyer, Isaiah Greenacre, and the state's attorney. She rented a stenographic machine and typewriter but the first machine broke down. Worse, the min-ister who lodged in the adjoining room hated tobacco smoke and Greenacre could not work without smoking so they kept the window open as they worked although it was a cold day in November.[57]

Other incidents emphasized the awkward presence of women in a man's world. Living out of a suitcase on limited means meant that Haley was often without clean clothes, and she wrote back to Chicago for Goggin or her sister to send things down. Once, Haley carried into court a bag that she thought was filled with Greenacre's legal papers when in fact it was filled with her pink silk underwear that her sister had sent down from Chicago. And one morning before going to court Haley and Goggin had an accident with their hair curler—a small alcohol burning apparatus. The hair curler tipped over and set fire to the carpet, and in trying to put it out Haley burned her arms. She had to take off her ruined blouse and put on lighter one which was a brilliant red with gold bands and looked like a military uniform. The hearing took place in an uncomfortable court room that was, Haley recalled, "as cold as Greenland," but because of her burned arms, she could not bear the weight of her coat, so that she shivered in her brilliant red blouse with the military gold bands. "I looked militant," she recalled, "but I felt miserable. The Judge sat with his overcoat on, his collar turned up, and he sneezed most of the time and I sneezed all the time."[58]

LOCAL ORGANIZING

Haley and Goggin agreed that one key to their success was public education, and they devoted enormous amounts of time to identifying Federation rep-resentatives in each school and setting up communication networks in school districts, and maintaining reliable links with friendly newspaper reporters. Haley recalled that the teachers started out their work with little under-standing of political organization and that they were essentially "stumbling along in the dark."[59] They were, after all, working women with little expe-rience in or understanding of government systems. But the teachers soon learned to coordinate their political skills well.

The formation of a teachers' association was not a radical move in and of itself. Growing out of the early teachers' institutes and normal schools, teachers' associations flourished in many cities by the turn of the century as a way for teachers to meet to discuss professional issues, share teaching tips, and socialize. Across the country, teachers formed specialized associations and clubs for those who taught common subjects or grade levels, or who shared common interests. Some larger city organizations offered in-service educational courses, lectures, and trips to museums and professional conferences; others worked as less formal reading groups, social clubs, and information networks providing mutual support and collegiality.[60] Many of these associations were publicly identified as men's or women's only. Elementary teachers were predominantly female, and even in the new high schools where some women worked with men, social custom drove women to organize in their own gender-specific groups in order to discuss common interests and common problems.

The Chicago Teachers' Federation offered some social benefits to its members, but it was distinguished from other teachers' associations by its primary focus on legislative education and political activism. Reflecting the teachers' interest in the political process, the Federation developed a representative governing structure. Teachers formally joined the Federation by paying annual dues; representative vice presidents were elected from each of the school districts in the city (originally there were fourteen districts; in 1900 the number was reduced to six). The president was elected by the total membership. The vice presidents led monthly district meetings in local school buildings to inform members of the larger activities of the Federation, organize local petition signing and community meetings, and discuss a range of issues including curriculum, the management of student discipline, teacher education, and local and national educational topics. Federation officers met regularly as a board of managers to strategize policy and activities. Standing committees were formed to research and report on particular topics such as city finance issues, professional education, the pension, and Federation rules. All Federation members met once a month in a Saturday morning membership meeting, and in the midst of particularly pressing political campaigns, mass meetings were called more often to rally and organize teachers.

Because membership rosters from Federation meetings did not survive, it is almost impossible to confirm the numbers of teachers in these meetings or to identify the type of teacher who joined the Federation. Few individual records exist as well. All Federation officials except Haley and Goggin were full-time teachers who had little time to preserve records. As women and as teachers, their biographies were not preserved in private directories that listed notable Chicago business or political leaders; and no citywide newspaper covered their individual accomplishments, elections to Federation posts, or their deaths. In addition, as Margaret Haley worked to create a powerful public image for the Federation, she neglected to record the common day-to-day activities of the organization. Her powerful ego, too, prevented her from acknowledging the work of others. Ironically, then, the lives and work of thousands of women who made up the bulk of the Federation work are forgotten behind the larger-than-life image of their leader.

By its constitution, membership was permitted only to elementary teachers, and no supervising teacher or principal was allowed to be a member. Because most elementary teachers were women, all Federation leaders and most Federation members were women, although there was an informal tradition of assigning the few men teachers in the Federation the job of secretary. Through at least 1910, Federation membership included a significant number of the city's elementary teachers, if not a majority. In March 1899, Catherine Goggin reported a membership of 3,300, and through 1915, membership averaged between 3,500 to 4,000 out of a total of 6,000 elementary teachers.[61] A large percentage of the Federation's leadership and membership was Catholic; although it was also true that the leadership were publicly *perceived* as being Catholic by opponents who charged the Federation as part of a larger papal plot to take over American culture. One 1917 report charged that up to 80 percent of all Federation members were Catholic, a proportion that about equaled the representation of Catholics in the larger Chicago teaching force. Such figures were commonly used to undermine Haley's authority and to write off the women teachers' political claims as a religious conspiracy.[62]

Whatever the numbers, Catholicism played a defining role in the Federation's ability to forge allegiances with non-Catholic women. Federation teachers were largely absent from the burgeoning middle-class women's reform movement in early-twentieth-century Chicago, including Jane Addams's Hull House, the Chicago Women's Club, and women's suffrage groups. Catholic women had their own social reform groups; both Haley and Goggin were members of the Catholic Women's League, a citywide organization of middle-class Catholic women involved in settlement and social reform work. Up to half of all the League's single members were school teachers. These women heeded the Catholic Church's persistent criticism of Protestant women's clubs as the root of political and social anarchy, divorce and other family problems, and elitism. Ever conscious of the social distinctions that divided them, Protestant and Catholic women reformers essentially led parallel reform programs in Chicago, maintaining a cordial, but strained relationship. Haley herself was always suspicious of many Protestant women's club members, who she tended to see as elitist good-deed-doers who had little touch with real life issues.

Certainly the general population of the Federation were women with backgrounds much like Margaret Haley's: Raised in working-class families, their teaching careers offered them reliable, if modest financial security. Their education and occupation led them to a station of some upward mobility and drew them into work in charitable organizations such as the Catholic

Women's League, the Y.W.C.A., and volunteer settlement houses.[63] Some Federation leaders were married, although most were single women who were either self-supporting or the breadwinner for their parents and younger siblings. One common characteristic of many of the Federation leaders was that they lived and worked in the south and west side of Chicago where overcrowded schools and a growing population of poor immigrant children added particular stress to the work of teaching. One Federation member described the region as the locus of "shifting currents of population" which "brought added cares and perplexities," and drew teachers together in mutual "sympathies."[64] Anna Mary Murphy, for example, was one of the main writers for the Federation *Bulletin* and a long-time activist in the Federation. Nine years younger than Haley, Murphy was single, a first grade teacher, and shared her house with her sister Margaret, who was also a teacher. Like many of the Federation leaders, Murphy lived on the south side of Chicago and taught in one of the city's schools with an increasing population of immigrant and poor children. Elizabeth Burhmann, who began teaching the same year that Haley did, was also a single woman who eventually spent more than thirty years teaching in Chicago's south side schools. Like many other Federation leaders, Burhmann was an early activist in the pension movement and stayed involved in the Federation until her retirement. Other Federation leaders such as Kate O'Conor, Anna Rockford, Florence Tennery, and Nano Hickey taught in south side schools.[65] To these teachers, Federation work was more than legislative lobbying; it was also a social organization that brought purpose, unity, and valor to their lives.

One male figure stands out from all the women. Isaiah Thomas Greenacre, the Federation attorney, proved to be the teachers' most loyal friend and supporter. Two years younger than Haley, Greenacre was longtime Chicagoan of Scots ancestry. He was a graduate of the Union Law School, which later affiliated with Northwestern University, and a long-time city activist, centering on the legal processes of economic reform. As a city alderman in the late 1890s, he had introduced policies that standardized the city tax collection system to minimize corruption. In 1886, he was a founding member of the Knights of Labor in Englewood, where he may have known Michael Haley. His progressive vision extended to women's suffrage, which he advocated, and to his large family of seven children, which included two daughters who studied through college and professional school. Eccentric and somewhat abrasive in his personality, Greenacre remained loyal to the Federation and to Margaret Haley who for years would ask great works of him with irregular financial compensation.[66]

Margaret Haley's presence loomed large over all Federation work. She was constantly in the office, and constantly corralling teachers to help her prepare meticulous presentations of the data that she had collected in her fact-finding missions. In her vigor and enthusiasm for her work, she drew teachers into the importance of the cause, and in turn they described the intensity of working with Haley with a combination of awe and admiration. One teacher who spent long hours with Haley in the Federation office recalled that:

> She was merciless in her demands when we were helping her with some big and important project, and would listen to no complaints of hunger or fatigue or suggestions that she had done enough. There was no stopping until every last little detail had been gone over again and again and everything done beyond any human possibility of improvement.[67]

Part of Haley's appeal to her followers was her inspiration as a diligent professional who, although a disenfranchised woman, was able to drill her way into the public world. Although known for being impetuous and impatient in person, she was a scrupulous researcher who would not take action on a problem until "she had circled the subject many times."[68] Ever optimistic about the power of common people to enact change, she taught women teachers that they could become citizen activists if they worked hard enough at it. One Federation teacher remembered: "She would always say to us that those who put her work down to genius just did not know how to work. She considered her success was due to digging for facts and then working and working and working to find the best way to present them."[69] Haley's tenacity in the face of overwhelming odds impressed many women in the Federation whose previous lives had been as private daughters and classroom teachers. Teachers saw her as "towering, triumphant, Margaret Haley" who "left all of us gasping at her vision and wisdom."[70]

Hard work brought teachers the rewards of enjoying Haley's notorious sparkling humor. On the rare occasions when work was completed, a teacher recalled:

> [A] small group would go out with our gallant little leader for a holiday! The happiness that danced in her sparkling blue eyes, the ring of her joyous laughter, the keen appreciation that she had for every bit of humor . . . for Margaret Haley played as she worked, with her whole heart and soul.[71]

Haley's irrepressible humor helped her to brush off the criticisms of the public, as did her ability to drop caustic and sarcastic lines about her opponents. She said that "buffoonery" ran in her family, and she was able to use that inheritance to poke fun at her adversaries and further press her point. "The paper I wrote on was thick and heavy," she once wrote a friend, "like most boards of education."[72] Federation colleagues recalled the day a well-known politician tried to compliment Haley by saying, "Well, Miss Haley, in spite of all your fights, you've never lost your femininity," to which Haley retorted: "And I didn't lose many of my fights either."[73] Haley was aptly described by one friend as a "consummate actress" and indeed, part of her public authority came from her ability to deliver powerful speeches from the stage, to challenge male authorities in public, and to entice teachers into the cause with her great wit and passion.[74] She could also be overdramatic in her efforts to recruit supporters. The educator John Dewey recalled the time when Haley came to him to beg him to run for Chicago school superintendent, even though Dewey well knew he had none of the temperament and qualifications, and that Haley was only asking him to create a political scene that would work to her benefit. Dewey was amused by Haley's aping of "pomp and circumstance," and he had little sympathy for her passionate plotting.[75] But for Haley, such dramatics were not only necessary, but part of the thrill of politics. And dramatics was one of the few tools that she had. Her wit, charm, theatrics, and ability to play a sweetly feminine role and then turn into a ferocious and combative political animal were her key to success. Contrary to what she told her teachers, it wasn't just hard work that got her to the center of Chicago's political stage; it was also her personal style and skills. Margaret Haley was a great actor in a great part, and she played up her multiple roles as pugnacious leader, feminine teacher, sisterly friend, colleague at arms, and charismatic leader. Her great energy and high spirits allowed her to move undaunted from role to role: One reporter recalled that she had "perpetual strength, perpetual motion, perpetual charm."[76]

Haley's personal life also reinforced her leadership style. Although she did not marry, and there is no indication of a long-time lover, male or female, it is not accurate to say that Margaret Haley had no personal life. Her life was rich with colleagues with whom she spent intense days and nights over work, and with friends and admirers across the country. And work for Haley was much more than financial compensation: It was also a "thrilling joy," and "a great glowing adventure."[77] By choosing her passion for work over a traditional marriage, Haley also chose independence of mind and body. As an unmarried woman, she was free to work all the time, and to develop her character into a bold, unfettered, and dynamic personality. As she entered her forties, and her unmarried status was further confirmed, she became even more free to take personal risks.

THE FEDERATION

Haley's prominence in the Federation grew when in April 1903, the membership voted to create two full-time officers with salaries paid by Federation dues. Haley was appointed Business Agent and Goggin became Financial Secretary.[78] Since September 1900, the two women had been granted leaves of absences from the school system, but with this regular appointment and salary, and other teachers taking on the elected positions, the two could fully devote themselves to the work. As secretary, Goggin maintained the office, correspondence, and relations with local teachers, while Haley took on the political lobbying, public speaking, and advocacy work. The two complemented each other and their different characters modeled traditional gender roles in a family. According to a tribute poem that ran on the front page of the *Journal of Education* in May 1902, Goggin was "clothed in Justice, patient, gentle, wise, with strength of fruitful deeds wrought silently; the full and even light of Charity, the calm of Fate accepted in her eyes." In contrast, Haley was "the one with white soul passionate, a-thrill with eager search for all-compelling Truth—Instinct with vigor of eternal youth, urged on to danger by a selfless will."[79]

Haley and Goggin made great efforts to increase the teachers' public presence. Well aware of women teachers' lack of power in a man's world, their political tactics centered on the principles of relentless publicity. This campaign began with the placement of the Federation office. Located in the heart of the city at one of the busiest intersections, the office represented a commitment to move the Federation physically and politically into the center of the city. This was not to be an intellectual teachers' club, a reform association in a ladies' parlor, or a settlement house in a poor residential neighborhood. Rather, Haley and Goggin envisioned the Federation to be central to city politics, government, and economics. They saw the Federation as a city office, organized on city terms, both implicitly and literally stepping onto men's turf.[80]

A tiny room filled with women in a large office building filled with men, the Federation office was the boiler room of teacher politics. The office was located in the Unity Building, which was owned by former governor John Peter Altgeld and renowned for housing "young lawyers, radicals, and idealists," many of whom could not pay their rent, according to Clarence Darrow who as a young lawyer donated some of his time to the tax case.[81] Teachers supplied the office furniture, typewriters, a telephone, and a mimeograph machine.[82] Haley set up shop in a corner of the office, propping up a screen to create a makeshift workspace.

The Federation office was a beehive of activity. Teachers continually filed into the office with questions about the tax case and grievances about their own individual work situations. Taxpayers also came into the office to discuss the case, strangers who were visiting Chicago came as a matter of curiosity, and newspaper reporters came in for news scoops while teachers constantly rushed about trying to make copies of important documents.[83] The organization's bookkeeping demands alone were overwhelming. In the single year of 1903, the Federation collected the dues of four thousand teacher members, and led at least three fundraising drives.[84] The tiny office also published *The Chicago Teachers' Federation Bulletin* which came out weekly during the school year—a four to eight page journal packed with information about legal proceedings, Federation meetings, teaching tips, and entertaining stories for teachers. The office also mailed out scores of informational flyers to Federation members about upcoming events regarding legislative actions on which the Federation was taking a stand. In June 1903, the Federation sent out postcards to *every* Chicago teacher and principal in the city—more than six thousand people—reminding them to attend a special meeting to support the reappointment of a favored school trustee.[85] Teachers passed out pamphlets at church doors, tacked signs on telegraph poles, and left literature in barbershops, drugstores, meat markets, and saloons, and they convinced newsboys to fold flyers into their newspapers and merchants to roll them up in their packages.[86]

By its very nature, the Federation had strong community links. Through their work in city schools and their own communities, the teachers were able to immediately call upon their students' relatives in union halls and churches. Because their focus was on school improvement, and included blistering attacks on wealthy corporate leaders, the Federation was able to attract a broad cross-class and ethnic alliance, including Polish, Spanish, German, and Irish Catholic community groups, as well as the Phyllis Wheatley club— the prominent black women's club in the city. Haley and Goggin went to speak to many of these groups, sometimes accompanied by priests or other local dignitaries, and joining the community for dinner afterward. At these meetings, Haley gave updated reports on the case and called for support, enlisting the audience to share their pamphlets with their neighbors, to get their children to canvass the neighborhood, to sign support petitions, and to donate money. At one mass meeting in Central Music Hall in February 1900, for example, a minister's wife described her recent visit to a Chicago school where she saw water oozing through the floors and dark classrooms where children never saw the light of day. This was all excused by the board of education because they didn't have enough money, even as public utility companies escaped paying millions of dollars in taxes.[87] On the evening of November 15, 1901, the Southside Business Men's Association hosted Haley for a public talk at the Douglas School. A veritable pantheon of local dignitaries presided, including the alderman who offered statistics about the city's finances and the need for tax reform, the president of a county office who spoke about county revenue, and the Reverend Joseph Stolz, a member of the school board, who applauded the Federation's work and promised relief from overcrowded schools. Haley then spoke about the tax fight, and the eighth grade children sang a song.[88]

Haley claimed to have no hesitation about public speaking before hundreds of people, and she was by all accounts a gifted speaker. On stage she spoke rapidly and extemporaneously, with great animation, telling the legal background of the case, then the narrative of the tax fight interspersed with comical asides that drew laughter and applause.[89] Ever the classroom teacher, she often supplemented her lectures with graphs and charts that showed the values of the big city corporations and what they had escaped in taxation, and how the public had paid the price with increased streetcar and other public

Chicago Teachers' Federation

Bulletin

| ol. VII. | CHICAGO, ILL., MARCH AND APRIL, 1908. | No. 4 and 5. |

Increase in Salaries of Office Employes, March 25, 1908.

	1907	1908	Increase
Secretary of Board of Education,	$4,000	$5,000	$1,000
Assistant Secretary,	3,300	3,500	200
Assistant Business Manager,	1,900	2,500	600
Assistant Auditor,	2,500	3,000	500
Architect's Draftsmen,	1,320	1,820	500
" "	2,840	3,300	460
Secretary and Stenographer,	1,650	2,100	450
" " "	2,400	2,700	300
Book-keeper,	1,500	1,800	300
4 Engineers (each)	2,000	2,250	250

	1907	1908	Average Increase
16 Stenographers and Clerks,	$ 900 to $ 950	$ 950 to $1,050	68.75
10 " " "	1,000 " 1,100	1,050 " 1,200	70.
6 Clerks and Book-keepers,	1,250 " 1,650	1,300 " 1,800	116.66
2 Laborers,	$720	$780	60
2 Laborers,	900	960	60
2 Teamsters,	900	960	60

	1898		1908		Increase in 10 years
	Primary	Grammar	Primary	Grammar	
2,000 Experienced Teachers,	$875	$900	$875	$900	0

Ten Years of Ups and Downs in Salaries of 2,000 Experienced Chicago Teachers.

MAXIMUM YEARLY SALARY ACTUALLY PAID.

	Primary	Grammar				Primary	Grammar		
Jan. 1897—	$800	$825			Jan. 1904—	$850	$875	Stationary	
" 1898—	875	900	Raised	$75	" 1905—	850	875	Stationary	
" 1899—	875	900	Stationary		" 1906—	850	875	Stationary	
" 1900—	800	825	CUT	75	Feb. 1907—	900	925	Raised	$50
" 1901—	875	900	Raised	75	June 1907—	850	875	CUT	50
" 1902—	800	825	CUT	75	Jan. 1908—	875	900	Raised	25
" 1903—	850	875	Raised	50	(See Table On Next Page.)				

Front page of the weekly Federation *Bulletin*, 1908
(Courtesy Chicago Historical Society)

utility fees. One particularly popular handout conceived by Haley showed that in 1899 the railways of Cook County paid $640,000 *less* than the previous year, although the taxes on real estate and personal property had increased.[90]

At another mass meeting, the dramatics could not have been orches-
trated better when a member of the audience made himself known as Jawn
McKenna, a member of the board of equalization. The audience pushed him
up to the stage, and Haley proceeded to interrogate him on the difference
between the board 's assessment of the franchise of People's Gas Company
(which was zero) versus a public assessment which valued the franchise at
$50 million. As Haley continued to "twist him in an inextricable snarl," the
audience jeered, laughed, groaned, and hissed until McKenna raced off the
stage without his hat.[91]

When not busy with the ongoing legislative battles over the tax case,
Haley and Goggin continued to organize the teachers. Realizing that the
Federation could be denounced at any minute as a bunch of chattering
women, the two leaders were desperate to keep the teachers involved in
the Federation and to create a public face of solidarity. The power of the
teachers, Haley wrote, depended to a large extent on their own unity, but
also on "the public's estimate of their unity." Teachers needed to attend
rallies and meetings because it was "the only means the public has of
measuring our strength."[92]

Haley herself was surprised by the extent to which the Federation had
become a regular part of city operations within only a few years. As she wrote
her friend Franklin Edmonds of the Philadelphia Teachers' Association in
the spring of 1903:

> The funny thing about all this is that the business world with which
> we are daily coming into contact takes the whole thing for granted
> as if there were nothing unusual about it. The office of the Teach-
> ers' Federation and the Federation itself is as much an accepted fact
> and as essential a part of the business of Chicago now as the Board
> of Trade, the City Hall, or even the board of education itself.[93]

The expanding role of the Federation after about 1905 was reflected in
the Federation *Bulletin*. First published in November 1901 as a weekly during
the school year, in the early years the *Bulletin* covered local school issues, and
offered amusing stories and anecdotes for teachers. Haley edited the *Bulletin*
and wrote regular reports and editorials. Regular issues included updates by
Haley about the tax case, reports by teachers on curriculum and outlines of
courses of study, news of Federation meetings and transcripts of speeches,
copies of relevant school laws, notes on ongoing petitions and referendums,
memorials and obituaries of teachers, reports from Federation committees,
and the names of Federation officers.

The *Bulletin* also included commentary. In February 1903, a working
man wrote Haley asking if any teachers were available to marry him.[94] Haley's
response is not recorded, but a later publication in the *Bulletin* offers an
insight to the spirit of these working women, most of whom were single.

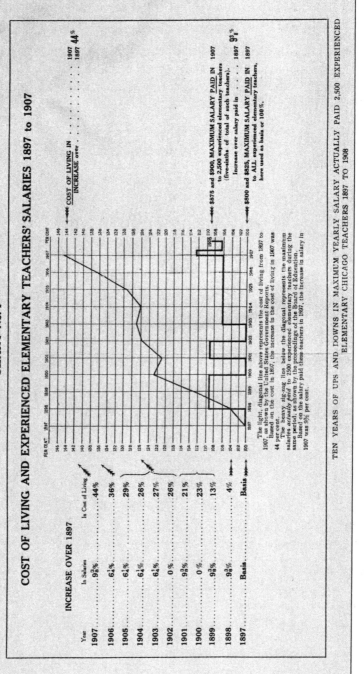

Margaret Haley supplemented her lectures with graphs and charts on the teachers' economic situation. (Courtesy Chicago Historical Society)

[I]f our school marms remain single, it is not because they can not
get husbands, but because they do not care to be bothered with
taking care of big, stupid men. They enjoy their freedom and independence and the knowledge that they are members of the most
useful and important of callings . . . why should she descend from
this high estate to become the keeper of a blundering, self-sufficient
male animal who will have to be watched all the time to keep him
out of mischief?[95]

Typical, too, in the *Bulletin*, were words of wisdom and inspiration,
such as a poem written in traditional verse, which was a powerful attack on
gender inequities in the pension:

"The Teacher"

The teacher spends her early years
In preparation for the strike
Of leading youthful minds to grasp
The knowledge which they need in life

She finds the pathway very steep,
And thorny, too, as day by day,
Courageously she plods along
Until her health and strength give way

And then, when old and feeble grown,
Her place a youthful maiden fills,
And she is turned adrift to bear
As best she may, life's cares and ills.

It may be there is naught ahead,
For others she has had to care,
And now when past her usefulness
Humiliation she must bear.

For firemen brace, and bluecoats too,
The city sets aside each year
A certain sum to help them through
So they the future need not fear.

For women, too, who spend their lives
In helping youthful minds to soar,
The city should provide a fund
To aid them when their work is o'er.[96]

In September 1905, the *Bulletin* announced that it was taking on a
"larger scope" than it had in the past. The journal was increasingly taken

over by Catherine Goggin and other Federation officers, and the number of signed pieces by Haley decreased. In subsequent issues, there was more news from around the country and world, including stories about vacation schools in London, teachers' lawsuits in Brooklyn, strikes by other women workers, and long essays on current issues in education that were written by Federation members or clipped from other journals. When the *Bulletin* became broader in its perspective, it gradually lost its connection to Chicago teachers; after 1905 there were fewer original articles from teachers about curriculum, local activities, poems, and commentaries. In late 1907, the *Bulletin* changed from a weekly to a monthly, with the explanation that the Federation officers needed to spend more time attending to legislative and political business. This shift reflected a change in the Federation itself: As it became more engaged in city and state political battles over education, it lost its earlier local, classroom-based character.

As the Federation expanded, its organizational capabilities became increasingly strained. Bookkeeping, correspondence, and record keeping stretched the physical limits of the organization and its two paid workers. At times of political crises and deadlines, Federation members stayed up late into the night preparing documents.[97] In the fray, regular business was pushed aside and the office often appeared to outsiders to be in a state of chronic disorganization. Because the Federation financed itself, its own economic state was always precarious. Teachers' membership dues paid for Haley's and Goggin's salaries, and fundraising drives were held at some mass meetings to pay for the lawyers, Haley's lodgings in Springfield, and the printing of pamphlets. But money was still scarce. Between 1900 and 1906, the Federation lawyer wrote numerous reminders to the office requesting to be paid. Other creditors were less polite, and they challenged the viability of the Federation. As one critic waiting for his long-overdue payment wrote angrily: "This does not seem to be just the way to establish woman's claim to business methods."[98] Poor bookkeeping also sent a few teachers away angry. In December 1903, Kate Tehan, a Federation officer, warned the office not to send her friend Miss Gunther another membership dues request. Not only was she indignant at being repeatedly billed, but it endangered the Federation itself because Miss Gunther was "a power in every way in our building and only by the greatest effort in all my art have I been able to have her join again."[99]

The intensity of the Federation work could also lead to personal misunderstandings. Haley's brusque and bossy attitude could often cause rifts among members, as a letter to her from one teacher indicates:

> I wish you would do something to mollify Miss Boyden's feelings. It was too bad we couldn't think of a kinder way of treating a report to which she had given so much time and attention. Can we reconsider the topic and maybe accept the report with the understanding that we focus on the first amendment. Whatever happens, can we

convince her to stay chair of the committee. She has worked hard
and her service to the teachers deserves recognition.[100]

The highly stressed working conditions that teachers worked under
intensified personal strains. When one teacher wrote a memo to Haley, she
apologized for not being very clear in her thoughts. She was writing from
school, and "a half dozen people are discussing grammar and interrupting me
to get my opinion."[101] Another teacher wrote to Haley that the demands of
her home life were making it difficult to attend to her Federation duties—
an example of the way in which many women teachers, although unmarried
and without children, were by no means without family responsibilities.

> My cares are numerous and pressing. My sister is away from home
> sick, has not been to school this year, my mother is not well neces-
> sitating my being home as much as possible. I have the secretaryship
> of the district council (which now numbers 38 schools) and my
> eighth grade is very large. I could see you on Saturday, but let me
> know in advance what the topic is, as even *Saturday* I should feel
> the cares of an unkempt home (we keep no help) haunting me.[102]

Haley did not seem to empathize with such troubles. So focused was
she on her political work that social protocol often fell by the wayside. Haley
had an aggressive and often belligerent political style, and she was more than
once chastised by her colleagues for being impatient. She had a unique tactic
of showing up at officials' houses early in the morning in order to grab their
attention, whether it was the president of the Chicago Board of Education,
whom she interrupted as he was doing his morning gardening, or the city's
lawyer, whom she caught at the breakfast table. With all of her interactions,
she struggled to follow through introductory pleasantries before she "plunged
into the school and tax situation."[103]

Haley's impatience could get her into trouble. Although she was wildly
popular on stage, she annoyed some of her colleagues with her bossiness. She
even crossed swords with Catherine Goggin and Isaiah Greenacre, the
Federation's loyal (and underpaid) lawyer, both of whom tended to consider
the broader political implications of Federation tactics and to follow a more
moderate course than Haley. Once, the three "thrashed out" their differing
opinions in front of a judge of the tax case.[104] To Haley, these compromises
were bitter pills to swallow, and years later she recalled them with lingering
resentment. For all that she was committed to the collective involvement of
the women teachers, her intense, confrontational, and combative style sometimes led her to act, ironically, in an imperious and arrogant fashion.

Haley and the Federation became increasingly popular outside of
Chicago during the tax campaign. Her cause was publicized widely in progressive circles, and reformers begged her to come and speak to their groups.

Single taxers, municipal reformers, and teacher activists alike heard Haley speak at public gatherings, or read articles about her, and they called on her to come speak to their community.[105] Teachers from around the country wrote Haley asking for information about how to organize, or about how to begin investigations of their local corporations. Some fledging organizations around the country simply asked for words of encouragement or advice. Campaigning politicians and school administrators also wrote Haley asking for tips, information, and support. A teacher in Kansas City wrote what many others were thinking as she joined with other teachers in her school to form an organization. Miss Goggin and Miss Haley, she wrote, "are known through the United States as the moving spirits among the Chicago teachers."[106] A tenth grader from Appleton, Wisconsin, asked Haley to help her out with her June oration on taxation. Her teacher had recommended that she contact Haley.[107] And a woman worker at the Wisconsin Bureau of Labor in Milwaukee wondered if Milwaukee teachers could organize against corporations as they had in Chicago. Such a campaign was possible, she mused, even though it was also true that "Margaret Haleys do not grow on every Milwaukee bush."[108]

Haley was constantly on the move in these years. In 1903 alone, she left Chicago for no fewer than thirty-five days on Federation business, traveling more than 7,500 miles, most of those miles by train, outside of the state, often to deliver public speeches. At a Labor Day march in Marinette, Wisconsin, in 1903, she spoke for two hours in the pouring rain, spinning tales of injustice, resistance, and redemption with humor and animation.[109] A reporter in Milwaukee described her talk there in December 1903 as being "full of sarcastic flings" and delivered in her "usual caustic, vigorous manner." It was true, she admitted in that speech, that some people believe that school administrators are educators, but it was also true that some people still believe that "the sun moved around the earth." It was teachers who knew best how schools should work. Administrators "ought to stimulate the teacher and not irritate her." "Irritators," she added, to her audience's great glee, "are not educators." As for those sincere school reformers who wanted to centralize the school system and take power out of the hands of parents and teachers, they are "the sincerest idiots that I have ever known."[110]

Public talks brought more than simple applause and ego-gratification. Haley's friends and colleagues in the movement knew her for her sparkling charm and great wit. "I do have such a good time with you," wrote the editor of a major journal of education whom Haley considered a good friend.[111] The organizer of a meeting where Haley spoke in 1903 wrote that her speech was "great, everybody loved it,"[112] and she herself wrote with delight about a speech in Philadelphia where she had "a great time" talking to fifteen hundred teachers who turned out even though it "rained cats and dogs."[113] It appeared that when she was in her stride, as she was in these years, nothing could get in Margaret Haley's way. She swung through her city and other cities, merrily slicing down opponents, receiving applause from her admirers, and enjoying a wild laugh with her friends.

As energetic as she was, Haley had a bad habit of overscheduling herself, forgetting meetings, and changing plans at the last minute. This became increasingly problematic as she took on national speaking engagements, even after she contracted with a speaking bureau to make arrangements for her outside of Chicago. She often realized that she was overbooked and tried to cancel at the last minute, which infuriated people who had built entire programs around her, and disappointed teachers who had flocked from near and far to hear her. More than once, she tried to avoid embarrassment and conflict by asking her friends to intervene for her.[114] To one of these friends she pleaded: "You will be my friend forever if you do this and I will never ask you for another favor—until the next time."[115] Such disorganization came to be expected among her friends, and they often lectured her about being more responsible and urged her to model her behavior more after Catherine Goggin, who was notoriously more levelheaded and responsible.

The multiple and varied expectations on Haley were a consequence of the complicated public image that she constructed. Part of Haley's tactic was to put forth an image of a simple schoolteacher and a common citizen who was only trying to right wrongs. Her public presence on the stage made her seem so personable that fans expected her to be an easygoing, everyday teacher whom they might find leisurely eating breakfast in her hotel or willing to visit a small-town fair for the weekend. In reality, Haley was increasingly busy, racing between cities and speaking engagements at a pace so fast that admirers rarely found ways to catch her attention.

Haley's own health often impeded her fast-paced schedule. She was occasionally bedridden with a cold, and one year she was laid up for ten days after being in a minor car accident.[116] These were among the few times that she saw her family, as she would retire to a sister's or brother's house to be nursed back to health. Given her intensity, Haley rarely took vacations, although usually she took off some weeks in July and August after the annual National Education Association convention. The Federation leadership was a close community of women who worked and often vacationed together. In the summer of 1902, the Federation board of managers spent a few weeks in a lakeside cottage in northern Wisconsin, a site that was so popular with vacationing teachers that local people called it "the teachers' lake."[117]

Even when she was on vacation, Haley worked. In August 1901, after the July NEA meeting in Detroit, Haley went to Buffalo for a few weeks vacation where she visited the Pan American Exhibition. But her time was not all relaxation. One night, she addressed the Buffalo Single Tax Club, and she conducted an interview with the local newspaper. She found it difficult to relax and she was at times lonely, and visited a friend of Goggin's who lived in the city.[118] She spent some of her time writing, and developed there a critique of U.S. Commissioner of Education William T. Harris's promotion of education in foreign countries, arguing that this was just another attempt to extend American business at the expense of attending to local problems.[119] And on her visit to Denmark and Norway in 1905—her one reported trip abroad—she wrote about observing the celebration in Oslo when the people voted by referendum to separate from Sweden. To the Federation *Bulletin*, she described visiting the national poll on election day, the nature of Norwegian democracy, and the celebrations in the streets.[120] For Haley, holidays allowed for time to catch up on work, or to explore new areas of her work.

TEACHERS AND ECONOMIC THEORY

Within the first years of the Federation's life, Margaret Haley and Catherine Goggin found that their organization had to fight for teachers on a number of fronts. First, they tried to protect and advance the material interests of teachers in their struggles for the pension and teachers' salaries. Second, they fought a broader campaign to conserve and augment the financial resources of the schools in such battles as the tax case. Thirdly, they sought to influence the formulation of educational policy.[121] Critics often saw the three struggles as distinct, arguing that the teachers spent too much time on "non education" issues. Haley saw all three as intricately related. Issues of classroom practice, she argued, could not be separated from educational policy. The training, support, and encouragement of teachers in the classroom, the use of classroom textbooks and the availability of other resources, and the guiding philosophy of schools were the battleground of opposing ideas. On one side, progressive educators promoted democratic school practices that prioritized the needs of the teachers and students. On the other side, business-influenced managers thought first of economic efficiency and the strict control of teachers' and students' work. The very struggle over educational policy, curriculum, and teachers' work in the classroom was a struggle between educational values and the controlling influences of business.

Haley's critique of business influence in education intersected with her critique of business in society at large. In both schools and society, she championed political reform in which government would monitor and reform business, regulating against corruption. This was her labor background shining through: her deep suspicion of unrestrained capital and her faith in the citizenry to do right. These ideas crystallized in the tax case and were furthered still in her involvement in municipal reform movements. Haley hoped to organize teachers and citizens together against what she saw as "the political machines and the entrenched vested interests of the city and state."[122]

The tax case epitomized Haley's application of economic theories to public schooling, and ultimately that broader vision transcended the complicated political and legal maneuverings of the Federation law suit. The results of that specific battle became a sideline to the larger cause, especially after

August 1904, when 2,300 teachers won their back salary in amounts ranging from $14 to $150.[123] That victory did not stop the larger fight. Haley's insistent equation of good schooling with fair taxation grounded her political motivations on the pragmatic goals of improving teachers' material working conditions and benefits such as salaries and pensions. But such tangible dividends were not the only goal of the tax fight. The Federation did not center on teachers' economic gains *instead of* broader social reform issues; rather, Haley saw the economic advancement of teachers as an intrinsic part of broad social reform. Improving the education of future citizens would lead to an improved society, and improving the working conditions of teachers would help improve that education. If teachers gained, all society gained.

Although obvious to her, the equation that linked the material gains of one occupational group to the betterment of society as a whole did not always translate clearly to the public. To critics, Haley was a self-interested labor boss trying to wring more money out of the public purse. The public saw the teachers' battle against economic corruption as admirable, but not necessarily because teachers would benefit. Elementary teachers, after all, still only taught small children, only nine months out of the year, and most of them were women who many people doubted should be paid at all for work that mothers did for free. So what Haley saw as one whole piece was dissected by a critical public.

Regardless of mixed public perception, the tax fight clarified Haley's thinking about teachers and economics in two main ways. First, Haley saw the tax fight as an educative struggle for women teachers to learn and practice their rights as citizens. She shared this understanding with her colleague Catherine Goggin who explained at a mass meeting that the radical implications of the tax fight was not merely for teachers to gain the $50 salary increase but for women to gain access to citizenship. Taxation, Goggin said, "is to most people sort of a hidden mystery, particularly so to women," and this was all the more reason for women to study taxes and law, so that they could become part of the civic structure of society.[124] To both Haley and Goggin, teachers needed to think about teachers' self-interest as part of a larger interest in civic betterment.[125] "Organization itself is educative," argued Haley.[126]

Haley reflected on the power of the tax fight after delivering a speech to three thousand teachers in Boston on the day of the judge's decision that supported the teachers' case in 1901. Unusually thrilled by the moment, Haley recalled that as she told the Boston teachers the tax story, she was suddenly aware of

> what it would mean to America if the spirit of that audience animated the entire teaching body. The fixed rungs of our government would soon be removed, for with accurate information, clear thinking, [and] determined purpose on the part of the teaching body of

the United States, no such condition as that revealed to the people of Illinois by the women teachers of Chicago could long continue to exist. These women teachers would demand and would secure the right to full citizenship and they would exercise it in the school room and out of the school room and from the public schools of America would come in one generation a body of pupils that would transform America.[127]

Women's fight for the just administration of taxes and the salaries that were legally due to them as civil servants was a powerful political act.

The second effect of the tax fight was that it solidified Haley's thinking about the primacy of economic issues in school reform. One example of her thinking on this matter was her response to a question by a school administrator about the importance of physical education in the school curriculum. Certainly physical education was important, she responded, but more important was securing the finances to compensate teachers for the additional training, preparation, and work. Otherwise, the reform would have no teeth and would only be another burden on teachers. [128] By the end of the tax fight, Haley saw the world through economic colored glasses. Changes in curriculum, developments in teacher education, and the nature of the organization of urban school systems raised for Haley the topic of economic compensation. Introductions of progressive education were, in her mind, regressive, if they were not accompanied by more resources for teachers.

An example of the centrality of economic thought in Haley's mind was her statement from the floor of the 1901 National Education Association meeting in Detroit. Haley had just heard a presenter express the hope that someday the Rockefellers or Carnegies of the country would see the value of sharing some of their wealth with the public schools, thereby improving education and sharing the wisdom of economic success with American school children. Haley had spent the previous year and a half engaged in the tax fight, charging wealthy corporations with tax dodging. But her objection to the proposal was not simply one of economic accounting, but also one of principle. She stood up from the membership seats and called out that she hoped that no Rockefeller or Carnegie would ever contribute from their "ill-gotten millions" to the public schools. Such a gift would "close the eyes and seal the mouth of the teachers," and they of all people should have their eyes open and their mouths free to state the facts. The public schools, she added emphatically, " should get their revenue and their support from public taxation and never from private gifts."[129] Public monies, equitably collected and judiciously delivered from all men and all women, should be the core of the public school.

CHAPTER FOUR

TREATIES AND SKIRMISHES

DURING THE TAX FIGHT, HALEY CONTINUED to clarify the meaning of citizenship for teachers, women, and the working class in two other great battles for what she believed was the soul of American education. The first fight was for teachers to organize as a labor union. If the tax fight represented the battle of the common people against the captains of industry, the teachers' affiliation with labor represented the consolidation of peoples' power. The affiliation of the Chicago Teachers' Federation with the Chicago Federation of Labor (CFL) in 1902 would become Haley's most public accomplishment—the work she was both praised and damned for decades afterward, and which would live on in the legacy of American teacher unionism. Haley's second great battle in these years was over the representation of women teachers within the National Education Association (NEA), the preeminent organization of professional educators that was, up to that time, run by school and university administrators, and that for half a century had excluded the voices of women teachers.

The two battles involved different types of allies and opponents, and Haley carefully negotiated her political maneuverings. With the affiliation with labor, Haley worked primarily on a local level, addressing the material needs of teachers in Chicago. With her work with the NEA, Haley stepped outside of Chicago and engaged in a wider professional debate about the role of women teachers in education as a whole. In both cases, Haley asserted her three main political themes: that school improvement could only happen with the equitable distribution of school financing and educational decision, that teachers' participation in such decision making reflected their responsibility as citizens in a democracy, and that teachers had the moral and political right to be activist participants in shaping their own working conditions. With both labor and the NEA however, Haley's immediate victories were short-lived, foreshadowing the marginalization of her educational vision in later years. Both cases reveal Haley's tendency to incite passionate political reaction against her cause. Union membership was a strategically risky move that brought the Federation national notoriety and immediate benefits, but over time, union affiliation brought the teachers up against political, economic, and ideological forces that scrambled their original intention. Some of those complicating forces were within the union community itself, which balked at the notion of white-collar women workers joining their ranks. The affiliation of teachers with working-class labor also challenged the powerful cultural myth of teachers' appropriate role as professionals who were "above" labor. Haley's work with the NEA touched the other side of the same coin of the professionalism concept. The NEA leadership conceived of teacher professionalism as political passivity. According to the NEA, women teachers should be quiet professionals, developing their expertise in the classroom, and leaving the leadership work of education to men. Haley challenged this notion, demanding that women teachers be equal to men school administrators in their professional organization. Her aggressive challenge to gendered occupational norms led to a bitter backlash.

LABOR

By 1902, Haley wrote in Battleground, Chicago's teachers had come to know all too well "the oppressiveness of political domination. We had learned the greed and the ruthlessness of corporate power. We had seen how entrenched, organized human avarice, working through the machinery of the law, had secured not only the resources of nature, oil wells, coal fields, and the iron mines, but the machinery of production and distribution, and the privileges of transportation, communication, intelligence, and the medium of exchange." Haley's analysis of the causes of social and economic injustice increasingly led her to look for powerful allies. As she well knew, "the school, alone, was powerless against organized wealth."[1] The teachers needed organized and powerful supports. In November 1902 the Chicago Teachers Federation affiliated with the Chicago Federation of Labor, becoming the first group of teachers to make a formal link with a labor union.

In her autobiography, Haley described the affiliation of the Federation with the CFL as almost a natural process, arguing that teachers and laborers had the same political perspective and the same interests at stake. Catherine Goggin and Margaret Haley both argued that since classroom teachers were the hardest working and poorest paid school employees, they had much in common with laborers and that their strength, too, lay in numbers.[2]

But the move to affiliate with labor was not as easy as Haley usually recounted. For one thing, at the turn of the century, the notion of teachers associating with labor was quite unthinkable. In 1902, the American Federation of Labor (AFL), barely fourteen years old, had organized one million skilled male workers to fight for specific employment protections and benefits for select groups. The AFL's leader, Samuel Gompers, rejected any role in broader progressive social movements, alliances with other reform groups, and the inclusion of middle class or white-collar workers. In fact, teachers were explicitly not welcome in the AFL, because Gompers's organizational strategy depended on a sharp division between working-class manual labor and middle-class white-collar work. In addition, Gompers was suspicious of women activists, whom he labeled "sentimental reformers" who would break picket lines or take jobs once reserved for men and thereby lower wages.[3]

The AFL was also distinctly male, and most Chicago teachers were women. If organized labor meant anything to women teachers in 1902, it meant a male collective organization that had earned so little authority in the legal world that it had to resort to contentious strikes. In contrast, the world of teachers was a largely feminine world of relatively prestigious if low paid work, heavily swathed in an imagery of caring and community, individuality and self-sacrifice. Thus, the popular conception of school teachers was in direct opposition to that of organized labor. Opponents to teachers' affiliation with labor inevitably raised the notion that teachers could strike— although in fact no teacher organization in these years ever supported the right to strike. It is not surprising, then, that while teachers in some cities had organized associations to work for health benefits, pensions, tenure, and higher wages, and in a few cities, teachers were in close communication with organized labor, in no city had any of those associations affiliated with a labor union.[4] Haley herself admitted that it did not occur to her to speak to Chicago's labor leaders until a teacher whose brother was a labor delegate suggested it in 1899. That visit proved to be "the opening wedge" of the affiliation of the teachers with labor three years later. Her initial visit was significant not only because of what it eventually led to, but because of the fact that it happened at all.[5]

In other ways, Chicago's women teachers were well positioned to affiliate with labor. Labor identification was deeply interwoven with ethnic and class identification, and Chicago's Irish Catholic population was among the most strongly identified with labor. Indeed, Irish Americans affirmed their racial and class superiority over newer immigrants and African American workers in part through union membership. For the Irish Catholic women teachers who made up the bulk of the Federation, the benefits of labor solidarity were familiar to them from their fathers and brothers who comprised the membership of the major labor unions of the city.

If women teachers' brothers and fathers were union members, they were also increasingly likely to have sisters who were members of newly organized women's unions in the city: In 1902 in Chicago, women milliners formed a union, and three thousand newly unionized women workers in the packing and box-making industries struck. The following spring, Chicago chorus girls, laundry workers, and waitresses organized into their own unions. After the Federation affiliated with labor, the National Women's Trade Union League was founded in 1903 and the Federation became the largest affiliate of the Chicago local.[6]

Still, for all that Haley spoke about the natural affinity of teachers and labor unions, it was the CFL's *differences* that proved most attractive to Haley. The main difference was that working men had the right to vote. Because women teachers could not vote, Federation political goals could be fought only by lobbying the legislature in Springfield, marching the streets to get signatures on petitions, and raising public awareness about schools in the newspapers and public meetings. Other working conditions in schools were determined by the Chicago Board of Education, which was appointed by an elected mayor. Women teachers' material working conditions were determined by men who had no political obligations to women.[7] In order to maintain the professional authority and independence of public schools, women teachers needed to make alliances with those with political power. Or, as Haley worded it in her characteristic belligerent imagery: "We had to fight the devil with fire."[8]

THE CHICAGO FEDERATION OF LABOR

The unique leadership of the Chicago Federation of Labor was one main reason why the Chicago teachers did organize. Since its founding in 1896, the CFL had played a central role as the political organizer and motivator of all Chicago labor. Through its monthly journal *The Labor Advocate*, and its biweekly meetings which attracted up to five hundred delegates, the CFL coordinated local political action and encouraged the formation of new unions. This uniquely inclusive vision was furthered by John Fitzpatrick, who became president of the CFL in 1902.

Fitzpatrick was committed to linking the CFL with broader social and political reform movements in the city. One of his first tasks was to sweep out the powerful and corrupt building trades unions, which had previously dominated CFL leadership, and he introduced a broader, more progressive tenor to the union, emphasizing the organization and inclusion of new unions, a commitment to democratic procedures, and broad intertrade solidarity.[9] Fitzpatrick reached out to organize unskilled industrial workers, and he welcomed the organization of women's unions—by 1904, more than sixty thousand Chicago working women (almost 20 percent of Chicago's unionized workforce) were union members, one-half of these in mixed unions and the other half in all-female locals of factory and other unskilled workers.[10] Simultaneously, he tried to link the labor movement with nonpartisan and progressive municipal reform movements.

One component of Fitzpatrick's progressive platform was the support of the Chicago city schools, a stand that may have been influenced by his wife Anna who was an elementary teacher and a member of the Federation.[11] In 1899, the Chicago Central Labor Council, the forerunner of the CFL, publicly opposed the Harper Bill, charging that it excluded working-class children from the educational system and promoted business interests in schools.

Further, the Labor Council argued that the proposed requirement that teachers have a college degree would severely limit the ability of working-class women to enter teaching, which was the principal avenue of social mobility for working-class daughters. One persistent theme of the CFL's position on education was the equalization of educational opportunities of the rich and poor. In response to charges that Chicago schools were too full of "frills and fads," the CFL argued that the school subjects that the rich denounced as "fads" in working-class schools were the same subjects that they praised in their own wealthy schools. The wealthy "delight in teaching their children music, art, and languages" while they criticized the same subjects as wasteful when implemented in working-class schools.[12]

Haley began to nurture her connections with organized labor soon after her first meeting with them in 1899. But what really motivated the teachers into union work was a radical change in their working conditions. When "Bulletin Ben" Andrews resigned as Chicago school superintendent in the spring of 1900, he was replaced by Edwin Cooley, who proved to be no better a friend to teachers. Cooley had been head of the Cook County Normal School and a high school principal in Indiana. These credentials gave him more experience in school buildings than Andrews, but no more affinity to women elementary teachers. Most suspicious about Cooley to the teachers was his great support by the business community. In fact, in his nine years as Superintendent, Cooley gradually accomplished much of the centralization objectives originally proposed in the Harper Bill.

Cooley set himself to tightening the administrative structure of the school system by reducing the number of district superintendents. These fourteen officers had held much of the control over their local districts, including curricular decision and the appointment of teachers. The Federation had approved of many of these officers—including Ella Flagg Young and William Speer, who had initiated progressive curriculum reform. Cooley gradually reduced the number of district superintendents to six, and he frequently shifted them from one district to another to undercut the development of personal loyalty between them and the teachers. In a further attempt to consolidate power, he reorganized his office to include three assistant superintendents who worked directly under him, and he trimmed the number of committees on the board of education.[13] He initiated a board of education *Bulletin*, which, between 1904 and 1908, presented curriculum outlines and recommended reading lists for teachers and offered statistical information about Chicago's school enrollment and average costs per pupil so that all principals and the public could see where school money was being spent. The *Bulletin's* cost-analysis approach confirmed Cooley's emphasis on standardization and accountability.[14]

In early 1902, Cooley recommended to the board the removal of William Speer, the popular district superintendent who promoted progressive learning in mathematics. The move raised a chorus of objections. John Dewey,

Francis Parker, and Thomas Shields, the progressive Catholic educator whom Haley had heard speak at the Sinsinawa Sisters' summer school, all wrote letters applauding Speer's work and objecting to his dismissal. The legislative committee of the CFL sent a delegation to Speer's district to evaluate his methods, and they wrote a letter to the board of education praising the student-centered work at his schools.[15] Haley went to Mayor Carter Harrison to lobby him to interfere in the firing of Speer, but she was unsuccessful. Haley suspected that it was Speer's independence from textbooks that earned him the wrath of the superintendent, and in this the treatment of Speer was reminiscent of that given to Josephine Locke, who, Haley believed, had also been chased out of the school system because she did not promote the art books recommended by textbook publishers.[16]

Added to the political fray over Speer was a combination of particularly difficult working conditions that teachers faced when school began in the fall of 1902. Over the summer, after the schools had closed and many teachers were out of town, the board had approved Cooley's new promotion scheme for teachers.[17] Under the new policy, teachers' salaries advanced from the first to the seventh year, but teachers in their eighth year were to be evaluated for efficiency by their principal and given "efficiency grades" on such professional characteristics as systematic work, cooperation with other teachers, and "school interest." Only those teachers who passed this efficiency evaluation were eligible to take a promotional exam to qualify for a raise. Three specific aspects of the new plan bothered the Teachers' Federation. First, the principals' efficiency grades were kept completely secret, supposedly to prevent teachers from unproductively comparing themselves with each other. Second, teachers who showed enough credits from degree-granting institutions or normal schools could be exempt from the efficiency rating, thereby privileging teachers who could afford to pay for extra coursework, and raising suspicions that the superintendent had coordinated with the University of Chicago, which had recently opened up its own teachers' college.[18] Thirdly, teacher transfers to different schools were based upon this rating, not teachers' interest. On a broader level, teachers objected to the undercutting of experienced teachers' seniority and the fact that the efficiency ratings failed to take into account their actual classroom skills gained over years of work.[19]

Even more galling to Haley was that the scheme was initiated by the board of education finance committee as a cost-saving measure, although the superintendent and the board promoted it publicly as a great educational reform. And save costs it did: In June 1905, three years after the scheme was put into effect, out of 2,600 teachers who had at least ten years of experience, only sixty-one received the maximum pay. In addition about one thousand teachers were paying for evening and summer courses. According to Haley, the teachers realized that the object of the new promotional plan was to force them "to put their heads down like the hens in the corn, into books and study" and to distract them from their recent political work in the tax investigations.[20] Teachers would be divided by their individual improvement plans, by the competition that grew from secret markings, and by the financial strain of paying for extra coursework.

To the public perception, however, Haley's opposition to Cooley's plan was simply the arrogant refusal of teachers to improve themselves. Advocates of the promotion system argued that such a plan was needed to maintain teacher quality and to introduce new ideas into the classroom. Even social reformer Jane Addams, who for many years was a friend of the Federation, scratched her head at the wisdom of the Federation positioning itself *against* further education.[21] Haley, focused as she was on the effect of the policy change on teachers, and by what she saw as the political motivations of the board, paid little attention to such criticism.

By September 1902, the teachers' anger was further enflamed for other reasons. By that time, they knew they would not be getting their raise from the tax suit because over the summer, the board decided to use the recently collected tax money for the cleaning of the schools and not for teachers' salaries.[22] Then, as school opened in late August, the city's department of health warned school officials that the school water was typhoid infected. The board shut off the schools' water supply and told students to bring bottles of water to school. But poor students did not have bottles so they drank from fire hydrants near the schools, which were also typhoid infected. Some principals and teachers boiled water for their students, but by October there were well over five thousand cases of the disease in the city.[23]

The tension reached a fever pitch in late October and early November 1902 when students led a series of strikes at eight public schools. The strikes began when the superintendent replaced the popular female principal of a west side school with a former male district superintendent. In protest, the students walked out of their classroom and threatened a general strike. The new principal appeased the students, but sent the truant officer into the neighborhood to search for malingerers. They rounded up two hundred children, but the community resisted and created a small riot. A few days later, about 250 students at the neighboring Andrew Jackson School held a three-day strike, boycotting their classes and setting up camp in the playground to protest the firing of their teacher, Jane McKoen, for insubordination and her replacement with an African American teacher, Julie Brown. Even after Brown was dismissed by the principal, the students maintained their strike, demanding the return of their teacher.[24] At another school, a Czech teacher was fired for becoming too close to her students in her largely Eastern European immigrant school. Students at other west side schools waged strikes too, and roamed the streets of the city calling broadly for more local control over the hiring of teachers and administrators. Jane McKoen's lawyer insisted that his client was fired simply because she was a supporter of the Teachers' Federation and of the recently fired District Superintendent Speer, and the conflict became framed in the public press as one of central office business-men trying to seize control from teachers and students.[25] Whatever the rea-sons for the strikes, they furthered the image of chaos in the schools and nudged the CFL along in their commitment to supporting the unionization of teachers. At the national AFL convention in New Orleans in late Octo-ber, George Lighthall of the CFL told his compatriots that with the union-ization of teachers, wild student strikes such as those that followed the dismissal of Jane McKoen would not happen.[26]

On October 16, 1902, Fitzpatrick sent the Teachers' Federation a letter inviting affiliation. "The time has come for the workingmen of Chicago to take a stand for their children's sake, and demand justice for the teachers and the children so that both may not be crushed by the power of corporate greed," he wrote. Then he clarified that the CFL had no authority under its constitution to call a strike, and that the CFL would not interfere in the policy of the Federation.[27]

The teachers considered affiliation for about five weeks. It was the biggest question that had ever come before the five-year-old organization and opinions were fiercely divided.[28] Arguments against affiliation raised various concerns. Some argued that unionization was in exact opposition to professionalism and professional ethics. Another argument was that teachers represented the people, while labor unions represented only a small special interest group of the people. Thus, the affiliation of teachers with labor meant aligning against parents and communities.[29] Federation president Ella Rowe, who would resign over the issue, believed that civil service workers should not unionize because their "boss" was not a specific body to be nego-tiated with, but a "great intangible, querulous, munificent public." Another teacher opposed the move because she opposed unions in general: "We are individuals and we ought to act as individuals and be treated accordingly."[30] But the most common argument drew on the perceived class differences between teachers and industrial workers. Teaching was white-collar work, and many teachers feared risking their newly won social status by aligning with a working-class labor union. Haley and Goggin knew quite well that one of the few compensations of teaching was a perceived class privilege, or "a certain social superiority over her non-teaching neighbors."[31] Typical of this position was that of an elementary principal who supported the Federation's work but who still insisted that she was not in favor of placing teachers "on a level with a hod carrier."[32]

In response, Goggin and Haley appealed to teachers to consider that working people *were* their allies, since they were the parents of their working-class students. Indeed, Haley argued, working people in the CFL consistently supported schools more than any other group in the city. Working men whose children attended public schools had direct interest in the public schools, and as working people, they also understood teachers' resistance to a board of education that acted like an all-powerful boss. Goggin made a special appeal to teachers' gender identity by reminding teachers that firemen and policemen received raises, but teachers did not. Why? Because they were men and men could vote. She argued: "Why shouldn't the City Council give our money to the firemen and policemen? Haven't they got votes?"[33] Until women got the vote, they needed to ally with men who could.

Haley and Goggin made a strategic move in inviting the popular Chicago reformer Jane Addams to speak to the teachers at the November 8 meeting. Addams's powerful social stature and her public commitment to social justice helped legitimate the cause. According to Haley, Addams "electrified" the members by telling them that, given their organizational and political strength, they were *already* a union. The only question now, she said, was whether they would not avail themselves of the help of other unions. Outside of the Federation, Addams was strongly criticized for her talk. Later, she told Haley that she was invited to the White House and was roundly criticized by Theodore Roosevelt for encouraging the teachers to affiliate with organized labor.[34] This news thrilled Haley, perhaps because it indicated the public effect of the teachers' action, and she longed to tell the teachers about it. But Federation lawyer Isaiah Greenacre talked her out of it, arguing that to publicly criticize the president might be considered in bad taste, and might alienate some supporters and exacerbate the Federation's already tenuous public standing. Familiar with Haley's firebrand political style, the lawyer gently admonished her: "Do not let your delight in contest invite you into a conflict, before you have grown large enough to win."[35] Greenacre's advice reinforced the stringent gender roles in which Haley remained confined as a woman leader and as a leader of teachers: Male labor leaders were hardly concerned about issues of inappropriate behavior in their politics.

In the meeting at which Addams spoke, the Chicago Teachers' Federation voted unanimously to join the CFL.[36] One week later, AFL delegates at their annual convention, endorsed the move and committed to making the Federation the nucleus of a national teachers' union.[37] But all was not well. The Federation president, Ella Rowe, was opposed to affiliation and she immediately resigned, charging that the Federation was being led by an unrepresentative group of radical leaders who ignored the interests of the majority of its membership. The meeting at which the vote was taken, Rowe charged, was packed with union sympathizers, and attended by less than half the regular Federation members, and many of these were "hypnotized" into acquiescence by Haley. Rowe said that Haley was "a dangerous leader" who believed that people who did not take her point of view had simply not thought enough about the issue. Haley explained to the press that Rowe had resigned for reasons of poor health, and Rowe cattily responded to the *Tribune* that if she had ill health, it was caused by her effort "to make the Federation a representative body."[38] In addition to the loss of Rowe, an unknown but large number of teachers resigned from the Federation.[39]

The teachers' affiliation with the CFL sent shock waves around the nation.[40] In Chicago, newspapers kept up their long-standing barrage, criticizing the teachers for their selfish desire for more money. The Chicago *Tribune* sarcastically editorialized that according to the Federation, it was not enough that a teacher taught students, she must also be a teacher unionist, social and economic reformer, and political activist. And as a result, the *Tribune* prophesized gloomily, "Discipline and efficiency in the schools will give way." Later that paper would charge the unionized teachers with teaching nothing less than "sedition, revolt against authority, disrespect for law, and subversion of private and public rights." Another Chicago daily claimed that courses in character and citizenship could not possibly be taught by a teacher in a labor union "which taught hatred of other classes."[41]

The teachers' first attendance at the CFL meeting in December 1902 was a moving affair. Five hundred male delegates applauded their entry. Teachers listened to the reports of their new colleagues, and clarified that they could not participate in a strike vote. Haley presented some of the features of an education bill under debate in the state legislature, and urged CFL members to look closely at the links between the bill and commercial and corporate interests.[42] One teacher was struck by the decency and politeness of the men, and the atmosphere of "frankness, sincerity and fair play" that gave her "a deep sense of satisfaction in the comradeship of men and women whose concern is with fundamental issues of life."[43] When in January 1903, the teachers received a $50 raise, that satisfaction may have deepened even more.

WHAT THE TEACHERS WON AND LOST

On one level, affiliation with labor was a tactical move to help expand the Federation's own political programs. The Federation's campaigns required expansive grassroots connections, and because women teachers could not vote, their political power rested in aligning with those who could. But the affiliation with labor was not merely a tactical move. By allying with the CFL, Haley also made a powerful statement about the nature of teaching as work. By emphasizing affiliation with a historically male, working-class organization, she positioned teachers as laborers more than as professionals or as female social reformers. At a very basic level, Haley saw the same force behind the horrors of the worst factory job and the injustice of teachers' low wages. Both industrial workers and teachers were pawns to the power of private capital and both needed to fight against the power of unregulated corporate interests. As she told the CFL: "You have demanded that the commercial interests take their hands off the child in the factory. I want you to say to those same commercial interests, 'Take your hands off the schools.'"[44]

Haley's analogies between teachers and factory workers made sense to her, although some might have thought it was a great leap of the imagination. During the massive Pennsylvania anthracite miners' strike of 1902, Haley equated the plight of unskilled male coal miners with that of educated women teachers. The Federation set up a miners' relief fund which raised over $600 to send to strikers and their families.[45] Haley urged teachers to contribute to the fund because, as she wrote in the *Bulletin*, miners were workers that were "not getting for their labor what it is worth to the community" and teachers, too, were "not getting proportion to what they give in the community." Furthermore, like the private corporations in Chicago that evaded taxes and regulation, the mine owners in Pennsylvania illustrated the evils of unregulated monopoly and "private ownership over natural resources."[46]

But the relationship between the teachers and labor remained prickly, in spite of Haley's great enthusiasm for the cause. In 1906, the Federation turned down an appeal from typographical workers to publicize their strike among teachers with the explanation that while they were in sympathy with them, their fight to affiliate with labor had "been so fierce that it does not seem prudent to invite further attacks." Haley wrote Fitzpatrick that labor unionists should not "fail to understand the difficulty of the teachers joining hands with the labor unions."[47]

And even Haley raised occasional doubts about the commonality of teachers and laborers. In April 1903, Haley and a half-dozen other teachers were asked by the CFL leadership to monitor their annual election and prevent the annual stealing of the ballots by a crooked unit in the union. This was the type of corruption that Fitzpatrick was committed to weeding out, and he apparently thought that the presence of the teachers and other women labor delegates would provide a cleansing influence on the election. The women supervised the ballot box through the afternoon and into the night, while a growing crowd of irritable men gathered around them. As men's tempers rose, Haley jumped onto a chair and gave the group a rousing speech, imploring them to stay honest for the sake of the thousands of men, women, and children whom they represented. Later in the night, the women lit candles to keep the room bright enough so that the ballot box would not be stolen.[48] The election was a success—the teachers had prevented another stolen election—but it added more worries to Haley's mind. In an unusual moment of self-reflection, she wrote about her concerns, wondering if she had done right to link the teachers with labor, given its great disorganization and internal strife. In a note to herself, she wrote: "That CF of L is turbulent, disorganized rather than unorganized, no co-ordination, full of suspicion of one another, hatred, discord, self-seeking, coarse, crude, and almost anarchistical—yet in it lies the hope of the workers."[49]

Affiliation with the CFL also drew dividing lines between the teachers and other groups. Like members of other ethnic working-class groups, Haley threw her hat in with her race and class identification, affiliating most strongly with the white ethnic working-class men in the Chicago Federation of Labor, which itself excluded black workers or segregated them in weak auxiliaries. The Federation and the CFL's promotion of the Jane McKoen case as one of local students and parents resisting the imposition of a school board decision blatantly ignored the racial character of the incident: Students and parents objected at least as much to the fact that her replacement was African American as to McKeon's firing. The Federation's single published comment about African Americans during the great teamsters' strike of 1905 displays exactly this kind of class and racial unity. During the strike, white industrialists hired black workers as strikebreakers, spurring a vicious race war.[50] White communities around the city organized against black strikebreakers, and one of the most violent incidents was at the Hendricks School, the building in which Haley had taught for sixteen years in the Stockyards district. On May 10, 1905, eight hundred white students at Hendricks walked out of their classrooms when they saw black strikebreakers delivering "scab coal" to their building. The students hurled rocks and pieces of wood at the drivers and at students who did not join the picket line, and they organized a "skilled pupils" union with a kindergarten local affiliated. Students wore paper badges that read, "We are on strike. Hurrah for the unions." The next day, despite threats from the principal, only 342 students attended school. More than three thousand school children from eight other schools, mostly on the south side, joined the "walkout." Many white parents supported the students' strike, and one south side school principal allegedly said that he would invite his pupils to join the strike "if the dirty 'niggers' deliver coal at this school."[51]

In Haley's lead article in the Federation *Bulletin* that month, she expressed solidarity with the striking teamsters, dismissed "the question of the negro's equal right to work," and blamed the riots on both "the plutocrats" and African Americans, whom she described as "strange" and "irresponsible."[52] In this, she shared the opinion of the Chicago Federation of Labor, which simultaneously criticized employers for their racial manipulation while also criticizing "irresponsible" African American workers.

The Federation's affiliation with labor also distanced this large group of women teachers from the middle-class women's reform movement that was so active in Chicago in these years. Irish Catholic teachers from working-class backgrounds were already socially distanced from middle-class Protestant women's clubs, and the linkage with men's labor unions only furthered that distance. This, of course, may not have been a loss to Haley, who already felt slighted by Protestant middle-class women who seemed to hold romantic views of the importance of children's experiences in schools, without considering the effect on working conditions of teachers. But this initial difference of opinion and allegiances would prove to be one of the fatal wedges in the Federation's work in later years.

Haley's authority as a leader, too, both won and lost in the affiliation with the CFL. Haley's conflict with Ella Rowe, who was one of the founding members of the Federation, echoed her earlier conflicts with Elizabeth Burdick in the Federation and with Elizabeth Rodgers in the Foresters. In each case, Haley went head to head with a prominent woman leader; in each case, Haley organized a dramatic opposition and was accused of manipulating the issues and political posturing. Characteristic of these interactions was Haley's inability to credit any value to her opponents' views, even as she drew upon rumor and innuendo to build up her own case. When any merits of her own argument were questioned, Haley accused the doubters of being traitors to her cause. These patterns of combative political conflict would mark the entirety of Haley's career and would eventually contribute to the undercutting of her authority.

In her written accounts of her life, Haley minimized such disputes and ignored the accusations about her character. Indeed, she would never admit to, and possibly never recognized, the recurring charge that what she saw as authority earned through representative democracy, others saw as sheer contrivance and abuse of power. The origins of this leadership style can only be imagined. Was it stubbornness inherited from her father that drove Margaret Haley into such contentious battles? Or was the cause Haley's overweening pride and ego, which led her to perfunctorily dismiss any idea that was not in agreement with her own? Or was she so unreflective that she simply was oblivious to what others thought of her? Perhaps Haley's behavior was the combined result of all three—stubbornness and hubris kept her from accepting others' perspectives, and her relentless focus on the Federation reinforced her belief that she was always right. In addition, Haley always saw herself in the marginalized, powerless position of a woman school teacher, and accordingly, she believed that she was justified in any method she used to gain authority.[53]

The conflict with Ella Rowe also speaks to a power imbalance within the Federation structure. The elected president tended to play a marginal role in the group, focusing on local organizing and management of teacher issues. Given the Federation's involvement in complex legal and political negotiations across the city and state, Haley's work often overshadowed the more day-to-day concerns of teachers. While presidents were elected regularly from the Federation local leadership, Haley became the long-time staff member who, although not elected by the whole, became the mouthpiece and titular head of the organization.

Furthermore, although Haley's difficult leadership style caused her trouble, it is useful to remember that even as she was condemned by her enemies, she was applauded by her supporters. When she led the Federation into affiliation with organized labor, her position was supported by Catherine Goggin, Jane Addams, and the CFL, as well as labor activists across the nation. What Rowe criticized as Haley's ability to "hypnotize" her membership was seen by others as the persuasive advocacy of a brilliant leader. Margaret Haley's fame came in part from her charismatic leadership skills, her highly focused commitment to her cause, and her famously domineering personality. It was these combined characteristics in a woman schoolteacher that captured the attention of the public and furthered publicity for the Federation. To some extent, the bitterness of Haley's opposition reflects the dramatic position that she represented: By advocating a more activist, political role for her women's organization, she was promoting distinctly nontraditional and controversial behavior for women. As a woman on the public political stage, each of her controversies was magnified and added to her larger public image as a loud, difficult woman. The radical nature of her decisions would inflame the critique of her behavior as a woman and as an organizational leader even more.

THE NEA

In some ways, Haley's battle with the National Education Association in these years was just as bloody as the battle to affiliate the teachers with labor, even though the stakes seemed less extreme and the opponents more refined. Issues of class and race were less at the forefront in Haley's battles with the NEA, and the issue of gender was far more paramount. Haley's struggle to open up the NEA leadership to the woman classroom teacher was a prime example of her vision of the expanded teachers' role in society—a vision that conflicted with a firmly entrenched educational establishment that positioned male school administrators at the front and center of educational policy making.

At the turn of the century, the NEA was a forty-year old education organization that functioned primarily as a networking agency for school administrators, university officials, and other educational leaders. At annual meetings held every summer, NEA speakers—all male, and almost all administrators—delivered speeches on particular educational topics of the day, from classroom matters to school organization. Schoolteachers attended NEA sessions, but they were prohibited from speaking. Their function was primarily to listen and learn from their superiors.

Haley attended her first NEA meeting in the summer of 1896 in Buffalo, New York, while she was in that city attending a teachers' institute. There she had heard a speech by Nicholas Murray Butler, the retiring president of the NEA, whom she found to be distinctly arrogant. Three years later, when the Federation began the battle against the Harper Bill, she saw the influence of another scion of the NEA crowd, William Rainey Harper. By this time she saw the NEA as a domineering tribunal of the educational world with an elitist, self-perpetuating leadership who were aligned with the same powers that were fighting democracy in the public schools. Haley joined a movement within the NEA to organize classroom teachers to stage a revolt against the leadership. In typical fashion, Haley explained this work as a necessary act in response to others' actions: "We Chicago teachers recognized that our experience was forcing us into leadership of the liberal forces within the national association. We didn't go out looking for it. It was just another of the heavily disguised blessings which were always being handed to us on pewter plates."[54]

The Federation used the 1899 NEA convention in Los Angeles to organize classroom teachers into a national political unit. Because the convention was held in summer, it had always attracted teachers who used the journey to the conference as a holiday. To encourage attendance at the Los Angeles meeting, the Federation put together a package trip with discount train and hotel accommodations. They attracted eight hundred teachers on the train journey, which stopped in Colorado Springs where some teachers hiked in the mountains and visited the mineral springs, and again in Salt Lake City where they visited a Mormon chapel.[55] Arriving in Los Angeles, the teachers began to organize a national group of classroom teachers which they called the National Federation of Teachers. Consisting mostly of classroom teachers from newly organized associations in urban districts in the east, the group planned its annual meetings to coincide with the NEA meeting. Their goal was to lobby the NEA to attend to the need to improve teachers' salaries and secure tenure and pensions.[56]

At the July 1901 NEA meeting in Detroit, Haley forced the issue of women teachers' right to representation in the NEA by speaking from the floor of the convention—the first time a woman and a classroom teacher spoke. Up to that moment, she recalled later, the meeting was like scores of other NEA conventions. William T. Harris, then commissioner of education, had given a long paper on the progress of education before a crowd of silent and restless teachers. "It was a hot day," she recalled, "and everybody was wondering how long he was going to keep it up, telling them the educational sky was without a cloud." After he finished, the chairman allowed five minutes for discussion, and Haley grabbed the opportunity, and in so doing, the NEA was "thrown open to the great unwashed." She recalled: "I was up in a second. I didn't weigh more than a hundred pounds at that time, or very little more, and I remember when I rose, I challenged the United States commissioner of education and three other men, and flung one challenge after another at them." In her speech, Haley challenged Harris's rosy vision, and argued for the case of tax revision, describing the Chicago tax fight. She sat down to thunderous applause. Harris rose and pointed his finger at Haley, charging that she was a tired and hysterical grade school teacher and that if there were any more outbursts from teachers, he would argue that the annual meeting not be held during summer break. He furthered dismissed Haley by identifying her as from Chicago, which he called a "morbid, cyclonic and hysterical" place that was in no way representative of the rest of the country.[57] Haley rose again in response, and pled guilty to being a common classroom teacher, and admitted that if what she had just done was hysterical, then she hoped it would be contagious so that teachers all over the country would rise up and claim their rights. It was at that meeting, Haley recalled, that "we, the elementary school teachers, had found out that we were another Estate."[58]

The teachers soon identified an effective method to organize that estate within the NEA. At each convention, members of the state chapters met and selected a representative to the nominating committee.[59] Women teachers had, by custom, never taken part in this "town meeting" structure. In 1901, this changed. As Haley later retold the story:

> Without any previous announcement and without the least hint to the men, so that it was a complete surprise, enough Chicago teachers, members of our Federation, quietly walked into the Illinois state headquarters at 5:30 o'clock on the evening of the first day, and wearing blue badges indicating active membership, voted for Miss Goggin and elected her a member of the Nominating Committee from Illinois, which actually took the men's breath away. It was done so quietly, so unexpectedly, and so good naturedly.

The men quickly caught on, and the next year they "mustered every occupant of a pair of trousers available and marched into the Illinois state headquarters." But the women were prepared and outnumbered them, and in the subsequent years, they continued to encourage teachers to attend the NEA meetings and pack the nominating sessions, and they continued offering vacation packages before and after the annual summer meeting.[60]

The NEA leadership was threatened by the growing voice of teachers. At the 1903 convention in Boston, Charles W. Eliot, president of Harvard University, presided at the meeting when Nicholas Murray Butler, president of Columbia University, presented an amendment that limited the participation of floor members from the nomination of NEA officials.[61] Haley was the first to the floor to challenge Butler's proposal, arguing that it would create "a self-perpetuating machine" of leadership. Butler argued that classroom teachers did not attend the nomination meetings anyway, to which Haley shot back that more than one hundred teachers were currently at the Illinois meeting.[62] Butler's proposal lost, and the NEA leadership responded to the teachers' pressure by forming a Committee on Teachers Salaries.[63] Classroom teachers had won their first foothold in the NEA. The *Chicago Record Herald* portrayed the teachers' victory in a cartoon where Margaret Haley was the stern and upright schoolmistress behind her desk overlooking the schoolboy versions of Eliot and Butler. But while some admirers praised the schoolteacher from Chicago who had "met and vanquished two of the leading university presidents of the country," others charged her with being a demagogue who was too ambitious and conceited.[64] "Give her enough rope and she will hang herself and ruin her cause all right" was one comment.[65]

There was little love lost between Haley and the two Ivy League college presidents who, like Chicago's William Rainey Harper, represented to

Cartoon of the 1903 meeting of the National Education Association, *Chicago Record Herald*, July 11, 1903

Haley the most elitist approach to education. She wrote Samuel Gompers, president of the AFL, that the NEA's promotion of vocational education programs was done under the guise of educators helping working people, when in fact, the programs were designed to train children to become docile and mechanical workers. In general, she explained to Gompers, the NEA was "undemocratic and not in sympathy with the workers whose children form the bulk of the pupils these people are hired to teach." Nowhere on the NEA program was there the topic of teachers' salaries, tenure, or any other issue related to the betterment of teachers' material conditions.[66] Furthermore, Haley argued, NEA leaders from private universities were trying to reduce the length of elementary schooling and lengthen high school and college courses, so that the children of the working poor who could only afford elementary education would spend less time in school. This she called a "university idea of education" that was "aristocratic" and diametrically opposed to the "kindergarten idea," which promoted more extensive early education for all children.[67] Once again, Haley positioned herself and her movement as standing for all citizens in opposition to elitist professional educators. In so doing, she widened the deep rift that already existed between elementary teachers and university educators.

Not surprisingly, Haley's promotion of her own occupational group at the expense of others was perceived by some of her potential supporters as exclusionary and divisive. At the 1902 NEA meeting in Minneapolis, the National Federation of Teachers held its charter meeting.[68] Founded with Haley's impetus, the National Federation was open only to elementary classroom teachers, and it was geared specifically toward women's interests: Their keynote speaker was suffragist Carrie Chapman Catt.[69] Some members disputed the wisdom of such specialization at a national level, particularly since in rural districts men and women high school teachers and administrators often shared working conditions and political perspectives. As a male school principal wrote to Haley:

> It occurs to me that whatever the position held in the teaching profession, interests are common and very closely allied: to divide forces therefore would seem to be a mistake. . . . some of the most aggressive men and women in the work are occupying positions as principals and to deny them a place in the federation would weaken its work. Separation is apt to engender misunderstanding and in the work ahead of us I deplore any such thing. In great cities like Chicago, your plan would be much stronger than in smaller places where the common interest and common bond is more strongly felt.[70]

Haley never addressed such concerns. It is possible she felt that she was in a bind: To extend her organizational impetus to friendly high school teachers and school administrators would run the risk of diluting the single-focus demands of women elementary teachers—the largest group in the nation's teaching force and the group that was by all accounts most marginalized and underpaid in American schools, often *by* school administrators, secondary teachers, and university educators. She was never able to fully trust the motives of supporters from outside of the elementary teaching staff; thus, however passionately she promoted her vision of a united teacher front, in practice she was far less inclusive.

WHY TEACHERS SHOULD ORGANIZE

It was at the NEA meeting in St. Louis in 1904 that Margaret Haley most clearly articulated her thinking about the rights of teachers to organize, and about the link to citizenship. Haley entitled her speech before the general session of the NEA "Why Teachers Should Organize," and in it she laid out her vision not only of teachers' right to form associations and unions, but of the necessity for teachers to organize to protect democracy.[71] It was the duty of teachers, Haley began, to take responsibility for the education of citizens about their political responsibilities. Referring to the power of private interests, Haley noted that the protection of democracy was especially important in America, a nation that had only recently freed itself of monarchial rule and was still tempted to fall into hierarchical practices. The struggle between monarchy and democracy was currently being played out in the battle between the industrial ideal that promoted the supremacy of commercialism by subordinating the worker to the product and to the machine, and the ideal of democracy, which "places humanity above all machines." The school was the site of democratic ideals, but schools could democratize society only if schools themselves were democratic. Teacher unions ensured just such a democratic structure in schools.

Haley qualified that unions in and of themselves were not automatically democratic or good for the social welfare because unions held in their organizational purpose selfish and self-protective motives. Unions that organized only for self-protection would only consider a narrow spectrum of teachers' needs, and not the broader responsibility of school and social betterment. Teacher unions thus needed a professional component that would allow the organization to "simultaneously pursue both the self-interest and the public interest." She cited the Federation's work in the tax case as an example of just such a partnership between self-protection and social reform: The teachers had rooted out corruption, improved the school life of Chicago's children, educated the citizenry about political reform, *and* helped their own cause.

Next, Haley outlined the support that teachers needed in order to develop this type of organization: an increase in salaries, the improvement of job security and pensions, the reduction of class size, and the inclusion of teachers in school decision making. Without such improvements, teachers had no initiative and no commitment to their work or to the children in their classrooms. Instead, they had only dissatisfaction and resentment. This was the current state in schools. Because of the types of administrative practices in schools today, there was little democratization and more "factoryization of education." As a result, the teacher became little more than a factory worker whose job was merely to carry out mechanically and unquestioningly the ideas and orders of those clothed with the authority of position and who may or may not know the needs of the children or how to minister to them.[72]

Such a condition oppressed both teachers and students, and ultimately it limited society which lost the opportunity for schools to model and teach democratic values to the next generation. A professional union that protected teachers' material interests would thus protect the nation's democracy.

Haley concluded with more condemnation of the "industrial ideal," which threatened to overwhelm the democratic ideal. Only one of these ideals could win the battle: Either educators would carry their vision of democracy into industry, or industry would be carried into schools. Educators faced a serious choice: "If the school can not bring joy to the work of the world, the joy must go out of its own life, and work in the school as in the industrial field, will become drudgery."

Haley's speech was followed by Aaron Grove, the superintendent of schools in Denver, who presented a sharp response entitled "The Limitation of the Superintendent's Authority and of Teachers' Independence." Making thinly veiled reference to the Chicago Teachers' Federation, Grove argued that school systems had clear lines of authority and duties that were laid out by the board of education. Neither superintendent nor teacher should be allowed to be independent of those assigned tasks: The administrator's job was to administrate, and the teacher's to teach. Certainly the more effective superintendent was one who administered his job with politeness and respect, but this was not always successful, because what one person saw as polite, others saw as despotic. Such misunderstanding was rife in "one of the large cities of the country," Grove said, where teachers were exhibiting a "dangerous tendency" to usurp power from the superintendent. These teachers believed that the public school system should be a democracy and that the teachers should constitute the actors of that democratic government. But Grove argued that this was "a false conception of true democracy." In fact, school systems were *already* democratic because school leaders were elected or appointed by elected officials, and a democratic line of command was already set up by school law. Teachers should be respected, and their advice must be heeded, but teachers needed to remember that they were independent only insofar as their job description entailed. Teacher's representation to their administrators should be advisory only, and

> this counsel, this giving of advice, which is essential, is not to be given in a formal way thru the orders and directions and laws and rules of an organized body like that of a trades union; but, on the other hand, it is to be given as a good daughter talks with the father and mother; as the kindly son participates in the counsels of the home.

Grove ended his talk with a stern warning about teacher unions that made life "sordid" by measuring their work as it was "gauged by the dollar," and making "the school world descend to a lower plane of social life, where the measurement of life's work cease to be honor, integrity, patriotism, and love, and become that which represent acquisitiveness, selfishness, and financial success at the expense of the neighbor."[73] In this speech, Haley's vision of teacher organizations as the agent of democratic citizenship was transformed to financial greed and selfishness embodied in the image of the disrespectful daughter.

The following year, Haley took up a different battle for democracy within the structure of the NEA. At the 1905 meeting in Asbury Park, New Jersey, members faced a major proposal for reorganization of the NEA that would incorporate it into a national charter and enhance the authority of the National Council, the oldest and most powerful committee in the Association, by giving it control over the permanent fund. The argument for the change was to give the NEA more national recognition and stabilize its operations and financial management. A former president of the NEA explained the move with implicit reference to the growing power of local teacher groups when he said that such a change would "prevent local meetings from squandering the savings of twenty years on something of no account."[74] Although a seemingly obscure bureaucratic change, Haley challenged it with full force. At the convention, she held up the vote, arguing that since the permanent fund came from members' dues, its use should be subject to the vote of all members, and that the National Council was an exclusive unrepresentative body whose members were appointed by the Council itself and included powerful university presidents and textbook company executives. The proposed changes would make the National Council "in perpetuity a self-perpetuating dynasty," whose authority could only be challenged by a special act of Congress, thus leaving the country's largest educational organization out of the control of most educators.[75] Six months later, Haley went to Washington, D.C., to testify in Congress against the granting of the national charter.[76] In February, Haley won her fight when Congress tabled the charter proposal.

By this time, Haley had become a significant fly in the NEA's ointment. She was the figurehead of mass gatherings of women teachers who voted as blocs on NEA issues; she challenged all efforts to minimize classroom teachers' votes; and she caused considerable public controversy and press whenever she appeared at NEA meetings. Furthermore, her public speeches levied sharp attacks at school administrators and their business and political associates. Chicago had indeed become a hotbed of teacher activism, and for many school administrators there was great fear that the plague would spread.

But, oddly enough, Haley's participation in the NEA waned in the years after 1905. The 1906 meeting in San Francisco was cancelled as a result of the devastating earthquake in that city, and Haley did not attend the 1907 meeting in Los Angeles. Indeed, her membership lapsed for a number of years. Haley was increasingly busy with political and legislative work in Chicago, and it is possible that she tired of the incessant battles on convention floors. Another explanation is that other women picked up the political work that Haley began, and accomplished some of her goals of democratizing the NEA. Ella Flagg Young was elected the NEA's first woman president in 1910; in 1912 the association endorsed woman's suffrage and appropriated money for research on salaries, tenure, and pensions, and a Department of Classroom Teachers was created. Haley remained active in certain campaigns within the NEA through the 1920s, but her withdrawal from major leadership positions adds another piece to the puzzle about her leadership.

Margaret Haley was a local leader. Although her vision for democratic change in education painted a large picture, she was in fact more comfortable with her particular, local, urban environment of Chicago. She was too passionate to be a good negotiator, and too impatient to wait for others' successes before she could fight for her own. Furthermore, with the exception of Catherine Goggin, Haley did not like to share the stage. Haley barely mentioned the work of the hundreds of women teachers from associations in St. Paul, New York, Boston, and New Jersey who made up the bulk of activist teachers in the NEA. Ironically, Haley may well have preferred to fight alone than to work collectively in peace.

THE POLITICAL OPERATOR

In her early forties, Haley was a striking figure in Chicago politics. She was involved in almost every aspect of Progressive Era Chicago, and she fought for or against almost every major Chicago political institution. Between 1900 and 1915, she was constantly in the news and always at work—making public speeches up to five times a week, and traveling across the city and the country to support fledging teacher organizations, speak before tax reform associations, and represent the teachers at national meetings.

Part of Haley's appeal was her physical presence. A small woman, with black hair and bright blue eyes, she dressed nicely, in formal, feminine clothes, and she often wore hats. She had enough vanity to believe that her appearance could help her political work. Or, as a woman contemporary recalled: "She was a most attractive little woman who knew how to use her dainty femininity effectively."[77] Although petite and feminine, she was hardly demure. Contemporaries often noted that more striking than her physical appearance was her energy. All descriptions of Margaret Haley note her as brave, spirited, resolute, and courageous—what turn-of-the century Americans called "pluck."[78] One reporter described Haley as a "short, tense, alert figure" that vibrated with energy, while her "blue eyes dart quick, penetrating glances at you," and another reporter described her as "a vigorous, energetic little body fabricked mostly of nerves."[79] Like Joan of Arc, with whom she was often compared, she was inevitably described by reporters by both her femininity as a school teacher, and simultaneously by her inherent masculinity as a union powerhouse from Chicago.[80] She was one of Chicago's "Five Maiden Aunts," wrote one reporter, while others called her a "lady labor slugger," a "rebel," and the "woman who stirred Chicago upside down until she had her way."[81] Her face revealed intelligence, intensity, endurance, and calculation, wrote one reporter in 1907, and "her mouth is set in lines that tell the story of long, bitter fights in which it was a test of manliness, as well as of womanliness, to be able to survive to the finish."[82]

In 1914, a Chicago *Daily News* story entitled "Women in Politics are Soldiers in Second American Revolution" highlighted Haley's double identity as a feminine teacher and a searing politician. She was described as "a trim little woman whose soft brown hair is silvered now, but whose blue eyes are soft except for the occasions when she is excoriating some especially repellant abuse, some dishonest politician or some time-serving interest." But she was "absolutely, entirely feminine," assured the reporter, offering as evidence that:

> While she directed the work of a corps of assistants in sending out registration appeals to tens of thousands of Chicago women, while she reviewed the history of the various petitions that she had set in circulation for the rousing of the public indignation against the corporations in the big tax fight, while she managed work that would have startled the manager of a great industry, she was intermittently refusing to pose for a photograph because her hair wasn't curled! A Joan of Arc setting her helmet on straight before the battle—but none the less a Joan![83]

The images of Haley were reinforced by her own dramatic and aggressive tactics. Her standard mode of argument was to aggressively press her point, and then flatly argue that anyone who disagreed with her was simply wrong, sorely misguided, or ignorant. Opponents testified to her abrasive and volcanic personality, and her tendency to be controlling and manipulative. Furthermore, she liked to pick a fight. She was known as impatient, restless, and a bit of a loose cannon: When a friend tried to help her schedule a special engagement, he teasingly begged her to be quiet, not irritate anybody, and do "*exactly as I say.*"[84] In later years, Haley described herself as someone who her own colleagues often had to restrain because she was like "dynamite."[85] She may have needed to feel like dynamite, given the heavy weaponry that was hurled at her by her enemies. Haley experienced the kind of public conflict that few women then, or now, could even imagine. Her name was already castigated by her opponents before the affiliation of the teachers with organized labor opened up a wave of vitriol from both outside and inside her organization.

Haley's ability to maneuver the complexity and intensity of city politics in these days was eased by her skillful relationships with newspapers. She worked hard at nurturing her relationships with reporters by sending them story tips and often writing home to Chicago when she was out of town with special greetings to the press corp. She wrote to her friend Richard Finnegan, a reporter at the Chicago *Daily Journal*, in early 1914, asking him to dig into a recent initiative by the board of education. Haley knew that there were underlying issues to the board's move, and "they all need the search light turned on them. . . . So long as one paper keeps its pages open to the truth we have nothing to fear." She closed with an affectionate salute to her reporter friend: "More power to your elbow."[86] Haley was a reporter's dream source, offering quick responses and dramatic details, and newspapers covered her often, whether or not they liked her.

Haley's enthusiasm and energy could not always make up for sloppy management skills and a tendency to abandon her responsibilities. As she continued her exhausting traveling and lobbying, some of her organizational inadequacies continued as well, leaving her supporters frustrated with her. The Federation continued to run on a shoestring budget in the overcrowded office in the Unity Building where papers and bills were often misplaced or overlooked by more immediate demands. The teachers tried to pay their bills promptly, she wrote a disgruntled stenographer who had not received his $57 due, "but anything that gets stalled is liable to fare pretty badly because we have such an enormous amount of different kinds of things doing and one crowds so fast on the other."[87] Other symptoms of chronic disorganization plagued the Federation: In March 1914, two hundred people gathered at a Chicago church to hear Haley speak about vocational education, but she never appeared, because she was in New Orleans for a conference on child labor.[88]

No incident better illustrates Haley's ability to direct change and then abandon her own responsibilities than the election campaign for Ella Flagg Young as NEA president in 1910. Early in the year, a number of teacher leaders around the country had written Haley asking if she would support a campaign to nominate Young as NEA president. Haley's leadership in the campaign would be critical: Young was famous for her progressive educational work in Chicago and for her support of teachers, and Haley could easily amass the membership of the Federation behind her. But Haley never responded to the pleas until late June, two weeks before the NEA convention, at which point she sent scores of frantic telegrams to everybody she knew to get the campaign going. She wrote to John Dewey, who then lived in New York City, to the founder of the Teachers' Association in Philadelphia, who, unbeknownst to her, had retired seven years previously, and to a number of teachers in New York City where the district superintendent .

Grace Strachan was also considering running for NEA President. In her last-minute enthusiasm, Haley succeeded in offending almost everybody.

A teacher in New Jersey responded that Haley's telegram had come too late to have any effect: Schools were already closed and it would be hard to get in touch with all the teachers. Furthermore, most teachers had given up on the NEA, being so discouraged by the way business was conducted that they felt there was "little advantage to be gained from the NEA by women teachers."[89] The president of the New Jersey Teachers' Association sharply rebuked Haley for ignoring the earlier campaign waged by the East Coast associations, and a New York City teacher activist complained that her people were resentful about organizing for a Chicagoan when the Chicago teachers had not lifted a finger to help them.[90] Haley tried to appease her critics by writing a letter explaining how busy she had been, listing a two-page litany of all her activities in Chicago.[91] For all her missteps, Haley remained powerful; not only did Young win the presidential bid, but Haley took the credit for it.

The discrepancy between Haley's leadership skills and flaws became more pronounced in these years. In many ways, Haley was an organizational genius. Her charisma drew people into a common cause and her sharp political skills directed them into action. She was savvy about political image, from her nurturance of reporters to her reliance on public forums to publicize the teachers' case, to her own personal presentation and performance. And she was punctilious in her legal and political research, obsessively studying case law, political precedent, and the weaknesses of her political opponents. But in other ways she was an organizational disaster. She was too self-centered to pay much attention to issues that did not immediately relate to her cause, and she never learned the value of compromise or political negotiations for long-term benefits. She was also a notoriously poor financial manager—ironically, given that she made her fame from calculating corporate taxes—and she never recognized how these characteristics undermined her cause. Even as Catherine Goggin, Isaiah Greenacre, and the Federation office tried to keep tabs on her, Haley's eccentricities still broke through, causing embarrassment to the organization.

In addition to the technical problems of organizational management, Haley struggled to carve out her own public identity. She had no role models of women teacher leaders, and she resorted to patchworking together leadership styles from male labor leaders, teacher educators, and some of the dynamic women leaders she observed in public service and social reform. But ultimately, she was on her own when considering how to approach male city and state legislative and political figures, university presidents and labor bureaucrats, and middle-class women reformers, as well as her own teachers. Was she a government lobbyist or the figurehead of a professional association, or the manager of a labor union? Were her primary loyalties to Chicago teachers or the nation's teachers? To women elementary teachers, or to men

and women educators from the kindergarten classroom to the university
president's office? To the social welfare of Chicago's children or the material
benefits of the city's teachers? To the laboring classes, educators, Irish Catholics, or women?

    In July 1909, Haley had a conversation that made her stop and reflect
on these questions. A member of the board of education asked her advice
about an upcoming vote to cut school principals' salaries. Haley told him to
vote *against* the proposal, arguing that even though she believed it was unfair
that school principals earned so much more than classroom teachers, on
principle, the salaries of working people should never be cut: "If the Board
once gives a salary, it should never cut it."[92] The board member, an Irish-
born doctor, admired Haley's savvy and praised her with the comment that
she was "a damn little Irish politician." Haley recalled that when she left the
office that afternoon and went out into the sunlit Chicago street, she began
to think about what the man had said and how far she had gone along "the
wide but rough road of public work." What did he mean by his taunt? "I
knew I was little and I knew I was Irish and I was afraid I was damned, but
I didn't like the idea that I had become a politician. I didn't like politicians.
I'd seen too many of them. I didn't want to be a public character." Haley's
reflection temporarily frightened her as she walked down the street, although
typical of her character, the fears were short-lived and she avoided any
resolution. "Appalled at the idea of myself which had suddenly been opened
to me, I paused at the corner of Dearborn and Washington Streets. I realized
that for nearly ten years I had been going along without thought of anything
except causes and conflicts. What, I asked myself, was I going to do about
it? I did what almost any woman under eighty would have done. I walked
over to a big store on State Street and bought myself a blue lace dress."[93]

CHAPTER FIVE

THE BATTLEFRONT WIDENS

ON WEDNESDAY, DECEMBER 30, 1903, a few dozen vacationing teachers accompanied their students to a matinee production at the newly built Iroquois Theater in downtown Chicago. The production was the newly opened "Mr. Bluebeard," a musical for children, and the theater was packed with women and children dressed in their holiday best. Midway through the performance, the scene darkened for the popular song "The Pale Moonlight" and the glamorous actors on the stage were bathed in a moon-like spotlight. Suddenly, the electric spotlight threw a spark, which lit on the heavy cloth drapery on the stage and started a small blaze. The band played on while stagehands tried in vain to stomp out the fire. Someone dropped the asbestos fire curtain, designed specifically to create a firewall between the audience and backstage, but it failed to drop all the way and as the actors escaped out the back door they created a draft that shot underneath the fire curtain and fanned the flames in the theater. Within seconds, the auditorium changed from "a dark, gloomy, smoke concealed scene of chaos into a seething volcano."[1]

Trapped in the furnace of heat, the audience stampeded the exit doors but some were locked and others were quickly choked with bodies. Within fifteen minutes, almost six hundred people were killed—twice the number of people lost in the Great Chicago Fire of 1871. Most of the victims were women and children, including ninety-six public school children and thirty-eight Chicago schoolteachers. All but one of those teachers was an elementary teacher. More than thirty schools lost teachers or students. Four city schools suffered the loss of more than one teacher, and many schools lost siblings who died together.

The Iroquois was located in downtown Chicago, only a few blocks from the Federation headquarters, and the Federation took on an active role in the post-fire activities. Margaret Haley had been in New Jersey on a speaking tour on the day of the fire. She rushed home to prepare a memorial service for the teachers and a special edition of the Federation *Bulletin*. In her editorial, Haley referred to the cruel democracy of the fire that indiscriminately killed people from all walks of life. She then linked the tragedy to a general negligence on the part of the city, arguing that the city is "in constant peril" due to weak safety ordinances. She noted that the new theater had specifically been advertised as a fireproof structure with adequate number of exits, although in fact the owners had rushed the opening of the theater in time for the Christmas season and skimped on safety.[2]

Haley's call to look to weak government and greedy businesses as the culprits was a popular cry in the weeks after the fire. In a city that still remembered the great city fire thirty years earlier, and that had taken such precautions to prevent its recurrence, it seemed incomprehensible that such a disaster could happen again, and terrified citizens demanded an investigation of all public buildings.[3] At a meeting of angry citizens held soon after the disaster, Eliza Haley furthered her sister's claim, arguing that the city government needed to be held criminally liable for allowing such terrible conditions to exist in the theater and other public buildings. She reported that many schools lacked any fire safety equipment and that many buildings were locked shut in the morning with only one exit left open. "Are not the mayor, the aldermen, and the trustees directly responsible for this state of things, and are they not the men who should be prosecuted along with the proprietors of that theater?" Eliza Haley asked.[4] In the following months, the *Bulletin* covered other stories of teachers injured at work, and of more school safety violations. In September, the *Bulletin* protested the reopening of the Iroquois Theater "before the first snow has fallen on the graves of the victims."[5]

Haley's response to the Iroquois Fire disaster wove naturally into her broader thinking about school reform and the role of government in checking the interests of business. As she continued her work with the Federation, Haley expanded her political analysis of economics outside of the particularity of the tax investigation to ongoing municipal reform. In so doing, she wove the teachers' cause and the cause of public school reform into the broader fabric of progressive municipal reform. To Haley, municipal reform and school reform were one and the same in that both drew on the common theory of democratizing city government and controlling corporate greed. This was what Haley referred to when she said in her autobiography that the battlefront widened. Whether fighting for increased teacher salaries, improved safety and working conditions inside schools, or for democratic electoral processes, the common struggle, she insisted, was the fight against "the political machines and the intrenched [sic] vested interests of the city and state."[6]

In the years after the terrible Iroquois Theater Fire, Haley consolidated her beliefs about the role of government in peoples' live, and the role of the school in government. Haley's response to the Iroquois Fire forecast her thinking about school and municipal issues in later years. As she wrote a friend two weeks after the fire, almost as depressing as the dreadful disaster itself was "the fear that Chicago may not rise to the moral height that such an experience demands, and learn and teach a lesson of civic consciousness and civic righteousness."[7]

MUNICIPAL REFORM: STREETCARS, LAND, AND POWER

Despite the way that Haley often spoke abut the tax case as a singular enterprise that she and her Federation colleagues discovered and investigated on their own, municipal reformers in Chicago had been debating the role of public utilities, the equity of tax codes, and the presence of graft and bribery in the city financial system for years. In turn-of-the-century Chicago, municipal reformers continued the economic question inspired by Henry George and the single taxers: How to allow private enterprise to grow while providing enough government regulations to help the common good? Teachers came to play an integral part in this movement as they drew connections between their plight and the city's municipal problems.[8]

In the last two decades of the 1800s, a cross-class urban reform movement took root in Chicago, led by reformers who advocated a democratic coalition of workers, consumers, and middle-class citizens with the object of abolishing corruption in municipal affairs and limiting the political and financial privileges of corporations. The first cohesive campaign for municipal reform in Chicago that garnered widespread support was over streetcars. Transportation became a critical urban issue for Chicago in the late nineteenth century as the city exploded in size. Between 1887 and 1893, Chicago's area tripled with the annexation of more than one hundred square miles of land, including Englewood, where Haley lived with her family. The civic problem was to find a method of transportation to help citizens traverse this large territory. Although in the 1890s, the old horse-drawn streetcar was replaced by cable cars, and then electric powered cars, it was hardly a sensible system of transportation.[9] The cars were run by a dozen or so private companies, and the different companies charged different fares and often had no connecting lines or free transfers. Furthermore, streetcars were uncomfortable and dangerous, and critics flooded the press with complaints about the crowded, unsanitary, and dangerous plight of the daily "straphanger." Streetcars cried out for regulation, not only to ease the daily transportation problems of thousands of workers, but also, reformers believed, to help create a more cohesive urban environment. A more efficient and affordable transportation system would help people move away from the slums, provide more personal and economic mobility, and raise the sense of pride in the city. For municipal reformers, the regulation of streetcars was often viewed as nothing less than the key to social harmony.

But reform was not so easy. Streetcar owners were loath to give up their lucrative franchises and they held strong political support from the legislature. What was called the "traction issue" was a classic case of independent business ownership holding political and economic influence in city politics. The issue came to a head in the 1890s in the person of the most notorious streetcar owner—Charles Tyson Yerkes, a railway traction magnate who owned a majority of Chicago's streetcar lines. Streetcar franchises were granted for a limit of twenty years, but in the spring of 1895, Yerkes persuaded the state legislature to extend his franchise for ninety-nine years without having to pay any extra compensation to the city. The governor vetoed the bill, but two years later the legislature passed the Allen Bill, which authorized Chicago's city council to grant streetcar franchises for terms of up to fifty years. Yerkes had essentially won his right to maintain control over Chicago streetcars for the next two generations.

But the popular tide was running against the traction magnate. In the three years after the passage of the Allen Bill, reformers lobbied for the transfer of public services and utilities from private ownership to city ownership—what was referred to generally as "municipal ownership." By the spring of 1897, the movement was so loud that Carter Harrison won his mayoral campaign under a pledge to veto franchises extensions. In city elections the following year, all candidates who supported the Allen Bill were defeated. The new state assembly immediately voted the Allen law null and void.[10]

Haley's residence in Englewood may have made her particularly attuned to developing political battles over the city's public transportation corporations. As the school system expanded in the 1890s, teachers were less likely to live in the communities in which they taught, making public transportation a key economic issue. Haley herself took a streetcar seventeen blocks north to the Hendricks School every day. Splashed across Chicago daily newspapers through the late 1890s was the issue of corporate graft, tax dodging, and the fight against "corporate arrogance." When Haley learned about corporations not paying their taxes, the pieces fit together and she saw how teachers, too, could be part of the larger progressive movement against "corporate arrogance." Indeed, the lessons in corruption came full circle when two of the five utilities companies sued by the Federation were railways.

Paralleling the municipal ownership movement was an organized movement for electoral reform. What was commonly called "initiative and referendum" was a movement designed to open up the political process by authorizing voters to petition a policy decision onto a ballot. In Illinois, reformers successfully supported a Public Policy Law, passed in 1901, whereby petitions for changes in public policy that were signed by 25 percent of legal voters in a city or district or by 10 percent of voters in the entire state could be placed on the ballot.[11] But in Illinois, unlike most other states that passed initiative and referendum laws, votes were only advisory to the legislature.[12] Even if an issue were placed on a ballot and voted for, it was still not law.

Nonetheless, Haley and other Chicago reformers saw the initiative and referendum movement as the mechanism by which to regulate corporate entities, democratize local government, and control corruption. To Haley, the campaign for electoral reform was a symbolic representation of the main conflicts in education: the narrow control of services by business interests versus popular democratic control. Not surprisingly, a major opponent to the initiative and referendum movement was Haley's old archenemy, Nicholas Murray Butler, whom she called in no uncertain terms a "shrewd, unprincipled, money serving, time serving, contemptible creature."[13] For Haley it was not a coincidence that people such as Butler who promoted an auto-cratic top-down form of rule in schools were also opposed to the initiative and referendum movement.

As she learned more about the broader movement for electoral reform, she saw the link with municipal ownership. Simply forcing corporations to pay their taxes was not enough: Citizens needed to gain control over corpo-rations that served basic public needs.[14] If the city itself owned public utili-ties, equitable services would be assured and the power of concentrated wealth would be restrained. But politicians were pressured by corporate powers not to do this. The only solution was to place the issue of municipal ownership on the ballot.

This, at least, was the solution proposed by other municipal reformers that Haley came to agree with in December 1901. The problem was that, according to the Public Policy Law, the petition to place the issue on a ballot had to be filed sixty days before the spring election, which meant that the reformers had only five weeks to collect one hundred thousand signatures from Chicago citizens.[15] Haley was sure that the designers of the law had made these rules to decrease the probability that many petitions would be successful. But the politicians had not taken into account the possibility that such a vast machinery as the public school system could be set in motion to distribute petitions. Teachers, after all, had direct contact with students who had direct contact with all the city's communities; teachers had the means to launch a giant grassroots petition campaign.[16] Already skilled in the de-sign, production, and distribution of petitions from earlier battles, Haley organized the teachers into a citywide democratic canvassing project.

In early January 1902, Haley called the teachers together and explained the principles of municipal ownership and delivered to them petitions to place city ownership of street railways and gas and electric light utilities on the spring ballot. The teachers delivered the petitions to their students out-side of school hours and off school grounds. The children proved to be good lobbyists, as they distilled the complicated policy initiative into its simplest form. One man told Haley that he met a little girl on the street who said to him: "Sir, do you want fifty cent gas and three cent car fare?" When he replied yes, the child told him: "Then Sir, sign this petition." Enough signa-tures were secured that the questions were put on a Chicago ballot in the election of April 1902 and voted for, five to one.[17] But the result was non-binding, and the movement continued through 1903 under the leadership of Henry Demerest Lloyd, the renowned advocate for municipal reform whose 1894 text *Wealth Against Commonwealth* set forth his antimonopoly stand.[18] Haley became an officer in Lloyd's Municipal Ownership League and lobbied for Lloyd's Mueller Law, which would authorize the legislature the take over the city's streetcar lines. Through the winter of 1903, Haley educated the teachers about the proposed law, helped Lloyd write petitions and legislative

Margaret Haley and the other referendum petitioners, Springfield, Illinois, *Times Magazine*, February 1907

proposals, and lobbied newspapers for positive coverage of the reformers' work.[19] In the heat of the campaign in early Fall 1903, the fifty-six-year-old Lloyd caught pneumonia and died. Haley characteristically used Lloyd's untimely death as a publicity mechanism. She pronounced that Lloyd "had put his frail body between the people of Chicago and the greedy, hungry corporations and their no less greedy, hungry tools, the peoples' representatives in the City Council." The Mueller Law was passed in April 1904. Now the people of Chicago could construct, own, and operate their own street railways.[20]

Municipal reform work made the complicated political structure of Chicago's laws all the more apparent to political activists such as Haley, and it inspired a movement to rewrite the city charter. Chicago's charter reform movement was an attempt to systematize and empower city government, which many urban reformers saw as a straitjacket restricting both efficient and effective urban reform. Chicago reformers were particularly frustrated that they were girded by the state constitution, what Haley called "an iron band around an iron band around any attempted spirit of expansion," severely limiting the city's ability to enact significant administrative and economic reform measures.[21] Home rule, which meant the clarification and empowerment of city government, promised not only more efficient lines of government administration, but also the creation of shared purpose in cities where local urban reform and community interest would develop hand in hand.

Having spent some time wrestling in the tangles of city and state politics, Haley was all too familiar with the difficulties of instituting reform in Chicago. It was state law that required that many proposed changes in Chicago school-based policy and teacher employment policies be approved by the legislators in the Springfield, forcing Chicago political battles to occur in both city and state political houses. Ideologically, Haley also approved of the goal of charter reform to make city government more democratic by opening up the process of policy making, including decision making about city schools, to local citizens.[22] Beginning in 1902, Chicago reformers began to organize for a revised city charter that would establish the city's legal and administrative framework independently from the state.

But one of the ironies of charter reform was that home rule was viewed differently by different groups. In particular, the conflicts over the charter highlighted the division among reformers about whether the priority of efficient government justified the restriction of popular participation. Working-class and labor organizations saw home rule as the expansion of the democratic process to the people who lived in the city. But middle-class social reformers and business representatives saw home rule as the control of civic functions by a consolidated group of urban professionals like themselves. And middle-class women reformers were infuriated that not only was women's suffrage not included in the reform package, but that they were not even permitted to take part in the writing of the new charter. These conflicts materialized in the creation of a charter convention in December 1905. Delegates were appointed by the city council and other legislative groups, and were not popularly elected representatives of communities, labor, or ethnic groups. This infuriated working-class activists. As Haley said, "The very persons and interests whom the new order sought to control were themselves controlling the convention."[23]

The battle over definitions of control was further epitomized in the charter convention debate over the function of Chicago's education system. Graham Taylor, the chair of the convention school committee, argued that the chief goal of educational administration was to protect the public interest by guarding against financial waste, shoddy facilities, and political factionalization. Taylor cautioned "that nothing can be worse for democracy than inefficiency." Middle-class members of the City Club of Chicago and the Commercial Club agreed and made recommendations for a strong central school administration that would "secure a more effective business administration and an education . . . more in accordance with the demands of modern society and business conditions."[24] Haley's nemesis Nicholas Murray Butler visited from New York to promote such school reorganization along a "rational and business-like basis." Butler argued that the key to the development of a good school system was the authorization of a strong superintendent. Teachers should be allowed little voice in school management, he asserted, and the very notion of democratizing education was simply ridiculous: one might as well talk about the "democratization of the treatment of appendicitis."[25]

Haley was suspicious of such calls for efficiency because they tended to promote the consolidation of school management *away* from teachers. She was not alone in her suspicions. The Chicago Federation of Labor linked business and professional support for the charter with the suppression of working-class democracy, stating in a public report that "the class who have most loudly demanded reform have the most to fear from the inauguration of any real reform. They constitute the class who fear the rule by the whole people. They are the class who in this charter seek to curb the power of the electorate."[26] Margaret Dreier Robins of the Women's Trade Union League, the wife of board of education member and Federation ally Raymond Robins, believed that the business community was using the charter debate to achieve its long-time goal of school centralization.[27] Raymond Robins also agreed with Haley that the charter convention placed business efficiency "as its supreme function." He promoted three proposals to the convention that had as their objective the broadening rather than narrowing of the control of schools. His first proposal was for the election of board members, a policy that had been the subject of other citizenry petitions.[28] Haley had been involved in these petition drives, arguing that it was useless for teachers to be fighting for improvements in schools when the board of education was appointed by and often in the pockets of tax-dodging corporations. In the charter convention, Robins's proposal for elected board of education members failed.

Robins's second proposal was that board of education members earn a salary of $2500, thereby allowing working-class people the opportunity to serve on the board and making board members immediately accountable to the citizens who paid their salaries. Clergyman Rufus A. White, who was a member of the school board, argued against this proposal, asserting that public service without compensation was an honor for responsible citizens. The introduction of salaried positions, he argued, would "deteriorate" the board of education. Chicago Federation of Labor representative James Linehan retorted that White's idea of public service installed millionaires on the school board while it disenfranchised the working people whose children were educated in Chicago public schools.[29] This proposal was rejected by the convention as well. Finally, Robins proposed a measure that would limit the authority of the superintendent to introduce textbooks, and to appoint, promote, and transfer teachers, and that would provide for teachers' direct access to the board for suggestions about education and a guarantee that teachers' salaries not be reduced during their tenure. This measure, too, was rejected by the convention.

These and other controversies undermined the success of the entire charter convention, particularly among working-class groups and women's groups, which argued that the charter was designed to limit their representation in city government. Two days before the popular election in September 1907, 35,000 Chicagoans rallied in Grant Park to denounce the charter. On September 17, the charter was firmly rejected by a two to one margin.[30] Haley saw the whole process as a tragedy: Pure democratic initiatives had been kidnapped by people in power who falsely claimed to be guardians of the public good.

THE NATIONAL STAGE:
SUFFRAGE, SOCIALISTS, LABOR, AND REFORM

Shadowing all of Haley's work in city politics was the issue of women's suffrage. There was a long historical link between women teachers and the struggle for the vote. Women teachers, who were economically independent and highly literate, made up the bulk of suffrage supporters and activists through the turn of the century.[31] Many of the earliest women's rights activists in the nineteenth century had been schoolteachers who had perfected their public speaking skills by standing in front of classrooms. As Katherine Blake, a New York City school principal and chair of her state's suffrage campaign said: "No school teacher needs to tell me that she can't make speeches, she makes them all day in the schoolroom, and she is well fitted for the work."[32]

This did not mean that all schoolteachers were pro-suffrage or even advocates for women's equal rights. Catherine Beecher, who championed the training and hiring of women teachers in the middle of the nineteenth century, was anti-suffrage on the grounds that women should focus their energies on developing their own nurturing qualities in the home and school-room. A contemporary of Haley's, Grace Strachan, who was a district super-intendent in New York City, led the battle for equal pay for women and men teachers, even while she was opposed to the hiring of married women teach-ers, and was equivocal about the necessity of women's suffrage.[33]

The women's suffrage movement was also plagued by many of the political fractures that were apparent in teachers' other organizations. The main proponents and activists for women's suffrage were middle-class Prot-estant women, some of whom held a patronizing attitude toward Irish Catho-lic, African American, and working-class women. Black women teachers organized their own caucuses, such as the Alpha Suffrage Club which was founded in Chicago in 1913 as an interracial counterforce to the racism present in many of the state's all-White state suffrage organizations.[34] Suf-frage was not universally supported among all working-class women. Many women labor activists argued that the suffrage movement was a middle-class diversion that distracted political action from the economic inequal-ity of the class system.

Women's right to vote in school elections was an important opening wedge to the larger suffrage movement. In the late nineteenth century, as school districts hired women teachers, suffragists argued that those teachers should have the right to vote for locally elected school officials. In fact, many of those school officials *were* women who won the elected positions on school boards and local superintendencies in rural and small town communities across the country. In 1900, up to 10 percent of local superintendents were women, so it was particularly obvious that they did not have the right to vote for themselves. By that year, when a half-million American women worked in education, many states saw a powerful wave of women teachers and school officials organized in political coalitions, clubs, and associations.[35] By 1910, twenty-four states had granted women school suffrage; Illinois women won the right to vote in school elections in 1891.[36]

Women's opportunities for both the vote and for professional appointments in education were enhanced in the underpopulated West. In new states with small populations, political parties recognized the opportunity to collect more voters by including women. In addition, the relatively freer social roles of the frontier allowed women more occasions to take on public work. By 1900 most of the western states had granted women the right to vote in state elections, and when Illinois passed woman's suffrage in 1913 it became the first state east of the Mississippi to do so. The question remaining for all states was the right of women to vote in federal elections, a right that was obtained only by the passage of the Nineteenth Amendment to the Constitution in 1920.

Illinois women had been fighting for suffrage since the 1860s but by 1910, the movement was stalled. The campaign was reinvigorated by a new multiclass alliance of traditionally conservative clubwomen, working-class and immigrant women, and middle-class women's reform groups. Organizations such as Jane Addams's Hull House, the Women's Trade Union League, and women's clubs and teachers' clubs joined in the larger movement to convince the Illinois State legislature to grant women the vote. One characteristic of this new political push in Illinois was that suffragists began to emphasize the pragmatic results of women's suffrage. Voting women would make the whole nation more efficient, suffrage leaders began to argue, because it would allow women to do their job as mothers and domestic caretakers, or "municipal housekeepers," more effectively. As the University of Chicago sociologist Sophonisba Breckinridge claimed, "the ballot was a labor-saving device, like the biscuit-machine."[37]

Despite this resort to more pragmatic nonideological arguments, opposition remained strong. A nonbinding referendum on women's suffrage in Chicago in early 1912 failed by almost a two to one margin.[38] Illinois suffragists then organized a high-energy campaign, which finally led to victory in June 1913. For the next seven years, the state organization continued its high-profile promotion of the federal Nineteenth Amendment.

In her autobiography, Margaret Haley identified the public debate about women's suffrage as one of her first political memories. When the family lived in Morris, Michael Haley took his three daughters to hear a lecturer on phrenology explain how different human traits could be determined by studying the shape of peoples' heads. The family secured seats in the front row of the crowded hall. In the course of his lecture, the phrenologist spoke scornfully of suffragist Susan B. Anthony, at which point Michael Haley instantly marshaled his children up from their seats and led them out of the hall. Facing the audience as they walked out, the three girls were suddenly "horribly conscious" of the unconventional nature of their father's actions and beliefs. Later, he explained to them that even though he did not know Anthony, he knew she was a woman working for a cause and he would not let his children hear "any half-baked nincompoop who sneers at her."[39] Years later, when Haley met Anthony, she was moved by the aged suffragist's recollection of her experience as a young teacher when she was denied the right to speak at the state teachers' association simply because she was a woman.[40]

Nonetheless, Haley did not always take an active stand on suffrage, primarily because her interests and energy were so singlemindedly set on the teachers' cause. The strong Irish Catholic base of the Federation worked against a natural affinity with the Protestant native-born leaders of the women's suffrage movement, some of whom held anti-Catholic biases. Catholic teachers were also torn by the pressure of their church, which opposed women's suffrage and often criticized its teachers who became involved in the movement. Haley opposed the church's involvement in political campaigns, seeing this as an inappropriate wielding of clerical power, and in 1912 she lobbied across Ohio against church interference in that state's suffrage campaign.[41] But overall, her involvement in suffrage campaigns was inconsistent and secondary to her primary focus on the Federation.

Haley also agreed with some male labor leaders that the focus on the vote was distracting from other more important issues. In her autobiography, she noted with some sympathy the critique of women's suffrage given to her by Andrew Furuseth, the powerful president of the International Seaman's Union of the Pacific. Furuseth felt that the debate over women's suffrage would distract voters from learning about the issue of labor. The labor fight was having enough troubles of its own without taking on the divisive issue of women's suffrage.[42] And while Haley recognized the power of the ballot, she also felt that the development of women's political abilities and consciousness was ultimately more powerful than the ballot. Haley believed that women's involvement in political activities—be it the Foresters or the Teachers' Federation or the campaign for initiative and referendum—did more to teach them about their responsibilities as citizens than did any experience in the voting booth.[43] Ironically, the very *absence* of the vote had mobilized women in a very dynamic way. Because women could not vote, they were forced to cajole, canvass, and educate the public. "If we had the vote and could go out and do as men do we could meet the men on men's terms," Haley wrote to a friend in 1911. But because men would not allow women to vote, women were forced to do their politics through other, more indirect means. "Man's law makes these means legitimate."[44] Haley believed that "woman suffrage was not an end in itself but a means to a more important end, the governmental establishment of fundamental justice to all men, women, and children of the nation."[45]

But Haley also recognized that ultimately women had no power without the vote. Ever the pragmatist, she realized that the vote meant power, because "men politicians care only for the fate of those who have the ballot in their hand."[46] Tax reform, school reorganization, or any other political change would only happen if women held the power of the vote.[47] Her support for suffrage came down to her faith in the law which she saw as "the machinery for the adjustment of social relations and the restoration of social equilibrium."[48]

Given the ambivalence about the vote from the labor movement, Haley was never full-throttle in her support for women's suffrage, and the way in which she chose her involvement in the work reflected her broader political strategies. She focused her suffrage energies on battles for the state and not national votes. In 1911, Haley traveled to California to campaign for the state vote there, and she was active in the Ohio campaign in 1912 and the Illinois campaign in 1913 where she served as state auditor for the Illinois State Suffrage Party.[49] She also supported the platform for suffrage in the charter reform bill, and joined other women at public speeches on behalf of suffrage. But although the Federation sent a squad of teachers to local parades, no Federation representative made an appearance at the National American Woman's Suffrage Association conference held in Chicago in February 1907, and there is no evidence that Haley was a member of that national group.[50]

Haley's great faith in legislative solutions to social problems centered on local and state politics. After years of struggling to organize teachers and citizens into political movements, Haley increasingly believed that individual lobbying work in the state house was more effective than broad-based populist movements or sweeping national campaigns. This strategy often put her on the side of more conservative political forces, and this was particularly the case in the state's suffrage campaign. In the battle for the state bill that was eventually passed in 1913, the Illinois suffrage movement split into two groups favoring opposing strategies. One group promoted unconventional and public tactics that gathered crowds of suffrage supporters together in mass meetings, automobile tours, parades, and public displays of force. Another group maneuvered the movement away from such controversial public politics to intense negotiating with individual legislatures. It was this latter, more conservative group of women whom Haley admired, particularly their leader, law school graduate Grace Trout, who stressed a quiet professional diplomacy that emphasized feminine attributes. As Trout explained: "We answered the claim that politics makes women unwomanly by making a

GOVERNOR DUNNE SIGNING BILL WHICH GIVES VOTE TO ILLINOIS WOMEN

Governor Edward F. Dunne signing the Illinois suffrage bill, June 26, 1913. Haley is seated across from the governor. *Chicago Record Herald*, June 27, 1913

quiet, pleasant campaign. We tried to argue that women would not argue by personality and hysteria."[51] To Haley, this meant that the women developed adept organizing and negotiating skills in Springfield—a talent that she admired above all others in political work. Familiar as she was with the legislative battlefield of the statehouse, Haley added a jolt of energy to this "quiet, pleasant campaign." Recalled a former lawmaker who observed the charge for suffrage in Springfield, "The sparkplug did not seem to flicker at all until Margaret Haley appeared upon the scene."[52]

This type of political campaign eventually won the state vote for women in Illinois. Haley was invited to the ceremony when her old friend Edward Dunne, the judge who had ruled for her in the Foresters case and in the tax case, who was now governor, signed the state suffrage bill in June 1913. Grace Trout and her lobbyists stood behind the table with the supporting legislators, while Haley took the seat at the table, across from Governor Dunne. The scene was certainly staged, and Dunne may have arranged it this way because he knew that although the suffragists had accomplished the final bill, as he stated publicly, it was the work of Margaret Haley and the Federation fighting for good government in the city and state that had converted him to the cause of women's suffrage.[53] The photograph evokes another image of Margaret Haley's leadership style: sitting alone, apart, and in front of other women.

VEERING LEFT

In the fall of 1911 Haley went to Los Angeles to join in that state's women's suffrage campaign and to observe one of the most dramatic political events of the new century. On October 1, 1910, a bomb at the *Los Angeles Times* printing plant building killed twenty-one men. Two brothers, labor union activists John and James McNamara, were arrested and charged with the crime. Unionists instantly portrayed the McNamaras as victims of a frame-up by industrial leaders. The brothers were active unionists and the publisher of the *Times* was a determined foe of organized labor. The running conspiracy theory was that by convicting the McNamaras of bombing his plant, the Los Angeles publisher and industrialist would demolish a recent upsurge in labor organizing in the city led by the American Federation of Labor.[54] The AFL took on unprecedented support of the McNamaras. Samuel Gompers declared that the brothers were the victims of a "the most diabolical plot ever hatched in our country" and he vowed to raise $350,000 for the defense team. Clarence Darrow was hired to defend them, and the Industrial Workers of the World called for a nationwide strike on the first day of the trial, and unionists across California were asked to contribute a full day's wages to the cause. On Labor Day 1911 (which the AFL named "McNamara Day") huge crowds in many major cities gathered to proclaim the brothers' innocence.[55]

Further electrifying Los Angeles in the fall of 1911 was the campaign of a dynamic and charismatic Socialist candidate for mayor. Job Harriman had run for vice president under Eugene Debs on the Socialist Party ticket in 1900 and was a seasoned labor lawyer. In his mayoral campaign, he was committed to linking labor and the Socialist Party together—a move that was not fully supported by either side. Laborites had long been suspicious of the radical position of Socialists, and Socialists saw the American labor movement as a compromising allegiance of workers with industry. Haley had experienced this split when the Federation affiliated with labor, and the local Socialist Party derided the teachers, arguing that affiliation with the CFL was merely a "side step" that was all but "uselessness."[56] Still, in this case, Haley supported the Socialist candidate, in part because she believed in labor *and* the political process represented by political parties, and if the Socialist Party could offer a platform for labor representation in government, she approved. In November, Haley traveled to Los Angeles where she joined a crowd of political activists who came expecting to observe the double victory for the Left of the acquittal of the McNamaras and the election of a Socialist mayor.[57] When Haley met Harriman, she was pleased to find him "well balanced" and likeable, and the campaign was "well conducted, no flurry, every one self contained, no one in a hurry but every one working effectively."[58]

Her rosy view was not to last long. Five days after her meeting with Harriman, the McNamara brothers pled guilty to the *Times* bombing and to involvement with other union officials in eighty-seven other bombings since 1906. The *New York World* called the confessions "the deadliest blow ever dealt to organized labor in the United States," and it delivered an equally deadly blow to Harriman's campaign, which immediately floundered and lost on election day the following week.[59]

The McNamara confessions were devastating to the Left, and it sent organized labor into a tailspin. For Haley, the McNamara case was a tragedy that convinced her even more that labor unions needed to abandon their backroom brawling politics and instead develop a formal political party. Haley had always been intrigued by the notion of a labor party comprised of unified labor interests who lobbied for their cause through legitimate political channels. Her father had supported the Greenback Labor Party, and their hero Henry George had also supported a labor party. Her inherent faith in the American political system left her eager to search for a way to improve that system by electing better representatives.[60] However devastating was the outcome in Los Angeles, Haley felt reassured about her broader vision that structural changes in the law could improve society.

Her faith was bolstered by a book she had recently read that inspired her thinking about governmental reform. Haley read J. Allen Smith's *The Spirit of American Government* soon after it was published in 1907 and she found it as inspiring as her first readings of Henry George. Smith was a professor of economics at the University of Washington, and he was a follower of Henry George and of the single tax idea, as well as municipal ownership and labor rights. But what most inspired Haley and others about Smith's treatise was his explanation of the cause of economic and political inequalities in the country. Smith identified the American Constitution as the source of the problem: He saw it as a document written by the wealthy to prevent the general population from access to government. Most undemocratic was the federal judiciary, which could with the swipe of a hand invalidate legislation that the public had fought for, but he also levied criticism at the system of checks and balances, which made it difficult to fix the blame on an independent organization and turned politics into a cauldron of deal making between government and political parties, excluding the common man. Party politics, in other words, created an oppressive force as powerful as that of private corporate interests. The solution, Smith argued, was the political education of all citizens, and the simultaneous limiting of federal power and enhancement of local government. Only in local communities, with voters who were educated about local issues, could real democracy happen. Like Haley, Smith argued that people needed to be educated in citizenship in order to maintain democracy and control political power, and with the enhancement of local governments, such empowerment might actually happen.[61] Smith's book also helped Haley work through her thinking

about the Socialist Party. She had mistrusted Socialists because she had faith
in the established political structures; but she had been drawn to socialism
because of the argument for popular ownership and against private monopolies. Smith provided a theory to secure private ownership while still controlling monopolies.

Smith invited Haley to visit him in Seattle and talk about her work.
She left Los Angeles in early December and stopped off in Oregon, where an
initiative and referendum bill was being reviewed by the courts. By December 15 she was in Seattle, where she decided to stay for some time to work
on local political campaigns and write about the tax case. The previous
summer, Haley had begun writing and dictating a narrative of the tax case,
but she had not accomplished much of the work. She had a few reasons for
writing the tax story, including further publicizing the cause. But her immediate reason was economic. The teachers' financial contributions to Haley
and Goggin were minimal, and this angered Haley not only because she was
running low on money but because she felt unappreciated by the teachers
who did not seem to realize that it was thanks to her work that they had
salary increases. She decided that by selling a book about the Federation, she
could become financially independent.

Haley found Seattle invigorating both personally and politically. She
wrote a friend that "the atmosphere of Seattle is charged with the spirit of
democracy and I know I can write our story here as I could no where else."[62]
The city was home to a wide variety of progressive reform movements. On
center stage that winter was Joe Smith, a political activist and former newspaper reporter and farmer who was an avid proponent of electoral reform and
single tax.[63] Supported by the Socialists, Joe Smith was campaigning for
governor. A mayoral campaign was also being battled in the winter of 1912,
as was a ballot initiative for the single tax. Haley threw herself into these
campaigns, speaking up to six times a day, and explaining the single tax
initiative to labor and women's groups in what she described as "a magnificent campaign of education, the best I have been in yet."[64]

Washington women were also notably active: they had won the state
vote in 1910 and women's groups had organized a recall vote against the
Seattle mayor, who was known for corruption and his support of brothels.
Most prolific among the Seattle women was Adele Parker, a former high
school teacher, who had earned a law degree in 1903 and now worked for
suffrage and municipal reform. She was also editor of the *Western Women
Voter*, which covered news about municipal reform, initiative and referendum, and education, as well as women's suffrage news. Nine years younger
than Haley, the two women had corresponded and they were close friends
during Haley's visit.[65]

Haley took an apartment on Capitol Hill with a view of the Olympic
mountains and within walking distance of Adele Parker's home. She heard
the British suffragist Emmeline Pankhurst speak in late December and spoke

to the Seattle Single Tax Club, the Labor Club, women's clubs, and Professor Smith's economics classes.[66] The time away from Chicago made her uncharacteristically giddy and evocative in her writing. As she wrote one friend in the middle of January,

> I am writing beside an open window, no fire, no wrap on, only my silk waist, a fly has just flown into my window, scores of them are flying around outside. The sun is shining in my south window, the grass and trees are a beautiful green, buds everywhere and birds singing. It's a beautiful spring day. I sympathize with you all from the bottom of my heart (and abundant freezing experience of my own in Chicago). . . . Wish I could share this delightful weather with you.

Later in the letter, she rhapsodized about her victory at a public debate a few days before, when she "wiped the earth up with one judge and could have demolished the other but had no chance to speak after he had spoken. Though I did manage to get in one good shaft at him."[67] Energized by this atmosphere, she wrote twenty installments about the tax case (almost three hundred double-spaced pages) that winter.

But she was lonely too. Margaret Haley did not enjoy reflective solitary time, and while her forays into municipal and state politics on the West Coast were inspiring, she missed her brothers and sisters. Because she rarely wrote about her family and because their names rarely appear in Federation papers, one can only gather a sense of their involvement in Haley's life. Scraps of evidence indicate that her brothers and sisters were engaged in a number of her professinal activities. Both Eliza and the third sister, Jenny Haley O'Reilly, were longtime teachers in Chicago schools and active Federation members. Eliza Haley was particularly involved, taking a leadership position in the Federation's response to the Iroquois Fire and later in her life attending law school. Haley's brothers, too, occasionally attended Federation meetings.[68] Her siblings' presence is also evidence on the sidelines of Haley's professional life: She wrote them regularly when she was away from Chicago, and when she fell ill, she went to one of her siblings' homes to be nursed. When she was away from them, she missed them, and longed for their mail and their company.

Impatient to see her family, and to get back into the work of the Federation, Margaret Haley headed home in March 1912. She arrived in Chicago just in time for a revitalized initiative and referendum campaign in the city. When she disembarked at the train station with her big trunk, she went immediately to the Federation office, trunk and all.[69]

CHAPTER SIX

ALLIES AND TRAITORS

IN HER BATTLES FOR municipal and electoral reform, Margaret Haley had not forgotten the schools. Indeed, she easily equated the political problems that she saw in government with those that she identified in school management. Haley wrote in her autobiography that the end of the nineteenth century had brought a great educational awakening that introduced democratic theories into classroom practice. But this awakening had extended only to the methods of teaching. School management had actually become *more* hierarchical, modeling itself on an industrial ideal that prioritized economic efficiency with an organizational model that was "essentially monarchial and military."[1] Even if classrooms had developed more democratic practices, the organization of the school system was "an autocracy in method."[2]

Haley's goal of making school management more democratic led her to forge alliances with other civic leaders in the hopes of reshaping all public institutions. In the years between 1905 and 1915, she experienced unprecedented access to Chicago city government when two of her friends became powerful city leaders. Between 1905 and 1907, her old friend Edward Dunne was mayor of Chicago and he appointed a board of education that was largely friendly to Federation interests. In 1909, Ella Flagg Young was appointed superintendent of Chicago schools and held the job for the next six years. Up to this time, Haley had been on the outside of city government, a tenacious gadfly flailing on the doors of hostile officials, so the advancement of her two friends harkened great successes. But the administrations of Mayor Dunne and Superintendent Young actually led to increased stress for the Federation, and by 1915, Haley was under full-fledged attack. There were two reasons for this intensified conflict.

First, as the Federation gained legitimacy in city offices, its organized opposition increased. The backbone of this opposition was the merger of business and middle-class reform interests, a coalition that the teachers had seen in the battle over the Harper Bill years earlier and that continued to gain strength. As seen in the debates over city charter reform in 1907, middle-class and business associations were able to position organized labor as a partisan special interest group, while identifying themselves as apolitical advocates for the common good. The Federation, which had always been suspected by its opponents of purely self-interested goals, fell under increasing attack when it gained access to city offices. That middle-class reform and business groups were able to create a distinction between their own role as "nonpartisan" and the teachers' interest as "political" in this period further undercut the Federation's ability to become a central player in school decision making.[3]

The second reason for the increased opposition to the Federation work in these years was Haley's political tactics. She forged allegiances with organizations and individuals in power, but she never developed the strategy of compromise. Repeatedly, she lost larger wars by refusing to concede a smaller battle, and she accused those who did compromise of being traitors to the larger cause of democracy. This practice of denouncing those who tried to negotiate frightened off some potential allies who might have helped the Federation. Haley's commitment to her principles was admirable, but it was also risky: Her staunch position often took precedence over more politically savvy bridge building. Her approach was also painfully ironic: As she argued for democratic processes in all sectors of the public, she herself refused to participate in just such practices and modeled instead the politics of a domineering power broker. Such behavior earned her her share of bitter enemies; as one reporter wrote in this period, whether or not you liked her or agreed with her, everyone in Chicago had to admit that Margaret Haley was "one of the most vital, as she has been one of the most disturbing, forces in the history of the women of Chicago."[4]

THE DUNNE BOARD, 1905–1907

According to Haley, Edwin Cooley, who replaced "Bulletin Ben" Andrews as superintendent of Chicago schools in 1900, was a potent threat to academic freedom. Within only a few years, Cooley had earned the teachers' distrust by centralizing city school management, firing popular district superintendent William Speer, and emphasizing an authoritarian economic efficiency regime. Depressed by this seemingly unending stream of antagonistic superintendents appointed by the city's board of education, the teachers saw the possibility of change in 1904, when Mayor Carter Harrison announced that he would not run for reelection. This opened up a backdoor to the Federation: The board of education was appointed by the mayor, and the new mayor who was to be elected in 1905 would be able to appoint seven new members to the board of twenty-one for each year of his two-year terms. Ultimately, Haley felt that the teachers' power was limited by the fact that the board of education held control over almost every facet of public education in Chicago, including the hiring, firing, and promotion of teachers, the selection of textbooks and curriculum, and control of the budget. Haley saw the election of a mayor who was favorable to the teachers as the opportunity to secure "a Board of Education instead of a Board of Big Business."[5]

Haley zeroed in on Edward F. Dunne as the best candidate. A circuit court judge in Cook County since 1892, Dunne was an Irish Catholic with a family of thirteen children, all of whom went to the public schools. His wife was a public school teacher, a Federation member, and with Haley and Catherine Goggin, a member of the Catholic Woman's League. Haley had first met Dunne during the Foresters fight, when he ruled for her injunction against the organization. In 1904 he had ruled for the Federation, preventing the board of education from using the returned tax money for anything but the teachers' overdue salary.[6] Haley had great faith in Dunne, whom she saw as "an expression of the awakened liberalism of Chicago." But she also felt he was hampered by "his own judicial temperament, always seeing both sides of every argument before he would make any decision."[7] Haley's critique of such "fairness" was typical of her single-focus politics. According to Haley, public officials who saw the teachers' side of the story were wise, but if they saw any merit to the other side of the argument, they were biased. Still, except for this minor flaw, Haley believed that Dunne was the man for the job and she pressured him to initiate a campaign.

In early 1905, Haley joined a chorus of progressive Chicagoans who convinced Dunne to run for mayor. She then fell sick and withdrew from public life for almost six months. She had first caught a cold while attending the funeral of her old school principal, John McCarthy. She recovered enough to go to congratulate Dunne on his election in April, and to remind him that although she had not mentioned to him anything about the board of education during the campaign, she urged him to check with her before he appointed any new board members. Then on May 6, Haley's father died, and she collapsed and withdrew from most of her work for a few more months. A friend later told Haley that her prognosis had seemed so grim that some reporters had written her obituary. By midsummer, Haley revived enough to advise Dunne on his board of education appointments.[8]

The new mayor made his appointees to the board in July 1905. Unlike previous board appointees, most of whom were city businessmen, Dunne's appointees represented a broad social and philosophical outlook and included women and union supporters.[9] The most famous of the appointees was Jane Addams, who presented both a great promise and a great challenge to Margaret Haley. Born one year apart, both in small towns in northern Illinois, Margaret Haley and Jane Addams were raised in strikingly different economic and cultural situations. Addams led a relatively sheltered and privileged life as a middle-class Protestant. She attended boarding school and Rockford College, and in her early twenties she traveled around Europe, caught in an emotional trauma that she later called "the family claim"—the

tension facing educated middle-class girls who wanted to do something purposeful with their life even as society pushed them back to the family. By this
time, the working-class Haley had been pushed *out* of her family by her
father's financial crisis, which led her to be a teacher. While Jane Addams
spent much of her young life in self-doubt, "weary of myself and sick of
asking what I am and what I ought to be," Haley spent the same years
teaching and reading the economic platforms of Henry George.[10] As young
women, their paths continued to follow their different economic and social
trajectories, albeit within a few miles of each other in the same city. Both
moved to Chicago, where in 1889, Addams and her friend Ellen Starr opened
the settlement Hull House on the west side of the city, where a core group
of middle-class women lived and provided services for the local immigrant
community. In these years, Haley worked in the Hendricks School in the
Stockyards. Both women worked with Chicago's poor, but Haley's teaching
was unheralded, while Addams became the figurehead of the national settlement house movement and advocate for social reform.

The two women's personality and leadership styles reflected their different backgrounds: Haley was a hard-boiled, uncompromising political activist, while Addams was known for her leadership style of compromise and
negotiation. The two women first communicated in 1902, after Haley had
made a name in the tax fight.[11] Addams praised the tax investigation, and
Haley was pleased in turn to hear that Addams shared her deep mistrust of
business involvement in city and state affairs. In her *Democracy and Social
Ethics*, written in 1902, Addams wrote: "It is possible that the business men,
whom we in America so tremendously admire, have really been dictating the
curriculum of our public schools, in spite of the conventions of educators and
the suggestions of university professors."[12] Addams saw the teachers' affiliation with the Chicago Federation of Labor as one way that teachers could
monitor such unscrupulous business interests and in November 1902, she
delivered a rousing speech at the Federation meeting endorsing the affiliation with the CFL. Still, Haley's take on Addams was guarded. Ultimately,
she mistrusted Addams because of her class background, which allowed her
to pick and choose her causes. More damning was Haley's belief that Addams
was a political weak link who was flawed by her insistence upon pleasing
everybody; she caustically referred to her as "Gentle Jane."[13]

Jane Addams was originally reluctant to join the board of education,
and Dunne dispatched Haley to Hull House to change her mind. Haley
roused herself from her sick room for the task. For all her doubts about
Addams's commitment to teachers, Haley still had good reason to support
her appointment. Addams had not only come out publicly in support of the
Teachers' Federation's affiliation with labor, but she had also critiqued the
controversial promotional system, arguing that evaluations of teachers must
be made in the classroom and not on a piece of paper.[14] Furthermore, by
1905 Addams was nationally famous for her activist work on behalf of

Chicago's poor and for her lectures and published writings that called for a new social ethic of urban reform. Haley clearly saw Addams's political stands and influence as an asset for the teachers.

Haley put on the pressure, telling Addams that not only did she owe the public schools her service, but she was the best person for the job. She made it clear to Addams that she would never ask her to do anything for the Federation, and that Addams's work on the board should be based on her own principles that the school system needed to become more democratic. The Federation wanted democracy too, Haley explained, but when they called for it, they were portrayed as selfish and politically oriented. The public would believe Addams because of her honorable reputation. Haley's assumption, of course, was that Addams would always be in agreement with the Federation.[15]

Haley's interest in using Addams as a mouthpiece was exactly what Addams most feared. She knew that the conservative members of the public already suspected that Dunne's newly appointed members of the board were merely representatives of the Teachers' Federation.[16] And she knew that whether she liked it or not, she would be considered part of that cabal. Addams eventually agreed to join the board, but only if Dunne also appointed her friend Anita McCormick Blaine.

Addams ultimately regretted taking on the job. Her first year on the board was "stormy and very unsatisfactory," she wrote to a friend, and she wondered if there was any way to make education more democratically self-governing.[17] Prior to her board experience, Addams had felt that all political problems could be negotiated, but on the Chicago school board she learned that "all such efforts were looked upon as compromising and unworthy, by both partisans."[18] Years later, she still found it difficult to write about her experience on the Chicago Board of Education because it was "dramatized in half a dozen strong personalities."[19] One of those, clearly, was Margaret Haley.

Haley was not disappointed by Dunne's other appointees. One was Jane Addams's friend Anita McCormick Blaine, the widow of a prominent Chicago businessman and the founder of a private elementary school run along the methods of Francis Parker.[20] Another appointee was Cornelia DeBey, an osteopathic physician and a former teacher who gained fame when she helped to mediate the great Chicago Stockyards strike of 1904. Even before she joined the board, DeBey had been involved in education matters, spearheading a state bill authorizing kindergartens as part of the public school system, working against a bill that would have fired married women teachers, and for a child labor law.[21] DeBey shared with Haley and Addams a suspicion of the power of business. In an interview in the *Chicago Teachers' Federation Bulletin* in 1904, DeBey asserted:

> There is a type of man who becomes nothing but a machine. Business is his god, and it rules him always. He loses his human faculty,

he has no sense of justice, and is powerless to analyze a situation . . . they have no blood to speak of in their veins, and no gray matter worth mentioning in their heads. They are the stumbling blocks set in the path of progress to teach us the lessons of sorrow and patience.

Nor did DeBey disguise her disdain of men politicians. As she began one of her campaigns, she told her friends that there had to be one male official who was "a little less of a fool than those around him," and when she found that man, she would move him over to her cause.[22] The tall and bony DeBey with her strident personality was a strong contrast to the rotund and warm Jane Addams. Haley remembered that the opinionated Cornelia DeBey was "a thorn in Gentle Jane's side" and that DeBey "had an uncanny ability in finding Jane's fallacies and of prodding her with the consciousness of them."[23]

Other appointees to the new board included John C. Harding from the Typographical Union and Emil Ritter, a former teacher, Federation member, and president of the Referendum League, which had organized for municipal reform. Almost all the appointees were recommended or approved by Haley. Dunne was ridiculed by the *Tribune* and others for having named a board of education that was composed "chiefly of avowed single taxers and socialists" and they lambasted the mayor's plan to "democratize" school government by submitting "all questions of educational policy to the teachers."[24] In a barely veiled attack on Haley and the predominantly Catholic Chicago Teachers' Federation, the press denounced the board as "tools of labor" that were "subservient to Roman Catholic interests."[25]

The first issue on the new board's table was the already controversial teachers' promotion scheme. First introduced by Superintendent Edwin Cooley in 1902, the plan had infuriated the teachers because it included a secret marking system conducted by the principal who determined whether or not teachers were eligible to take an exam that, if they passed, would earn them a raise. The teachers objected to this double-gated promotion system because of the secrecy of the principal's evaluation and the reliance on a written exam, neither of which captured teachers' skills in the classroom or provided teachers with suggestions for improvement. In the winter of 1906, Cooley recommended a modification of the plan under which teachers were still marked secretly by the principal, but now if they were deemed eligible, they had an option of taking the exam or of taking five courses at institutions accredited by the superintendent and the Chicago Normal School.[26]

The Federation was not pleased by the revised plan. They objected to the coursework option because it measured teachers' capabilities as a student and not as a professional and because the coursework was to be taken at the expense of teachers' time and money. Furthermore, the secret markings by the principal remained. Haley saw the new promotional plan as a continued attempt to cut school costs, now disguised in a scheme that looked as though it promoted increased academics. It was, she insisted, yet another "money-shaving and teacher-punishing plan."[27]

Jane Adams, ca. 1900

But according to Addams, much of the public approved of the revised plan because it assured advanced education for teachers who only three years earlier had risked their professional status by aligning with the Chicago Federation of Labor.[28] Addams was chair of the school management committee to which Cooley submitted the modified promotional scheme and her political alliance with the teachers was immediately on the line. In the spirit

Dr. Cornelia DeBey

A physician by profession; by avocation an educator; a member of the Board of Education

Cornelia DeBey, *American Magazine*, September 1906

of compromise, Addams invited Haley to Hull House for a conference with her, Cornelia DeBey, and Ella Flagg Young, who was then principal of the Normal School. Haley made her case against the new plan by arguing that it had been designed without any input from teachers. She proposed to

Addams that in order to develop a true democratic principle in Chicago schools, the scheme should be presented to small groups of teachers where they could freely study and comment on the proposal. The others agreed with the idea, but Addams said she feared that Cooley would not go along with it, and she believed it imprudent to cross the mayor in this instance. Haley then lectured Addams that it was her responsibility to convince Cooley, and that she had the authority to do so.[29]

Haley's lecture must have been pointed, because two days later she wrote Addams an apology for her rudeness at the meeting, saying that her history of "irritations" with school politics often made her lose her temper and that she had expressed "ugly feelings" of which she was deeply ashamed. The problem, she explained, was that her passion for democratic principles was so strong and the work was often so discouraging, that she fell prey to small feelings of "prejudices and antagonism." She hoped that Addams did not interpret Haley's impatience at school politics as a criticism of Addams herself or as a desire to force Addams to Haley's position. Addams may very well have thought exactly that, since Haley's point *was* to change her mind.[30]

Addams did go to Superintendent Cooley, and asked him to submit the revised plan to teachers for their opinion. Cooley flatly refused and submitted it to the board the next week—so quickly that one board member complained that he didn't even have the chance to read it. The board passed the revised plan, but only after they voted against a proposal by DeBey to discuss it further. Addams not only voted against the proposal for discussion, but she voted for the new promotion scheme.[31]

Haley was astounded. She arranged a meeting with Addams, DeBey, and Catherine Goggin at the Federation headquarters and the group debated the matter for more than two hours. Addams began by saying that the new promotion plan was a compromise and that she believed in compromises. Haley retorted that she did not believe in any compromise that compromised a principle, and that Addams had done exactly that by voting for a plan that barely a year before she had denounced publicly. Haley interpreted Addams's next remark as evidence of her lack of a backbone. According to Haley, Addams admitted that she had often been pressured by the teachers to say more than she wanted to, and to take more radical stands than what she actually believed. This was apparently the case when Addams had encouraged the teachers to join with the Chicago Federation of Labor: She hadn't really felt that strongly about the case, but she was pressured to support it publicly. As a result, she had been put on the defensive, risked losing financial donations to Hull House, and had been lectured by President Roosevelt in the White House.[32] This, at least, was Haley's report, but Addams herself wrote in her autobiography that she had fully supported the affiliation. Clearly, the two women disagreed not only on political positions, but also on their interpretation of motivations.

Although Haley sharply criticized Addams publicly, privately she recognized that Addams had a very rational reason for her vote. In a few months,

Mayor Dunne would have the opportunity to appoint seven more members to the board, thereby creating a strong majority of his appointees. It was probable that the new Dunne board would abolish the promotion scheme anyway. Addams believed that she needed to vote for the new promotion plan to make the Dunne appointees appear not to be simply puppets of the Federation. This temporary compromise would allow more leverage for bargaining in the future. Eventually Haley admitted that Addams was right, but she never acknowledged this to Addams. Rather, she insisted that

> as a matter of principle and not of policy I felt and I still feel that Miss Addams made a mistake and a serious one. Miss Addams if she is anything to Chicago is an ethical and moral leader not a compromiser. It was as such that the people of Chicago looked up [to] her in this and this incident simply demonstrates the difference between my view of Jane Addams and her view of her place in the activities of our city.[33]

The issue was one of principle, and not practical politics. "I believe in compromises," Haley stated, "but not a compromise of principle. That was the difference."[34] On closer inspection, it is more likely that Haley, the highly practical political operator who often negotiated behind the scenes, believed strongly in principle only when it was *her* principle that was at stake.

Relations between Haley and Addams deteriorated in the following months. In July 1906, Dunne appointed his second batch of board members after inviting Adams, Haley, DeBey, and his other past appointees to his house to discuss the nominations. Appointed were Raymond Robins, a social worker from the Northwestern University settlement house whom Haley had worked with on municipal reform issues. His wife was Margaret Drier Robins, who was a founder of the Women's Trade Union League. Also appointed was Wiley Wright Mills, a single taxer who had run unsuccessfully for the city council on a platform on municipal ownership of Chicago's streetcars; Philip Angsten, who was an advocate of municipal ownership; John J. Stonsteby, president of the garment cutters' union; Dr. John Guerin, an Irish-born doctor; and Louis Post, editor of *The Public*, a progressive weekly newspaper based in Cleveland where Haley's friend Mayor Tom Johnson was developing single tax policies. Haley was so enthusiastic about Post that she took a night train to Cleveland to ask Johnson to release Post from his duties as editor so he could join the board.[35] Post accepted the offer and moved to Chicago, explaining that he would try to "change a despotic business man's education policy that makes automatic marionettes of teachers to one that recognizes their human dignity and value as the real educational guardians of the school children."[36] The conservative public felt differently. The *Tribune* continued its attack on Dunne for packing the board of education with "freaks, cranks, monomaniacs, and boodlers," thereby putting Chicago's name into "disrepute" and inviting labor unrest.[37] The portrayal of Haley as a controlling force of the board remained prominent. The *Tribune* referred to her as "Deputy Assistant Margaret Haley," and the "long haired" men on the board were satirized as being feminine pawns to bossy and masculine women such as Haley and DeBey.[38]

Although Dunne and his appointees insisted on their independence, Haley's presence in city politics was notable in both policy and daily practice. A contemporary reporter described a visit to the Chicago Board of Education in late 1906, where any visitor might see Margaret Haley "quite frequently" sitting at one side of the boardroom.

> He will see her eagerly noting the votes cast by the members. He will see the reporters go over to her and interview her for the purpose of getting a forecast of the future policy of the Board. He will see some of the Board members go over to her and consult with her on the subjects under discussion. He will observe that while Margaret Haley is not a member of the Board she is the most important person in the room.[39]

The new board immediately set up a committee, chaired by Louis Post, to investigate the promotion plan. Post consulted closely with Haley on the plan, asking her advice, and drawing on evidence that the Federation had collected. In general, Haley wrote to the committee, the concept of grading teachers showed that the board had lost sight of the ideal of "what a teacher should be and what her ideals should be." Teachers were always being told that "they must not teach for money," that their work was worth *more* than mere financial recompense. But the testing and perfunctory requirements that might lead to a raise merely reduced teachers to mercenaries.[40] The secret nature of the marking was terrible, but marking teachers in and of itself was wrong because it reduced the evaluation of teachers to a specific moment in time, and it did not connect evaluation with any kind of support. If there was no institutionalized stimulant to encourage teachers to do their best, then there was something wrong with the system, not with teachers. Teachers needed ongoing, encouraging supervision; "Marking and examining is small and cheap in comparison."[41] Haley's proposal for long-term substantial support for teaching and learning in schools remained her suggestion for teacher improvement. But as Haley well knew, long-term support meant higher costs than the occasional raise for some teachers, which reinforced her belief that Cooley's new promotion plan was designed as a cost-saving measure more than any pedagogical reform.

The findings of the Post Report, completed in December 1906, were no surprise to the teachers. The report found that barely one-fifth of all elementary teachers (493 teachers) with seven years or more experience had been recommended by their principals to take the promotion exam; they had all passed the examination and were earning $1000. But the vast majority of teachers with seven years or more experience (2,600 elementary teachers) had not been recommended to take the exam, and most of these were primary teachers who earned an annual salary of $450. Furthermore, a study of the principals' secret efficiency marks of teachers found that many teachers who earned high efficiency marks from their principal still had not been recommended to take the exam. Because the efficiency marking was secret, and no teacher could apply for promotion unless the principal said that her marks were high, principals were able to recommend whom they wanted to take the promotion exam for any reason whatsoever. The Post Report found that "teachers were being tested on their loyalty to immediate authority rather than on their loyalty to ethical and educational principle."[42]

The Post committee recommended a new promotional plan that would include a three-year probationary period, at the end of which the teacher would get a certificate; annual written evaluations of each teacher by her principal and district superintendent, which would be presented to the teacher; automatic pay raises granted for the first seven years; and for subsequent raises, regular observations of classroom work by two superintendents and the principal of the Chicago Normal School. Teachers would be encouraged to take courses at the Chicago Normal School and given ten half-days off each six months for that purpose. The report also recommended that all principals report inefficient teachers and that those teachers so identified should have a reasonable probation period, with written evaluations, and if they did not improve they should be dismissed.[43]

The Teachers' Federation liked Post's plan, and not surprisingly, Superintendent Cooley strongly opposed it and the press continued its charge that the board was under the control of the Federation.[44] Louis Post, who never hid his admiration for Haley, the woman who had taken a midnight train to Cleveland to convince his boss to let him take the job on the board, publicly mocked the notion that he was under her control. In a meeting before the Chicago Federation of Labor in December 1906, he praised Haley's work to great applause and cheering, and said that he "would rather be bossed by Margaret Haley, who has brought two hundred and fifty thousands of dollars a year into the school fund, than by these 'financeers' who have never done anything but take money out!"[45]

And as it turned out, the teachers' suspicion that Cooley's promotion plan was motivated by economic rationale was validated when the chair of the board's finance committee announced that the additional raises that would result from the Post report recommendations would bankrupt the board. It was now obvious that Cooley's plan had been oriented more around the school budget than around teacher quality. In February 1907, the board adopted the Post Report anyway, and authorized raises for 2,600 teachers.[46] But they never collected, because in April, Mayor Dunne was voted out of office and the new mayor, Fred Busse, threw out most of the Dunne board.

Busse's supporters cheered the election of "a good, straight, hard headed businessman" as mayor.[47] On her side, Haley described the new mayor with disgust as "the absolutely perfect personification of a political machine. Fred was 'One of the Boys.' He came into office with the declared and fixed intention of making the world safe for the other boys."[48] One of the first things he did was fire the Dunne board of education. Busse will "Oust 'Longhairs'" read the gleeful front page of the *Interocean* over a degrading cartoon of a sobbing African American child in fairy dress holding a sign that read, "I want work." Although the board members may have had good intentions, the editors reported, their fatal flaw was that they "subordinated their educational aims to the commercial purposes of a trade union."[49] By dismissing Dunne's board, the *Tribune* crowed, Chicago had finally rejected "petticoat government and pipe dream government" and denounced "the whole crew of female politicians and other long haired freaks."[50]

The new mayor demanded the resignation of twelve members of the board before the expiration of their terms. When seven members refused to resign, he announced their removal anyway. Included in the purge were Louis Post, Raymond Robins, and Cornelia DeBey. He retained Jane Addams and Anita Blaine. Immediately after his announcement, some of the surviving members of the Dunne board met at Blaine's house. Blaine volunteered to challenge the legality of the firing of the members at the next board meeting, but when the board met, she remained silent. Worse, the board decided to postpone the meeting of the school management committee so that its chair, Jane Addams, would not be pressured to take any public position regarding Mayor Busse's move. To the horror of the deposed members of the board, their former colleagues made no formal challenge to their firing.[51] The *Chicago Record-Herald* observed that Addams "diplomatically avoided a sharp clash by announcing that she would adopt the course of the board's executive head . . . she took the middle ground."[52]

As soon as Haley heard about this chain of events, she called a meeting with Addams in Cornelia DeBey's office. Addams explained her side of the story in a way that left Haley uncharacteristically confused about what had actually happened. After the meeting the three women went out to the street, and Haley heard Addams casually tell her: "Do you know that I'm not at all ashamed to be seen walking along the same street with you?" Haley then realized that Addams saw her as some kind of a dangerous, immoral person.[53] When Addams left, DeBey explained the whole story more fully to Haley. Never afraid of confrontation, Haley telephoned Addams and yelled at her for her refusal to confront Mayor Busse. When the new board met a week later, they hired two dozen police officers to control a crowd of three hundred infuriated teachers who protested at the door.[54]

Haley was not the only one who saw Addams's position as supercilious and divisive. Social reformer Mary Dreier wrote her brother-in-law, the recently dismissed board member Raymond Robins, "What a dreadful backward step has been taken because of St. Jane." Robins's wife, Margaret Dreier Robins, was also disturbed by Addams's failure to stand for principle. Thinking that Addams's position was due to her fear of losing donations to Hull House, Robins offered to give the settlement $20,000 if Addams changed her vote. But it was not fear of losing money that led to Addams's vote; Jane Addams preferred compromise to conflict, a characteristic that inevitably led Haley to dismiss her as "a social rather than a moral leader" who was no more than "a sensitive plate reflecting the feelings of others and having unusual power of putting herself in the other fellow's place."[55] Haley saw such sensitivity—which would lead to Addams's 1931 award of the Nobel Peace Prize—as weak leadership.

Addams herself recalled that she played "a most inglorious part" in the board's conflict. She felt that in her first year on the board the majority of members were "exasperatingly conservative," and the next year they were "frustratingly radical," and "I was of course highly unsatisfactory to both."[56] Anita McCormick Blaine shared Addams's frustration with the board, and with school politics in general. To both women, who were well experienced in organizational work in reform groups, the board of education was rife with wire pulling, cliques, and conspiracy theories. The experience made Blaine question the very notion of participatory democracy, particularly in the case of the board where citizens with no specific experience in school management were given final authority. Certainly public education had to be accountable to the public, but there had to be a better way.[57]

With Fred Busse's election, the teachers' influence in City Hall was abruptly terminated. The new board, installed in June 1907, repealed the Post committee's promotion plan and the salary raise for the 2,600 teachers, rejected architectural plans for school buildings with smaller classrooms, and it reinstated the Cooley scheme of secret marks and promotional exams. Worst of all was the Busse board's decision about a problem that Haley considered to be the most egregious financial dealing in all Chicago school politics. What became known as the "Land Lease" issue became one of the keystone pieces in Haley's understanding of the manipulative role of business in school matters.[58]

The land lease issue had origins in the original legal designation of public school land. Under the Ordinance of 1787, in the new federally procured lands of the Northwest Territory, one square mile in every thirty-six square miles was designated for use for public education. Throughout the area that became the American Midwest, district boards of education were authorized to use that property for schools, or else to rent, or lease, the land and use the income to support the public schools. What had happened in Chicago over the years was that powerful interests had pressured the board into renting them those school lands at far below market value. Many of the properties were located in the middle of what was now the expensive business section of the city—the Loop—and some businesses secured long leases at below-value rates. The most flagrant offenders were the very powerful newspaper companies that had close ties to the board of education. In 1895, the chairman of the board of education, who was also the chairman of the board's committee on school fund property, was also the Chicago *Tribune* attorney who had negotiated a ninety-nine year lease for the *Tribune* from the board of education on valuable property in the center of Chicago's downtown. Because the rented land was school property, there was no tax charged, although in fact it was the board that was tax exempt, not the renters. So the *Tribune* not only paid low rent, but they also paid no taxes to the city. In an additional bizarre twist, in 1902 the board rented one floor of the *Tribune* building for its offices and paid the *Tribune* $1000 a year, which meant that the board was essentially renting from its own renter, and paying significantly more than the *Tribune* was paying to itself.[59]

By 1905, the issue was at a boiling point, in part because companies that had not been able to negotiate long leases were suing in the courts to have that right. After investigating the issue, the Federation found that the annual rent received from all school lands was only $500,000, estimated to be one-half of what it could have been at current land values. "Had the land been retained," Haley wrote, "there would now be far more than enough money in school treasuries to give every child in Illinois a first-class grammar school education without one cent of taxation on the people of the city or state."[60]

In late 1906, Louis Post initiated a lawsuit on behalf of the board of education against the *Tribune* Company to invalidate its ninety-nine-year lease. The case was on its way to the state Supreme Court when Busse won the mayoral election, and his new board stopped the suit. Even though the court refused to drop the case, in 1910 the state court ruled for the *Tribune* Company, denying any impropriety between it and the board, arguing that any valuation of land values over the years were mere speculation, and denying the claim that under the Fourteenth Amendment, the land leases had deprived the children of Chicago of their due property. As school started in the fall of 1907, Federation teachers returned to work greatly discouraged. Haley grimly stated: "The future of justice looked dark."[61]

SABOTAGE

"There was, however, a gleam of light already glowing on the horizon, although it was no bigger than a pin point," Haley recalled, as she described one of her most devious plans for undermining Superintendent Cooley.[62] According to the revised promotional plan, teachers who wanted a raise were given a choice between taking an exam at the end of their seventh year or enrolling in five education courses. Only teachers who were qualified by their principals' secret marking could apply for the raise by taking the examination or the courses. But during the three months that the Post promotion plan had been in implementation, a large number of teachers became qualified because their principals, no longer shielded by the secret marking system, delivered them high ratings.[63] The question for the Federation was how to get as many teachers as possible prepared for the raise before the new board found a way to deny them.

Haley had earlier critiqued Cooley's promotion plan that rewarded teachers' extra course work with a raise, because it forced teachers to see extra education classes as mere hurdles to leap in order to earn more money. As she wrote a friend: "It is pitiful to see the teachers of this day grasping and grabbing and crowding each other to get into classes . . . to get a money reward."[64] In the autumn of 1907, however, with the Cooley promotion system back in place, Haley shrewdly decided to beat the superintendent at his own game. If teachers were being forced to take classes to get a raise, she would make sure that they did it as quickly and painlessly as possible.

Among the schools approved by the board to offer coursework was the Chicago Art Institute, and some teachers reported to Haley that the Art Institute was planning to offer five courses concurrently. These teachers planned to take all five courses and apply for their raise in January 1908. The Superintendent had once specified that teachers could not get credit for more than two courses taken during a single school year, but teachers hoped to quietly slide their credits through without the superintendent noticing.[65] Haley encouraged them. The group of teachers took their five classes and in January, they received their raise.

Haley then asked the registrar at the Art Institute to increase the number of courses, and that winter, 1,300 teachers swarmed to the building on Michigan Avenue to take a series of night classes. The scheme worked in part because Superintendent Cooley was on sick leave in Europe in the beginning of the year, and the teachers did not publicize what they were doing. Still, during those months, when Haley passed the Art Institute at night and watched the crowds of teachers pour out of the building, she was amazed that the board of education did not learn of the affair. When the 1,300 teachers finished their course work in early May, they filed their applications for raises and, because of the precedent set by first group of teachers in January, the board was forced to grant them.[66] When Cooley returned from Europe to hear the news, he was furious, but the only thing he could do in his rage was remove the Art Institute from the list of accredited institutions. As one commentator noted, Cooley had set a trap for the teachers and they walked off with the trap.[67] "The financial scheme to keep down the salary of the teachers had broken of its own weight," Haley crowed. "The one small hole in the dike had enlarged and the flood of teachers had gone through."[68]

The Federation was vindicated. Their long-running insistence that teachers' raises should be based on seniority was based both on a respect for older teachers and on continued mistrust of other types of promotional devices. No teachers were earning what they deserved, Haley argued, and to fix the system so that teachers had to jump through more hoops to earn pennies more was further humiliation and injustice, especially when those hoops were designed not by teachers but by business-minded bureaucrats whose main objective was to save money. Like policemen, firemen, and other civil service workers, teachers' wages should be based on years of service alone, because otherwise teachers' promotions would be based on the board's financial exigencies or local administrators' petty disagreements with teachers. Haley was not opposed to extra studies for teachers, but she believed they should be optional only, and provided free of charge for teachers. But Haley's argument was not particularly popular. Critics expressed dismay that educators would be opposed to advanced education that was designed to improve the educational experiences of students. And Jane Addams worried that in large school systems such as Chicago's, teachers would grow "mechanical and indifferent" without ongoing education.[69]

REVENGE AND RETRIBUTION

When Fred Busse retired from his job as mayor in 1911, former mayor Carter Harrison announced his candidacy. Harrison's first term (1897–1905) had coincided with Haley's first years in the Federation and the great tax fight, and in all those years, he had not been a friend of progressive groups. Haley was unrestrained in her hatred for Harrison, the son of the mayor by the same name, and she constantly referred to him by his aristocratic sounding full name: Carter Henry Harrison II. Haley claimed that Harrison's refusal to support the tax fight had driven innumerable women teachers "to the hospital, the insane asylum, and to their graves." She called Harrison a "cowardly, subservient tool to big business; indolent, slovenly, [and] irresponsible."[70]

Harrison's reemergence raised all of Haley's worst suspicions. In early 1911, she was told by one of Harrison's supporters that if she organized the teachers to support his candidacy, she could dictate her own terms in the board of education as she had with Mayor Dunne. Haley adamantly refused, calling Harrison a liar and a cheat who could not be trusted. When she heard a rumor that Elizabeth Burdick, her old foe in the Teachers' Federation, had left her position in the schools to work for Harrison's nomination and election, she was convinced that Harrison was out to demolish the Federation for good.[71]

But the teachers' spirits were bolstered by their new superintendent. Edwin Cooley had retired in 1909, exhausted from nine years of school battles, and in a surprise move the board appointed Ella Flagg Young as superintendent. Young became not only the first woman superintendent of a major American city, but also the first superintendent in Chicago who expressed public loyalties to the teachers. At age sixty-five, she was indeed an unusual choice.

Few Chicago superintendents came to the office with more experience or more intellectual and political acumen. By the time she retired in 1915, Ella Flagg Young had held virtually every instructional and administrative position in the Chicago school system. Ella Flagg was born in 1845 in upstate New York into a family of Scottish descent. When she was thirteen years old, the family moved to Chicago where she attended high school and the Chicago Normal School, graduated in 1862, and took a job teaching grade school. Two years later she was appointed principal of the practice school associated with the Normal School. In 1868, she married William Young, who died within a few years, and Young returned to her work in schools. Over the next twenty years she taught high school, became principal of two elementary schools, and taught at the Normal School. She was appointed district superintendent 1887, a position she held until she resigned in 1899 as a protest against the administration of "Bulletin Ben" Andrews. By this time, she had already been taking classes with John Dewey at the University of Chicago, where she eventually earned her Ph.D. She later taught at the University of Chicago, and between 1905 and 1909 she was principal of the Cook County Normal School. Meanwhile, Young had been active in the Illinois State Board of Education for twenty-five years, and in 1909 she was elected president of the State Teachers' Association of Illinois.[72]

Young was a deeply intellectual woman. Jane Addams, whose circle included the best educated and most articulate women in America, described Young as having "more general intelligence and character than any other woman I knew." John Dewey, Young's dissertation advisor at the University of Chicago, described her as one of his best students and the wisest person in school matters with whom he had ever worked, and she helped him develop his ideas about the role of the teacher in the democratic school.[73] Dewey had long emphasized the creation of an egalitarian classroom through reforms of teachers' pedagogical practice, and argued that the democratic classroom could only occur in a democratic school; where every teacher was able to contribute to the decision making on all educational matters, not just classroom matters. "What does democracy mean save that the individual is to have a share in determining the conditions and the aims of his own work?" Dewey asked in an essay that was reprinted in the Chicago Teachers' Federation Bulletin in 1904.[74]

But Dewey's interests as a philosopher and his location in higher education made him less adept at applying his theories to educational practice, and Ella Flagg Young worked in effect as his translating agent to public schools. Her University of Chicago dissertation, which was published in 1900 under the title "Isolation in the Schools," argued that schools had become highly differentiated and disjointed institutions in a variety of ways. Students were divided arbitrarily by grades, curriculum was disjointed between subjects, and teachers were separated from each other and from those administrators who held sole authority to make educational decisions. The

Ella Flagg Young, 1911 (Courtesy Chicago Historical Society)

result, Young argued, was an institution that was isolated both within and without. Schools were organized in a piecemeal fashion that alienated teachers to such an extent that they acted merely as "operatives" within a system overburdened by heavy-handed administrative supervision.[75] "The parts have been brought together mechanically," she wrote, so that the school is not a community but "an aggregation of independent units."[76] The worst effect of this isolation was that individuals were being underestimated in their abilities to contribute to the schools. A solution to this problem, Young argued, was the creation of cooperative representative groups called teacher councils where teachers could discuss and deliberate matters of school legislation as a group, and later as a representative assembly to the administration. Young's proposals for structural change in school organization appealed to Haley, who called Young's text "the Bible of the teachers of the United States [on] the question of academic freedom."[77] Haley reproduced in her autobiography one of her favorite statements by Young, delivered in a speech near the end of her career as superintendent:

> In order that teachers may delight in awakening the spirits of children, they must themselves be awake. We have tried to free the teachers. Some day the system will be such that the child and the teacher will go to school with elastic joy. At home in the evening, the child will talk about the things done during the day and will talk with pride. I want to make the school the great instrument of democracy.[78]

As a person, Young was described as "brusque and plain looking with piercing looking eyes that could read people through and through."[79] Another contemporary recalled that "in fighting for a principle, Mrs. Young could be as 'hard as nails,' and she could match her wits with anyone."[80] Haley greatly admired Young, whom she saw as a skilled "manipulator" whose work was the nearest she had ever seen to "thought in instantaneous action. . . . Her intellect was a machine gun," but it was her "moral courage rather than her mental capacity that made her a leader of women."[81] Young was also a good judge of character, and more than once she played a mediating, moderating role to Haley's firebrand personality.

As a public figure, Ella Flagg Young stood as a champion of and for women. With her lifelong companion Laura Brayton, she lived and worked for women's rights. As superintendent, she unabashedly promoted women's suffrage; before an election in 1914—the first election in which Illinois women had the right to vote—she sent a note to all teachers requesting them to tell their students to urge their mothers to vote.[82] Young saw her appointment as superintendent to be the breaking down of a wall of male prestige. Women, she felt, were naturally more qualified for administrative positions in education than were men. "Women are destined to rule the schools of every city," she wrote upon her appointment.

> I look for a majority of the big cities to follow the lead of Chicago in choosing a woman for superintendent. In the near future we will have more women than men in executive charge of the vast educational system It is women's natural field, and she is no longer satisfied to do the greatest part of the work and yet be denied lead-

ership. As the first woman to be placed in control of the schools of a big city, it will be my aim to prove that no mistake has been made and to show cities and friends alike that a woman is better qualified for this work than is a man.[83]

To Haley, Young's appointment as superintendent was sweet revenge for the autocratic anti-teacher superintendents of the past. But Young's appointment was not without controversy. Men teachers, principals, and even school engineers and janitors, "would rather have had a man over them" reported one observer, and they "would have felt the same about any woman, no matter how efficient."[84] Some men's fear about a conspiracy of women materialized in 1913 when Young resigned her appointment out of frustration with the board, and in response, the city's women's clubs held a packed mass meeting and called on the mayor to bring Young back. Young did return, but the board never forgave her or her women supporters for the way they "squawked and screeched" to "put Feminism and fads" on the school agenda, and they harassed her mercilessly until her final resignation two years later.[85]

Young initiated her superintendency with an investigation of the land lease issue. She also defended the Federation over a new attack on the pension, and opposed a proposal to reduce teachers' salaries so as to meet the board's financial deficit.[86] She won teachers' praise with her institution of a system of teacher councils. As she had argued in "Isolation in Schools," the impersonality and confusion of large city school systems were best addressed by the establishment of representative teacher councils that would work as advisory bodies to school administrations. Councils were originally approved by the board of education in 1898, but they received minimal support from the superintendent's office until 1907 when the Dunne board tried to reenact them, only to be ignored by Superintendent Cooley. Only when Young took office in 1913 was the plan fully enacted. Elementary teachers met regularly without administrators in a local council within each school; a group council of local school representatives met regularly; and a general council composed of one delegate from each of group councils met with the superintendent every five weeks. Each of the councils met during school hours for at least forty-five minutes.[87] Issues under discussion in the councils ranged from salary and working conditions to curriculum and classroom responsibilities. In practice, many local council meetings were slow and unproductive gatherings of tired teachers at the end of the day, and their decisions were only advisory recommendations to the board. Still, teachers liked the councils if only for the symbolism that they were asked their views. Haley thought that teacher councils were the best device yet invented to allow for effective communication between teacher and administrator. For years, she had complained that teachers did not have a voice in schools and she identified the Federation as the teachers' only representative body. Teacher councils institutionalized a democratic process through in-school organization. Still, because councils had no real authority, for most of Young's tenure they were accepted by school administrators as a method of diverting teachers' more aggressive activities in the Federation.[88]

Young's greatest battle was over her predecessor Edwin Cooley's long campaign for vocational education. To Haley and other progressive educators and unionists, vocational education (also known as manual training) was not in and of itself bad. The reality was that between child labor laws and the creation of labor-saving devices, fewer young children were learning skilled trades and there was a legitimate reason for schools to take on the responsibility of preparing children for their eventual place in the workforce. Both the Teachers' Federation and the Chicago Federation of Labor supported vocational education as a way to minimize class differences because poor children would learn a trade well, and schools would not be the preserve of the rich who could afford liberal education. Indeed, some teachers and unionists argued that schools were already classist in centering their education on the academic, thereby excluding children from the working class whose interests might lie in the industrial or commercial, and they argued that the incorporation of vocational education in schools would provide a motive for children to stay in school in a system where in 1910 almost one-half of Chicago children did not complete eighth grade.[89] As a consortium of Chicago teachers' organizations stated in 1913: "Each child of the democracy, whatever his life work is to be, has the right to full exploration before choice and full preparation after choice."[90] To Haley, manual training meant more than preparation for labor; coursework should be centered around activities that helped the whole development of the child, both "his brain and his hand."[91] A democratic education should provide the opportunity for all children to explore different choices in life.

The concern of teachers, unionists, and progressive educators was that the type of vocational education introduced into schools would not be led by educators but by business leaders who would advocate a functionalist job training program. In fact, business involvement in vocational education *was* growing. In 1910, the Commercial Club, with a membership of ninety of the most prominent businessmen in the city, hired the recently retired Superintendent Cooley to study vocational education in Europe. He returned in 1911 convinced that the best plan for instituting vocational education was to create a system of separate trade and continuation schools, called a "dual system," that would be run by an independent school board and superintendent. The Federation strongly critiqued the plan for the way it would heighten class difference by dividing children "into classes and masses."[92] Superintendent Young joined the teachers in the charge that the dual plan was a ploy to divide teachers into different categories and reduce their salaries to pay for the plan.[93] The Federation organized a mass of opponents to the dual system proposal and in the spring of 1913, the bill was defeated in the state legislature.

A backdrop to all of these skirmishes was a continued battle over control of the teachers' pension. In 1909, a legislative committee proposed a bill that essentially disabled the original pension law. Haley characteristically denounced the bill with a character assassination of its promoters, charging three women lobbyists with scandalous sexual behavior and insurance fraud. More damning than such scurrilous gossip was her organized attack on one of the backers of the bill, William Rothman, a board of education member who wanted the teachers' pension to be taken away from the control of teachers and put under the control of the board. The Federation instigated a public investigation of Rothman's financial activities when he was chair of the police pension fund, discovering that Rothman had personally pocketed $20,000 of the interest money from that fund. The Federation printed up a report of Rothman's misdeed to deliver to teachers. According to Haley, Rothman then tried to bribe the teachers by offering a salary increase if they withheld the publication, but he was rebuffed and eventually every teacher in the system received a copy of the report and spread the news to the press. Rothman's pension bill lost in the legislature.[94]

Rothman was humiliated but far from defeated, and his animus against the teachers created trouble for the Federation for the next few years. Rothman's retribution was facilitated in 1915 by the mayoral election of William Hale Thompson, who filled the board with antiunion activists. Rothman teamed up with board member Jacob Loeb and they proposed a full-scale investigation of Chicago's schools, including the board of education. The senate established an investigation commission chaired by Percy Baldwin, but typical of the politics of the day, the Baldwin Commission immediately came under the influence of the very members that it was designed to investigate, and it ultimately gave only one day's hearings to activities in the board of education, and committed the rest of its sessions through the summer of 1915 to investigating the Chicago Teachers' Federation. Board member Jacob Loeb was the star witness, laying out a series of charges against the Federation. Loeb testified that the Teachers' Federation was "a curse to the school system of Chicago," that the school system ran on a deficit budget that was the product of "frenzied feminine finance," and that the entire school system was "in the grip of Margaret Haley."[95] Referring to the Federation's attack on his friend Rothman, Loeb, charged that "a labor slugger will go out and hit a man over the head with a lead pipe, and he has got a chance at recovery, but the lady slugger has a poisoned tongue and assassinates a man's reputation, from which he can not recover. The Teachers' Federation has assassinated character."[96] Loeb also had important words for Federation supporters who claimed to care more about children than about politics. Labor unions, he insisted, were "contemptuous and rebellious toward those in authority," and teacher unions would thus lead innocent children to lose respect for authority, law, and order. Margaret Haley herself, he charged "preaches anarchy."[97]

Haley recognized that Loeb was trying to portray the Teachers Federation as an old-fashioned power mongering "boodler" that controlled the board of education—just like the corporate giants that Haley herself had made a career of demonizing. And this is exactly what happened, as newspapers published stories that the Federation had regularly used intimidation against the board, referring to the Federation leaders as "Dictators."[98] The Chicago *Tribune* ran a story that between 1900 and 1907 Haley had received two salaries—one from the board of education as a teacher and one from the Federation. Two days after the article appeared, Mayor Thompson announced his support of Jacob Loeb's forthcoming proposal to the board of education to prohibit teachers from union membership.[99]

On September 1, 1915, the board of education adopted the infamous Loeb Rule which prohibited teachers from membership in a labor union or an association that was affiliated with a labor union. In a direct attack on Haley and Goggin, the ruling also prohibited teachers from membership in any teachers' organization that had paid "officers, business agents, or other representatives" who were not members of the teaching force.[100] In order to keep their jobs, teachers were required to sign a pledge that they were not members of any such organization. Haley understood that the Loeb ruling looked merely like a political scuffle between the leadership of the board of education and the Teachers' Federation, but to Haley, the Loeb Rule was yet another example of a powerful elite trying to gain control of democratic processes in the city. It was clear to her that since their affiliation with the Chicago Federation of Labor, disenfranchised women teachers had gained access to political power. The influence of organized labor had helped the teachers defeat the Cooley promotion plan and vocational education bill and to maintain control over their pensions. According to Haley, opposing powers knew that they had to "divorce us from the general Labor movement if they were to win their war against us and against what we represented. They seized their opportunity in using the class consciousness of a Thompson, the stupidity of a Loeb, and the vindictiveness of a Rothman."[101]

To add to the onslaught, the antilabor ruling enflamed anti-Catholic prejudice. A group of Methodist ministers endorsed the Loeb Rule because, while claiming not to "appeal to sectarian or religious prejudice," the ministers had long worried about the preponderance of Catholics on the Federation leadership.[102] This was not the first time that anti-Catholic prejudice was used by anti-Federation forces. Hate mail to the Federation office in recent years described Haley as "the dirtiest specimen of rotten irish [sic] politics I ever knew" and charged that the Catholic Church had always been against education. The writer promised a "religious war when eighty million Protestants will annihilate you or drive you all back to your own ignorant catholic countries."[103] In a city where a large proportion of all labor activists were of working-class immigrant Catholic origin, anti-Catholicism was often a veiled attack on working-class labor politics.

The Chicago progressive community immediately reacted to the Loeb ruling. The Chicago Federation of Labor held special protest meetings attended by American Federation of Labor president Samuel Gompers, John Fitzpatrick of the CFL, and Louis Post, now assistant secretary of the Department of Labor. Gompers railed against corporate interests that were trying to manipulate schoolteachers and the curriculum. How, he asked the cheering crowd, had the Teachers' Federation shown that it was "inimical to the proper discipline" or detrimental to the welfare of the public school system? Had teachers been absent from work more often since the Federation was organized, he asked? "Are the teachers less competent in teaching the children? Are they inferior in their deportment? Are they inferior in their character? Are they inferior in their manners? Are they inferior in their dignity? Are they less cordial? . . . . Is the children's education neglected?" He condemned those who wanted public education to ask children to sing not "My Country "Tis of Thee," but "Hail to the Almighty Dollar."[104]

Other progressive movements supported the teachers. Carl Sandburg published a poem in the Chicago *Day Book* that accused Loeb, a Jewish immigrant, of denying his heritage of persecution by turning to persecute others. To Jacob M. Loeb, Sandburg wrote:

> You came from Kovno in Russia and you ought to know something about liberty
>
> And how school boards, police boards, military boards and czars have gone on year after year,
>
> To choke the Jews from having societies, organizations, labor unions,
>
> Shoving bayonets into the faces of the Jews and driving them to the ghettos. . .
>
> And now you, a Jew, stand up here in Chicago and act proud
>
> Because you have in effect spit in the faces of Chicago women, accused them, belittled them....
>
> You belong in the trash of history, the oppressors and the killjoys.[105]

On September 23, the Federation won a court injunction. The judge found that the Loeb ruling was so broad that it prohibited teachers from belonging to the National Educational Association and the Illinois State Teachers Association because these groups, too, had paid staff members.[106] In response, the board rewrote the Loeb Rule to forbid membership in organizations that included nonteachers, such as the CFL. In late November the court ruled again against the board of education, with the judge reminding the board that the Supreme Court had upheld the legal right of labor to organize. Carl Sandburg reported on this victory with the exultant cry "Margaret Haley wins again!"

> For fifteen years this one little woman has flung her clenched fists
> into the faces of contractors, school land lease holders, tax dodgers
> and their politicians, fixers, go-betweens and stool pigeons. . . . Over
> the years the *Tribune*, the *News*, and the ramified gang of manipu-
> lators who hate Margaret Haley have not been able to smutch her
> once in the eyes of decent men and women of this town who do
> their own thinking.[107]

The thrill of victory was quickly followed by a terrible loss. On December 11, 1915, Ella Flagg Young resigned from the superintendency after the board rejected her reappointment.[108] Young reported that in her final two years she had been harassed continuously by board members. She claimed that the Baldwin Commission instigated rumors that she was a Catholic who went to daily mass, had an altar in her room, and had a son who was a Catholic priest. Young responded that not only was the charge incorrect (she was a Presbyterian and had no children) but that she respected many Catholics, and that the charge was clearly designed to imply "something disgraceful in being a Catholic."[109] She told Haley that she was also harassed on a daily basis by Rothman himself who would come into her office "pestering her with questions of no importance to her or to the public welfare, but which had nagging value."[110]

The tenacious Haley kept up the attack on her enemy. When she heard that one of Rothman and Loeb's most active supporters on the board of education, Ernest Kruetgen, was a candidate for the federally appointed office of Chicago postmaster, she took a train to Washington, D.C., and arranged a meeting with President Woodrow Wilson to lobby him against the appointment.[111] Since 1913, Illinois women could vote for state candidates and Haley felt her influence on Wilson's Democratic Party carried some weight. In her absence, Kreutgen went to the Chicago Federation of Labor and lobbied John Fitzpatrick and the CFL secretary Ed Nockels for their support. Fitzpatrick invited Goggin to the meeting and she later told Haley how the candidate came in and called Nockels by his first name and slapped him on the back, just like insider politicians getting ready to grease each others' palms. Goggin enjoyed telling Haley this story about male privilege, with an additional comment that betrayed both Goggin's admiration for Haley's power and her amusement at the idiocy of such a man. "If you'd been there," Goggin said with a sly little wink, "he would have slapped you on the back and said, 'Maggie, what can you do?'"[112]

THE POWER BROKER

At the close of 1915, Haley was losing legal battles, but she was still winning the popular war. She was at the apex of her career, a formidable player in Chicago politics who wielded great power. Her political influence affected the nature of teachers' hiring practices, employment qualifications, salary, and pension, and she influenced educational policies from vocational education to teacher certification. With the Loeb decision, Haley stood at the epicenter of a major legal debate about the professional definition of teachers and the legal rights of public employees. Haley's political weight extended to broader progressive causes, including child labor, women's suffrage, municipal reform, and electoral reform. She was invited to deliver her invigorating speeches at numerous progressive meetings and conferences across the country, at which she ignited local political fires. As an educator wrote after her talk to Boston teachers, Haley's presentation did a lot of good, "though it scared a lot of perfectly good teachers within an inch of their lives."[113]

Although Haley cared about broader causes and a national movement, she prioritized her local activities. As she wrote a friend in early 1914, "There is always something doing in Chicago."[114] Indeed there was. In the years 1914 and 1915, the Federation fought a revised version of the Cooley vocational bill, a board of education–proposed salary cut of $7\frac{1}{2}$ percent for all teachers, a proposal to reduce clerical assistance for principals, and threats to the teachers' pension, and it faced the Baldwin Commission investigation and Loeb ruling. In these years, Haley also initiated a libel suit against the *Chicago Tribune* for its story that she had received two salaries (from the Federation and the board of education). In 1914 alone, the Federation led a failed effort to have Catherine Goggin appointed to the board of education, and they took a leadership role in a progressive movement for public ownership of telephone wires. Meanwhile, the Federation continued its regular educative work for teachers, introducing a monthly series on parliamentary law, producing regular "legislative bulletins," running monthly meetings, and shouldering the work of the teacher councils.

Of greatest significance was the Loeb ruling, which pushed the longboiling conflicts between the Federation and what Haley referred to generically as business interests into the spotlight. The immediate issue was teachers' right to organize into labor unions; the underlying issue was teachers' right to engage in educational policy making. Haley's opponents argued that the Federation had destroyed the purity of education by dragging economic and political concerns into the classroom, and that teachers must return to the original intent of schools: the academic instruction of the city's children. The Federation continued to press an opposing case: that teachers needed to take a leadership role in school reform, and particularly the reform of those business interests that controlled schools. Teachers would never return to the simplistic classroom of old, wrote one reporter in 1915 in an imaginary dialogue between Haley and her opponents in the board of education: "They will go forward. They will go into your factories and they will change your factories. They will go into the hideous slums which you have created and they will clean them out. They will go into the politics which you have corrupted and they will make that pure. You must go back or you must change. The schools will advance."[115] This was what organization meant to teachers, and with the dawn of 1916, fifty-five-year-old Margaret Haley was rolling up her sleeves for the ultimate battle.

CHAPTER SEVEN

CASUALTIES

THE YEAR 1916 STARTED BADLY. Ella Flagg Young's last day as superintendent was the first of January. A few days later, the Federation held its regular board of managers meeting at the office. Catherine Goggin was at the meeting that afternoon, sharing the couch with Margaret Haley. Goggin had been ill and in semiretirement since September, but her health had recently improved, and the meeting was her first public activity in two weeks. At age sixty-one, she was the senior stateswoman of the Federation, and still greatly admired for her wit and charm. That afternoon, she reminded the group of the necessity of guarding the interests of all rank and file classroom teachers who constituted the bulk of the school system. Elementary teachers, she believed, were discriminated against particularly *because* there were so many of them, and this was both the strength and the weakness of the group, as it also was for the great mass of laboring people. This was the link that teachers had with other workers, and the reason why teachers always had to consider the financial needs of the *entire* system, not just their own salaries.[1] After this impassioned reminder, Goggin broke the tension with a joke—her classic style of following a powerful statement with unifying laughter. She left the meeting early to visit a sick friend. Later that evening, as she left her friend and began to cross the dark street to head home, she was struck by a passing delivery truck. Her legs were caught under the truck's frame and she was dragged for twenty-five feet before the driver noticed her. She died almost instantly.

A dozen women friends, including a distraught Haley, visited Goggin's body at the morgue that night. Ever the public figure, Haley quickly regrouped to tell reporters about Goggin's life and popularity among teachers, adding that Goggin's recent illness was the result of the Federation's battle with the board of education over the Loeb ruling in the previous months. The next day, she hurled the blame for Goggin's death on a more specific and familiar cause: the city's refusal to enforce its public welfare laws. If the truck had a fender, as was legally required, Haley charged, Goggin may only

165

have suffered broken bones instead of being mangled to death. It was the fault of self-serving business interests that her friend was dead. "How can those store managers hesitate to spend a few of their dollars when the lives of women like Catherine Goggin are at stake?" she demanded.[2] Days later, the Federation itself would reiterate this charge in their letter to the driver, whom they absolved of blame for the accident. The fault was not his, a lowly worker, but the corporate entity for which he worked. "In death as in life," the Federation president Ida Fursman wrote, Catherine Goggin "was struck by the power that disregards everything in this brutal race for money."[3] Haley continued to grasp desperately for other explanations for Goggin's death. A few weeks later, she would expand her blame to former Mayor Harrison, whose hateful political positions had led Goggin to leave retirement to fight for the teachers.[4]

Goggin's great popularity was evidenced by the hordes that attended her viewing and funeral. City Hall accepted the teachers' petition to hold her wake in the large City Council Chambers—a right reserved only for mayors and celebrities. More than ten thousand people paid their last respects in one day, including delegations of teachers and students from Chicago schools, labor leaders, women's suffragists and reformers, school administrators, city officials, Catholic clergy, and the city's most prominent politicians. Seventy members of a teachers' chorus sang in the evening, and by the end of the wake parts of the room were covered in flowers, including a five-foot panel of more than one thousand roses and carnations from the CFL with a banner reading "Her Spirit Lives," a flower tribute from labor leaders in Ireland, and a blanket of roses from the Federation with a banner reading "Our Miss Goggin." A guard of honor made up of teachers and clubwomen stayed with the body through the night and Haley stood at attendance, receiving condolences. The next day, hundreds attended the funeral at Holy Name Cathedral, the largest Catholic church in Chicago, and a procession of vehicles paraded to the gravesite at Calvary Cemetery on the north side of the city. Goggin had purchased the plot in 1880 to bury her younger sister, Margaret, and later her cousin and mentor, Judge James Goggin. The teachers ordered the inscription on the gravestone: "Life shaped her for a task, a trust, sublime—Just, patient, fearless, sure in word and deed."[5]

Condolence letters and telegrams flooded the Federation office and were reproduced in a fifty-page memorial edition of the *Bulletin*. Many testimonies spoke to this Catholic woman leader's devotion, unselfishness, modesty, and unassuming loyalty, but others spoke specifically to Goggin's particular skills as a leader. Some letters praised Goggin for her "citizenship," describing her as a public-spirited citizen, whose regular monitoring of city politics made her a patriot. She was praised for having such a sharp legal mind that, had she been a man, she surely would have made a skilled judge. Goggin was also described in more personal terms as a friend and mentor, a "peerless leader, wise counselor, sane advisor, and best friend." She was "the teachers' good fairy." So caring was she that young teachers looked to her for advice, and her death left many feeling grief as with the loss of a mother. Newspapers around the city reported on "a humble, unknown teacher" who attended Goggin's wake and said: "I am only an ordinary unheard-of school teacher, and my name would mean nothing to anyone. But I do want to say that she was so gentle and sweet and kind that she was loved by everyone."[6] However motherly, Goggin was also seen as a tough and visionary leader who was repeatedly referred to in masculine terms as "the little general," "the quiet general," and "a fellow soldier in a great cause."[7] Mother, military general, citizen, good fairy—Goggin's ability to embody both masculine and feminine images had furthered her ability to take highly controversial political stands.

Other testimonials spoke to the joint leadership of Goggin and Haley. It was Catherine Goggin who had "the legal type of mind coupled with a soundness of judgment that comes to few men," wrote the *Chicago Evening Post*. The tax fight was undoubtedly the creature of her mind, while it was Margaret Haley who "did the hard and more spectacular field work for it."[8] Louis Post wrote Haley that what affected him most as he reflected on Goggin's life and work was the sense of Haley's own personality "moving through the whole story, arm in arm with Miss Goggin, from the beginning over the whole stretch of fifteen years." There was "a singleness of purpose" in Haley's "double work with Miss Goggin."[9]

The public perceptions of Goggin and Haley's relationship were that Goggin provided a tempering influence to Haley's flamboyant and prickly style. It was Goggin who would lighten the mood at a Federation meeting, or who would salve the hurt feelings of a teacher or political leader who had been rebuffed by Haley. It was Goggin who kept up relations with the middle-class women's reform and suffrage movement, and Goggin who was able to please and appease political leaders with her gracious style. Ironically, perhaps it was because Goggin appeared more "motherly" than Haley that she was also seen as such an effective "general."

Characteristically, Haley wrote nothing about her own personal reaction to her friend's death. Newspapers reported her as grief stricken, but she was just as able to report on political matters, and in early March, barely two months after Goggin's death, she was talking to teachers in New York City. These actions speak as much to Haley's personality as they do to anything she might have recorded about her grief. That Haley was able to turn Goggin's accidental death into a political critique of the city implies that Haley processed her emotional life through politics. Ultimately, Haley's private life *was* her public life, and the meaning that she made out of Goggin's death was persistently public.

But certainly Haley experienced a great loss with Goggin's death, and it was a loss that would intrinsically shape the progress of the Federation for years to come. Haley had lost not only a confidant and supporter, but also a person who mediated her own intense and ricocheting activism. She had also lost a woman friend who linked her to the breadth of women's social reform movements, and she lost a contact with the older generation. At fifty-five years old, with her closest ally of more than a dozen years gone, Haley now faced one of the biggest battles of her career.

THE AFT

Four months after Goggin's death, eight teachers' associations joined together to form the American Federation of Teachers. Ten delegates from the Federation, including Haley, met in Chicago with delegates from two Chicago high school associations and the Gary, Indiana, Teachers' Union. On the table too were documents of agreement from federations in New York City, Washington, D.C., Scranton, Pennsylvania, Oklahoma City, and Waycross, Georgia. On May 9, the American Federation of Teachers (AFT) was granted a charter by the American Federation of Labor. As the oldest and largest member organization, the Federation was designated Local 1 of the AFT.

The teacher organizations that joined to form the AFT were unique in that they took an activist position on improving teachers' material conditions. Teachers' voluntary associations had existed in many cities for years, but most of these were organized for professional interest and advocacy and did not take aggressive stands on economic or political issues. Rather, they were self-interested protective groups that tended to hold mainstream views about the role of teachers in schools and focused on providing continuing education and social opportunities for teachers. Many of them were open to school administrators as well as teachers, and most of the groups opposed the affiliation of teachers with labor. For such groups, the key to improving the occupation of teaching was not union organization but professionalization; the solution was not to link with industrial laborers but with school administrators and university professors to further the professional stature and reputation of teaching. For many of these teachers, the work of Margaret Haley in Chicago was an example of where teachers should *not* go.[10]

The Chicago teachers had been discussing a national union for some time, at least since the affiliation with the CFL in 1902 and the formation of the National Federation of Teachers within the NEA in that same year. By 1910, there was a need for a new and more powerful network because the number of teachers' associations had grown—at least thirty one cities had at least one such association—and many of these had begun to turn their energies to lobbying for increased wages and benefits for the expanding teaching force. These new activist associations addressed the specific problems of the new urban teaching force. Since 1900, the growth of urban school systems had radically changed the nature of teaching from a small, community-based occupation to a standardized job in a large bureaucratic system. Haley had seen some of these developments in her own career at Hendricks School, including the decline of informal and local hiring practices and the increase of curricular and personnel regulations, teacher preparation requirements, and centralized administrative structures. Some of these changes had brought benefits to teachers, such as the pension and the salary scale, but in other ways, teachers' working conditions worsened under the intensified demands of the expanded curriculum, increasingly diverse student body, and complicated managerial structures. The question that drove all teacher politics in these years was how to respond to these changes: by trying to professionalize the occupation as had doctors and lawyers, or by aligning with labor unions.

Disagreements among teachers about the appropriate approach to take reflected other divisions within the occupation. The main division was between elementary and high school teachers. High schools, which were originally conceived as public colleges for the elite, had grown in number in the early twentieth century, but they still maintained their exceptional status, primarily because they serviced only a minority of students: In 1910, barely fourteen per cent of all fourteen- to seventeen-year-olds were enrolled in high school.[11] High school and elementary teachers had significantly different training, and status, and in many districts high school teachers earned almost twice what elementary teachers earned.[12] Required to hold a college degree, high school teachers tended to come from a higher class background than elementary teachers. Although originally most high school teachers were men, as more girls entered the public high schools as students, women were hired, making high school teaching an unusually gender-mixed occupation as opposed to the predominantly female elementary teaching staff. The day-to-day working experience of elementary and secondary teachers differed too: High school teachers taught and were identified by their specific subject and department area, while elementary teachers were generalists. Elementary teachers in Chicago were keenly aware of these distinctions: From its founding date, the Federation represented and lobbied for only elementary teachers. Secondary teachers proceeded to establish their own protective organizations: In 1912, a Federation of Men Teachers was formed, and two years later the Chicago Federation of Women High School Teachers was founded.

The difference between the Federation and the high school groups materialized in the next few years in the battle over salaries. High school teachers were paid on a different, and higher, salary schedule than were elementary teachers. In 1914, as Superintendent Ella Flagg Young had tried to negotiate a salary increase for all teachers, Haley promoted a single salary scale in which elementary and high school teachers would have identical starting salaries and raises. The high school teachers, not surprisingly, sought to maintain their traditionally higher salary scale, arguing that the advanced education required for their work should earn them more money. Although neither group earned a raise, the issue furthered the divisions between them.[13] Ironically, the Chicago Federation of Men Teachers was founded as a reaction to the board's threat to increase the discrepancy between men and women teachers' salaries. The men teachers objected, but not out of concern for the women: They believed that the result would be that men's jobs in high schools would be replaced with lower-paid women workers. To protect themselves, they formed their own association.[14]

But conflict existed not only between men and women teachers: women teachers were also divided among themselves by the class lines between elementary and secondary teaching. Women high school teachers had more education than elementary teachers and worked in environments where they were afforded more professional stature. They also tended to come from more diverse backgrounds than the primarily white Catholic elementary teachers corps, and had greater affiliation with activities outside of education, such as women's social settlement work and political organizations. For example, Lillian Herstein, a Jewish high school teacher, was a founder of the Farmer Labor party in Illinois, and Jennie Wilcox, who fought to equate women high school teachers' salary with men's, fought for industrial safety as a member of the Women's Trade Union League and the Consumer's League in Chicago.[15] Some white high school women developed connections with African American women teachers with whom they were more likely to teach in the new high schools. While elementary school staffs were increasingly racially segregated, by the 1920s some African American college graduates were hired to teach at Wendall Phillips and Du Sable High School, which were informally but effectively designated as the city's African American high schools. The Federation of Women High School Teachers was racially integrated from its founding in 1914, and the group's leader, Mary Herrick, was a white woman who taught social studies at Du Sable and actively recruited black women teachers.[16]

In contrast, Federation members tended to distrust movements that distracted from the cause of the economic improvement of elementary teachers who earned less than and seemed to work more than high school teachers. Elementary teachers were also not used to working with men, and they were mistrustful of men leaders. The fact that African American women high school teachers were college-educated women who earned double the salary of white women in the elementary schools did not appeal to Catholic elementary teachers who already held prejudiced views against black workers. Haley made little effort to recruit African American elementary teachers to the Federation.[17]

The Federation also faced competition from other women elementary teachers. For years the Federation had been shadowed by the Chicago Teachers' League, a smaller organization of about one thousand elementary teachers that regarded itself as a rival to the Federation. Membership in the League was open to any member of the school staff, including administrators, and its politics tended to be more in line with administrative policy. To make the League even more suspicious to Haley, the group consisted primarily of middle-

Margaret Haley, on telephone, 1922 (Courtesy Chicago Historical Society)

class Protestant teachers, many of whose experience was only in private schools, and who concentrated not on teachers' working conditions but on broader school improvement issues such as the development of kindergartens, parent-teacher organizations, school lunch programs, and guidance for delinquent girls. Their relationship with the opinionated and legalistic Haley was not an easy one. One Teachers' League member identified Haley's sister Jenny O'Reilley as a more likely ally to their group because, compared to her strong-headed elder sister, Jenny seemed more "sensible."[18] Haley herself rarely even stooped to acknowledge the League's existence, except to comment that its sole purpose was to destroy "the bona fide labor union of the teachers, namely the Chicago Teachers' Federation."[19]

By 1916, then, the Federation was not the only option in Chicago teacher politics. But Haley never tried to link her association with the others, or even to align their political stands. Fiercely independent and jealous of competition, Haley remained aloof from most other Chicago teachers until the founding of the AFT, and it is possible that she joined that group only because she thought that a larger, central organization could be a more effective way for her to influence competing organizations. Certainly the intensifying Loeb crisis also furthered her interest in a national union, if only to show to Loeb and his allies that teachers would organize in spite of him.

But if Haley believed that she could dominate the new group, she was soon to be disappointed. Competing for political leverage with the Chicago Federation was the New York City Teachers' League. Founded in 1913, the League was run by two male high school teachers, Henry R. Linville and Abraham Lefkowitz. The League, which changed its name to the Teachers' Union when it affiliated with the AFT in 1916, identified itself as a militant trade union with a political mandate to support teachers' academic freedom and political rights in the workplace. More aggressive and radical than the Chicago group, the League was popular among some of New York City's most public political figures: The educator John Dewey, now working at Columbia University, and the feminist writer Charlotte Perkins Gilman spoke at the founding meeting in February 1913. But however notorious among political activists, the Teachers' League never attracted more than 5 percent of New York City teachers into its membership ranks. Radicalism, a leadership drawn from male high school teachers and university professors, and the predominant number of Jewish teachers in the League alienated the more conservative, Catholic, female elementary school teachers who still dominated the ranks in New York.[20]

These same dynamics set up a barrier between Haley and the New York group. Haley's emphasis on local and state initiatives and her commitment to specific improvements in teachers' working conditions were not shared by the New York League. Where the New York group offered a direct challenge to the established political system, Haley's Federation had a record of reforming the educational and political structure through persistent legislative work.

Yet another variable discouraged any matchmaking attempt between Haley and the New York Teachers' League. One of the central planks of the newly emerging national group was the abolition of political influence in schools. Of course, Haley had fought relentlessly against the role of business, the upper class, and other commercial and political interests in the management of the school system. Yet by the late teens, the Federation held such a powerful public presence in Chicago that its enemies could turn and accuse Haley and the Federation itself of doing exactly that: of being insiders, "boodlers," and political power brokers in city government. The rise of other organized teachers' groups and the Federation's growing distance from them furthered the impression that the Federation was an entrenched "insider" that stood in opposition to progressive reforms. Margaret Haley, now in her mid-fiftys, and increasingly marginalized by her younger cohorts, was a perfect setup for that role.

The shape that the new AFT would take was confirmed with the election of the new president at the founding meeting in April 1916. Ida Fursman, president of the Federation, submitted Haley's name to the nominating committee, assuming that Haley's national reputation would make her the logical choice. But the committee disagreed and chose Charles

Stillman, a high school teacher from the Chicago Federation of Men Teachers. The choice of a male high school teacher from Chicago instead of Haley made a powerful statement that the new organization would not be a replica of the Federation. The high school teachers tried to explain that their choice was not because of a lack of appreciation for Haley's work, "but rather because of the differences over the scope of the national organization," by which they meant Haley's tradition of supporting local organizing.[21]

But personality conflicts also surely played a part in the decision. Haley's own strong character and her distrust of high school teachers and administrators made her no easy comrade for the new locals. Further, Haley's sense of proprietary control over teacher politics, and her sixteen years in the limelight of national education news, must have made her an intimidating force to newcomers. The absence of the politically savvy Goggin must only have furthered the division in the new AFT, in spite of the cordial relations between other Federation members, especially Ida Fursman, with the AFT leadership.

Haley had good reason to be insulted by her rejection. Not only did the Federation membership of more than 1,600 dwarf the smaller locals—the Federation of Men Teachers had 195 members, and the Federation of Women High School Teachers had ninety three—but it had been in existence much longer than any other organization, and had been sending some thirty-five delegates to the Chicago Federation of Labor meetings for more than ten years. Worse, the AFT dues structure required each member to pay a penny per month, and this meant that the Federation was paying over one-half the dues of the new organization. The Federation was already burdened with fees from battling the Loeb ruling in court, and it was all but broke. Relations only worsened when the Federation faced a new attack from the Loeb forces later that spring.

THE DRED SCOTT DECISION OF EDUCATION

Although the Loeb ruling that prohibited teachers from membership in any labor unions or associations affiliated with a labor union had been thrown out of court in the fall of 1915, the board of education devised a way to effectively accomplish the ruling's objectives. Their actions were eased by the passivity of the newly appointed superintendent, John Shoop, who had replaced Ella Flagg Young. Rather than attempt a new bill to prohibit unionization, the board found a way to rewrite the 1895 law that provided teachers with job security. The revision essentially dismantled tenure by authorizing the board to hire teachers only on annual contracts. Accordingly, in June 1916, the board simply denied reappointment to sixty-five teachers, thirty-eight of whom had been or were still officers of the Federation. Those fired included Ida Fursmann, president of the Federation, the five main officers, and two members of the teachers' pension committee. Haley's sister Eliza was among the fired. All the Federation teachers had been rated good or above by their superiors.[22] Furthering the distance between the secondary and elementary teachers was the fact that only one of those fired was a high school teacher. The high school teachers promised to help the Federation raise money to support the cause, but the burden of the case still rested on the Federation and elementary teachers.[23]

The progressive community organized on behalf of the teachers. On June 17, a mass meeting was held in Chicago Auditorium to protest both the board's new policy and the firing of the teachers. The settlement worker Mary McDowell chaired the meeting, and speakers included Jane Addams, John Fitzpatrick, and other city reformers.[24] At the regular meeting of the CFL on July 2, Margaret Dreier Robins from the Women's Trade Union League harshly condemned the board's actions and two male labor delegates spoke for the teachers, after which Haley took the stand to thunderous applause. She praised the fired teachers, condemned her old enemies Loeb and Rothman, and told the group that it was good that some newspapers had published the high efficiency markings of many of the teachers who were fired because "if they shoot down our officers they must shoot down the efficient ones and not the weaklings."[25] In a grand finale to this passionate gathering, the elderly and beloved radical activist Mother Jones entered the hall to great applause.

The Federation filed suit against the board over the firings. The battle ended badly for the teachers one year later with a court decision on April 19, 1917—which Haley ironically noted as the anniversary of the first battle of the war for American independence in Concord and Lexington in 1775. Ella Flagg Young drew on a different image from American history when she called the court ruling the "Dred Scott Decision of Education," referring to the 1857 Supreme Court decision that African Americans could not be citizens. In the decision, the State Supreme Court of Illinois held that the board of education was free to elect any teachers by any means it chose. Haley sardonically commented that this decision legally allowed boards of education all over the state to refuse to appoint anyone except "blue-eyed teachers or red-haired teachers or tall teachers or short teachers or thin teachers or stout teachers or spectacled teachers or Ziegfield chorus girls. If any board of education in the state wanted torch singers instead of educators, it was at liberty to have them." The court also affirmed the ruling that teachers could be hired on an annual contract, thereby voiding the tenure provisions that Chicago teachers had enjoyed for the previous twenty-two years. This meant that when teachers left their classrooms in June, they were officially unemployed until the board sent them a reappointment letter. Haley, who had seen a lot of court decisions go against the teachers in her time, called this one "the most devilish, dastardly, and devastating opinion ever leveled against American public school education."[26]

But in fact the effect of the court decision was muted because at the same time the legislature passed the Otis Law, which gave Chicago teachers tenure after three years and a legal process for dismissal. Ralph Otis, the sponsor of the bill, was a school board member who had voted for the Loeb ruling, but later regretted it after the firing of the teachers. He proposed a compromise measure that promised administrative efficiency and centralization on one side, and protections for the teachers on the other. Under the law, the board of education was reduced in size and the superintendent's power was enhanced—two provisions which the Federation had opposed for over a dozen years. The teachers compromised on these issues because the law provided job security. Employing an uncharacteristic tact, Haley kept a low profile in the lobbying process for the Otis bill in Springfield, recognizing that her public support might mean its death knell. According to Chester Dodge, then head of the Chicago Principals' Club, which actively lobbied for the bill, the Speaker of the House was particularly peeved at Haley for coming down to his district and lobbying to defeat him in a prior election. The speaker drilled Dodge on whether or not Haley supported the Otis bill, because "if so, I'm against it." Dodge kept quiet on the subject and other teacher advocates carefully avoided Haley's name and references to the Federation. Haley attended the hearings, but sat silent, taking on the role of the interested reformer—a sharp contrast to the bullying image that had prevailed in the papers in recent months.[27]

For all that the teachers gained with the Otis Law, it still did not overturn the board's right to dismiss teachers who were members of unions, and in May 1917 the Federation, beaten and battered by the two-year-long battle, withdrew from the Chicago Federation of Labor, the Illinois State Federation of Labor, the American Federation of Teachers, and the Women's Trade Union League. The fired teachers were rehired the next month. Federation leadership had already expressed interest in the separation, noting that the sixty eight teachers had suffered enough, and that the majority of the teachers were eager to make the break as well. Indeed, many of the women elementary teachers who were committed Federation members drew a line at the contentious and public political controversy that had left the organization almost bankrupt. The Federation needed to compromise, counseled some of its leadership, or else lose a majority of its membership and financial support. The writing was on the wall: Between 1915 and 1917 Federation membership halved. Under repeated attacks, Haley may have felt that she did not have a choice about cutting the relationship between the teachers and labor; she may have seen disaffiliation as a compromise that would allow the Federation to dig itself out of the political disaster caused by the Loeb Rule.[28]

Haley's withdrawal of the Federation from the CFL indicated her recognition of the changing political playing field. After fifteen years of trying to make the marriage with labor work, she had reasons to suspect that a separation was inevitable. Many women teachers were still wary of their allegiance with male-dominated labor, and in the years since 1902, competing and more conservative teachers' associations had been formed. Furthermore, the Federation's local battles for municipal and school reform had never received full support from the AFL. Although Haley intended to keep the teachers closely aligned with labor after 1917, there was in fact a gradual distancing of the Federation from other elements of organized labor.

Most significantly, the separation of the Federation from the AFT furthered its distance from the high school groups which, with the selection of Stillman as AFT president, had already made implicit their own opinion about Margaret Haley. Haley did not attend the first AFT meeting in New York City in the summer of 1916, and she and Stillman agreed that the Federation's *Bulletin* would continue to cover Federation news while the new AFT publication *The American Teacher* would cover all other AFT reports. This meant that the September publication of *The American Teacher* included articles by John Dewey, Charles Stillman, and two New York City principals who were members of the AFT and none by Federation members.[29] Even a short article on the dismissal of the Chicago teachers referred only to the support that the men and women high school teachers would give the fired Federation members. In the next issue, essays by Ella Flagg Young and Ida Fursman were included, but in what could only be seen as a slam to Haley, an announcement entitled "What Federation Means to Chicago Teachers" directed the reader to contact the Federation of Men Teachers and the Federation of Women High School Teachers, and not Haley's Federation. From its initial publication, then, *The American Teacher* contained no Federation news, symbolizing the increasingly isolated political pathway of the Teachers' Federation.

Along with her ongoing suspicions of men labor leaders and high school teachers, Haley ultimately doubted the wisdom of a national organization that would surpass local authority. The power of local politics was both Haley's strength and weakness. She was adept at organizing a homogenous group of women elementary teachers in cities across the country and knitting them together into a single-purpose cause. Her charismatic leadership inspired women teachers around the nation to take their first political stand. But she lost her footing when she had to engage activists with established agendas and different tactics. Ultimately, she was not able to see beyond the Federation as the template for all teacher organizations. Haley's peers recognized her limitations all too well. Freeland Strecker, one of the founding AFT members from the Federation of Men Teachers, believed that for Haley "every problem was one of local solution, that Chicago was the testing ground, and that little could be gained by nation-wide organization."[30]

WAR

Haley wrote in her autobiography that the American entrance into World War I "accomplished what Jacob Loeb and William Rothman had not been able to do": It finalized the Federation's separation from organized labor.[31] Haley already had some interest in the emerging pacifist movement; in 1914, she met with a coalition of Chicago women activists and Jane Addams to found an Emergency Peace Committee, and although she did not maintain much contact with the peace movement afterward, her lifelong support of Ireland's nationalistic cause kept her attuned to international affairs in Europe.[32] One of her suspicions about the AFL head, English-born Samuel Gompers, was his interest in war. The British intensification of their control over Ireland made American Irish Catholics especially loath to support British military endeavors, particularly after the harsh repression of the Irish rebellion in Dublin during Easter week of April 1916, when British forces executed rebel leaders. One of those executed was the Irish patriot and educator Padraic Pearse, founder of St. Enda's School outside of Dublin. Pearse established St. Enda's in 1908 as a nationalist school that taught the Gaelic language and Irish politics, literature, and folklore. In her autobiography, Haley claimed that she met Pearse at the door of the school, and heard him say prophetically, "I hope that I may die some day for Ireland."[33] In fact, it is unclear when, or if, she met him on a trip she might have taken to Ireland or during his one trip to the United States in the spring of 1914 when he toured the East Coast raising funds for his school. No documentation exists to confirm either possibility, and it is very likely that in her zeal to write a dramatic life story, Haley drew on her father's legacy of creative story-telling and simply invented her meeting with Pearse. There was good reason for her to spin such a connection. The two shared ideas about education as a social and political force in a democracy, and Pearse drew on Francis Parker in his school philosophy.[34] Haley's reference to him made public her commitment to Irish nationalism and to her own version of education for democratic rights. In terms of the impending war, the execution of Pearse by British forces would certainly not have endeared Haley to any British cause.

So when Charles Stillman, the newly elected president of the AFT, attended an AFL conference in April 1917 to discuss American involvement in the war, Haley was appalled. According to Haley, the AFL's alignment with the federal government's war effort without consulting their members led to a great sense of betrayal within the labor movement at large, including the teachers.

The war had other effects that worked against the teachers. Haley saw many of the great liberal measures that had been promoted by progressives in the first two decades of the twentieth century "swept away by the mighty flood of conflict."[35] During the war, labor shortage brought a great surge in labor activism. In 1919 alone, four million workers, or one-fifth of the nation's work force, held labor strikes, and alternative political parties such as the Socialist Party and the Labor Party gained in strength. Between 1919 and 1920, more than 143 local teachers' unions were organized.[36] But the Left was quickly undercut by a combination of mediation and repression. Through the late teens and early 1920s, business and government developed alliances with labor by offering certain protections and benefits in exchange for a compromised peace. The lesson learned by management was that high pay and other benefits would effectively silence labor radicals. For those who were not appeased, there were harsher means. Under the 1917 Espionage Act and the 1918 Sedition Act, the government was given a wide latitude on the persecution of political dissenters, including pacifists, socialists, and labor activists. The prosecution of radicals under Attorney General A. Mitchell Palmer's notorious "Red Scare" saw thousands of activists arrested, deported, and imprisoned. Supporters of the government founded "100% American-ism" groups that furthered the intimidation of dissenters. The pressure ex-tended into schools, where thousands of teachers were suspended or dismissed for not signing school loyalty codes, for teaching pacifism or alternative ideas about the war or the government, or for not showing adequate patriotism.[37]

Economic stress accompanied political stress. Wartime inflation increased the cost of living 100 percent, but between 1914 and 1919, American teachers' salaries rose only 16 percent.[38] A 1918 government report showed the average American teacher's salary was less than that of an average scrubwoman, street cleaner, or garbage man.[39] Between the financial losses and political restraints occasioned by the war, teaching lost much of its appeal, and at the dawn of the 1920s, American schools faced a national teacher shortage. Four hundred and sixty Chicago teachers quit their jobs in 1919—more than double the highest previous record. That year, the Federation sent out a flyer with a poem titled "Why is There Unrest Among the Teachers?"

> The Teachers of Chicago are flitting
> Not waiting around and just sitting
> Til a strike is here—
> Oh! no, no, my dear
> Not striking, but just merely quitting.[40]

Haley saw not only liberal legislation, but "the spirit of liberalism" destroyed by the war.[41] Antilabor sentiment undercut CFL leader John Fitzpatrick's bid for Chicago mayor on the Labor Party ticket in 1919. The Labor Party, fulfilling Haley's long-held dream of a legitimate political party for labor interests, supported equal rights for men and women, public own-ership of utilities and nationalization of natural resources, and the abolition of "Kaiserism" in education. For Haley, the Labor Party was a last best hope for broad, political labor action, especially in the place of her own lost attempts at unity with the CFL and within the new AFT. Fitzpatrick and the Labor Party's failure in 1919, and again in 1923, further confirmed the de-mise of labor's unification.[42] When the Illinois Equal Suffrage Association denied a representative of the Labor Party the opportunity to speak at the state convention in October 1920, Haley experienced another painful gap in her vision of unity.[43]

The war killed more than political movements and military soldiers. In a seven-month period in 1918, more than a half-million Americans died in a massive influenza epidemic. Over 8,500 died in Chicago alone.[44] Haley's long-time friend and ally Ella Flagg Young was one of its victims; she died in late October 1918 at age seventy three. Since her retirement from the Chicago superintendency in 1915, Young had remained prominent in the news, traveling the nation as a representative of the wartime Women's Liberty Loan Committee. She had attended and spoken at the NEA meeting in Pittsburgh that summer, and only a week before her death, she spoke at a gathering at the Auditorium in Chicago.[45]

Even in death, Young inspired her followers. After her funeral, some teachers went to the cemetery and found a huge wreath that had been sent from Jacob Loeb resting on Young's gravesite. Indignant, one teacher snatched the wreath from the grave and put it on another, saying that Ella Flagg Young could not rest in peace under those flowers. Another teacher saw that her colleague had placed the wreath on a headstone that bore an Irish name, and she picked up the wreath and moved it again, saying, "No Irishman could lie under that." Haley reflected on Young "as a symbol for the time through which she had lived, a woman of genuine greatness, of magnificent vision, of tremendous accomplishment. She had been the old America marching onward in hope, in courage, in clarity of vision. Now she was dead."[46] Haley might as well have been speaking of the teachers' movement that she, Young, and Goggin had once shared and led, and that itself seemed to be on the decline.

STEAMROLLER

There was yet another loss. Although Haley was uneasy about a national movement within the AFT, she had continued her connection to the National Education Association, focusing on improving the opportunities for teacher representation within the organization. Although preoccupied with Chicago business most of the time, she was active in the creation of the National Federation of Teachers in 1902 and the Department of Classroom Teachers in 1912 both of which were attempts to increase the representation of teachers—especially women elementary teachers—within the NEA. And the women had made significant gains: They won the election of Ella Flagg Young as the first woman president of the NEA in 1910; in 1912 they successfully lobbied the NEA to endorse women's suffrage; and in 1915 they enacted a policy of alternating male and female presidents of the organization.[47]

The teachers' new political power presented a great threat to the NEA, not only to its older, male members who still believed in the original purpose of the organization as a professional association for men school and university administrators, but also to the very idea of teacher professionalism. The women teachers' continued emphasis on material concerns challenged the NEA leaderships' vision of education as a respectable profession, not a militant labor group. Reformers within the NEA identified the problem as an organizational one: Teachers felt that their concerns were not legitimately represented within the association and as a result they were forced to create the Department of Classroom Teachers or worse, labor unions such as the AFT. Teachers had essentially been driven to radical means because the NEA had not sufficiently addressed teachers' material and professional needs in one body. The solution, first introduced at the 1913 NEA meeting by Teachers College professor Henry Suzallo, was a revised organizational structure that would address teachers' economic and material needs *and* educational and professional issues The new NEA would be neither a self-interested union nor an academic group that discussed educational theory, but both merged together. Suzallo proposed restructuring the organization so that local teachers' groups would be better connected with state and national bodies through an elected delegate system of representation. With this structure, all local teachers would have a vote through their elected representative on the NEA floor. Teachers' concerns would be heard not through the haphazard packing of the NEA floor once a year, but through delegates and committee processes. In this way, the NEA would become a more streamlined and stable organization that could systematically address current educational issues.[48]

Haley adamantly opposed the reform and she urged her sister activists in other associations to oppose it as well. For years, Haley had supported the development of women teachers' associations in other cities. She nurtured the leadership of other women activists such as Florence Rood of the Grade Teachers' Association in St. Paul and Ethel Gardner of the Milwaukee Teachers' Association, both of whom became good friends and political allies over the years.[49] Haley and her peers saw that the NEA reorganization was designed specifically to marginalize these independent city organizations led by women elementary teachers by funneling teachers' concerns into NEA affiliated-state organizations which, like the national NEA group, were traditionally controlled by male administrators.

The reorganization was first proposed at the 1919 meeting in Milwaukee, but a large body of teachers from the Milwaukee, St. Paul, and Chicago Federations opposed it from the floor. Frustrated by these tactics, the NEA leaders intentionally chose Salt Lake City for the site of the 1920 meeting because it was remote enough to keep the bulk of midwestern and eastern city teachers from attending, and because the Utah teachers' association was notably conservative.[50] Ironically, the leaders figured they could use their own version of local control to eliminate teachers' local control in the future. Having packed the Salt Lake City meeting with their own supporters, the NEA leadership refused to recognize Haley from the floor, and the proposal for reorganization won.

For Haley, the meeting in Salt Lake City was both a literal disaster and a symbolic victory. The reorganization vote was essentially a vote on whether the NEA would intentionally disassociate from the local teacher-centered activist format represented by the Federation and the larger AFT. Her cause was hopeless from the beginning: Fewer than 1 percent of all NEA members were affiliated with the AFT, and most of those were from Chicago and Milwaukee.[51] Furthermore, the notorious failure of the policeman's strike in Boston the year before had affirmed the message that public sector employees should not unionize, and administrators repeated this theme throughout the meeting.[52] So adamant was the NEA leadership in forcing through the reorganization and silencing Haley that observers referred to the meeting as a "steam roller." One attendee mocked the powerful male leaders for being so "scared to a panic" by the little woman whom they seemed to see as nothing less than a "Holy Terror." The NEA leaders even winced when Haley submitted a general resolution supporting teaching tenure that was assured unanimous support. Haley characteristically used their response to her benefit by publicly mocking their paranoia when she asked the crowd if the NEA leaders would be suspicious if she offered them the Lord's Prayer as a resolution.[53] Even a self-identified opponent of Haley's, Annie Webb Blanton, a state superintendent in Texas, wrote her a personal letter admiring her skills in such a tense political situation.[54]

With the passage of the reorganization, it appeared that Haley would never return to the NEA, a prospect that made one member wonder: "What can we do now that we'll not have Margaret Haley to scare us?"[55] This was, in fact, wishful thinking, as Haley remained a presence in national meetings over subsequent years, repeatedly badgering the NEA leadership for recognition, and turning her questions into miniature speeches about the Chicago teachers' situation. At the 1922 meeting in Boston, for example, Haley led a move to reorganize the Department of Classroom Teachers to regain constitutional authority within the NEA and elect Ethel Gardner from Milwaukee as president. Haley debated procedural processes from the floor, arguing that the meeting was illegal because it was run by the incoming NEA president who as of yet had no authority. She lost both her case and Gardner's election. The incident was referred to in the *School Board Journal* as "the only rift in the harmony" in the meeting.[56] Such behavior only furthered Haley's already waning popularity. Women and men organizers in the expanding NEA saw her as an obnoxious gadfly who stood in the face of progress. Indeed, the NEA that developed in the 1920s *was* notably more progressive and attentive to the needs of teachers. The newly appointed full-time secretary of the organization, J. W. Crabtree, hired women staff to promote NEA membership among women teachers, and he developed a research bureau that conducted national studies of teachers' salaries and working conditions. With this new commitment to make the NEA "the instrument of the teachers of the nation," Crabtree criticized Haley's "political manipulations" of a small circle of teachers, "who have never done anything whatever for the Association except to seek to use it for selfish ends."[57] Haley stayed aloof from the women activists in the NEA, including Field Secretary Charl Williams, who developed networks between teachers, social reform organizations, and the federal government. To these educators, who saw value in the newly professionalized and energized NEA, Haley's critiques made her simply a "chronic obstructionist."[58]

Haley's vision of unity was, ironically, hers alone. The newly reorganized and empowered AFT and NEA did not fit with her vision, in part because they did not put her at the center, and this objection raised Haley's least admirable personal qualities, thus furthering the division between the Federation and other teacher organizations. Yet however imperious her responses, Haley's fear of a loss of focus on local teachers' material needs was legitimate. As the new NEA and AFT grew into large, national organizations, they lost the spit and vinegar of local organizing, including the late-night envelope stuffing, rousing speeches in union halls, and intense lobbying of local legislatures. This was the price of national recognition: more widespread power meant more compromise, and Haley hated that.

CHAPTER EIGHT

SIEGE

MARGARET HALEY WROTE IN HER autobiography that the story of Chicago schools through "the torrential Twenties and the troubled Thirties" was the story of a siege. She believed that the world war had changed the essential purpose of schooling by replacing the progressive movement for academic freedom with an ever more increased emphasis on business objectives. Outside of schools, too, the postwar period saw the repression of labor unions and radical movements, and the exchange of social welfare initiatives for the dominant creed of the 1920s: that the business of America was business. As teachers fought the changes, Haley recalled, Chicago schools came to be a battlefield for the warring factions of public welfare and private interests.[1] What Haley was more likely to ignore in her rampage against the enemy in these years was that the Federation was also beset by internal conflict as allies turned on one another, and Haley herself furthered the disunity.

The Federation's politics of the 1920s were deeply entwined with the complicated and dramatic political maneuverings of the board of education, superintendent, and Chicago mayors of the decade, especially the notorious political operator William Hale Thompson whose first terms as mayor ran from 1915 and 1923. Mayor "Big Bill" Thompson's disdainful attitude toward public schools was epitomized in his recounting of his experience as a student at the school where Ella Flagg Young was principal. According to this apocryphal tale, he came to school one morning and found some of the smaller boys playing marbles on the school grounds. As he watched, a big bully came up to the group and stole the marbles. Young Thompson was offended and challenged the bully to a fight, which Thompson won. The little boys got back their marbles but the bully ran to Principal Young and tattled on his opponent. Mrs. Young, without even talking to Thompson, sent him home to his parents as punishment for starting a fight. Insulted at the injustice, Thompson refused to go to school again. Out of this experience, Mayor Thompson zealously supported the building of more public playgrounds, and he just as zealously mistrusted the word or intentions of schoolteachers and principals.[2] Beyond his disdainful approach to education, Thompson's two decades of political leadership in Chicago were marked by unprecedented scandal. The Chicago *Tribune* encapsulated in no uncertain terms that Thompson's three terms as mayor were distinguished by "filth, corruption, obscenity, idiocy, and bankruptcy. He has given the city an international reputation for moronic buffoonery, barbaric crime, triumphant hoodlumism, unchecked graft, and a dejected citizenship. . . . He made Chicago a byword of the collapse of American civilization."[3]

There were more specific reasons why Haley did not like Thompson. He supported Jacob Loeb, opposed the right of city employees to unionize, and he made it no secret that one of his goals as mayor was to "get rid of the army of catholic school teachers" and to shut down the Chicago Teachers' Federation and Margaret Haley.[4] On the other hand, Thompson was a dynamic political presence and an opportunist, and when he swung around to be on Haley's side, she just as opportunely aligned herself with him. Indeed, Haley's relationship with Thompson in these years reflected both her own strengths and weaknesses as a political leader: She was so staunchly committed to teachers that, like Thompson, she switched allegiances to develop stronger allies. Her hubris in believing that she could do righteously what she criticized others for doing furthered public dissatisfaction with her leadership.

BIG BILL THOMPSON

City reformers had seen the passage of the Otis Law of 1917 as the beginning of the end of political patronage and corruption in the city school system. The bill's authorization of teacher tenure, a four-year term for the superintendent, a leaner school board, and clarified responsibilities for the mayor in school affairs, promised not only efficiency but also improved working relations between teachers and administrators. All educational and civic groups, including the Federation, had approved the bill, a circumstance that heralded a new era of collaboration. Mayor Thompson himself assured school reformers and other civic organizations that they would be consulted on all his major educational decisions. But after the initial enthusiasm invoked by passage of the Otis Law, reformers saw that Chicago education retained its deeply political character. Thompson used the law to increase his power over the board. His dominance was furthered by the weak leadership of Superintendent John Shoop, who had been appointed after the resignation of Ella Flagg Young in 1916 and who was ill for most of his three years of service.[5]

Thompson made a flamboyant debut into educational politics. In May 1917, barely a month after the Otis bill became law, he appointed a new board of education without consulting any educational or civic groups. The city council did not approve the appointments and the previous board sued to be reinstated. Through 1918 and 1919 the two boards wrangled with each other and with the mayor in court. In the midst of the chaos, Superintendent Shoop died, and a search committee recommended the hiring of Charles E. Chadsey, the

(Courtesy Chicago Historical Society)

school superintendent of Detroit. But Thompson disapproved of the committee's choice and when Chadsey arrived at work in March 1919, he faced opposition from the mayor, who had reconstructed the board of education yet again, hired a different superintendent, and locked Chadsey out of his office by order of the

(Courtesy Chicago Historical Society)

city police. Thompson initiated his 1919 mayoral campaign with the promise to "kick Chadsey out," for no reason except that he had not appointed him. Chadsey was reinstated by the courts but was stripped of his duties and powers by Thompson's board. Chadsey finally gave up and resigned in disgust, but not before he took the matter to court and had six members of the

Salary Number

Margaret Haley's
Weekly Bulletin

VOL. II.   CHICAGO, ILL, APRIL 16, 1925   No. 2

When a Feller Needs a Friend
With apologies to Briggs

Class Room Teacher: "Oh, Santa Claus, don't I get my maximum, too?"
Santa Claus: "No, little girl, there are too many of you!"

(Courtesy Chicago Historical Society)

board and the board attorney given five-day jail sentences. In the middle of this fantastic series of events, Jacob Loeb, whom Thompson had appointed to his board, turned on his patron and defended Chadsey's case.[6]

Thompson's choice as superintendent was Peter Mortenson, who tried to pour oil on the waters and win over the teachers by reviving the teacher councils—the representative body that Ella Flagg Young had introduced during her tenure as superintendent but which had since lapsed. Mortenson expanded the

(Courtesy Chicago Historical Society)

councils to the high schools and reinstituted Young's provisions that the councils meet on school time and that the superintendent meet regularly with the general council. During Mortenson's five years as superintendent, the teachers used the councils to articulate a host of problems in schools, and they made requests for teachers' participation in choosing textbooks, for more clerical help, and for increased salaries. To the councils, the superintendent promised more textbooks, electric lighting in all schools, and improvements in teacher education. By early 1923, when Mortenson announced his resignation, he had won the support and praise of the teachers.[7]

However popular he was with teachers, Mortenson's tenure was marred by myriad charges of corruption. Under his tenure, board members were accused of illegally selling school lands, purchasing unneeded supplies at quadruple their cost, stealing school furniture, and bribing school janitors by raising their salaries. In one year alone, 1921, the board spent more than $8 million in the category of "incidentals."[8] The situation became a public scandal and in May 1922, civic groups demanded an investigation. Members of the board of education were brought before a grand jury on the charge of conspiracy. The Federation lawyer, Isaiah Greenacre, was appointed assistant state's attorney for the case against the board, and he discovered a slush fund gathered by engineers of the public schools for distribution to certain members of the board. The money had been delivered to the board members during what was purported to be the awarding of a silver tea service to a board member. Stuffed inside the teapot was the cash. In August 1922, the Thompson board was indicted; ultimately, the board attorney was sentenced to prison and others were indicted for defrauding the schools of more than a million dollars. In disgrace, Mayor Thompson said that he would not run for reelection in the 1923 election, and superintendent Mortenson resigned.[9]

Even without such activities, Chicago schools faced enormous pressures in the years after the war. Enrollment shot up between 1915 and 1925, a result of the 21 percent growth in the city's population, the enforcement of child labor laws, and the expansion of high schools. By 1929, Chicago housed the second-largest school system in the country, and the schools employed nearly twelve thousand teachers in an array of technical and night schools, elementary and high schools, and schools for children with disabilities.[10] The inadequate funding of schools that had always plagued Chicago's schools was exacerbated by wartime inflation.

Elementary teachers claimed that the strains of postwar schooling affected them most. In teacher council meetings across the city, elementary teachers levied consistent complaints about their overcrowded schools, low salaries, and multiplicity of tasks. Elementary teachers faced up to fifty children in a classroom, and children came with a variety of abilities and skills, and from a variety of linguistic and cultural backgrounds. Unlike high school teachers, who focused on their specialty subject area, elementary teachers juggled a variety of subject topics, often with out-of-date books and with no free class period to prepare. They also repeatedly described the lack of respect they faced in their buildings, and they often referred resentfully to high school teachers who had less students but were paid more and received higher status and social authority than they did. Elementary teachers, declared the council from one school in 1921, "find ourselves occupying the lowest place in the educational system."[11] Teachers in another council made

a resolution "deploring the low status of the elementary teacher" and requested of the superintendent that

> [i]n order to minimize as far as possible, the assumption on the part
> of certain principals that that office carries with it the right to be an
> autocrat, a boss, or a czar, instead of leaders in educational ideals, and
> to end the abuses of authority on the part of such principals by super-
> imposing upon teachers methods of instruction which time and expe-
> rience have proven fallacious and inefficient, and by impairing the
> efficiency of the teachers by creating conditions detrimental to proper
> discipline and by crushing all initiative on the part of the teachers,
> reducing her to a human machine, the Council voted unanimously in
> favor of a resolution giving teachers a right to be heard in the edu-
> cational and administrative policies of the school.[12]

Haley was furious to hear such reports from her constituents. After twenty
years of fighting to improve elementary teachers' status, by the mid-1920s
they appeared to be as underappreciated and overworked as ever. That high
school teachers did not suffer as harsh a fate made the Federation's cause
even more desperate. As elementary teachers came to her complaining of
overcrowded classrooms, increasing discipline problems, the hiring of untrained substitutes instead of qualified teachers, and intensified workloads,
the sixty-year-old Haley told her teachers: "I am crazy to roll up my sleeves
for this fight."[13]

CARPETBAGGER

William Dever succeeded Thompson as mayor, and he immediately identified a candidate for the superintendency who would restore the public faith
in schools and appeal to teachers and reformers. On first glance, he seemed
to have succeeded. William McAndrew had a Ph.D. from the University of
Michigan and was a former teacher and administrator in the Hyde Park
community in Chicago. In 1889 he had been dismissed as principal of the
Hyde Park High School because of a dispute with board members, which he
described as his refusal to alter the grades and diploma of the son of a
textbook company executive. He then moved to Michigan where he took a
small town superintendency and then to New York City where he was a high
school principal and then associate superintendent. Like Ella Flagg Young,
McAndrew was able to maintain his sympathy with teachers for much of his
administrative career, joining a teachers' rally in Boston in 1903 to criticize
"woodenhead administrators who paid teachers next to nothing."[14] McAndrew
was part of the founding organization of the AFT in 1916 and had stood on
the stage with John Dewey and Ella Flagg Young supporting teachers' right
to organize.

Although in her autobiography she claimed she never trusted him, Haley was actually a longtime friend and admirer of the sixty-year-old McAndrew, and she publicly welcomed him back to Chicago. The two had known each other since 1902 when McAndrew spoke at a special Federation meeting on the subject of "The Wages of Teachers," where he argued strenuously for a salary increase for teachers.[15] In 1905, he had worked on an NEA salary committee with Catherine Goggin, and he and Haley had corresponded on various political issues over the years. The two had an affectionate and playful friendship. McAndrew liked to tease Haley, who he called "Lady Margaret" or "Professor," writing once that her recent interview with Chicago's Superintendent Shoop was "exceedingly hot stuff. Chicago is not likely to be at peace, educationally or politically, for several days."[16] Haley enjoyed his plays on words, recalling his comical reference to Jacob Loeb's board of education as the "Low-Ebb Board." McAndrew once told Haley that he never had an interest in being a superintendent—that he had never contracted the disease of "superintendentitis" as he put it—given the way that they were treated, even though they did earn "$16,896,943,980,000,000 a year."[17] In turn, upon his appointment as Chicago's school chief, Haley praised McAndrew as one of the foremost educators in the country. McAndrew was on record as supporting higher teachers' salaries and the right of teachers to unionize. A distinguished, experienced, and amiable man, McAndrew seemed like a good catch for Chicago's teachers. Haley never imagined how bitterly she would be disappointed.

Haley might have suspected that McAndrew would act differently as superintendent if she had paid closer attention to his thinking. Although McAndrew had always supported teachers' rights to organize in order to balance the authority of boards of education and politicians, he had also consistently upheld the right of school administrators to maintain authority in a school system. According to McAndrew, teachers needed better salaries and more opportunities to express themselves, but it was the ultimate task of the superintendent to establish economic efficiency in the school system. He also believed that poor teaching was not solely the result of poor working conditions, but also of irresponsible and lazy educators: Only when teachers broke away from professional "narrowness" would they also be able to break away from "harassment, poverty and discontent."[18] Nor was McAndrew's affinity for adopting business methods of organization to schools a secret: Only two years before he moved back to Chicago, he linked the role of school administrators to that of financiers, describing the superintendent's role as similar to "a captain of big business."[19]

McAndrew's concern for fiscal efficiency may have been less obvious in his role as administrator in New York, but given the extreme financial mismanagement and bitter political disagreements that he found in the Chicago school system, he decided to take a strong upper hand. McAndrew himself believed that he was brought to Chicago to loose the hold "that certain outside agencies and the city hall had on the school system."[20] He believed that Chicago had "an invisible empire" within the schools, "a weird system, a selfish system" that was a political machine as powerful as those of most corrupt governments. Included in his conception of the machine was the Chicago Teachers' Federation. It would have surprised and disheartened his old friend Margaret Haley if she knew that McAndrew felt that he had been brought to Chicago to "steamroller" the Chicago Teachers' Federation into submission.[21]

Haley never wrote about her disappointment of McAndrew. Indeed, in typical fashion, she later brusquely wrote him off as a "devil in the schools" who was hired merely because he would be subservient to business interests. In her autobiography, she described him as a "carpetbagger," referring to the derisive name for greedy northern whites who moved south after the Civil War to take advantage of the defeated southerners. A more emotionally sensitive person than Haley might have felt personal loss and resentment, or even an interest in understanding what made a person such as McAndrew tick. Haley channeled such emotions into rage. As with Goggin's death and her father's financial failures, she articulated her loss into trenchant political analysis.

McAndrew took up his job on February 1, 1924, and immediately instituted an administrative regime with a newly streamlined staff organization, close supervision of instruction, and opposition to political influence in schools. He also promoted the use of intelligence tests and a salary scale that favored school principals and high school teachers over elementary teachers. Enforcing rigor and efficiency in the work day, he adopted the slogan "every man on the job," reduced the number of holidays in schools, introduced time clocks for all employees, and enforced the use of objective tests in appraisal of the work of teachers and principals.[22] But his three most controversial moves were his promotion of the platoon plan and the junior high school and his abolition of the teacher councils.

Because it was originally conceived by the superintendent of schools in Gary, Indiana, platoon schooling was commonly referred to as "the Gary Plan." Platooning was a scheduling scheme that combined curricular and administrative reform by dividing up the school population into two groups, or platoons, of roughly equal size, with one group engaged half the day in traditional academic work in regular classrooms while the other group pursued creative or athletic work in the auditorium, workshops, and gymnasium. The results were both the doubling of student time in innovative classroom settings and the doubling of the number of students that could use a school building simultaneously, thus doubling the cost efficiency of the building. However much the plan impressed some school administrators, the platoon plan faced tremendous opposition: In New York City parents and educators were suspicious that the plan was merely a well-dressed way to economize on school funding and to funnel working-class children into inferior schools, and it was never fully introduced into New York or other cities.[23]

Not surprisingly, the platoon plan was also criticized by Chicago's teachers and organized labor as a scheme to reduce school costs while offering less to children, especially poor children.[24] In a series of protest meetings at schools, and at a mass meeting of four thousand teachers in October 1924, opponents made a direct link between McAndrew's proposals for platooning with increased economic class division. The Chicago Federation of Labor warned that platoon schools would be made over "into a replica of the Ford automobile plant, pouring little children into the hopper at one end and grinding them out at the other end as perfect parts of an industrial machine."[25]

Haley's critique of platoon schools echoed her commentary on other school reforms: she saw the initiative as an economic cost-saving device disguised as an educational improvement. For one thing, she argued, platoon schools were a pedagogical travesty. The entire school day was organized like a factory in short, disconnected periods that worked against children's natural learning process. Children moved from teacher to teacher, so that no single teacher was able to develop a full understanding of the child, and teachers themselves could see as many as four hundred pupils a day who rolled past them like widgets on an assembly line. Indeed, she asserted, the battle over platoon schools was itself "a deadly conflict between two hostile American institutions struggling for supremacy—the public school and the factory."[26] Rather than a curricular reform, Haley charged, platoon schools were simply a response to overcrowded schools, and they were a cheaper response than building the new schools needed for the great surge in school enrollments in the 1920s. Platoon schools addressed this problem by doubling the capacity of school buildings for minimal cost. Haley said this was "a cowardly, unintelligent, indefensible, misleading way of keeping from the public the fact that children's school opportunities are being limited."[27]

Haley also condemned the way in which the public was duped into thinking that something progressive was being done in platoon schools. She was increasingly frustrated by the absence of any public dialogue about school financing, management, and educational principles. "There is no intelligent, critical faculty developed in the people so they can detect any weakness in the school," she wrote in exasperation in 1923. Expanding Ella Flagg Young's diagnosis of "isolation in the schools," she argued that "the people are isolated from the schools and the schools are isolated from the activities of the community."[28] So too did people take for granted that there was no solution to the financial problems in schools, given that government officials refused to address the inequities of the tax system. Even more than during the first tax fight twenty years before, Haley interpreted the current political situation as one of government officials perverting public understanding of school finance in order to preserve economic inequities. Citizens believed that the only solution to poor school funding was to raise taxes, thereby increasing the burden on working people. But the real solution, Haley repeated, was to completely revise the tax codes. The current method of tax assessment was completely antiquated; it was "more useless and out of date than the tallow candle or the prairie schooner, in an age of automobiles and airplanes."[29] A revised tax assessment plan would both equalize the weight of taxation between businesses and individuals, and would abolish the graft and political pull that had so long dominated the taxation process.

McAndrew's proposal for junior high schools also came under attack by the Federation, especially when he explained his support as, first, a cost-saving measure, and second as a way to upgrade teachers in upper level elementary classrooms by requiring that they earn a college degree. This, the Federation saw immediately, was a way to both demean elementary school teachers and create more divisions within the teaching force. Because the junior high school would work as a shorter alternative to the four-year high school, Haley saw the proposal as a veiled attempt to reintroduce the Cooley vocational education plan, funneling working-class children into the more vocationally oriented junior high schools. Like the platoon plan, she believed that the junior high school proposal was designed "to industrialize the public schools."[30]

No move earned McAndrew more wrath from teachers than his abolition of the teacher councils. In March 1924, barely a month after he took office, the general council reported to him that it had discussed and unanimously disapproved of his proposed platoon system. The general council also requested more information about the junior high school proposal before they would decide on its value.[31] The superintendent responded by promptly abolishing the teacher councils. So extreme was his response that even McAndrew's supporters cautioned him to reconsider. Former superintendent Mortenson advised McAndrew to think of the councils less for what they discussed and more for "the spirit of harmony and cooperation induced."[32] The *Tribune*, which was usually highly critical of the Federation, warned McAndrew that "a conquered teaching force will be worse than useless."[33]

McAndrew didn't seem to care about these concerns. Indeed, his adamant refusal to compromise furthered a popular rumor that he had been hired by big business to silence teachers, cut expenses, and reduce the educational opportunities available to working people. His allegiance to business became more pronounced in his language as he touted phrases like "the purpose of a school system is not to please us who are in it, but as with all public service corporations, to satisfy the customers."[34] He promoted a "100% mastery" program under which students were drilled in basic skills until they reached "100% efficiency in reading, writing, and arithmetic."[35] When teachers complained that they needed more resources in schools if they were to improve their instruction, McAndrew scoffed at them.

Epitomizing McAndrew's style was his 1926 production of Chicago Citizen's Sampling Day of the Public Schools. The event took place in the Chicago Art Institute auditorium where an audience of three hundred school principals observed a group of randomly chosen Chicago eighth graders answer questions chosen by representatives of prominent social and business clubs. Over the course of two hours, students demonstrated knowledge in music and art appreciation, arithmetic, spelling, problem solving, and sewing (girls only). The object, according to the superintendent, was to show school principals what citizens expected of Chicago schoolchildren and to align student performance with those expectations. Superintendent McAndrew believed that this experience gave school administrators the opportunity to observe how "your human output meets requirements, proposed by your customers."[36]

McAndrew later made the poor decision to invite John Fitzpatrick, the longtime president of the Chicago Federation of Labor, to participate in a follow-up Sample Day. "You are a stockholder in the public schools," the school superintendent wrote the labor leader, and "the output should be brought up to your requirements." McAndrew explained that the next Sampling Day would include a slide show presentation at which students would have to identify historical figures such as George Washington, Florence Nightingale, Rutherford B. Hayes, Louis Pasteur, and Samuel Gompers. Fitzpatrick wrote back and dryly suggested a modification to the test that would include slides of a picture of the *Daily News* and the *Tribune* and asking students how much money the school system had lost because these newspapers had rented school lands at below market cost. Fitzpatrick also suggested that a picture of former superintendent Ella Flagg Young be accompanied by a question why her representative teacher councils were abolished by the present superintendent, and that a picture of a new junior high school be aligned with a question about whether the school board ever took seriously the Chicago Federation of Labor's critique of these schools as a "blind alley in education." Finally, Fitzpatrick blasted McAndrew: "I can not understand what you and your assistants are thinking about when you talk about your 'output, customers, stockholders, and sampling day,' unless you imagine that you are running some kind of a mill or factory while you are grinding out a certain kind of product or material and you are going to get the 'stockholders and customers' together and bring forth your 'samples' as an exhibit of your 'output.'"[37]

McAndrew boasted about his controversial reception in Chicago. In his 1925 annual report, he reprinted the newspaper headlines of his conflict with the teachers, and noted that in spite of the ruckus, he had successfully reduced the political influence in schools. He reported that in his first year on the job, there had been 520 attempts by board members and others to influence him, but that in the most recent year only five attempts had occurred. The complaints of his opponents he called a hysterical and "noisy lampoon" of selfish interests.[38]

Haley, of course, came in for special criticism by McAndrew and his supporters. Her critiques of McAndrew were immediately derided as the old

"Haleyism" that protected incompetent teachers.[39] The *Chicago Daily Journal* called her the "Carrie Nation" of the schools, referring to the vigilante prohibitionist who charged into bars with an ax aimed at bottles of alcohol.[40] Educators at the University of Chicago claimed that the Federation's opposition to junior high schools was merely based on the fear that seventh and eighth grade teachers who would no longer be classified as elementary teachers would be placed where "the high priestess of that organization cannot dictate teachers' judgments and pronouncements."[41] And the *Tribune* agreed with McAndrew that "Margaret Haley, leader of the teachers, has been bellicose and unreasonable," and that her opposition to the superintendent's plans was "motivated less by educational ideals than by a desire to obstruct Mr. McAndrew."[42]

That the bulk of middle-class reform organizations supported McAndrew's efforts did not help Haley's cause. In a move that certainly did not make Haley any more fond of middle-class women reformers, the Chicago Women's Club members accepted the superintendent's invitation to be on the judging board of "Sampling Day."[43] As other reform groups circled around McAndrew, supporting his proposals and opposing a tax increase for school building construction, the great ideological differences between labor and business ideas about educational efficiency emerged. Haley had always insisted that efficiency should be measured by the degree of social justice achieved. No society could be seen as efficient if there were vast disparities in wealth and education between groups of people. Raising the standard of living of the poorest and weakest members of society was surely the most efficient government policy. In terms of education, she argued that low salaries for teachers meant "a low standard of efficiency" because it led to poor work by the teacher.[44] This perspective differed radically from the notion of financial efficiency promoted by McAndrew, which emphasized immediate cost accounting. These different understandings of the nature of effective management of schools created a deep rift between teachers and reform groups, particularly in a political climate that prioritized economic accountability.

Haley articulated her views in a series of articles that *The Daily News* published in early January 1928. In these columns, Haley repeatedly attacked McAndrew by referring to the previous four years of his leadership as a period of both "standstill" and "retrogression." The Chicago school system was stymied by an authoritarian administration that tried to rule by edict and which silenced teachers into "sullen submission." Platooning was one example of this authoritarianism, and Haley let loose her most lurid metaphors when she described the classroom teacher who was made to be merely "a cog in a vast machine of many moving parts, operated from above," and children who were seen as "unfinished parts placed on the conveyor belt like the nuts and bolts in a Ford factory." She cited the overload of tests for students and paper work for teachers, the abolition of the teacher councils which "killed" the "only intelligent contact between teachers and administrators," and she

mocked McAndrew's use of business terminology when referring to the learning processes of children.

In her final two columns, Haley cast her critique more widely to address the issue of politics in schools, asserting the Federation's right and
responsibility to continue its work. To the campaign pledges of political
candidates that they would "take the politics out of schools," Haley argued
that politics would *always* be in schools and that teachers and students lived
and worked with that politics every day. The Chicago teacher whose fifty-
three students were jammed in a room with forty-eight seats worked in the
middle of such "politics in schools." Such a teacher, Haley wrote,

> knows that the board of education that put those fifty-three chil-
> dren in that room knows that she can teach no more than thirty
> children and give them individual attention. . . . She knows that
> the reason she faces fifty-three children a day instead of thirty is
> that the board of assessors, the board of review and the other taxing
> officials are not doing their duty under the law to those fifty-three
> children, to their parents and to other taxpayers. . . . When thou-
> sands of other teachers face the same kind of living evidence of
> "politics in the schools" . . . these teachers know it is time to take
> the schools into politics and go after the robbers.

The struggle over this kind of experiential politics that teachers faced
every day was what placed the actual teaching of children on the "battlefront" of education.[45]

"Big Bill" Thompson, who was considering a campaign to return to the
mayor's office, seized on the controversy stirred up by McAndrew. The wily
Thompson furthered his affinity with the Irish Catholic teachers by specifically charging McAndrew with allowing "pro-British propaganda" in the
schools, and promoting unpatriotic textbooks produced by intellectual snobs
at the University of Chicago. The fact that these textbooks had been approved by Thompson's own board of education four years earlier was little
noticed by the press. So much did Haley hate McAndrew that she sided with
Thompson, her old enemy and once supporter of Jacob Loeb, and helped
him win his election.[46] Back in his mayor's seat, Thompson encouraged the
superintendent's enemies to organize their assault, and McAndrew resigned
a few months later.

Although relieved that McAndrew was gone, Haley knew that he had
left a dangerous legacy. She believed that William McAndrew had accomplished what "Bulletin Ben" Andrews, Edwin Cooley, and Jacob Loeb had
failed to do: create the environment wherein the opposition to teachers'
material interests was perceived to be not only acceptable but progressive.
McAndrew was able to link together the interests of reformers and business, and
to position the Federation on the other side of the fence, and in opposition to

the majority of Chicago citizens. Part of McAndrew's success was due to the politics of the period: Labor was on the defensive in the 1920s, and business was in the ascendancy. McAndrew's accomplishment was not merely his implementation of specific policies, but also his development of a politic of business-minded school reform. This is what Haley meant when she wrote that "McAndrew put into effect a machine as disruptive as an army of tanks."[47]

TRAITORS

Through the 1920s, Haley's ability to represent teachers as a progressive force was further undercut by internal divisions between teachers. Since the Federation disaffiliated from the AFT and the CFL in 1917, the separation between the older Federation and newer teachers' unions had become more pronounced. Much of the distance was carved by Haley, who became increasingly eccentric in her political tactics during the McAndrew years. Her notion that all teachers were under siege made her suspicious about competing interests, and she intensified her attacks on anyone who disagreed with her by charging that their proposal was a plot to hoodwink teachers into supporting a self-destructive policy. Her personal leadership style reflected her political concerns. She became so obsessed with details that one observer noted that her methods were that of "forensic combat" as she drew on legislative advisors, her store of office files that documented every move of the board of education, and stenographic transcripts that she ordered for every meeting of potential interest to teachers. Her suspicion of other groups veered on paranoia as she solicited written testimonies from teachers reporting about internal strife in the other unions. With her years of connections with reporters, judges, and politicians, Haley's was probably the best informed of all teachers' organizations, furthering the image that she was an entrenched political crony.[48]

Haley's corrosive leadership style further undermined her popularity. She dominated meetings with long speeches and allowed little discussion from the floor. Relying on her skill of interpreting rules, she called out for points of order as elections were taking place and weighed in with long diatribes about parliamentary procedure. In the NEA, she became so notorious for clogging up proceedings that when she stood up to be recognized, other members called the vote to question, hoping to avoid a lecture. As the president of the NEA said wryly at the 1922 meeting after cutting Haley off, if he had given her the floor "she would have talked indefinitely" and "when you are shooting the rapids, you have to take care of yourself."[49] Much of her talk relied on the past: She referred repeatedly to the tax case and to the continued need for tax reform, and she often harkened to the golden days of Ella Flagg Young's superintendency which, by the mid-1920s, was before the time of any young Chicago teacher.

Such behavior aggravated other teachers on a day-to-day level and alienated potential allies. Mary Herrick, who worked in the Chicago Federation of Women High School Teachers found Haley very difficult to get along with, and felt that she had an "unwillingness to cooperate in any activity she could not control."[50] Jennie Wilcox of the AFT specifically criticized the way that Haley kept the Federation teachers isolated both from other teachers and from new ideas in politics. "Leaders may come and leaders may go," Wilcox wrote a friend in 1928, "but the movement lives on. I hardly think Margaret has ever thought of what her scheme of 'going it alone' is doing to her membership. We can not live in isolation and really grow—neither can we afford to lose the desire of cooperation." The Federation still had power in its large numbers, but its members seemed staunchly isolated and petrified in their positions.[51] Florence Hanson, AFT Secretary-Treasurer, believed that by 1928, Haley had lost all her support from labor, having "antagonized the labor men here in Chicago as well as nearly everyone else."[52] In 1931, Hanson gave Mary C. Barker, the AFT President, a description of Haley's leadership style in her report on teacher organizations in Milwaukee:

> The Milwaukee situation and method is almost identical with the Chicago Teachers' Federation situation and method. They have a Milwaukee Teachers' Association headed by Miss Ethel Gardner which employs an attorney who does their lobbying for them at the state capitol. They have developed a large organization which is decidedly self-sufficient. It hasn't an idea outside of Milwaukee or outside of its own particular group. . . . [T]he fact remains that for themselves alone they have secured some benefits and no other group in the state that talks about organizing and affiliating is discouraged from doing so by this Association which directly tells them "look at us. All you need to do is to organize like we are organized." Miss Gardner regards Miss Haley as the greatest person on earth and patterns her life and conduct on Miss Haley's.[53]

The general antipathy toward Haley was captured by Susan Dorsey, the popular superintendent of Los Angeles schools, who simply refused to engage with Haley in a public debate at the 1920 NEA meeting , stating that Haley was little more than a "soap box orator."[54]

Haley's suspicion of outside groups was not new. She had worried about the teachers losing authority with the affiliation with the CFL in 1902, and with the creation of the AFT in 1916. She knew from her own experience that teachers were not inclined toward unity: Young teachers came to the occupation educated in different ideas than their elders, and administrative changes in school organizations pitted teachers against each other over salary and status. Furthermore, she had seen that women teachers were never inclined to political activism, and that men teachers were often inclined to seek their own interests over women's. So too had she seen organized politicians and labor work against Irish American interests, and she maintained her lifelong suspicion of high school teachers, who she believed only wanted to maintain their superior status over elementary teachers. She apparently did not see the irony that her continued rebuff of the high school teachers paralleled the tactics of AFL leader Samuel Gompers who had resisted bringing all teachers into the larger labor movement for similar reasons. Like Gompers, Haley feared the introduction of a more "professionalized" group that would steer the union movement away from the material needs of the common worker, in her case, the rank and file elementary teacher.

Haley also belittled the newer teacher unionists for their youth and inexperience. With thirty years of legislative lobbying under her belt, Haley believed that the new AFT leaders were presumptuous and arrogant, coming to political work with no understanding of process and only an "overweening ambition and a terrific hunger for publicity." She described the other unions as "little groups" who "speak for their people without consulting them." In a transcript autobiography that Haley dictated a few years before her death, when age and isolation either exacerbated her feelings or took away whatever restraint she once had, Haley described these leaders with vicious hatred: She called Mary Herrick a "cheap little nincompoop" and Agnes Clohesy, the president of a competing elementary teachers' union, a "deliberate rascal." Charles Stillman, the first president of the AFT, she had unreserved disdain for, calling him traitorous.[55] Their worst crime, according to a bitter Haley, was that they did not have her three decades of experience lobbying the legislature and their politics changed depending on the wind. She was convinced that the AFT locals were either the creation of her political opponents or that they were simpletons in search of fame. Haley knew full well that the unity of all teachers was the only way that real change could come about, but she believed that her Federation *was* unity, while the other groups were merely the creations of men and women who were "blinded by flattery or by a mistaken idea of self interest, [who] break away from the ranks and make terms with the enemy."[56]

In 1926 Haley made a tactical error that lost her the support of the other teachers forever. The financial problems of Chicago's school system were particularly acute in the 1920s because of rising school costs. Since 1915, elementary enrollment had increased by 30 percent and high school enrollment by 130 percent, leaving schools overcrowded. Schools in the 1920s had also expanded their roles, offering commercial and technical courses, manual training and domestic science, physical education, classes for children with disabilities, and kindergartens. Other reforms increased school costs, including the availability of free textbooks, new school playgrounds, bus transportation, and community services in schools, all of which needed increased staffing and maintenance. The addition of non-teaching employees to the Chicago school system since the war had increased over 300 percent as compared to the 176 percent increase in instructional costs. Exacerbating these additional costs was the fact that since 1915, the board of education had been spending tax money before it actually arrived. In so doing, the board had used up almost eleven years of tax income in ten years time, was paying up to one million dollars a year in interest, and was on the edge of bankruptcy.[57]

Much of the problem, city officials were forced to admit, was the school board's overwhelming reliance on local property taxes, which accounted for 90 percent of school income. This point led Haley immediately back to her refrain that the underassessment of corporate properties undercut the amount of school income generated, and she advocated a full-fledged investigation, reassessment, and reform of Illinois' tax structure. Meanwhile, the high school teachers began to raise money for a lawsuit against the board, taking as a precedent the Firefighters Union of Chicago, which had won such a suit the previous year and reaped $800,000. At the teachers' meeting of the Illinois State Teachers Association in November 1927, the division between the Federation and the high school teachers solidified when Haley made an impassioned two-hour speech, critiquing the high school plan and promising all Chicago teachers fourteen million more dollars for schools from her proposed tax reassessment. The solution was not the piecemeal rewards of a lawsuit, she argued, but long-term tax equity. She won the day at the Association meeting by four to one, carrying the votes of all the elementary teachers. The high school teachers still decided to levy the lawsuit on their own.[58]

Haley's pushiness on this issue got the best of even her oldest friends. A few months later, James Meade, a longtime activist for the Federation of Men Teachers, penned a letter to Haley to explain how divisive she was. Meade had great concerns about what Haley was doing to the teacher union movement, yet his longtime respect for her led him to carefully write and rewrite his letter, trying to compose his criticism as delicately as possible. For all his respect and admiration of her, Meade wrote, he was tired of being lectured by her. She denounced his colleagues, charging that he was "the simple minded victim of a bunch of crooks," and then was amazed that he did not believe her. He had always agreed with her until recently when, as the new president of the men's teachers' association, he wrote, "I had the humiliation of finding out for myself what all my predecessors in this office had told me: that it is practically impossible for any other organization of teachers to cooperate with the Chicago Teachers' Federation." He had supported the men and women teachers' fight for teacher councils, smaller classes, better salaries, and improved teaching conditions. But now Haley demanded that he abandon these campaigns and get behind the Federation activities. Meade charged Haley with threatening to undermine the other groups if they did not do what she wanted, and with pursuing "vindictively these bitter personal attacks on people with whom you disagree on public questions." Her threats were misguided and ineffective, he concluded. The other teacher groups would continue with their work.[59] Meade's letter was a draft, and there is no evidence that he rewrote and sent the letter, or what Haley's response to it was. If she received it, it is likely she rejected it as quickly as she had rejected other suggestions to temper her style.

Haley was correct in arguing that tax inequities were a major source of Chicago's tremendous financial problems, but her plan for reassessment would not be the solution.[60] The hearing for the tax assessment was scheduled for November 1927, but legal and bureaucratic snags postponed it until May 1928 and then again until April 1930, six months after the stock market crash. Although the review found that Illinois' tax assessments were substantially undervalued, it also found that the rate of assessment was higher in Chicago than in the rest of Cook County, and after equalizing that difference, the tax rate for Chicago actually *declined*, and the school board suffered an even greater loss. According to Mary Herrick, "Haley's promised fourteen millions of additional annual income if the assessment were redone had proved to be a mirage; instead, future income would be millions less. There were not only no pots of gold at the end of the rainbow; by October, 1929, there were no rainbows in sight in any direction."[61]

The distance between the Federation and the AFT union was hammered home in late 1927 with the chartering of AFT Local #199, the Chicago Elementary Teachers' Union. The Federation was invited to join, but refused. Indeed, according to Florence Hanson of the AFT, Haley did not consider the invitation even worth a reply.[62] In response, AFT president Mary C. Barker announced the formation of the new union with a statement that completely ignored the past history of the Federation.[63] If the Federation stood for anything, it stood for the representation of elementary teachers, but here an entirely new union was formed outside of the Federation to do exactly that. Haley responded by intensifying her investigations of the competition, asking teachers to report when Union members tried to recruit in schools. Loyal Federation members dutifully wrote their observations to Haley, including criticisms that Union organizers reportedly made about Haley ("He said we have only one person to blame for this whole chaotic situation and you know who she is"), and their own gallant defense of their cause ("I told him . . . we were 100% Federationists—which is not true as we are in the minority but I did not wish to let him know that").[64] The other teacher groups ignored Haley, holding meetings and conducting studies about the crisis in Chicago's school system without mentioning the Federation. When the twelfth Annual Convention of the AFT was held in Chicago in June 1928 and 1929, no Federation members attended.[65]

Haley's support for "Big Bill" Thompson's reelection in 1927 after he promised to fire McAndrew further hurt her reputation, as did her decision to turn around yet again and *oppose* Thompson in the 1931 election. With the effects of the stock market crash hitting Chicago, teachers' monthly paychecks were repeatedly postponed in what were called "payless pay days." In 1931, Haley favored mayoral candidate Anton Cermak, and she sent out a last-minute flyer to all teachers stating that the election of Thompson would mean more "payless pay days" whereas Cermak would ensure the payment of teachers' salaries. The Teachers' Union quickly responded with its own flyer which denounced Haley, and argued that her promises were merely her way of getting teachers to sign up with the Federation.[66] As one AFT administrator confessed sadly in 1935, it would take no one less than Moses to bring all the Chicago locals together.[67]

Yet over the years, all Chicago locals *except* the Federation did join together. In 1924 the board of education officially allowed teachers to join labor unions, and the superintendent who replaced McAndrew in 1927, William Brogan, developed a close and cordial relationship with the Chicago AFT locals.[68] Through the 1930s, while the financial crisis in Chicago grew increasingly severe, the Federation concentrated on obscure court cases and new legislation, while AFT locals took on popular militant responses to the economic crises. Between December 1929 and August 1934, Chicago teachers received only nine paychecks on time, and delays ran from one week to ten months. Salaries were reduced 23 percent during this period, and in 1931 the city was so bankrupt that they paid teachers in scrip. In July 1932, the board of education cut $15 million from the proposed $90 million budget, and cut $4.5 million a few months later. In July 1933, the board voted to fire 1,400 teachers (ten percent of the total), which Haley later called the "School-Wrecking Program."[69] The AFT locals organized mass meetings and strikes in 1932 and 1933, culminating in a series of rallies and marches involving up to fifteen thousand teachers in the city center. This political action motivated Chicago teachers to unify their locals, and in October 1937 the Chicago Teachers' Union was formed with a membership of more than five thousand members, including principals and high school teachers. Haley promptly accused the Teachers' Union of opposing a salary increase for elementary teachers, a charge the Union immediately denied.[70] By October 1938, more than one-half of Chicago's elementary teachers had joined the new union, which took on the old Federation's designation as AFT Local #1.

LOYALISTS

Although most of her prestige collapsed around her in the 1930s, Haley remained the charismatic heroine of a surviving cohort of elderly Irish American women elementary teachers who stayed loyal to the Federation. For more than thirty years, the Federation had offered these teachers not simply activities to do, but a cohesive identity and purpose behind those activities. Women Federation members felt part of a whole and aligned with a cause. Much of Federation teachers' unity was shaped by their distance from other teachers, including other women teachers. By the 1920s, Federation members differed from AFT teachers in age, ethnicity, training, social identity, and beliefs about organization. Their political experience

was grounded in the Federation, which had generally eschewed the political radicalism of the AFT as well as the more militant organizing
strategies of the left wing of the women's suffrage movement. Their primary focus had always been the assertion of women teachers' working
rights and citizenship, staying carefully within the boundaries of the current
political structure.

In contrast, women teachers hired since World War I were trained in
modern teacher training schools, and were more likely to come from socially,
economically, and ethnically diverse backgrounds and more likely to hold
modern values and attitudes, including contemporary notions of gender equity. They were also more likely to be married. Simultaneously, the image of
the older single woman teacher came under suspicion as a sexual deviant or,
at the very least, a social outsider, thus creating another barrier between the
generations of women. This cultural shift furthered the division between
older and younger women teacher activists. Jennie Wilcox described how
women in the AFT experienced a "sense of companionship" and creativity
as they worked with men and other union and reform groups. But Wilcox
believed that Haley kept her teachers on a tight social and well as political
rein, restricting Federation teachers' "personal life."[71] This is not to say that
Federation teachers could not be described as feminist, or that they did not
unite with other women on particular causes. Indeed, the Federation upheld
its all-female cohort as a unique and empowering aspect of their work. But
they held distinctly unique histories and understandings of political work that
undercut their ability to align with many modern movements. Federation teachers in the 1920s and 1930s were older women teachers with ideological origins
in the late-nineteenth-century labor aristocracy; many were Irish Catholic
women who stepped lightly around issues that the Catholic church opposed;
many were unmarried and unaccustomed to working with men; and they all
shared common political experiences of diligently following Federation projects
for citizenship rights and civic improvement. They also shared the Federation
history of mistrusting outsiders, be they secondary teachers, school administrators, men educators, middle-class women, or Protestants.

Through the 1920s, the Federation leadership concentrated on rebuilding membership. The Federation *Bulletin*, which had lapsed around 1908, was
briefly revived in 1915 and 1916, to cover the Loeb decision and Catherine
Goggin's death. In 1924 it was renamed *Margaret Haley's Weekly Bulletin*, and
covered stories about the platoon plan, salaries, tax assessment, and stenographic reports from Federation meetings. One clever addition to the new
Bulletin was a full-page cartoon on the cover page that captured current
debates. In one cartoon, the Teachers' Federation was portrayed as a savvy
modern woman who discovers between the pages of a volume of tax records
a rotund businessman in a cheap suit, labeled as a "tax fixer."[72] In a twist on
feminine imagery, two other cartoons portrayed the teachers as innocent
little girls hoping to find a prize on the street, or to receive a present from

Margaret Haley, the great orator, 1920s (Courtesy Chicago Historical Society)

Santa Claus, only to find sneering and scowling men yanking away their dreams.[73] The *Bulletin* was published irregularly and eventually stopped in the mid-1920s in part because, according to Haley, it could not keep up with the rush of information that she wanted published.[74]

As the Federation declined in public authority, surviving members produced entertaining activities that reinforced their common experience. One *Bulletin* issue included a crossword puzzle with clues referring to Federation inside jokes and history.[75] They held a Silver Jubilee luncheon in honor of the Federation's twenty-five years of service in 1925, and another anniversary luncheon in 1928. Both events included speeches by the current president of the Federation and by Haley, poetic tributes to Haley, and communal singing of popular songs rewritten with comical lyrics, such as a parody on "Over There" with the words "supervise, supervise, don't let up, don't let up, if you're wise." Dominating the programs were affectionate tributes to Haley, such as this verse sung to "Reuben, Reuben, I've been thinking:"

> Margaret, Margaret, we're all thinking
> With your courage, zeal, and grace
> All the Board of Ed's conniving
> Never can eclipse our "ace"[76]

The Federation leadership also entertained its members with its traditional mocking of the opponents in dramatic performances. In 1931 they put on a "tragedy in one overt act" called "How to be Happy Tho Married," starring the "Pedagogical Players" with star performances by the current president of the Federation, playing Haley, and the long-time lawyer Isaiah Greenacre playing himself. The comedy revolved around a potential teacher candidate and her search for benefits, with accompanying characters including the superintendent, board members, and representatives of group insurance agencies.[77] In 1932 they put on a performance entitled "School Scandels of 1932," featuring an operatic comedy drawn loosely from Gilbert and Sullivan called "Bored of Education." Songs included "We are teachers, tired and blue," "I am the chairman of this board," and "Little tax warrant."[78]

For all her combative relationships with many contemporary political activists, Haley was hardly a social pariah, and she maintained some political alliances through the 1920s and 30s. Some women high school teachers took part in the Federation celebratory activities and dramatics, and she stayed in touch with key legislators and city reformers and supported the candidacy of Agnes Nestor from the Women's Trade Union League for state representative in 1928.[79]

Nor did she lose any of her notorious political energy and tenacity. In a five-day period in June 1935, the 74-year-old Haley led a lobbying rampage in Springfield to pass a bill that would increase school funding. Although she spent Monday, June 17, in bed in Chicago with a cold, she revived by Tuesday to take a midnight train to Springfield. On Wednesday and Thursday, she met in the governor's office with a group of teachers and state representatives, arguing for three hours for the passage of the bill. Then she met with the secretary of state and with a group of teachers and lawyers to write up a revised bill. On Friday, Haley continued to work on the bill and showed it to the governor and key legislative supporters. The bill was introduced that afternoon and passed. Haley returned to Chicago on the Friday night train, and spent all Saturday morning on the telephone reporting about the bill. Sunday, she met with board of education and Federation members for four or five hours. She stayed up until midnight chronicling the weeks' activities.[80]

Such energy earned her praise by reporters, who portrayed her as an aged soldier who refused to retire. One 1920 interview described Haley with affection as "alert-eyed, always modishly dressed woman, with a rapier-like keenness of wit; charming to meet socially, and a power to reckon with officially if she opposes you. Miss Haley loves a good fight, it might seem, for its own sake, as a warhorse loves the fray; her eyes snap, her color rises, her words come faster and more scintillatingly the greater the demand upon them; she goes into a 'scrap,' and comes out of it, smiling."[81] Eleven years later, she had not faded: a reporter described Haley as white haired, and a little frail, "but the blue eyes laugh and flash; the saucy tongue has lost none of its Irish piquancy, and the chin rides high as ever." Such dynamism helped the Federation maintain membership rosters of between one and two thousand in the late 1930s, against all odds.[82]

THE BATTLE OVER

Haley remained focused on tax reform and the board's leasing of lands, including the sale of a plot of school land on the south side of Chicago that would be used to make Midway Airport.[83] She also maintained her monitoring of the state legislature, and in 1935 battled a revised bill on pensions and retirement and a proposed bill that would require teachers to sign loyalty oaths. She continued to hold forth at Federation meetings, lecturing teachers at length about legislative and political details, and interspersing her talks with long references to Federation history. She was occasionally interrupted by the chair of the meeting who asked if Haley really needed to cover such ancient history. To Haley, this history was vitally important—it explained not only the context of the situation, but also the context of the injustice. Although she might have exhausted her audience, such talks invigorated the aging Haley, who ended a long harangue in 1933 by promising to continue at the next meeting. "We ought to stay here all day," she admonished, "I never stop anyway."[84]

Although still ablaze with activity, Haley was now in her early seventies and suffering from heart disease. In June 1934, she traveled to Los Angeles to stay with her old friend and Federation colleague Frances Harden and to undergo medical treatment. On the journey, the once indefatigable Haley fell sick and went straight from the station to the hospital. For the next few months, she stayed at Harden's home. In recovery and out of town, she was still connected enough to Chicago politics to send the Federation leadership a long telegram instructing them to support an alderman who was running for county assessor. Her reasoning reflected the way that her politics were still mired in the past. She telegraphed a lengthy biography of the candidate's political activities, starting in 1917 when he had been one of the four aldermen who voted against the board's reappointment of Jacob Loeb and continuing through the recent tax reassessment case.[85] Through February and March she fired off more telegrams instructing the Federation about political tactics, and advising them to learn the lessons of Federation history.

Haley's other goal was to complete her autobiography. She was obsessed with chronicling the past and present actions of the Federation, and she had begun to dictate memoranda of recent events and to transcribe telephone calls. For six hot afternoons in late July 1929, she had sat in the Federation office and dictated the story of her 1926 attempt at a tax reassessment, producing almost six hundred pages of double-spaced typed text. Haley spoke constantly, although she was in a room attended by at least two people all the time. With almost no hesitations or tangents, she methodically related the tale of political maneuverings, including specific details about

meetings, legislative hearings, legal codes, tax rate information, and her lobbying of legislatures and reporters. At times she reenacted whole conversations, taking the part of the other participants. Present, but almost completely
silent, at these meetings was Emma McCredie, a Chicago teacher who would
later help Haley write another version of her autobiography.[86]

Five years later, in California, Haley set to work on her autobiography
again with the help of McCredie, who was now studying for a master's degree
in sociology in Los Angeles. Even at seventy three, Haley was known for her
hyperactivity, and McCredie had some trouble getting her to focus. She
asked Haley's friends if there was any possibility of "holding Miss Haley down
long enough" to get any of the work done, and if it was appropriate to call
Haley early in the morning, although "of course she dares to call others at
any hour she gets up."[87] About Haley's visit to California, McCredie wrote
a friend that she would make all the preparations and then let her "run the
show the way she wants it . . . (She will anyhow)."[88]

Eliza Haley died in May 1935 in Chicago, and her sister raced home
from Los Angeles for the funeral. If Margaret Haley had any life partner, it
was her younger sister Eliza who had taught at the Hendricks School and was
a lifelong member of the Federation and one of the teachers fired under the
Loeb Ruling in 1916. Equally as important was Eliza's role supporting her
sister's active work life, taking care of her when she was sick and attending
to her domestic needs. When still a schoolteacher, Haley was able to move
out of the family home in part because Eliza stayed home to care for their
widowed father. Eliza was the third of Haley's five younger siblings to die
before her, leaving her increasingly alone. She secured a plot for the two to
share at Olivet Cemetery in Joliet, the town of their birth. In a sharp irony,
Eliza died when Jane Addams was gravely ill, and the front page of the
newspapers that published Eliza's obituary were covered with news about
Addams's impending death.[89] For Haley, both friends and foes were disap-
pearing quickly.

Haley stayed in Chicago and made another attempt at her autobiography, dictating a long, rambling monologue to Alice Adams. The disjointed
nature of the text suggests that Haley was suffering some dementia. Ever
obsessed with details, she directed Adams to write an index of important
names and events, and she commissioned reporter Mary Synon, to combine
all her writings into a final manuscript to be published under the title of
"Forty Fighting Years."[90] In 1936 she sent out flyers to teachers advertising
the forthcoming book and offering advance purchasing for $3 a copy.[91] But
the book was not published in her lifetime.

In late December 1938, Haley's heart took a turn for the worse and she
was admitted to Englewood Hospital, where she died on January 5, 1939,
almost twenty-three years to the day after Catherine Goggin's death. She was
seventy-seven years old and financially destitute. The personal property that
she left behind was $25 and the unpublished manuscript.[92] A funeral was

held at her old parish, St. Bernard's Catholic Church in Englewood and she was buried in Joliet next to Eliza. Superintendent William Johnson told teachers that they could leave their classes to attend the funeral, which attracted more than two thousand people.[93] Two months later, the Federation held a memorial service, where friends and colleagues remembered Haley's strengths, energy, and accomplishments.

Isaiah Greenacre, one of Haley's oldest and most loyal friends, appropriately delivered one of the first speeches at the memorial. Greenacre first met Haley in 1899 in the early days of the Federation, and he had steadfastly stood by Haley as the Federation's legal counsel through years of battles. Greenacre's influence extended beyond writing legal briefs: an advocate of women's suffrage, he provided legal counsel for state suffrage groups, and he was a steadfast advisor to Haley and Goggin as they designed their political strategies. His liberal influence extended to his family of seven children: His daughter Phyllis graduated from the University of Chicago in 1913 and became a nationally renowned psychoanalyst, and his daughter Alice became an attorney in Chicago. He shared with Haley an abrasive and independent character, although he also had the patience of Job, since he handled a seemingly endless array of Federation legal cases often with late, or no, payment. After forty years working together, Greenacre had only praise for Haley. She was, he said, "absolutely fearless," and she was honest and insightful. Her positive effect on Chicago was inestimable, "not merely by example and precept, but in dollars and cents."[94]

In obituaries and memorial testimonies, Haley was remembered for her fortitude and dynamism. She was "Tireless in Fight for Teachers," wrote one reporter, "a feminine Don Quixote" who "knew how to make the politicians wish she had never been born."[95] The *Daily News* recalled her energy and diligence, "a formidable opponent of recreant or blundering boards of education [and] dictatorial or generally unfit school superintendents." She clung "passionately" to principles of sound finance, and her hatred of tax dodging was "boundless." She was "the embodiment of alert, informed and fearless citizenship in action," and she mapped out "the method by which well-administered government is to be gained and kept."[96] Recalled a friend, she had "the energy of a dynamo, the wisdom of a seer, the integrity of a Lincoln, and the courage that knew neither retreat nor defeat."[97] A lead reporter of one of Chicago's daily papers recalled that in covering the news beat of Margaret Haley, "a newspaper man was privileged to observe and to write one of the great stories of Chicago."[98]

But others remembered her differently, or not at all. At the twenty third Annual Convention of the American Federation of Teachers, held in Buffalo in August 1939, only eight months after her death, there was no mention of Haley's passing.[99] Nor did the National Education Association make any notice of her death in their literature. The Federation struggled on for another thirty years under the leadership of Frances Kenney, who held

Haley's title from 1948 to her death in 1968, monitoring the pension and taking conservative stands on the persecution of communist teachers in the 1950s and on racial integration of schools in the 1960s. The Federation was a shadow of its former self, and when the Chicago Teachers' Union was elected by public school teachers to be their collective bargaining agent in 1960, the Federation collapsed. It formally disbanded in 1968, with the death of Kenney.[100]

Haley's penniless death is a poignant irony, given that she had spent her life fighting against corporate greed. Her last years appear to be frustrating ones, with no success in publication, health problems that kept her physically from the center of action, and younger political leaders who dismissed her knowledge and experience. But characteristically, Haley did not seem to notice her increasing marginalization. Her continued focus on the cause kept her from analyzing the cause itself or reflecting on the best tactics of an aged warrior in an ongoing battle. Never a sentimental woman, she equated the pain of the death of her friends and family with the treacheries of professional colleagues that, she claimed, left "a deeper sadness than does loss." With each of life's blows, she wrote, "I have met the next day with the courage to take up the banner again."[101]

In one of her autobiographical writings, Haley closed with a short reflection on her own life, recalling her origins on the wide and open Illinois prairie, her travels into villages, towns, and finally the city, and the way in which, as a young woman, she fell in "with the surging cavalcade of my generation." Drawing on her familiar military metaphors, she described her years of work for the teachers as forty years upon a battleground. Now that her work was almost done, the best service she could do was inspire others to hold the battlefield and to continue the fight for justice that extended far beyond immediate material gain. She herself promised to continue that fight in heaven, where she hoped to "be looking down from some high rampart of eternity when the last war for man's freedom has been won."[102]

CONCLUSION

TEACHER LEADER

"TO ME," MARGARET HALEY WROTE in the final chapter of her autobiography, *Battleground*, the city of Chicago was "the proving ground of American democracy" and the battleground for two opposing forces in American life: "the defenders and the exploiters of true popular government." In this short chapter, Haley laid out her philosophy of political organizing for teachers and emphasized their responsibility to maintain the American heritage of freedom and citizenship. The final pages were her call to arms for future teachers and her guidelines or "fieldmap" for battle. "If our democracy is to continue," she wrote with foreboding, "the teachers of this nation must teach the children of the nation the obligations of citizenship in a true democracy." Such lessons in citizenship should not merely be the structures of government or passing political issues, but "enduring questions of economic and social existence: taxation, the land system, the money system."[1]

Economics was central to political education because it was economics that remained so obscure to the mass of people. Haley argued that this confusion was intentional on the part of those who controlled money: By filling economic discourse with confusing nomenclature and scientific terms, common people were left ignorant of what was the backbone of the American social fabric: public taxation for the civic good. Throughout history, groups in power had used education to control the thoughts of children by restricting their knowledge. Such an education kept citizens from recognizing the ways in which the wealthy took advantage of the poor through graft, political pressure, and unequal taxation. It was the teachers' job to clarify these principles to children by relating economic principles to everyday life.

But teachers could only teach clearly about economics if they understood their own condition. This was the goal of teacher education, but not in the sense that teacher education had so far been defined. "Instead of running like hares to classes which give them nothing but promotional credits," Haley argued, teachers "must study intensely and intensively the real

211

problems of our time and our country." Haley set forth her program for the political education of teachers:

> They must familiarize themselves with the methods and purposes of public utilities. They must find out who are the enemies of the republic, both in and out of office. They must scan the existing laws, discover why some of them can't be changed, and devise methods for their revision. They must find out what Initiative and Referendum and Recall mean, and how these methods may be exercised to secure better laws and put out dishonest administrators and legislators. They must inform themselves about the thieves and thieveries which are putting the high burden of taxation upon the little man and letting the big fellow escape. Then, having learned their lesson, they must teach it.[2]

In this way, school teachers would pave the way for a bloodless revolution.

Teachers could only accomplish this through unity. Teachers needed to organize in councils and unions where they could collectively shape and control their own profession. It was teachers, not boards of education or other elected officials, who should be in charge of their work, setting and enforcing standards of admission, performance, the course of study, and working conditions. In curriculum development, teachers had to recognize that "the human heart seeks beauty as much as the human soul seeks justice." Respect for children's culture, pleasure, and aesthetics was as important as formal course work.

Most importantly, teachers needed to become educational activists, and they needed to rebel against the notion that *others* should lead in schools. Haley wrote: "Teachers have the obligation, by virtue of their position, to fight against that machine civilization which tries to extinguish all leadership other than its own. They must throw off the inferiority complex which they have developed under school systems which have oppressed them." The crisis in American education was due to the fact that educational leadership came from administrators, higher education, and government; teachers had been prevented from taking up their responsibility and had become apathetic and passive cogs in an undemocratic administrative system. To reinvigorate schools, teachers needed to develop a code of ethics that would presuppose activism in educational issues. Teachers' material conditions, such as salary, pension, and tenure, were certainly important subjects of a teachers' organization, but more important was the development of teachers' consciousness about citizenship and responsibility. "This," she wrote, "is the real meaning of academic freedom."[3]

LEGACY

Three main themes emerge in this biography of Margaret Haley's life and leadership. The first theme is Haley's advocacy of school finance reform and her belief that public funding for public schools is an integral part of the American civic identity. The second theme is her vision of schools as the generative engine of a democratic society and her belief that teachers should be activist citizens in American society. The third theme is Haley's insistence that public school teachers have the right to shape and control their own working conditions. An additional theme emerges at the conclusion of this study, and that is the resounding failure of all of Haley's propositions. For all her significance during her own lifetime, for all of her rhetorical power and political influence, Margaret Haley's legacy is hard to discern in today's schools and teacher organizations.

Why did Haley fail, leaving teacher activists today as politically marginalized as they were one hundred years ago? Why have her proposals for economic and organizational reform not become standard policy in American schools today? In this biography, I have tried to show that Margaret Haley was a visionary leader who was also a tragic figure bowled over by forces greater than herself and by the political complexities of her time and her profession. Her loss was the loss of all public schools. But contemporary educators still have much to learn Haley's failures, because the problems that she faced then continue in today's schools. Four main obstacles to Haley's work one hundred years ago persist in contemporary education. By studying those barriers, educators today can develop strategies to reenergize and promote Haley's vision.

Haley herself identified the first barrier to her work during the McAndrew superintendency, although in fact she had seen it looming since her first introduction to politics with the Harper Bill. This was her opponents' success at rhetorically identifying teachers' interests as selfish "special interests," a notion that was diametrically opposed to Haley's conception of teachers as citizens who acted for the public good. Haley asserted that "the cause of the teacher is the cause of the people and vice versa, and their common cause is that of the children," arguing that if teachers' working conditions in schools were improved, so too would the daily experiences of students in those schools.[4] But neither Haley nor any teacher activist since her has been able to persuade the public that what was good for teachers was also good for children.

The second challenge that Haley faced was that of shaping a teacher politics that reflected both teachers' labor needs and their professional aspirations. Unlike the medical and legal professions, which were able to gain self-regulatory and cultural authority over their work in the early twentieth century, teachers have never been able to gain more than ambivalent professional status. Teachers continue today in a netherworld between civil service workers who are subject to others' authority and highly educated professionals with self-determined professional expectations. As Christine Murray wryly notes, the whole concept of teacher professionalism is "equated with teachers assuming their assigned roles in the education hierarchy and following directions without complaint."[5] Margaret Haley identified this problem from the beginning of her career as she observed the cultural pressures that discouraged women teachers from adopting activist political roles in their work. Convinced of their own slim hold on privilege as white-collar workers, excluded from discussions of politics or economics, and denied the vote, most women elementary teachers were fearful to even believe that they had rights as citizens or workers. Today's women teachers have the right to vote, but they remain a politically passive force under a hierarchy of school administrative policy, legal regulations, and legislative financial control. Margaret Haley came the closest of any leader, then or since, to mobilizing an activist force of teachers through her charisma, political savvy, and single-focused commitment to education.

The third challenge to Haley's vision was her own leadership strategies, and here it is important to locate her work in a broader political context. Haley was both highly effective at creating local group cohesion and she was tragically polarizing. Like a ferocious lioness, she charged against intimidating male legislatures and educational administrators and in the process energized women teachers into a self-confident political force. In her passion to create that community, however, Haley eschewed alliances with school administrators, secondary teachers, middle-class women, and African American activists, and in so doing, she ultimately undercut her own progressive vision. This strategy was in part a consequence of her combative character and powerful ego, both of which reinforced her public activism in a men's political world, even as it isolated her from potential allies. The divisiveness of much of Haley's leadership also speaks to the continuing tension facing teachers in progressive movements. In her work with the Federation, Margaret Haley covered a wide range of political playing fields, linking teachers with the male-dominated labor movement, the Irish Catholic reform community, feminist activists, local and state political legislators, and progressive educators. None of these movements fully understood or accommodated to the unique political and cultural status of women elementary school teachers, and as Haley persistently forefronted the teachers' agenda, she tended to slip away from other groups' agendas. Haley always identified as a teacher first, so that her commitment to other movements was often secondary, particularly if those other movements marginalized teachers. This dynamic did not die with the twentieth century; it continues to this day in the occupation of teaching, which moves in and out of movements in organized labor, school reform, feminism, and social reform.

The fourth and most intransigent reason why Haley's work with the Federation did not become embedded in American educational policy is that Margaret Haley organized her civic vision on a significant challenge to capitalist ideology. Although she never embraced a socialist platform for reorganizing the economy, her critique of the tax system attacked the power structure of modern corporate capitalism. However persuasive she was with teachers and other progressives, she was not powerful enough to dismantle corporate influence in legislation, and most of the barriers to school finance equity that she identified one hundred years ago remain today. School funding continues to be too complicated for the common citizen to understand. The corporate franchise tax exemptions that Haley condemned one hundred years ago continue today with corporate tax abatements that shift the burden of school support from business to individuals. A public culture that condemns taxation as government intrusion into private lives further discourages a progressive vision of collective investment in communities. Contemporary "tax revolts" exemplify the persistence of the ideology that Haley critiqued but could not change. In a painful irony, citizens across the nation have used the populist mechanisms promoted by Haley—the popular referendum—to limit public taxation. On a national average, local property taxes today contribute about one-half of all school funds, leading to great educational inequalities between property poor and property wealthy districts. Judicial courts in more than thirty states have declared such school funding systems to be illegal or inadequate, but the courts have not been able to move legislative bodies to revise those systems.[6] These intensifying problems may be less the legacy of Haley's failure and more of a legacy of economic inequality that runs like an iron rod through American educational policy.

Were she alive today, Margaret Haley would argue that teachers should take the lead on fighting against such economic disparities. She would identify organized women elementary teachers as the leaders of a movement that would untangle confusing school finance laws and educate the public about the social good and economic benefits of equitable taxation. She would position teacher unions as advocates to reform policies that undercut school resources. She would mobilize classroom teachers to fight for their own professional standards and for the right to participate in school governance and curriculum decisions. Up to the day she died, Margaret Haley believed that teachers would educate citizens to protect democracy by supporting public schools.

Haley died before she could be fully disappointed. Although teachers continued to organize through the 1930s and then in another burst of activity beginning in the 1960s, Haley's vision that women elementary teachers would become the vanguard of democratic activism in education has not yet come to pass. Too many cultural, economic, and political forces worked against them, and without the dynamic leadership of Margaret Haley, many women teachers receded back into their classrooms to observe the political battle from a distance. It is time to bring Margaret Haley's vision of civic activism and teacher leadership back to the forefront of educational work.

NOTES

INTRODUCTION. CITIZEN TEACHER

1. Margaret Haley, "Why Teachers Should Organize," *Journal of the Addresses and Proceedings of the National Education Association* (1904): 148.

2. Ibid., 151.

3. "Modern Knight in a Gown," *St. Paul Pioneer Press*, 27 December 1901, 6.

4. Robert L. Reid, ed., *Battleground: The Autobiography of Margaret Haley* (Urbana: University of Illinois Press: 1982), 3.

5. *Ibid.*, 230.

6. Ohio Coalition for Educational Equity, www.ohiocoalition.org.

CHAPTER 1. THE EDUCATION OF A TEACHER

1. *Battleground*, 23.

2. John J. Halsey, ed., *A History of Lake County, Illinois* (Chicago: Harmegnies and Howell, 1912), 35, 572.

3. Kerby A. Miller, *Immigrants and Exiles: Ireland and the Irish Exodus to North America* (New York: Oxford University Press, 1985).

4. Ruth W. Gregory, ed., *Waukegan Illinois; Its Past, Its Present* (Waukegan: League of Women Voters, 1967), 27, 65; Ruth Mogg, *First Land Purchases in Lake County, Illinois* (Waukegan, IL: Midwest Crafts, 1979), 90; Halsey, *A History of Lake County*, 572.

5. *Battleground*, 7. The 1850 Illinois census notes Michael Haley born in 1827 in Toronto. In the 1900 census the seventy-three-year-old Michael Haley reported that he was born in New York. Michael Haley's obituary is in the *Chicago Tribune*, 6 May 1905, and the *Chicago Daily News*, 6 May 1905. Nancy Lusignan Schultz, *Fire and Roses: The Burning of the Charlestown Convent, 1834* (Boston: Northeastern University Press, 2002).

6. Eugene Staley, *History of the Illinois State Federation of Labor* (Chicago: University of Chicago Press, 1930), 29–30.

7. Lawrence J. McCaffrey, *The Irish Catholic Diaspora in America* (Washington, DC: Catholic University Press, 1997), 3. According to the Patron's *Directory of*

the *Combination Atlas Map of Will County, Illinois* (Elgin, IL: Thompson Brothers and Burr, 1873), Michael Haley came to Will County, Illinois, in 1837.

8. George W. Woodruff, *Forty Years Ago! A Contribution to the Early History of Joliet and Will County* (Joliet: Joliet Republican Steam Printing, 1874), 67; Catherine Tobin, "The Lowly Muscular Digger: Irish Canal Workers in Nineteenth Century America." PhD diss., University of Notre Dame, 1987; Elizabeth Kytle, *Home on the Canal* (Cabin John, MD: Seven Locks Press, 1983).

9. Mark Wyman, *Immigrants in the Valley: Irish, Germans, and Americans in the Upper Mississippi Country, 1830–1860* (Chicago: Nelson-Hall, 1984), 75–84.

10. Ibid., 94–96.

11. Ibid., 83.

12. *Battleground*, 7; Autobiography of Margaret Haley, 1934, box 33, folder 1, Chicago Teachers' Federation Papers [CTF Papers], Chicago Historical Society, 8.

13. Haley Autobiography, 1934, 8–9; Harry E. Pratt, ed., *Illinois as Lincoln Knew It: A Boston Reporters' Record of a Trip in 1847* (Springfield, IL: 1838), 24. The 1850 census notes Michael Haley, laborer, worth $500, living in the household of James Tyrrell in Lockport. See also Linda T. Pote, "'The Celebrated Joliet Marble Fields': An Historical Geography of the Lower Des Plaines Valley Limestone Industry," in *Time and Place in Joliet: Essays on the Geographical Evolution of the City*, ed. Michael P. Conzen (Studies of the Illinois and Michigan Canal Corridor, No. 2). (Chicago: University of Chicago, Committee on Geographical Studies: 1988).

14. *Battleground*, 4.

15. Jane Addams, *Twenty Years at Hull House* (New York: Signet, 1981), 33.

16. Victor Searcher, *The Farewell to Lincoln* (New York: Abingdon Press, 1965), 240.

17. Theodore J. Karamanski, *Rally 'Round the Flag: Chicago and the Civil War* (Chicago: Nelson-Hall, 1993), 77–83, 180.

18. *Battleground*, 3–4.

19. Franklin L. Yoder, "Beyond the Towpath: Farming Along the Illinois and Michigan Canal," in *Settling the Upper Illinois Valley*, ed. Michael P. Conzen and Melissa J. Morales (Studies of the Illinois and Michigan Canal Corridor, No. 3). (Chicago: University of Chicago, Committee on Geographical Studies: 1989).

20. In the 1870 Illinois Census, the Haley family is listed as living in Joliet.

21. *Battleground*, 5.

22. Ibid., 4, 10.

23. Ibid., 11. Death dates of Thomas and Mary Haley from gravestone in the Haley-Tiernan family plot, St. Mary's Cemetery, Waukegan, Illinois.

24. S. S. Schoff, *The Glory of Chicago: Her Manufactories* (Chicago: Knight and Leonard, 1873), 135; *The History of Will County, Illinois* (Chicago: William LeBaron, Jr., and Co, 1878), 598; Haley Autobiography, 1934, 8.

25. *Battleground*, 11.

26. Marjorie Murphy, "Progress of the Poverty of Philosophy: Two Generations of Labor Reform Politics: Michael and Margaret Haley" paper delivered at Knights of Labor Centennial Symposium, Chicago, May 17–19, 1979, 17–18.

27. Richard Schneirov, "Rethinking the Relation of Labor to the Politics of Urban Social Reform in Late Nineteenth-Century America: The Case of Chicago," *International Labor and Working-Class History* 46 (Fall 1994): 94; Philip S. Foner, *Organized Labor and the Black Worker, 1619–1973* (New York: Praeger, 1974), 62–63.

28. *Joliet Signal*, 29 May 1855.

29. Eric Foner, "Class, Ethnicity, and Radicalism in the Gilded Age: the Land League and Irish-America," in Eric Foner, *Politics and Ideology in the Age of the Civil War* (New York: Oxford University Press, 1980), 156.

30. *Battleground*, 5.

31. Ibid., 11–12.

32. Autobiography of Margaret Haley, 1935, box 34, Chicago Historical Society, 715.

33. *Battleground*, 12; Leslie Joseph Farrington, "Development of Public School Administration in the Public Schools of Will County, Illinois as Shown in a Comparison of three selected years, 1877, 1920, and 1965," PhD diss., Northern Illinois University, 1967, 80; Diary of County Superintendent of Schools, Inspection Visits to Joint Wilmington-Channahon Township District No. 3 and Channahon Township District No. 3, January 1872, Will County School Records, Illinois Regional Archives Depository (IRAD), Northern Illinois University, DeKalb, Illinois.

34. Ninth Biennial Report of the Superintendent of Public Instruction of the State of Illinois, 1871–1872, County Statistics and Report of Will County.

35. Helen E. Hittle, "History of Channahon Elementary Public School from Its Inception, 1837–1956." Masters thesis, DePaul University, 1958, 31; Farrington, "Development of Public School Administration," 81; *Battleground*, 12–13. Description of school building in *The History of Will County Illinois*, 598.

36. Cyrus W. Brown, *Essays and Papers Read Before the Illinois Commandery of the Military Order of the Loyal Legion of the United States*. Vol 9, 1906–1909 (Chicago: 1923), 438–39.

37. Cyrus Winthrop Brown was born in West Behavia, N.Y., July 20, 1844, and died in Joliet, January 10, 1921. He was First Lieutenant and Adjutant Third, United States Colored Troops. After the war, Brown studied law, was admitted to the bar in 1875, and became state's attorney of Will County in 1880. He was a practicing lawyer until his death. *Memorials of Deceased Companions of the Commandery of the State of Illinois Military Order of the Loyal Legion of the United States*, from January 1, 1912, to December 31, 1922. (Chicago: 1923), 629–31.

38. D. S. Lawrence and A. R. Thompson, *Lawrence and Thompson's Grundy County Directory, 1877–1878*, 23.

39. David C. McCabe, "Creating Downtown: Lots and Buildings, to 1927," in *Canal Town and County Seat: The Historical Geography of Morris*, ed. Michael P. Conzen and Valerie M. McKay (Studies of the Illinois and Michigan Canal Corridor, No. 8). (Chicago: University of Chicago, Committee on Geographical Studies, 1994), 38–39.

40. *Grundy County Directory, 1877–1878*; Warren Kozak, "Building Faith in Morris: Collective History of Denominations and Churches," in *Canal Town and County Seat: The Historical Geography of Morris*, ed. Michael P. Conzen and Valerie M. McKay (Studies of the Illinois and Michigan Canal Corridor, No. 8). (Chicago: University of Chicago, Committee on Geographical Studies: 1994).

41. David R. Roediger, *The Wages of Whiteness: Race and the Making of the American Working Class* (New York: Verso, 1991); Noel Ignatiev, *How the Irish Became White* (New York: Routledge, 1995).

42. John F. Whitehead, "East Side, West Side: The Evolution of Residential Architecture," in *Canal Town and County Seat: The Historical Geography of Morris*, ed. Michael P. Conzen and Valerie M. McKay (Studies of the Illinois and Michigan

Canal Corridor, No. 8). (Chicago: University of Chicago, Committee on Geographical Studies, 1994).

43. Jeremy S. Hodess, "The Community on the Eve of the Civil War," and Risa Carley Whitson, "Mining in Morris: Proprietors and Miners in the Coal Trade," in *Canal Town and County Seat: The Historical Geography of Morris*, ed. Michael P. Conzen and Valerie M. McKay (Studies of the Illinois and Michigan Canal Corridor, No. 8). (Chicago: University of Chicago, Committee on Geographical Studies, 1994).

44. Quoted in James W. Sanders, *The Education of an Urban Minority: Catholics in Chicago, 1833–1965* (New York: Oxford University Press, 1977), 21.

45. Evidence that Haley attended St. Angela's can be found in archive narrative of St. Angela's Academy, St. Mary's College Archives, Notre Dame, Indiana, and "The Academy," *Morris Herald*, 28 June 1878.

46. Anna Shannon McAllister, *Flame in the Wilderness: Life and Letters of Mother Angela Gillespie, C.S.C., 1824–1887* (Notre Dame: Sisters of the Holy Cross, 1944), 147–49.

47. Eileen Mary Brewer, *Nuns and the Education of American Catholic Women, 1860–1920* (Chicago: Loyola University Press, 1987), 45–77; *Morris Herald*, 28 June 1878.

48. *Chicago Teachers' Federation Memorial Tribute to Margaret Haley* (Chicago: Chicago Teachers Federation, 1939), 67.

49. *Battleground*, 14.

50. Haley Autobiography, 1935, 413.

51. *Battleground*, 14.

52. Eric J. Hobsbawm, "The Labour Aristocracy in Nineteenth-Century Britain," in Eric J. Hobsbawm, *Laboring Men: Studies in the History of Labour* (London: Weidenfeld and Nicolson, 1964). For discussions on the concept of labor aristocracy and women teachers see Dina M. Copelman, *London's Women Teachers: Gender, Class, and Feminism, 1870–1930* (New York: Routledge, 1996) and Marjorie Murphy, "The Aristocracy of Women's Labor in America," *History Workshop* 22 (August 1986): 56–69.

53. Ignatiev, *How the Irish Became White*.

54. *History of Will County*, 996.

55. Woodruff, *Forty Years Ago*, 19; *History of Will County*, 594.

56. Haley Autobiography, 1935, 725.

57. Haley Autobiography, 1934, 8.

58. *Morris Herald*, 19 July 1878.

59. "Letter to the Editor," *Morris Herald and Advertiser*, 9 May 1874.

60. Twelfth Biennial Report, Superintendent of Public Instruction of the State of Illinois, 1877–1878, Table XI, 122.

61. Laura Doctor Thornburg and Christine A. Ogren, "Normal Schools," in *Historical Dictionary of American Education*, ed. Richard Altenbaugh (Westport, CT: Greenwood Press, 1999), 260–62.

62. "The Morris Normal and Scientific School," *Morris Herald*, 31 May 1878.

63. *Morris Herald*, 6 December 1878.

64. Walter Ray Sanders, "History of Education in Greene County Illinois, 1840–1940," Masters thesis, University of Illinois, 1942, 244–45.

65. *Chicago and its Resources: Twenty Years After, 1871–1891* (Chicago: Chicago Times Co., 1892), 230.

66. *Fourth Annual Announcement of the Normal and Scientific School*, Morris, Grundy County, Illinois, 1881–1882 (Morris, IL: Herald Stern, 1881).

67. Haley Autobiography, 1935, 414.

68. Ibid., 408.

69. Men teachers' average monthly wage was about $40. Twelfth Biennial Report of the Superintendent of Public Instruction of the State of Illinois, 1877–1878, Table IX, 118.

70. *Battleground*, 15; Haley Autobiography, 1935, 8–11.

71. Twelfth Biennial Report of the Superintendent of Public Instruction of the State of Illinois, 1877–1878, 125, 135; *Battleground*, 15–17; Haley Autobiography, 1935, 415.

72. Diary of County Superintendent of Schools, Inspection Visits, 19 May 1880 and 18 February 1881, Will County School Records. Illinois Regional Archives Depository, Illinois Northern University, DeKalb, IL.

73. *Battleground*, 19.

74. Names and Addresses of Persons Attending the August Term at Normal, 1882, *Illinois School Journal* September 1882, 156.

75. Herbart M. Kliebard, "Dewey and the Herbartians: The Genesis of a Theory of Curriculum," in Herbert M. Kliebard, *Forging the American Curriculum: Essays in Curriculum Theory and History* (New York: Routledge, 1992), 68–82; George H. Howe, "The Summer School, *"Semi-Centennial History of the Illinois State Normal University* (David Felmey, 1907), 122. Haley's actual dates of attendance at Normal are unclear. She registered for the summer and may have stayed for the fall semester, which was how she attended James's class, since there is no evidence that he taught in the summer. But Cook County records have her teaching in Cook County schools in the fall of 1882.

76. Of the 261 students from Illinois counties, well over half were women. Haley's name is listed in the catalogue for Special Term for August 1882, meaning that she spent at least six days in the four-week term. Twenty-Fifth Annual Catalogue of the Illinois State Normal University, Normal Illinois, for the year ending May 31, 1883, 32–37.

77. Nathan A. Harvey, "My Early Impressions of Normal," in *Semi-Centennial History of the Illinois State Normal University*, 203–205.

78. Richard Allen Swanson, "Edmund J. James, 1855–1925: A 'Conservative Progressive' in American Education." PhD diss., University of Illinois, 1966.

79. *Battleground*, 20; "Normal News," *Illinois School Journal* (January 1883), 284; Daniel T. Rodgers, *Atlantic Crossings: Social Politics in a Progressive Age* (Cambridge: Harvard University Press, 1998), 84–85, 107–108. James may have had an influence on Haley, but apparently he did not recall her. James's career later crisscrossed Haley's; he would write extensively about municipal reform and school reform issues, and he later moved to Chicago to teach at the University of Chicago and become dean of the newly founded Teachers College there in 1898, president of Northwestern University in 1902, and president of the University of Illinois Champaign-Urbana in 1905. But he and Haley apparently never met again; and his Chicago address book of 1900–01 does not contain Haley's name, although it does contain the names of Ella Rowe, president of the Chicago Teachers' Federation at the time, and Catherine Goggin, Secretary. Manuscript collection of Edmund Janes James, University of Illinois Archives, Champaign-Urbana, IL.

80. *Battleground*, 20–21. In Will County in January 1883, the average woman teacher's salary was $25 to $35 with at least one woman teacher earning $40, or what Haley was asking. Men teachers earned $40 a month. Will County Superintendent's Diary, January 1883, Illinois Regional Archives Depository (IRAD), Illinois Northern University, Dekalb, IL.

81. Theodore Dreiser, *A Book About Myself* (New York: Boni and Liveright, 1922), 1–2.

82. Hasia Diner, *Erin's Daughters in America: Irish Immigrant Women in the Nineteenth Century* (Baltimore: Johns Hopkins University Press, 1983); Sanders, *Education of an Urban Minority*, 130–135. See also Janet Nolan, *Servants of the Poor: Teachers and Mobility in Ireland and Irish America* (Notre Dame, IN: University of Notre Dame Press, 2004); Ellen Skerrett, "The Development of Catholic Identity among Irish Americans in Chicago, 1880–1920," in *From Paddy to Studs: Irish American Communities in the Turn of the Century Era, 1880–1920*, ed. Timothy J. Meagher (New York: Greenwood Press, 1986), 117–38 and Ellen Skerrett, "The Irish in Chicago: The Catholic Dimension," in *Catholicism, Chicago Style*, ed. Ellen Skerrett, Edward R. Kantowicz, and Steven M. Avella (Chicago: Loyola University Press, 1993), 29–62.

83. Haley Autobiography, 1935, 714.

84. Biennial Report of the County Superintendent of Schools, Lemont, 1 July 1882 to 30 June 1884, 46.

85. *Battleground*, 25. In her autobiography, Haley describes this school as Hendricks, but she was mistaken. Hendricks was a much larger school and had a male principal whom Haley admired.

86. Robert Eugene Tostberg, "Educational Ferment in Chicago, 1883–1904," PhD diss., University of Wisconsin, 1960, 53–54.

87. David Hogan, *Class and Reform: School and Society in Chicago, 1880–1930* (Philadelphia: University of Pennsylvania Press, 1985), 85–86.

88. Tostberg, "Educational Ferment in Chicago," 75–76.

89. Francis W. Parker, "An Account of the Work of the Cook County and Chicago Normal School from 1883–1899," *Elementary School Teacher* 2 (June 1902): 752; Tostberg, "Educational Ferment in Chicago," 86.

90. Parker, "An Account of the Work," 754.

91. Ida Cassa Heffron, *Francis Wayland Parker: An Interpretive Biography* (Los Angeles: Ivan Deach, 1934); J. M. Rice, *The Public School System of the United States* (New York: Arno Press, 1969 [1893]), 209–16.

92. Haley Autobiography, 1934, 2.

93. Tostberg, "Educational Ferment in Chicago," 75.

94. Haley Autobiography, 1934, 2.

95. Margaret Haley, "From a Personal Letter Written on March 4," reprinted in *Chicago Teachers' Federation Bulletin* 1 (4 April 1902): 2; *Battleground*, 23–24.

96. James R. Barrett, *Work and Community in the Jungle: Chicago's Packinghouse Workers, 1894–1922* (Urbana: University of Illinois Press, 1987), 19.

97. Howard E. Wilson, *Mary McDowell: Neighbor* (Chicago: University of Chicago Press, 1928), 26–27.

98. Donald L. Miller, *City of the Century: The Epic of Chicago and the Making of America* (New York: Simon and Schuster, 1996), 218–24.

99. Mary McDowell, "Reminiscing on Stock Yards Area," (10 February 1914), Mary McDowell Papers, Chicago Historical Society.

100. *Battleground*, 24.

101. Quoted in Louise Carroll Wade, *Chicago's Pride: The Stockyards, Packingtown, and Environs in the Nineteenth Century* (Urbana: University of Illinois Press, 1987), 183. The Hendricks School was located on the far east side of the Stockyards district, in a neighborhood that was often referred to as Canaryville. See Glen E. Holt and Dominic Pacyga, *Chicago: A Historical Guide to the Neighborhoods* (Chicago: Chicago Historical Society, 1979), 132–39.

102. *Battleground*, 24.

103. Upton Sinclair quoted in Miller, *City of the Century*, 219.

104. Haley Autobiography, 1935, 693.

105. Mary McDowell,"A Quarter of a Century in the Stockyards District" (1919), Mary McDowell Papers, Chicago Historical Society, 17.

106. Wade, *Chicago's Pride*, 233 58

107. Hannah B. Clark, *The Public Schools of Chicago: A Sociological Study* (Chicago: University of Chicago Press, 1897), 99–100; Barrett, *Work and Community in the Jungle*, 19–117.

108. The description of the interior of a typical Chicago school building in 1897 is in Clark, *Public Schools of Chicago*, 90. Other data about the school building was drawn from the 37th Annual Report of Board of Education, 1890–91, and Tract Atlases of the City of Chicago, 1872–1910, Illinois Regional Archives Depository (IRAD), Chicago Branch, Northeastern Illinois University, Chicago.

109. The following information about school facilities and repairs is drawn from the Proceedings of the Board of Education of the City of Chicago, 1891–97.

110. Clark, *Public Schools of Chicago*, 113–14.

111. Rules and Regulations of the Board of Education, Chicago, 1896.

112. Rice, *The Public School System of the United States*, 166–83.

113. Clark, *Public Schools of Chicago*, 31–32, 77–78.

114. *Battleground*, 23.

115. Mary J. Herrick, *The Chicago Schools: A Social and Political History* (Beverly Hills: Sage, 1971), 72–73.

116. Josephine Locke to Ethel Sturgis Dummer, n.d. Ethel Sturgis Dummer Collection, box 20, folder 318, Schlesinger Library, Radcliffe College, Cambridge, MA; "Art in the Public Schools," *Chicago Tribune*, 16 December 16, 1899; "Aroused by Cut" *The Chicago Times*, 9 January 1896.

117. Josephine Locke to Ethel Sturgis Dummer, 7 August 1916, Ethel Sturgis Dummer Collection, box 20, folder 318, Schlesinger Library, Radcliffe College, Cambridge, MA.

118. *Battleground*, 23.

119. *A History of Marshall County, Iowa* (Chicago: Western Historical Society, 1878), 571; Clarence Ray Aurner, *History of Education in Iowa* (Iowa Historical Society, 1916), 136; W. W. Speer, "Observation and Natural Science," *Biennial Report of the Superintendent of Public Instruction, State of Iowa* (Des Moines, 1881), 49–52.

120. *Battleground*, 23; Carolyn Terry Bashaw, "Ella Flagg Young," *Historical Dictionary of Women's Education in the United States*, ed. Linda Eisenmann (Westport CT: Greenwood Press, 1998), 496–98.

121. *Battleground*, 36.

122. Ibid., 22; List of teachers' names from board of education annual reports for inclusive years.

123. Marjorie Murphy, *Blackboard Unions : The AFT and the NEA, 1900–1980* (Ithaca: Cornell University Press, 1990), 42.

124. Herrick, *Chicago Schools*, 72.

125. Clark, *Public Schools of Chicago*, 97.

126. Rice, *Public School System of the United States*, 166–83.

127. Murphy, *Blackboard Unions*, 34–43.

CHAPTER 2. THE EDUCATION OF AN ACTIVIST

1. *Battleground*, 22.

2. Haley Autobiography, 1934, 3

3. *Battleground*, 40.

4. *Battleground*, 26; Skerrett, "The Development of Catholic Identity," 117–38; Skerrett, "The Irish in Chicago," 29–62; Maria Lettiere Roberts and Richard Stamz, *Chicago's Englewood Neighborhood at the Junction* (Chicago: Arcadia, 2002).

5. *Battleground*, 27.

6. Haley Autobiography, 1934, 16; Elizabeth Haley obituary, *Joliet Daily Republic and Sun*, 21 January 1888.

7. Jackie M. Blount, "Manly Men and Womanly Women: Deviance, Gender Role Polarization, and the Shift in Women's School Employment, 1900–1976," *Harvard Educational Review* 66 (Summer 1996); Diner, *Erin's Daughters*.

8. John K. Folger and Charles B. Nam, *Education of the American Population: a 1960 Census Monograph* (Washington, DC: U.S. Bureau of the Census, 1967), 81.

9. Margaret Haley probate records, Office of the Circuit Court Clerk of Cook County, Chicago.

10. Catherine Goggin, "Early Days," n.d., box 35, CTF Papers. For more on singleness and working women see Ruth Freeman and Patrcia Klaus, "Blessed or Not? The New Spinster in England and the United States in the Late Nineteenth and Early Twentieth Centuries," *Journal of Family History* 9 (Winter 1984): 394–414.

11. Blount, "Manly Men and Womenly Women"; Martha Vicinis, "Lesbian History: All Theory and No Facts or All Facts and No Theory?" *Radical History Review* 60 (1994); Carol Smith-Rosenberg, "The Female World of Love and Ritual: Relations Between Women in Nineteenth-Century America," in her *Disorderly Conduct: Visions of Gender in Victorian America* (New York: Knopf, 1985).

12. Joanne J. Meyerowitz, *Women Adrift: Independent Wage Earners in Chicago, 1880–1930* (Chicago: University of Chicago Press, 1988), 4–5, 7.

13. Don T. Davis, "The Chicago Teachers Federation and the School Board," n.d., box 1, folder 2, CTF Papers.

14. Public Schools of the City of Chicago, Annual Reports of the Board of Education for years 1894–1897.

15. Gary Cross and Peter Shergold, "We Think We Are of the Oppressed: Gender, White Collar Work, and Grievances of Late Nineteenth-Century Women," *Labor History* 28 (Winter 1987): 23–53.

16. Salary figures from Proceedings of the Board of Education of the City of Chicago, 1894–1895.

17. In 1880, Michael Haley was identified as a "Greenbacker" who was a prominent player in Chicago's 8th Ward Land League Club. *Chicago Tribune*, 22 December 1880.

18. Lawrence J. McCaffrey, "The Irish-American Dimension," and Michael F. Funchion, "The Political and Nationalist Dimensions," in *The Irish in Chicago*, ed. Lawrence J. McCaffrey, Ellen Skerrett, Michael F. Funchion, and Charles Fanning (Chicago: University of Illinois Press, 1987).

19. Sanders, *Education of an Urban Minority*, 130–135.

20. Diner, *Erin's Daughters*, 142–49.

21. Susan Levine, *Labor's True Woman: Carpet Weavers, Industrialization, and Labor Reform in the Gilded Age* (Philadelphia: Temple University Press, 1984).

22. Ralph Scharnau, "Elizabeth Morgan, Crusader for Labor Reform," *Labor History* 14 (Summer 1973): 340–51; Meredith Tax, *The Rising of the Women: Feminist Solidarity and Class Conflict, 1880–1917* (New York: Monthly Review Press, 1980), ch. 4; Alice Henry, "Corinne Brown," *Life and Labor* 14 (June 1914): 188–89.

23. Marjorie Murphy, "From Artisan to Semi-Professional: White Collar Unionism Among Chicago Public School Teachers, 1870–1930," PhD diss., University of California, Davis, 171.

24. On teachers as labor aristocracy see Copelman, *London's Women Teachers*: and Kate Rousmaniere, "Where Haley Stood: Margaret Haley, Teachers' Work, and the Problem of Teacher Identity," in *Telling Women's Lives: Narrative Inquiries in the History of Women's Education*, ed. Kathleen Weiler and Sue Middleton (Philadelphia: Open University Press, 1999).

25. Herrick, *Chicago Schools*, 75; Clark, *Public Schools of Chicago*, 88–90.

26. Kate Rousmaniere, "Good Teachers Are Born, Not Made: Self-Regulation in the Work of Nineteenth-Century American Women Teachers," in *Discipline, Moral Regulation, and Schooling: A Social History*, ed. Kate Rousmaniere, Kari Dehli, and Ning de Coninck-Smith (New York: Garland Press, 1997), 117–33.

27. "Inaugural Address of Miss Catherine Goggin, President of the Chicago Teachers' Federation," *The Chicago Teacher and School Board Journal* 1 (June 1899): 307.

28. Theda Skocpol, *Protecting Soldiers and Mothers: The Political Origins of Social Policy in the United States* (Cambridge: Harvard University Press, 1992).

29. Chicago city police and firemen got a pension in 1890. Lillian C. Flint, "Pensions for Women Teachers," *The Century Magazine* (1901): 618–20; Elizabeth A. Allen, "Teachers' Pensions—The Story of a Women's Campaign," *The Review of Reviews* 15 (1897): 700–711.

30. Public Schools of the City of Chicago, Forty-First Annual Report of the Board of Education, 1895, 47–51.

31. Murphy, "From Artisan to Semi-Professional," 106–107.

32. In 1895 there were 4,326 teachers employed by the Chicago public school system. 4,027 (95%) of these were women. Of men teachers, more than half taught in the city's ten high schools, where they worked in about equal proportion to women. The remaining eighty eight men taught in primary and grammar schools and as special education teachers. All high school principals were male, but half of elementary principals were female. Public Schools of the City of Chicago, Forty-First Annual Report of the Board of Education, 1895, 34. For discussions about the fear

of "feminization" of male children see "Are There Too Many Women Teachers," *Educational Review* 28 (June 1904): 98–99; C. W. Bardeen, "Why Teaching Repels Men," *Educational Review* 35 (April 1908): 352–57.

33. William Graebner, "Retirement in Education: The Economic and Social Function of the Teachers' Pension," *History of Education Quarterly* 18 (Winter 1978): 397–418.

34. Arvilla C. DeLuce, "Brief Account of the Pension Movement," box 1, folder 2, CTF papers.

35. DeLuce, "Brief Account of the Pension Movement," *Chicago Times Herald*, 14 November 1895. Catherine Goggin, "The Chicago Pension Law," *School Journal* 54 (1 May 1897): 542.

36. Goggin, "The Chicago Pension Law"; *Battleground*, 34; Herrick, *Chicago Schools*, 96; Clark, *Public Schools of Chicago*, 47.

37. Goggin, "The Chicago Pension Law."

38. Proceedings of the Board of Education of the City of Chicago, 1896–1897, 246.

39. Herbert M. Kliebard, "John Dewey," in *Historical Dictionary of American Education*, ed. Richard Altenbaugh (Westport, CT: Greenwood Press, 1999), 111–13.

40. Charles R. J. Collins, "The University of Buffalo School of Pedagogy, 1895–1898," *Niagara Frontier* 19 (Summer 1972): 30–41; *Battleground*, 27.

41. Haley attended at least two Catholic summer institutes for teachers—one at Lake Champlain, possibly in the summer of 1896 right after she left Buffalo, and the Sinsinawa summer school in Madison, probably in the summer of 1897. "Summer School at Sinsinawa," *The Young Eagle*, St. Clara Academy, Sinsinawa, Wisconsin, September 1897. Sinsinawa Dominican Archives, Sinsinawa, Wisconsin.

42. Robert D. Cross, *The Emergence of Liberal Catholicism in America* (Cambridge: Harvard University Press, 1958); Henry J. Browne, *The Catholic Church and the Knights of Labor* (Washington, DC: Catholic University of America Press, 1949).

43. Thomas Edward Shields, *Teachers' Manual of Primary Methods* (Washington, DC: The Catholic Education Press, 1912), 35; Justine Ward, *Thomas Edward Shields: Biologist, Psychologist, Educator* (New York: Scribners, 1947), 125–214.

44. *Battleground*, 28.

45. Karen M. Kennelly, C.S.J., "Women Religious, the Intellectual Life, and Anti-Intellectualism: History and Present Situation," in *Women Religious and the Intellectual Life: The North American Achievement*, ed. Bridget Puzon, O.S.U. (San Francisco: International Scholars Publications, 1996), 46–48; Sister Mary Nona McGreal, O.P., M.A., "The Role of a Teaching Sisterhood in American Education," PhD diss., Catholic University of America, 1951, 50–54; Janet Margaret Welsh, O.P., B.A., M.A., "Where the Spirit Dwells: Catholic and Protestant Women and the Development of Christianity in the Upper Mississippi River Valley Lead Region, 1830–1870," PhD diss., University of Notre Dame, 1995.

46. The Women's Catholic Order of Foresters (chartered in 1894), like its brother institution the Men's Catholic Order of Foresters, was formed for the purpose of providing death benefits to families of deceased members. Both organizations allowed Catholic membership only. In April 1897 it had 7,500 members. *The Women's Catholic Forester* 2 (25 May 1897): 5.

47. Haley Autobiography, 1935, 633.

48. Levine, *Labors' True Woman*, 136–38, 140; Archie Jones, "Elizabeth Flynn Rodgers," *Notable American Women*, Vol. 3 (Cambridge: Harvard University Press, 1971), 187–88; "Mrs. Rodgers is dead at 92," *Chicago Tribune*, 28 August 1939.

49. *Battleground*, 30.

50. Don H. Doyle, "Rules of Order: Henry Martyn Robert and the Popularization of American Parliamentary Law," *American Quarterly* 32 (Spring 1980): 3–18.

51. Haley's version of the debate in *Battleground* ignores the work of her colleagues, and describes the story as one of her own solitary attack on the autocratic procedures of the Foresters. Although the incident happened in 1898, the account of it can be found in the Women's Catholic Order of Foresters Verbatim Report, Biennial Session, May 1900. Archives of the National Catholic Society of Foresters, Mt. Prospect, Illinois.

52. *Battleground*, 30.

53. Haley Autobiography, 1911, 205; *Battleground*, 30–31; Women's Catholic Order of Foresters, Verbatim Report.

54. *The Women's Catholic Forester* 2 (25 May 1897), 5.

55. Haley Autobiography, 1911, 206.

56. *Battleground*, 32–33.

57. Women's Catholic Order of Foresters Verbatim Report.

58. Haley Autobiography, 1911, 205.

59. Leila J. Rupp, "Is Feminism the Province of Old (or Middle-Aged) Women?" *Journal of Women's History* 12 (Winter 2001): 164–73; Kay Whitehead and Stephen Thorpe, "The Function of Age and the History of Women's Work: The Career of an Australian Teacher, 1907–1947," *Gender and History* 16 (April 2004): 172–97.

60. Herrick, *Chicago Schools*, 96; Catherine Goggin, "The Chicago Teachers' Federation," 1906, box 1, folder 2, CTF Papers.

61. *Chicago Tribune*, 16 March 1899.

62. Catherine Goggin, draft manuscript, 3 November 1906, box 1, folder 2, CTF papers. In 1897 there were 4,216 elementary teachers who taught primary school (grades 1–4) and grammar school (grades 5–8). Also welcomed by the Federation were about one hundred special teachers who taught Kindergarten (108 women), deaf-mute, or special classes for crippled children. *Chicago Board of Education Annual Report* 1897, 28.

63. Davis, "The Chicago Teachers' Federation"; Goggin, "The Chicago Teachers' Federation."

64. Goggin, draft manuscript, 1906; Herrick, *Chicago Schools*, 96.

65. "Gallery of Local Characters: Catherine Goggin," *Chicago Tribune*, 3 November 1901; Catherine Goggin probate records, Office of the Circuit Court Clerk of Cook County, Chicago; Shepherd Johnston, *Historical Sketches of the Public School System of the City of Chicago* (Chicago: Clark and Edwards, 1880), 43; Clark, *Chicago Schools*, 23.

66. Clark, *Public Schools of Chicago*, 52–58.

67. Obituary for Margaret L. Goggin, *Chicago Daily News*, 27 August 1880.

68. Obituary for James Goggin, *Chicago Daily News*, 29 March, 1898; Johnston, *Historical Sketches*, 46; Haley Autobiography, 1934, 5.

69. *Thirty-Sixth Annual Report of the Board of Education of the City of Chicago*, 1890, 219; *Public Schools of the City of Chicago Monthly Summaries of Statistics for School Year 1896–97*; Jones School, Board of Education Records, Illinois

Regional Archives Depository (IRAD), Chicago Branch, Northeastern Illinois University, Chicago.

70. M. Bunton, "Professions," 1942, Illinois Writers' Project, box 35, folder 1, Carter Woodson Library, Chicago.

71. "Gallery of Local Characters."

72. Haley Autobiography, 1911, 250.

73. Haley Autobiography, 1934, 2–3.

74. Haley Autobiography, 1935, 222.

75. Catherine Goggin, "The Report of the Educational Commission," *Chicago Teacher and School Board Journal* 1 (February 1899): 85, 87–88; Julia Wrigley, *Class Politics and the Public Schools: Chicago, 1900–1950* (New Brunswick, NJ: Rutgers University Press, 1982), 92–104.

76. *Battleground*, 35.

77. Haley Autobiography, 1935, 517; *Battleground*, 35–36.

78. Haley Autobiography, 1911, 218–19.

79. Haley Autobiography, 1911, 206–207; Haley Autobiography, 1935, 516; *Battleground*, 36.

80. *Chicago Tribune*, 11 February 1899; William Hard, "Margaret Haley, Rebel," *The Times Magazine* 1 (January 1907): 233.

81. Haley Autobiography, 1911, 212.

82. Ibid., 213.

83. *Battleground*, 36–37.

84. *Chicago Tribune*, 25 March 1899.

85. *Chicago Tribune*, 19 June 1899; quoted in Hogan, *Class and Reform*, 197; Maureen A. Flanagan, *Seeing with Their Hearts: Chicago Women and the Vision of a Good City, 1871–1933* (Princeton: Princeton University Press, 2002), 67–68.

86. Haley Autobiography, 1911, 216–17.

87. Haley Autobiography, 1911, 244–46; *Battleground*, 37; Haley Autobiography, 1935, 517.

88. *Battleground*, 87; *Chicago Tribune*, 6 June 1899.

89. Chicago Teachers' Federation minutes, 28 May 1898– 24 June 1898, box 1, CTF Papers; "February meetings of the Chicago Teachers' Associations," *The Chicago Teacher and School Board Journal* 1 (March 1899): 14.

90. Haley Autobiography, 1935, 521; Haley Autobiography, 1911, 257–58.

91. CTF minutes, 28 January, 1899, box 1, CTF Papers.

92. Resignation letter by Elizabeth Burdick, CTF minutes, February 4, 1899, box 1, CTF Papers; "Miss Burdick is Out," *Chicago Tribune*, 5 February 1899.

93. Haley Autobiography, 1911, 249.

94. Ibid., 247–49.

95. Haley Autobiography, 1911, 254–56; Hard, "Margaret Haley, Rebel," 234–35.

96. Haley Autobiography, 1911, 257–62; CTF Minutes, 29 April 1899, box 1, CTF Papers.

97. W. O. Chapman, "Miss Goggin Beloved by Host of Teachers," *Chicago Herald* (January 5, 1916), reprinted in *Margaret A. Haley's Bulletin* (27 January 1916): 29.

98. Hogan, *Class and Reform*, 197–98.

99. Catherine Goggin to Ella Flagg Young, 21 June 1899, box 35, folder 1, CTF Papers.

100. *Chicago Tribune*, 18 June 1899.

101. Robert E. Knoll, *Prairie University: A History of the University of Nebraska* (Lincoln: University of Nebraska Press, 1995), 41–55.

102 . Haley Autobiography, 1911, 252–65; "Miss Goggin Wins Fight," *Chicago Tribune*, 26 March 1899.

103. *Battleground*, 37.

104. Hard, "Margaret Haley, Rebel," 234–35

105. "Democracy in Education," *The Public* (5 May 1906): 100–103.

106. *Battleground*, 86.

107. Ibid., 40.

108. Ibid., 30.

109. Ibid., 41.

CHAPTER 3. BATTLEGROUND

1. The most detailed secondary accounts of the teachers' tax case are Marjorie Murphy, "Taxation and Social Conflict: Teacher Unionism and Public School Finance in Chicago, 1898–1934," *Journal of the Illinois State Historical Society* 74 (1981): 242–60; and John F. Lyons, "The Limits of Professionalism: The Response of Chicago Schoolteachers to Cuts in Education Expenditures, 1929–1933," *Journal of Illinois History* 1 (Autumn 1998): 4–22.

2. The term *franchise* in this case was directed primarily at public utility corporations and meant the right or privilege of a corporation "to use the public streets of the city, to burrow beneath them, or to go above them." The franchise was both the opportunity to use property and "that indefinable something" that gave property its value—be it location, access to other locations, or other advantages. Edwin R. A. Seligman, "Taxation of Franchise Values," *Municipal Affairs* 6 (1902): 765–73. The topic of franchise values obsessed economic theorists at the turn of the century. See the first six volumes of *Municipal Affairs*, a journal "devoted to the consideration of urban problems from the standpoint of the taxpayer and citizen" (1897–1902).

3. Robert Murray Haig, "A History of the General Property Tax in Illinois," *University of Illinois Bulletin* 11 (June 1914): 200–216; Hiram B. Loomis, "Franchise Taxation in Illinois," *Municipal Affairs* 5 (June 1901): 398–400; Joel Roscoe Moore, *Taxation of Corporations in Illinois Other Than Railroads Since 1872* (University of Illinois Press, 1913).

4. Haig, "A History of General Property Tax," 205.

5. Sidney I. Roberts, "The Municipal Voters' League and Chicago's Boodlers," *Journal of Illinois State Historical Society* 2 (Summer 1960): 117–48.

6. Autobiography of Margaret Haley, 1910, box 32, CTF Papers, Chicago Historical Society, installment 3, 5.

7. Ibid., installment 6, 2.

8. *Chicago Tribune*, 23 August 1904.

9. Staley, *History of the Illinois State Federation of Labor*, 29–30.

10. John L. Thomas, *Alternative America: Henry George, Edward Bellamy, Henry Demarest Lloyd, and the Adversary Tradition* (Cambridge: Harvard University Press, 1983); William J. Reese, *Power and the Promise of School Reform: Grassroots Movements During the Progressive Era* (Boston: Routledge, 1986), esp. ch. 3.

11. Robert M . Bremner, "The Single Tax Philosophy in Cleveland and Toledo," *American Journal of Economics and Sociology* 9 (April 1950): 369–76; Byron W. Holt, "The Single Tax Applied to Cities," *Municipal Affairs* 3 (June 1899): 328–49; Eugene C. Murdock, *Tom Johnson of Cleveland* (Dayton: Wright State University Press, 1994); M. Barclay, "Reform in Toledo: The Political Career of Samuel M. Jones," *Northwest Ohio Quarterly* 50 (Summer 1978): 79–89; Eugene M. Tobin, "In Pusuit of Equal Taxation: Jersey City's Struggle Against Corporate Arrogance and Tax-Dodging by the Railroad Trust," *American Journal of Economics and Sociology* 34 (April 1975): 213–24.

12. Bremner, "The Single Tax Philosophy"; Robert H. Bremner, "The Civic Revival In Ohio: Municipal Ownership and Economic Privilege," *American Journal of Economics and Sociology* 7 (July 1950): 213–24.

13. Elizabeth J. Hauser, ed., *My Story, by Tom L. Johnson* (New York, B. W. Huebsch, 1911), 48.

14. Tom L. Johnson to Catherine Goggin and Margaret Haley, 7 November 1901, box 36, folder 3, CTF Papers.

15. Quoted in Reese, *Power and the Promise*, 119.

16. Haley Autobiography, 1935, 430–31.

17. *Battleground*, 20.

18. Haley Autobiography, 1911, 8; Hiram B. Loomis, "Franchise Taxation in Illinois," *Municipal Affairs* 5 (June 1901): 388–400.

19. Linda K. Kerber, *No Constitutional Right to be Ladies* (New York: Hill and Wang, 1998), ch. 3.

20. "Inaugural Address of Miss Catherine Goggin," *The Chicago Teacher and School Board Journal* 1 (June 1899): 310.

21. Herrick, *Chicago Schools*, 102.

22. Rheta Childe Dorr quoted in Paula Baker, "The Domestication of Politics: Women and American Political Society, 1780–1920," *American Historical Review* 89 (April 1984): 632.

23. Maureen A. Flanagan, "Gender and Urban Political Reform: The City Club and the Woman's City Club of Chicago in the Progressive Era," *American Historical Review* 95 (October 1990): 1032–50.

24. *The School Weekly*, 3 May 1901.

25. Maureen A. Flanagan, *Charter Reform in Chicago* (Carbondale: Southern Illinois University Press, 1987), 41–42.

26. *Chicago Journal*, 18 October 1900.

27. "The Tax War," *Chicago Teachers' Federation Bulletin* 1 (31 January 1902).

28. Josiah Cratty to Margaret Haley and Catharine Goggin, 23 March 1901, box 36, folder 1, CTF Papers.

29. *The New World*, 4 May 1901.

30. J. L. Spalding, Bishop of Peoria, to Katharine [sic] Goggin, 11 November 1901, box 36, folder 3, CTF Papers.

31. A. J. Phillips to Margaret Haley, 20 March 1903, box 37, folder 3, CTF Papers.

32. Sarah M. Perkins to Margaret Haley, 23 November 1901, box 36, folder 3, CTF Papers; Edward M. Bemis to Margaret Haley, 4 December 1901, box 36, folder 3, CTF Papers.

33. Susan B. Anthony to Margaret Haley, July 1903 (handwritten copy of original), box, 37, folder 3, CTF Papers.

34. Address of Miss Margaret A. Haley before Public Ownership League of the Chicago Federation of Labor, 29 August 1915, box 43, folder 3, CTF Papers.

35. A. E. Winship, "A Woman's Victory for Schools," *Everybody's Magazine* 7 (October 1902): 395.

36. Haley Autobiography, 1910, installment 7, 1–4; *Battleground*, 63–64.

37. *Battleground*, 71.

38. Ibid., 72.

39. Quoted in Herrick, *The Chicago Schools*, 103.

40. Haley Autobiography, 1910, installment 2, 1–2.

41. Ibid., 3–5.

42. S. J. Duncan Clark, "Militant Miss Haley: Still Fighting After Thirty Years," *Chicago Daily News*, 17 April 1931.

43. *Battleground*, 68.

44. Haley Autobiography, 1911, 10; *Battleground*, 68.

45. *Battleground*, 71.

46. Haley Autobiography, 1911, 74.

47. Ibid., 81.

48. Ibid., 78–79.

49. Ibid., 4.

50. Ibid., 34.

51. Ibid., 12.

52. Ibid., 20.

53. Ibid., 30–31.

54. Kate M. O'Conor to Margaret Haley, 5 February 1902, box 36, folder, 4, CTF Papers; Haley Autobiography, 1910, installment 8, 5.

55. Margaret Haley to Catherine Goggin, 1 February 1901, box 36, folder 1, CTF Papers.

56. Margaret Haley to Catherine Goggin , n.d. box, 35, folder, 4, CTF Papers; Margaret Haley to Catherine Goggin, 12 November 1900, box 35, folder 4, CTF Papers.

57. Haley Autobiography, 1911, 15.

58. Haley Autobiography, 1911, 35; *Battleground*, 74.

59. *Battleground*, 60.

60. Carter Alexander, *Some Present Aspects of the Work of Teachers' Voluntary Associations in the United States* (New York: Teachers College Press, 1910).

61. "Miss Goggin Wins Fight," *Chicago Tribune*, 26 March 1899; "Inaugural Address of Miss Catherine Goggin, President of the Chicago Teachers' Federation," *The Chicago Teacher and School Board Journal* 1, (June 1899): 307; William W. Thompson to Max Loeb, 23 November 1915, box 43, folder 5, CTF Papers.

62. Don T. Davis, "The Chicago Teachers' Federation and the School Board," n.d., box 1, folder 2, CTF Papers; William W. Wattenberg, *On the Educational Front: The Reactions of Teachers' Associations in New York and Chicago* (New York: Columbia University Press, 1936), 128–29.

63. Deborah Ann Skok, "Catholic Ladies Bountiful: Chicago's Catholic Settlement Houses and Day Nurseries, 1892–1930," PhD diss. University of Chicago, 2001.

64. "Memorial Meeting in Honor of Florence E. Tennery," *Chicago Teachers' Federation Bulletin* 6 (24 May 1907), 7.

65. "Elizabeth C. Buhmann Honored by Teachers," *Margaret Haley's Bulletin* 7 (15 April 1930): 219, 229; information about Anna Murphy and other teachers is from Chicago census.

66. Isaiah T. Greenacre obituary, *New York Times*, 10 April 1944; Biographical information about Isaiah T. Greenacre from Englewood Community Collection, 1870–1966, series IX, box 2, folder 9, Special Collections, Chicago Public Library, Harold Washington Library Center; Isaiah T. Greenacre, "Argument for Woman Suffrage," *Chicago Teachers' Federation Bulletin* 6 (31 May 1907). Personal insights about Greenacre are from a helpful conversation with Greenacre's grandson, Peter Richter, 30 June, 2003.

67. F. Blanche Preble, "Our Gallant Leader," *Memorial Bulletin for Margaret Haley*, 1939, box 71, folder 3, CTF Papers, p. 41.

68. "Mr McCahey's Message," *Memorial Bulletin for Margaret Haley*, 27.

69. Preble, "Our Gallant Leader," 42.

70. Mary E. Dutton, *Memorial Bulletin for Margaret Haley*, 64.

71. Preble, "Our Gallant Leader," 43.

72. Margaret Haley to Mr. Ferguson, 22 August 1920, box 48, folder 2, CTF Papers.

73. "Femininity and Fights" *Memorial Bulletin for Margaret Haley*, 35.

74. Robert C. Kennan, "Miss Haley," *Memorial Bulletin for Margaret Haley*, 32.

75. John Dewey to Alice Dewey, 16 April 1907, John Dewey papers, Morris Library, University of Southern Illinois, Carbondale.

76. Richard Finnegan, *Memorial Bulletin for Margaret Haley*, 17.

77. *Battleground*, 275.

78. "Miss Haley, Business Agent," *Chicago Tribune*, 12 April 1903.

79. "Catherine Goggin and Margaret Haley," *Journal of Education* 55 (22 May 1902).

80. Sarah Deutsch "Learning to Talk More Like a Man: Boston Women's Class-Bridging Organizations, 1870–1940," *American Historical Review* 97 (April 1992): 397; Michael McGerr, "Political Style and Women's Power, 1830–1930," *Journal of American History* 77 (December 1990): 864–85.

81. Clarence Darrow, *The Story of My Life* (New York: Scribners, 1932),105.

82. "Miss Haley, Business Agent," *Chicago Tribune*, 12 April 1903. Margaret Haley to Franklin Edmonds, 2 June 1903, box 37, folder 3, CTF Papers; Haley Autobiography, 1910, installment 9, 6.

83. Haley autobiography, 1910, installment 9, 6; *Battleground*, 61.

84. Report of the Educational Department of the Chicago Teachers' Federation, 2 April 1903, box 37, folder 3, CTF Papers.

85. "Out to Aid Gallagher," *Chicago Tribune*, 14 June 1903.

86. *Battleground*, 61.

87. Haley Autobiography, 1911, 40.

88. *Chicago Teachers' Federation Bulletin* 1 (November 15, 1901), 2.

89. "Miss Haley at the Davidson," *Milwaukee Sentinel*, 28 December 1901.

90. Haley Autobiography, 1911, 41–42.

91. Winship, "A Woman's Victory," 395; Haley Autobiography, 1911, 42–44.

92. Margaret Haley, "Dear Friend," 19 November 1902, box 36, folder 5, CTF Papers.

93. Margaret Haley to Franklin S. Edmonds, 2 June 1903, box 37, folder 3, CTF Papers.

94. Charles Viana to Margaret Haley, 11 February 1903, box 37, folder 3, CTF Papers.

95. "Why Our Schoolmarms Don't Get Married," *Chicago Teachers' Federation Bulletin* 6 (8 November 1907): 5.

96. M. Louise Garcia, "The Teacher," *Chicago Teachers' Federation Bulletin* 3 (29 November 1903): 3.

97. R. E. Freeman to Chicago Teachers' Federation, 20 January 1902, box 36, folder 4, CTF Papers.

98. C. W. Bailey to Margaret Haley, 10 February 1903, box 37, folder 3, CTF Papers.

99. Kate Tehan to Chicago Teachers' Federation, 28 December 1903, box 37, folder 4, CTF Papers.

100. Mary J. Collins to Margaret Haley, 29 September 1902, box 36, folder 5, CTF Papers.

101. Ibid.

102. Anna McKillop to Margaret Haley, 18 September 1902, box 36, folder 5, CTF Papers.

103. Haley Autobiography, 1910, installment 8, 2

104. Haley Autobiography, 1910, installment 8, 2; Haley Autobiography, 1911, 36.

105. John Sinclair to Margaret Haley, 18 December 1901, box 36, folder 3, CTF Papers.

106. Genevieve Turk to Catherine Goggin, 1902, box 36, folder 5, CTF Papers.

107. Emma Tracy to Margaret Haley, 11 February 1902, box 36, folder 4, CTF Papers.

108. Ida M. Jackson to Margaret Haley, 28 December 1901, box 36, folder 3, CTF Papers.

109. "Labor Unions Parade in the Pouring Rain," *The Daily Eagle*, Marinette, Wisconsin, 8 September 1903.

110. "Election will be held today," *Milwaukee Sentinel*, 30 December 1903.

111. A. E. Winship to Margaret Haley, 17 March 1903, box 37, folder 3, CTF Papers.

112. George W. Hanley to Margaret Haley, 20 August 1903, box 37, folder 4, CTF Papers.

113. Margaret Haley to E. W. Krackowizer, 12 October 1903, box 37, folder 4, CTF Papers.

114. Margaret Haley to E. W. Krackowizer, 7 October 1903, box 37, folder 4, CTF Papers.

115. Margaret Haley to Mr. William G. Bruce, 7 October 1903, box 37, folder 4, CTF Papers.

116. Margaret Haley to Thomas Boyce, 23 September 1903, box 37, folder 4, CTF Papers; Catherine Goggin to unknown, 12 April 1906, box 39, folder 1, CTF Papers.

117. *Chicago Teachers' Federation Bulletin* 1 (16 May 1902): 3.

118. Marie Coe to Catherine Goggin, 11 August 1901, box 36, folder 2, CTF Papers; "Woman Beats Chicago's Franchise Tax Dodgers," *Buffalo Courier*, 19 August 1901.

119. Handwritten note by Margaret Haley, 3 August 1901, Buffalo, N.Y., box 36, folder 2, CTF Papers.

120. Margaret Haley, "How Norway Voted 'Yes' for Disunion from Sweden," *Chicago Teachers' Federation Bulletin* 4 (15 September 1905): 5–6.

121. This argument was pointed out in George Counts, *School and Society in Chicago* (New York: Harcourt, Brace), 90.

122. Haley Autobiography, 1911, 118.

123. *Chicago Tribune*, 23 August 1904.

124. Catherine Goggin, "Mass Teachers Meeting," 29 October 1900, box 35, folder 5, CTF Papers.

125. Catherine Goggin, "The Chicago Teachers Federation," *Chicago Teacher and School Board Journal* 1 (May 1899): 258.

126. David Ricker, "The School-Teacher Unionized," *Educational Review* 30 (November 1905), 356; Lois Weiner, "Teachers, Unions, and School Reform: Examining Margaret Haley's Vision," *Educational Foundations* 10 (Summer 1996): 87. Cherry Collins makes a similar observation about Haley's and Goggin's role as women trying to change the public world from which they were excluded in "Regaining the Past for the Present: The Legacy of the Chicago Teachers' Federation," *History of Education Review* 13 (1984).

127. Haley Autobiography, 1911, 64.

128. Margaret Haley to the Ohio Superintendent of Physical Education, 4 May 1902, box 36, folder 4, CTF Papers.

129. *Battleground*, 132.

CHAPTER 4. TREATIES AND SKIRMISHES

1. *Battleground*, 90.

2. Margaret Haley, "Catherine Goggin," *Margaret A. Haley's Bulletin* 2 (January 27, 1916): 3.

3. Murphy, *Blackboard Unions*, 72; David Montgomery, *Beyond Equality* (New York: Vintage, 1967), 387–424.

4. Teachers in San Antonio, San Francisco, St. Paul, and Milwaukee were closely affiliated with organized labor. *Chicago Teachers' Federation Bulletin* 3 (October 1902); Harriet Talan, "San Francisco Federation of Teachers: 1919–1949," Masters thesis, San Francisco State University, 1982.

5. Haley Autobiography, 1911, 265–66.

6. Murphy, *Blackboard Unions*, 68

7. Corinne S. Brown, "Why the Teachers Did It," *The Socialist Spirit* 2 (January 1903): 24.

8. *Battleground*, 90.

9. Wrigley, *Class Politics and the Public Schools*, 23, 26–27.

10. Anna Nichols, "Women and Trade Unions," *The Commons* 9 (June 1904): 268–73.

11 . Mary Herrick to Carl Megel, 19 September 1973, Carl Megel papers, box 21, folder 5, Archives of the American Federation of Teachers, Archives of Labor and Urban Affairs, Walter Reuther Library, Detroit, Michigan.

12. *Chicago Tribune*, 8 May 1899; Wrigley, *Class Politics and the Public Schools*, 48–60.

13. Wrigley, *Class Politics and the Public Schools*, 110–13.

14. Murphy, "From Artisan to Semi-Professional," 58–60.

15. Copies of letters from Dewey, Parker, and Shields, box 37, folder 3, CTF Archives; CFL letter in *Board of Education Proceedings*, 3 September 1902, 63.

16. *Battleground*, 37, 87–88; J. H. Bowman, "Chicago Public Schools: What the Cleveland Educators Think of the Speer System," *Union Labor Advocate* 2 (April 1902).

17. Haley Autobiography, 1911, 11; "Offers Bonus for Merit," *Chicago Tribune*, 3 July 1902.

18. W. D. MacClintock to William Rainey Harper, 24 October 1903, President's papers 1889–1925, Joseph Regenstein Library, University of Chicago.

19. Wayne J. Urban, *Why Teachers Organized* (Detroit: Wayne State University Press, 1982), 39; Hogan, *Class and Reform*, 199–200.

20. Haley Autobiography, 1911, 112–13; Herrick, *The Chicago Schools*, 106.

21. Robert Lowe, "The Chicago Teachers' Federation and its Legacy," in *Transforming Teacher Unions: Fighting for Better Schools and Social Justice*, ed. Bob Peterson and Michael Charney (Milwaukee: Rethinking Schools, 1999), 78–85.

22. *Battleground*, 80; Haley Autobiography, 1911, 113; *Chicago Tribune*, 3 July 1902.

23. *Chicago Tribune*, 3, 8, 19 September 1902, 1 October 1902.

24. *Chicago Board of Education Proceedings*, 29 October 1902, 186; "Striking Students," *Chicago Tribune*, 7 November 1902.

25. *Blackboard Unions*, 9–10; "Calls Teachers a Victim of Plot," *Chicago Tribune*, 14 November 1902.

26. *Chicago Tribune*, 1 November 1902.

27. "Letter of Mr. John Fitzpatrick Inviting the Chicago Teachers' Federation to Affiliate with Organized Labor," in Report of Fifteen Years of Organization, box 39, folder 1908, CTF Papers; Haley Autobiography, 1911, 113.

28. "Why Chicago's Teachers Unionized," *Harper's Weekly* 60 (19 June 1915): 598–600.

29. "Editorial Notes," *The Elementary School Teacher* 5 (March 1905): 442.

30. "Teachers Differ on 'Unionizing,'" *Chicago Tribune*, 12 November 1902; *The Public* 5 (15 November 1902): 499.

31. *Battleground*, 91.

32. "Teachers Differ on 'Unionizing,'" 1902; *The Public* 5 (November 15, 1902), 499.

33. Haley Autobiography, 1911, 113.

34. Ibid., 1911, 114–15.

35. Isaiah Greenacre to Margaret Haley, 4 December 1902, box 36, folder 5, CTF Papers.

36. *Chicago Tribune*, 9 November 1902.

37. "Teachers Form National Union," *Chicago Tribune*, 15 November 1902.

38. "Teachers Differ on 'Unionizing,'" 1902; Murphy, "From Artisan to Semi-Professional," 176–78.

39. Urban, *Why Teachers Organized*, 82. Catherine Goggin to Carter Alexander, 27 May 1910, Box 40, folder 2, CTF Papers.

40. "Chicago Teachers in the Union," *Appeal to Reason* (6 December 1902).

41. Quoted in Herrick, *Chicago Schools*, 108.

42. "Snap Shots Taken by Delegate," *Chicago Teachers' Federation Bulletin* 2 (19 December 1902): 5.

43. "Chicago Federation of Labor: Impressions of a New Delegate," *Chicago Teachers' Federation Bulletin* 2 (27 February 1903): 4–5.

44. *Chicago Tribune*, 22 September 1902.

45. *Chicago Teachers' Federation Bulletin* 1 (14 November 1902): 2.

46. Haley, "Why the Federation Voted to Aid the Striking Miners," *Chicago Teachers' Federation Bulletin* 1 (3 October 1902).

47. Catherine Goggin to N. C. O'Connor, 13 February 1906, box 39, folder 1, CTF Papers; Margaret Haley to John Fitzpatrick, 28 March 1906, box 39, folder 1, CTF Papers.

48. *Battleground*, 91–93; Haley Autobiography, 1911, 153–58; William Hard, "The Fight for the Schools," *The Times Magazine* 1 (February, 1907): 364.

49. Margaret Haley, unsigned handwritten fragment, 19 April 1903, box 37, folder 3, CTF Papers.

50. William M. Tuttle, *Race Riot: Chicago in the Red Summer of 1919* (New York: Atheneum, 1970), 120–24.

51. William M. Tuttle, "Labor Conflict and Racial Violence: The Black Workers in Chicago, 1894–1919," *Labor History* 10 (1969): 417; "Striking Students Terrorize School" *Chicago Tribune*, 3, 7, 9 November 1905.

52. Margaret Haley, "The Chicago Strike," *Chicago Teachers' Federation Bulletin* 4 (1905): 1.

53. *Battleground*, 230.

54. Ibid., 129–30.

55. Murphy, *Blackboard Unions*, 53; "Fail to Climb Peak," *Chicago Tribune*, 8 July 1899; "Chicago Teachers Here," *Deseret Evening News*, 10 July 1899.

56. Urban, *Why Teachers Organized*, 113–14.

57. Haley Autobiography, 1935, 266–68; *Battleground*, 132–33.

58. *Battleground*, 134; Murphy, *Blackboard Unions*, 54–55.

59. Wayne J. Urban, *Gender, Race, and the National Education Association: Professionalism and its Limitations* (New York: Routledge Falmer, 2000), 1–19.

60. Margaret Haley, "To the Editor," *The Woman's Journal* (4 June 1903).

61. *Battleground*, 135–36.

62. *Battleground*, 136; Murphy, *Blackboard Unions*, 57; *Journal of Proceedings and Addresses of the National Education Association*, 1903, 24–31.

63. Urban, *Why Teachers Organized*, 113–14.

64. "Teacher Wins a Point," *Chicago Tribune*, 8 July 1903.

65. Charles Cornell Ramsay, "Impressions of the NEA Convention for 1903," *Education* 24 (September 1903): 44–49.

66. Margaret Haley to Samuel Gompers, 13 May 1903, box 47, "Teachers Associations," National and International Union Correspondence, American Federation of Labor Papers, State Historical Society of Wisconsin, Madison, Wisconsin.

67. Margaret Haley to Samuel Gompers, 15 May 1903, box 47, "Teachers Associations," National and International Union Correspondence, American Federa-

tion of Labor Papers, State Historical Society of Wisconsin, Madison, Wisconsin; Samuel Gompers, "The Point of View" *Scribners* 33 (June 1903): 764.

68. "National Federation of Teachers," *Chicago Teachers' Federation Bulletin* 1 (5 September 1902).

69. *Minneapolis Tribune*, 11 July 1902.

70. J. H. Francis to Margaret Haley, 22 May 1902, Box 36, folder 4, CTF Papers.

71. Weiner, "Teachers, Unions, and School Reform" 85–96.

72. Haley, "Why Teachers Should Organize," 145–52.

73. Aaron Grove, "Limitations of the Superintendent's Authority and of the Teacher's Independence," *Journal of the Addresses and Proceedings of the National Education Association*, 1904, 152–57.

74. N. C. Dougherty, quoted in "Conflict in the National Education Association," *The Public* (15 July 1905): 233.

75. "Editorial," *The Public* 8 (15 July 1905): 225.

76. "The NEA Charter," *Chicago Teachers' Federation Bulletin* (2 March 1906): 4–5.

77. Herrick, *Chicago Schools*, 108; George Creel, "Why Chicago's Teachers Unionized," *Harper's Weekly* (19 June 1915).

78. Jane Addams referred to Haley as having "pluck and energy." Jane Addams to Anita McCormick Blaine, 20 November 1903, Anita McCormick Blaine Papers, State Historical Society of Wisconsin; Haley was described as "plucky" in "Woman Bears Chicago's Franchise Tax Dodgers," *Buffalo Courier*, 10 August 1901.

79. Hard, "Margaret Haley, Rebel," 231; Ricker, "The School-Teacher Unionized," 344.

80. "A brave little woman" who was nothing less than a "modern Joan of Arc." *The Daily Eagle*, Marinette, Wisconsin, 4 August 1903; Haley's friend Josephine Locke wrote Haley in July 1903 applauding her challenge to the National Education Association and reminding her that "The University of Paris condemned Joan of Arc, and never forget this." Josephine C. Locke to Margaret Haley, 14 July, 1903, box 37, folder 3, CTF Papers.

81. William Hard, "Chicago's Five Maiden Aunts," *American Magazine* 62 (September 1906): 481–89; Hard, "Margaret Haley, Rebel"; "Margaret A. Haley in Boston," *Journal of Education* 65 (7 November 1901).

82. Hard, "Margaret Haley, Rebel," 231.

83. Mary Synon, "Women in Politics are Soldiers in Second American Revolution," *Chicago Daily Journal*, 2 February 1914.

84. E. W. Krackowizer to Margaret Haley, 7 October, 1903. Box 37, folder 4, CTF Papers.

85. Haley once described herself as "the dynamite and the danger signal" in many of the Federation's political situations. Haley Autobiography, 1934, 2.

86. Margaret Haley to Richard Finnegan, 8 January 1914, box 42, folder 2, CTF Papers.

87. Margaret Haley to Mr. W. L. Corris, 22 December, 1914, box 42, folder 5, CTF Papers.

88. Bernard Bell to Margaret Haley, 16 March 1914, box 42, folder 2, CTF Papers.

89. Mary A. Burrough to Margaret Haley, 25 June 1910, box 40, folder 2, CTF Papers.

90. Elizabeth A. Allen to Margaret Haley, 19 June 1910, box 40, folder 2, CTF Papers; Katherine D. Blake to Margaret Haley, 21 June 1910, box 40, folder 2, CTF Papers.

91. Margaret Haley to Grace Strachan, 21 June 1910, box 40, folder 2, CTF Papers.

92. *Battleground*, 126–27.

93. Ibid., 127.

CHAPTER 5. THE BATTLEFRONT WIDENS

1. Marshall Everett, *The Great Chicago Theater Disaster* (Publishers Union of America, 1904), 36.

2. "Burning of the Iroquois Theater," *Chicago Teachers' Federation Bulletin* 3 (8 January 1904).

3. "Danger Arouses School Trustees," *Chicago Tribune*, 9 January 1904; "Few Lack Fire Escapes," *Chicago Tribune*, 14 January 1904.

4. "Join to Avenge Victims of Fire," *Chicago Tribune*, 10 January 1904.

5. *Chicago Teachers' Federation Bulletin* 3 (22 January 1904); *Chicago Teachers' Federation Bulletin* 3 (20 May 1904); *Chicago Teachers' Federation Bulletin* 3 (23 September 1904).

6. Haley Autobiography, 1911, 118.

7. Margaret Haley to Franklin S. Edmonds, 15 January 1904, Box 37, Folder 5, CTF Papers.

8. Flanagan, *Charter Reform in Chicago*, 41–42.

9. Thomas R. Pegram, *Partisans and Progressives: Private Interest and Public Policy in Illinois, 1870–1922* (Urbana, University of Illinois Press, 1992), 137–44.

10. Flanagan, *Charter Reform in Chicago*, 42–43; Pegram, *Partisans and Progressives*, 137–38.

11. "If you want 2-cent fare," *Chicago Teachers' Federation Bulletin* 1 (December 1901), 2.

12. William Bennett Munro, ed., *The Initiative, Referendum, and Recall* (New York: D. Appleton and Co., 1912), 12.

13. Haley Autobiography, 1911, 233.

14. Haley Autobiography, 1911, 119–21, 228–29; Daniel L. Cruice, "Direct Legislation in Illinois: A Story of Triumph for Popular Government," *Arena* 31 (June 1904): 561–68.

15. Haley Autobiography, 1911, 120.

16. Ibid., 229.

17. Haley Autobiography, 1911, 121–22; "Address of Miss Margaret Haley Before Public Ownership League of the Chicago Federation of Labor," 29 August 1915, box 43, folder 3, CTF Papers.

18. Pegram, *Partisans and Progressives*, 139; Haley Autobiography, 1911, 122–23; Herrick, *Chicago Schools*, 107–109.

19. Haley Autobiography, 1911, 124; Henry Demerest Lloyd to Margaret Haley, 10 February 1903, Henry Demerest Lloyd Papers, Wisconsin Historical Society, Madison, Wisconsin.

20. Haley Autobiography, 1911, 125–26; Thomas, *Alternative America*, 352–53; *Battleground*, 96–97.

21. *Battleground*, 121.

22. Flanagan, *Charter Reform in Chicago*, 23–27; Pegram, *Partisans and Progressives*, 92.

23. *Battleground*, 122; Flanagan, *Seeing with Their Hearts*, 75–81.

24. "Report of the Committee on Public Education," 1 April 1907, City Club of Chicago Papers, Chicago Historical Society.

25. Nicholas Murray Butler, "Remarks of Dr. Butler, President of Columbia University, Before the Merchant's Club on Saturday, December 8th, at the Auditorium," in Merchants' Club, *Public Schools and their Administration* (Chicago: Merchants' Club, 1906), 45.

26. Quoted in Pegram, *Partisans and Progressives*, 115.

27. Mary E. Dreier, *Margaret Dreier Robins: Her Life, Letters, and Work* (New York: Island Press Cooperative 1950), 96.

28. Flanagan, *Charter Reform in Chicago*, 79–81; Pegram, *Partisans and Progressives*, 103–104.

29. Pegram, *Partisans and Progressives*, 104.

30. Ibid., 117.

31. Jackie M. Blount, *Destined to Rule the Schools: Women and the Superintendency, 1873–1995* (Albany: State Univesity of New York Press, 1998), 63–64; Patricia A. Carter, *"Everybody's Paid but the Teacher": The Teaching Profession and the Women's Movement* (New York: Teachers College Press, 2002).

32. "School for Suffrage," *Woman's Journal* 42 (1911): 298.

33. Robert E. Doherty, "Tempest on the Hudson: The Struggle for 'Equal Pay for Equal Work' in the New York City Schools, 1907–1911," *History of Education Quarterly* 19 (Winter 1979): 413–34.

34. Wanda Hendricks, "The Alpha Suffrage Club," in *Black Women in America: an Historical Encyclopedia*, ed. Darlene Clark Hine et al. (Bloomington: Indiana University Press, 1993), 1242–46.

35. Carter, *Everybody's Paid but the Teacher*, 78; Blount, *Destined to Rule the Schools*, 74.

36. Blount, *Destined to Rule the Schools*, 65–67; Adade Mitchell Wheeler, "Conflict in the Illinois Woman Suffrage Movement of 1913," *Journal of the Illinois State Historical Society* 76 (Summer 1983).

37. Quoted in Steven M. Buechler, *The Transformation of the Woman Suffrage Movement: The Case of Illinois, 1850–1920* (New Brunswick, NJ: Rutgers University Press, 1986), 170.

38. Buechler, *Transformation of the Woman Suffrage Movement*, 175.

39. *Battleground*, 13.

40. Ibid., 132

41. Carter, *Everybody's Paid but the Teacher*, 89.

42. *Battleground*, 159.

43. Ibid., 36. This belief was shared by other suffragists in England and America. See Caitriona Beaumont, "Citizens, Not Feminists: The Boundary Negotiated Between Citizenship and Feminism by Mainstream Women's Organizations in England," *Women's History Review* 9 (2000): 411–29, and Ellen Carol DuBois, *Feminism and*

Suffrage: The Emergence of an Independent Women's Movement in America, 1848–1869 (Ithaca: Cornell University Press, 1978).

44. Margaret Haley to Hon. Owen Thompson, 2 May 1911, box 41, folder 2, CTF Papers.

45. *Battleground*, 148.

46. *Journal of Education* 80 (July 13 1914): 91.

47. *Chicago Teachers' Federation Bulletin* 1 (3 October 1902): 5; "Tax-Paying Women and the Ballot," *Chicago Teachers' Federation Bulletin* 1 (10 October 1902): 3.

48. *Battleground*, 90.

49. *The Public* (29 September 1911): 1005; "News Notes," *The Public* (17 November 1911).

50. Margery Currey, "The Suffrage Parade," *Life and Labor* (July 1916): 104–105; Flanagan, *Seeing with Their Hearts*, 128.

51. Quoted in Wheeler, "Conflict in the Illinois Woman Suffrage Movement": 105.

52. Judge Michael L. Igoe, "Miss Haley as I knew her in Springfield," *Margaret Haley Memorial Bulletin*, 1939, 22.

53. *Chicago Record-Herald*, 27 June 1913.

54. Michael Kazin, "McNamara Case," in *The Encyclopedia of the American Left*, ed. MariJo Buhle, Paul Buhle, and Dan Georgakas (Urbana: University of Illinois Press, 1990), 463–64; James P. Kraft, "The Fall of Job Harriman's Socialist Party: Violence, Gender, and Politics in Los Angeles, 1911," *Southern California Quarterly* 70 (Spring 1988).

55. Kazin, "McNamara Case"; Gompers quoted in Geoffrey Cohen, *The People v. Clarence Darrow* (New York: Times Books, 1993), 169–70.

56. "Chicago Teachers in the Union," *Appeal to Reason* (6 December 1902).

57. Cohen, *The People v. Clarence Darrow*, 148–50.

58. Margaret Haley to Catherine Goggin, 26 November 1911, box 41, folder 2, CTF Papers.

59. Quoted in Cohen, *The People v. Clarence Darrow*, 263; Kraft, "The Fall of Job Harriman's Socialist Party," 273.

60. "Labor Party," in *The Encyclopedia of the American Left*, ed. MariJo Buhle, Paul Buhle, and Dan Georgakas (Urbana: University of Illinois Press, 1990).

61. Eric F. Goldman, "J. Allen Smith: The Reformer and His Dilemma," *The Pacific Northwest Quarterly* 35 (July 1944): 195–214.

62. Margaret Haley to Mrs. Fursman, 26 December 1911, box 41, folder 2, CTF Papers.

63. Joseph E. Smith to Louis Post, 8 May 1911, Joseph E. Smith Papers, box 2, folder 9, University of Washington Archives; Warren B. Johnson, "Muckraking in the Northwest: Joe Smith and Seattle Reform," *Pacific Historical Review* 40 (November 1971): 481–87.

64. Margaret Haley, "Single Tax Campaign in Seattle," *The Public* 15 (15 March 1912): 246.

65. Gary Lee Geiger, *Adele Parker: The Case Study of a Woman in the Progressive Era*, Masters thesis, University of Washington, 1971; C. H. Baily, "How Washington Women Regained the Ballot," *Pacific Monthly* 26 (July 1911): 1–11.

66. "Good Government News," *The Western Woman Voter* 2 (January 1912): 7; "To Friends of Single Tax," from the Single Tax Club, Seattle, 12 January 1912, Joseph Smith Papers, University of Washington, Box 2, Folder 17; Margaret Haley to Miss Platt, 27 December 1911, box 41, folder, 2, CTF Papers.

67. Margaret Haley to Miss Platt, 21 January 1912, box 41, folder, 3, CTF Papers.

68. Catherine Goggin to Margaret Haley, 9 February 1912, box 41, folder 3, CTF Papers; untitled Margaret Haley transcription, 1911, box 41, folder 1, CTF Papers.

69. Haley Autobiography, 1934, 5; Haley Autobiography, 1935, 33–36.

CHAPTER 6. ALLIES AND TRAITORS

1. *Battleground*, 86.
2. Ibid., 87.
3. Marvin Lazerson, "Teachers Organize: What Margaret Haley Lost," *History of Education Quarterly* 24 (Summer 1984): 261–70.
4. Synon, "Women in Politics": 3–4.
5. Haley Autobiography, 1911, 139.
6. *Chicago Teachers' Federation Bulletin* 3 (9 September 1904).
7. *Battleground*, 102.
8. John D. Buenker, "Edward F. Dunne: The Limits of Municipal Reform," in *The Mayors: The Chicago Political Tradition*, ed. Paul M. Green and Melvin G. Holli (Carbondale: Southern Illinois University Press, 1987), 37. John McCarthy died February 24, 1905; Haley's father died May 6, 1905. Haley Autobiography, 1911, 144; E. S. Smith to Catherine Goggin, 17 July 1905, box 38, folder 4, CTF Papers; Catherine Goggin to Cynthia P. Leet, 8 December 1905, box 38, folder 5, CTF Papers; Margaret Haley to Mr. Gillian, 28 June 1905, box 38, folder 4, CTF Papers.
9. Board members held three-year terms. Mary C. Schiltz, "Women on the Chicago Board of Education: A Collective Biography of Three Members in the Early Twentieth Century," *Journal of the Midwest History of Education Society* 21 (1994): 215–27.
10. Addams, *Twenty Years at Hull House*, 68.
11. Jane Addams to Anita McCormick Blaine, 20 November 1903, Anita McCormick Blaine papers, State Historical Society of Wisconsin.
12. Jane Addams, *Democracy and Social Ethics* (Cambridge: Harvard University Press, 1964), 190–91.
13. *Battleground*, 102; Haley Autobiography, 1911, 145.
14. Haley Autobiography, 1911, 182–83.
15. Ibid., 1911, 46, 187–89.
16. Addams, *Twenty Years at Hull House*, 230.
17. Jane Addams to Graham Wallace, 1 July, 1906, Jane Addams Memorial Collection, University of Illinois at Chicago.
18. Addams, *Twenty Years at Hull House*, 235.
19. Ibid., 229.
20. Gilbert H. Harrison, *A Timeless Affair: The Life of Antia McCormick Blaine* (Chicago: University of Chicago Press, 1979), 84–102; Schiltz, "Women on the Chicago Board of Education."

21. *Chicago Record Herald*, 11 September 1904; Cornelia DeBey, "The Relation of the Teaching Force," *Elementary School Teacher* 6 (January 1905); Schiltz, "Women on the Chicago Board of Education."

22. Quoted in *Chicago Teachers' Federation Bulletin* 3 (16 September 1904): 4–5.

23. *Battleground*, 103; Hard, "Chicago's Five Maiden Aunts": 489; "Editorial Notes," *The Elementary School Teacher* 6 (January, 1906): 265–74.

24. *Chicago Tribune*, 22 March 1907.

25. Allen F. Davis, *American Heroine: The Life and Legend of Jane Addams* (New York: Oxford University Press, 1973), 132; *Chicago Tribune*, 19 October 1907.

26. *Battleground*, 104–105; Haley Autobiography, 1911, 167; *Chicago Teachers' Federation Bulletin* 5 (11 May 1906); *The Chicago Board of Education Bulletin* (11 June 1906): 249–51.

27. Haley Autobiography, 1911, 165.

28. Addams, *Twenty Years at Hull House*, 232.

29. *Battleground*, 105; Haley Autobiography, 1911, 165.

30. Margaret Haley to Jane Addams, 4 May 1906, Anita McCormick Blaine papers, Box 281, Wisconsin Historical Society.

31. *Chicago Board of Education Proceedings*, 1905–1906, 773–76 and 813–15; Haley Autobiography, 1911, 166.

32. Haley Autobiography, 1911, 183.

33. Ibid., 187.

34. Ibid., 189.

35. *Battleground*, 118; Haley Autobiography, 1911, 186.

36. Louis Post, "A Personal Editorial," *The Public* 9 (1906): 625; Dominic Candeloro, "The Chicago School Board Crisis of 1907," *Journal of Illinois State Historical Society* 68 (November 1975): 396–406.

37. *Chicago Tribune*, 10 October 1906.

38. Chicago *Tribune*, 16 January 1907.

39. Hard, "The Fight for the Schools," 367.

40. Margaret Haley to Mr. Robins, 27 September 1906, box 39, folder 2, CTF Papers.

41. Note by Margaret Haley, 26 July 1906, box 39, folder 1, CTF Papers.

42. *Battleground*, 106; Haley Autobiography, 1911, 170–71; *Chicago Board of Education Proceedings*, 1906–1907, 490–534.

43. *Chicago Board of Education Proceedings*, 1906–1907, 510.

44. *Chicago Tribune*, 3 December 1906; *Chicago Daily News*, 7 December 1906; Margaret Haley to John Fitzpatrick, 28 March 1906, box 39, folder 1, CTF Papers.

45. Report of a meeting held at the rooms of the Federation of Labor, Chicago, 2 December, 1906, box 39, folder 2, CTF Papers.

46. Haley Autobiography, 1911, 150–52; *Battleground*, 107; *Chicago Tribune*, 1 December 1906.

47. *Chicago Tribune*, 31 March 1907.

48. *Battleground*, 119.

49. "Why the Dunne School Board Goes," *Interocean*, 20 May 1907.

50. Chicago *Tribune*, 3 April 1907.

51. *Battleground*, 108; Harrison, *A Timeless Affair*, 125–27; Candeloro, "Chicago School Board Crisis of 1907," 402–403.

52. *Chicago Record-Herald*, 23 May 1907; Davis, *American Heroine*, 133–34.

53. *Battleground*, 109.

54. "New Board Takes Reins, Guarded by Police Deadline," *Interocean*, 30 May 1907.

55. *Battleground*, 103; Davis, *American Heroine*, 133.

56. Addams, *Twenty Years at Hull House*, 234.

57. Harrison, *A Timeless Affair*, 127.

58. *Battleground*, 100.

59. "The School-Land Leases of Chicago," *The Public* (5 January 1907): 939–40; *Battleground*, 114–17; Herrick, *Chicago Schools*, 104–105.

60. *Battleground*, 100; Herrick, *Chicago Schools*, 104–105.

61. *Battleground*, 107.

62. Ibid.

63. *Battleground*,104–105; Haley Autobiography, 1911, 167; *Chicago Teachers' Federation Bulletin* 5 (11 May 1906).

64. Haley to Robins, 27 September 1906; note by Margaret Haley, 26 July 1906, box 39, folder 1, CTF Papers.

65. *Battleground*, 107; Haley Autobiography, 1911, 175.

66. *Chicago Board of Education Proceedings*, 1907–1908, 814–28, 883–85, 957–58; Haley Autobiography, 1911, 177–78.

67. *Battleground*, 108.

68. Haley Autobiography, 1911, 178.

69. Addams, *Twenty Years at Hull House*, 232; Lowe, "The Chicago Teachers' Federation and Its Legacy," 83.

70. Margaret Haley to Hon. Owen Thompson, 2 May 1911, box 41, folder 2, CTF Papers.

71. Margaret Haley to Hon. Owen Thompson, 2 May 1911.

72. Jackie M. Blount, "Ella Flagg Young and the Chicago Schools," in *Founding Mothers and Others: Women Educational Leaders During the Progressive Era*, ed. Alan R. Sadovnik and Susan F. Semel (New York: Palgrave, 2002); Joan K. Smith, *Ella Flagg Young: Portrait of a Leader* (Ames, IA: Educational Studies Press, 1979).

73. Ellen Condliffe Lagemann, "Experimenting with Education: John Dewey and Ella Flagg Young at the University of Chicago," *American Journal of Education* 104 (May 1996): 171–85; Necrology, *Proceedings and Addresses of the National Education Association for the Year 1918* (Washington, DC: NEA, 1918), 685; Jane M. Dewey, "Biography of John Dewey," in *The Philosophy of John Dewey*, ed. Paul A. Schilpp (New York: The Tudor Publishing Co., 1951), 29.

74. John Dewey, "Democracy in Education" *Chicago Teachers' Federation Bulletin* 2 (February 26, 1904): 1–3, 5–6.

75. Ella Flagg Young, *Isolation in the Schools* (Chicago: University of Chicago Press, 1901), 25.

76. Ibid., 13

77. Haley Autobiography, 1934, 3.

78. Quoted in *Battleground*, 174–75.

79. Dora Wells quoted in Rosemary V. Donatelli, "The Contrbutions of Ella Flagg Young to the Educational Enterprise," PhD diss., University of Chicago, 1971, 89.

80. Elmer A. Morrow in Donatelli, "The Contributions of Ella Flagg Young," 241–42.

81. *Battleground*, 140–41.

82. Alice Henry, "Registration Day in Chicago," *Life and Labor* 14 (March 1914): 68–70.

83. "The Highest Salaried Woman in the World," *The Western Journal of Education* 14 (1909): 515.

84. Mrs. George Bass, "Mrs. Young and the Chicago Schools," *School and Society* 2 (23 October, 1915), 605–606.

85. "Chicago's New Lesson," *Journal of Education* 78 (14 August 1913): 126; B. V. Hubbard, *Socialism, Feminism, and Suffragism, the Terrible Triplet Connected by the Same Umbilical Cord and Fed from the Same Nursing Bottle* (Chicago: American Publishing, 1915), 282–84.

86. John T. McManis, *Ella Flagg Young And a Half-Century of the Chicago Public Schools* (Chicago: A.C. McClurg and Co., 1916), 159–62.

87. Counts, *School and Society in Chicago*, 107–15.

88. Urban, *Why Teachers Organized*, 155.

89. Stephen Provasnik, "Compulsory Schooling, from Idea to Institution: A Case Study of the Development of Compulsory Attendance in Illinois, 1857–1907," PhD diss., University of Chicago, 1999; Ernest A. Wreidt, William J. Bogan, and George H. Mead, *A Report on Vocational Training in Chicago and Other Cities* (Chicago: City Club, 1912), p. 29.

90. "Vocational Education in Illinois," issued by the Publicity Committee of the Joint Conference Committee on Vocational Education Consisting of Representative of All Chicago Public School Teachers' Organizations, Leaflet Number One (14 February 1913), box 41, folder 5, CTF Papers.

91. *Battleground*, 160.

92. "5,500 Teachers Organized to Fight Proposed Laws," *Chicago Tribune*, 10 November 1912.

93. "Mrs. Young Heads Cooley Bill Fight," *Interocean* 23 October 1912; "To Fight Cooley Bill," *Chicago Record-Herald*, 23 October 1912.

94. *Battleground*, 149–58.

95. *Chicago Tribune*, 9 July 1915.

96. *Chicago Tribune*, 22 July 1915.

97. Jacob Loeb, "Stenographic Report of Address," 2 February 1917, box 46, folder 1, CTF Papers.

98. *Chicago Daily News*, 23 July 1915; *Chicago Tribune*, 23 July 1915.

99. *Chicago Tribune*, 26 August 1915.

100. *Chicago Tribune*, 24 August 1915; *Chicago Board of Education Proceedings*, 1915–1916, 734.

101. *Battleground*, 170.

102. *Chicago Tribune*, 27 June, 1916, as quoted in Douglas Bukowski, *Big Bill Thompson, Chicago, and the Politics of Image* (Urbana: University of Illinois Press, 1998), 46.

103. Martha Wilkinson O'Brien to Margaret Haley, 24 December 1913, box 42, folder 1, CTF Papers.

104. Speech of Samuel Gompers, Chicago Federation of Labor meeting, 8 September 1915, box 43, folder 3, CTF Papers; Mary O'Reilly, "What Organization of the Teachers Means to Labor," *Life and Labor* 5 (November 1915): 166.

105. Carl Sandburg, "Sandberg to Loeb," *Day Book* (8 September 1915).

106. Wrigley, *Class Politics and Public Schools*, 132; *Chicago Board of Education Proceedings*, 1915–1916, 885–86.

107. Carl Sandburg, *Day Book* (24 September 1915): 445.

108. *Chicago Board of Education Proceedings*, 1915–1916, 1274–75.

109. Quoted in McManis, *Ella Flagg Young*, 163–64.

110. *Battleground*, 163.

111. *Battleground, 175*; *Chicago Tribune*, 3 December 1915.

112. *Battleground*, 176.

113. Mary C. Crawford to Margaret Haley, 11 December 1913, box 42, folder 1, CTF Papers.

114. Margaret Haley to Minnie Reynolds, 5 January 1914, box 42, folder 2, CTF Papers.

115. William R. Chenery, "Adulterated Education," *The New Republic* (23 October 1915): 304.

CHAPTER 7. CASUALITIES

1. *Battleground, 177*.

2. *Margaret A. Haley's Bulletin* (27 January 1916): 32.

3. Ida Fursman, "Letter to Mr. John Hood," *Margaret A. Haley's Bulletin* (27 January 1916): 44.

4. Margaret Haley to Carter Harrison, 28 January, 1916, Carter H. Harrison IV Papers, Newberry Library, Chicago.

5. "Catherine Goggin, " *The Journal of Education* 83 (13 January 1916): 44; Catherine Goggin's grave is at Calvery Cemetery, now in Evanston. Lot 7, Block 4, Section S.

6. "Teachers' Friend Dead," *The New World* (7 January 1916): 1; *Margaret A. Haley's Bulletin* (27 January 1916): 30.

7. *Margaret A. Haley's Bulletin* (27 January 1916); William L. Chenery, "Catherine Goggin," *Life and Labor* (February 1916): 23.

8. *Chicago Evening Post*, 8 January 1916.

9. Louis Post to Margaret Haley, 13 February 1916, box 45, folder 1, CTF Papers.

10. "The American Federation of Teachers," *Life and Labor* (June 1916): 85.

11. David L. Angus and Jeffrey E. Mirel, *The Failed Promise of the American High School* (New York: Teachers College Press, 1999), 203.

12. Herrick, *Chicago Schools*, 404–406.

13. Murphy, "From Artisan to Semi-Professional," 216.

14. Freeland G. Stecker, "Early History of the American Federation of Teachers," n.d., box 32, folder 13, Carl J. Megel Collection, Archives of Labor and Urban Affairs, Walter Reuther Library, Detroit.

15. Jennie Wilcox to Mrs. Trowbridge, "Thursday morning," ca. 1920s, AFT series 6, box 2, Chicago Women's Teachers Union, Archives of Labor and Urban Affairs, Walter Reuther Library, Detroit.

16. Harry Jones, Interview with Mary Herrick, 11 June, 1937, box 14, folder 12, Illinois Writers' Project, Carter Woodson Library, Chicago.

17. In 1931, Mary Herrick reported that although there were 278 African American elementary teachers (out of ten thousand elementary teachers total) who

were eligible for membership in the Chicago Teachers' Federation, there were no African American leaders in the organization and "no Negroes were visible" among the one thousand women teachers at a Federation meeting. Mary Herrick, "Negro Employees of the Chicago Board of Education," PhD diss. University of Chicago, 1931, 77–78.

18. "My Dear Mrs. Dummer," ca. 1916, box 21, folder 329, Ethel Sturgis Dummer Papers, Schlesinger Library, Radcliffe Institute, Harvard University; Counts, *School and Society in Chicago*, 104–105.

19. Margaret Haley to Hon. Joseph Z. Uhlir, 9 December 1914, box 42, folder 5, CTF Papers.

20. Urban, *Why Teachers Organized*, 89–108.

21. Stecker, "Early History of the American Federation of Teachers."

22. *Chicago Daily Tribune*, 28 June 1916.

23. Charles Stillman to J. E. Mayman, 11 September 1916, series 6, box 3, New York Teachers Union folder, AFT Archives, Archives of Labor and Urban Affairs, Walter Reuther Library, Detroit.

24. "Report of Public Demonstration Held in the Auditorium on Saturday June 17, 1916," box 45, folder 2, CTF Papers.

25. "Report of Meeting of the Chicago Federation of Labor," 2 July, 1916, box 45, folder 3, CTF Papers.

26. *Battleground*, 179.

27. Chester C. Dodge, *Reminisences of a Schoolmaster* (Chicago: Ralph Fletcher Seymour, 1941), 85–86; Herrick, *Chicago Schools*, 131–34.

28. Urban, *Why Teachers Organized*, 85–86.

29. Charles Stillman to Margaret Haley, 3 August, 1916, box 45, folder 3, CTF Papers.

30. "Stecker, "Early History of the American Federation of Teachers."

31. *Battleground*, 180.

32. Minutes, Emergency Peace Committee, Chicago, 21 December 1914, Jane Addams Memorial Collection, University of Illinois at Chicago.

33. *Battleground*, 273.

34. Ruth Dudley Edwards, *Patrick Pearse: The Triumph of Failure* (London: Victor Gollancz, 1977).

35. *Battleground*, 181.

36. Urban, *Why Teachers Organized*, 151–53.

37. Howard K. Beale, *Are American Teachers Free?* (New York: Scribners, 1936).

38. E. S. Evenden, "The Payment of American Teachers," *Nation* 109 (30 August 1919), 295.

39. Mary Badger Wilson, "What About Teachers' Pay Envelop?" *McCall's Magazine* (September 1919), 2, 24; President Hibben, Princeton University, "Are Cheap Teachers Going to be Good for Your Children?" *The American Magazine* (September 1919), 15–16, 80–81.

40. CTF Flyer, 1919 box 1, AFT series 6 (Old correspondence), Archives of Labor and Urban Affairs, Walter Reuther Library, Detroit.

41. *Battleground*, 181.

42. Murphy, "From Artisans to Semi-Professionals," 248–54.

43. Margaret Haley to J. W. McGraw, 7 October 1920, box 48, folder 3, CTF Papers.

44. Bukowski, *Big Bill Thompson*, 75.

45. Ethel Sturges Dummer to Mrs. James Flower, 20 October 1916, box 22, folder 344, Ethel Sturges Dummer papers; Smith, *Ella Flagg Young*, 228–29.

46. *Battleground*, 182.

47. Murphy, *Blackboard Unions*, 77–78; Edgar B. Wesley, *NEA: The First Hundred Years* (New York: Harper and Brothers, 1957), 280–82.

48. Urban, *Gender, Race, and the National Education Association*, 3–5.

49. Paula O'Connor, "Grade-School Teachers Become Labor Leaders: Margaret Haley, Florence Rood, and Mary Barker of the AFT," *Labor's Heritage* 7 (Fall 1995): 4–17.

50. Urban, *Gender, Race, and the National Education Association*, 12–19.

51. "Utah Charged with Railroading," *Utah Educational Review* 14 (September 1920), 21.

52. "Nation's Educators Open Session Today," *The Salt Lake Tribune*, 5 July 1920.

53. "Final Meeting of the NEA as It Has Been since 1856," *Journal of Education* 42 (19 August 1920): 20–21; "Utah Charged with Railroading,"*Utah Educational Review* 14 (September 1920); Frederick S. Buchanan, "Unpacking the NEA: The Role of Utah's Teachers at the 1920 Convention," *Utah Historical Quarterly* 41 (Spring 1973):150–61.

54. Annie Webb Blanton to Margaret Haley, 17 July, 1920, box 48, folder 2, CTF Papers.

55. "Final Meeting of the NEA," 121.

56. "From the School Board Journal," box 50, folder 3, CTF Papers; Transcript of Department of Classroom Teachers Meeting, box 50, folder 5, CTF Papers.

57. "Effective Professional Organizations," *NEA Journal* 10 (September 1921): 119–20; J. W. Crabtree to Joseph Swain, 18 March 1922, NEA Archives, Washington, DC.

58. Wayne J. Urban, "Charl Williams and the National Education Association," in *Founding Mothers and Others: Women Educational Leaders during the Progressive Era*, ed. Alan R. Sadovnik and Susan F. Semel, (New York: Palgrave, 2002). Fannie McLean, report to Berkeley teachers about the 1921 NEA meeting, carton 9, Fannie McLean Papers, Bancroft Library, University of California, Berkley, California. I am grateful to Geraldine Clifford for identifying this source.

CHAPTER 8. SIEGE

1. *Battleground*, 183.

2. Dodge, *Reminiscences of a Schoolmaster*, 95–96.

3. *Chicago Tribune*, 8 April 1931.

4. Memorandum by Margaret A. Haley, dictated 2 December 1934, box 67, folder 3, CTF Papers; Thompson quoted in Herrick, *Chicago Schools*, 121.

5. Herrick, *Chicago Schools*, 137–38.

6. Counts, *School and Society in Chicago*, 68–69; Herrick, *Chicago Schools*, 137–39.

7. Herrick, *Chicago Schools*, 139–41.

8. Ibid., 142.

9. *Chicago Tribune,* 9 September 1922, 27 January 1923; Counts, *School and Society in Chicago,* 259–63; Herrick, *Chicago Schools,* 141–43.

10. Counts, *School and Society in Chicago,* 28–31.

11. Ravenswood Group Council, 21 October 1921, box 48, folder 5, CTF Papers.

12. Ibid.

13. CTF Minutes, 2 October 1923, box 2, folder 8, CTF Papers.

14. *Chicago Teachers' Federation Bulletin* 2 (11 September 1903).

15. William McAndrew, "The Wages of Teachers," *Chicago Teachers' Federation Bulletin* 1, (28 February 1902): 16; William McAndrew, "Plain Words on Teachers' Wages," *Chicago Teachers' Federation Bulletin* 1 (7 March 1902); *Chicago Teachers' Federation Bulletin* 2 (6 November 1903): 1–3; *Chicago Teachers' Federation Bulletin* 4 (10 February 1905).

16. William McAndrew to Margaret Haley, n.d., box 42, folder 2, CTF Papers.

17. Haley Autobiography, 1934, 18; William McAndrew to Margaret Haley, 21 January 1914, box 42, folder 2, CTF Papers.

18. William McAndrew, "Breaking Away," *Chicago Teachers' Federation Bulletin* 2 (3 July 3, 1903): 7.

19. William McAndrew, "The Schoolman's Loins," *Educational Review* (September 1922): 114.

20. Quoted in Counts, *School and Society in Chicago,* 247.

21. *Chicago Daily Journal,* 18 April 1927; *Chicago Daily Tribune,* 16 May 1927; *Margaret Haley's Bulletin* (15 May 1927): 246, 255; Urban, *Why Teachers Organized,* 165–68.

22. Counts, *School and Society in Chicago,* 71–84.

23. Herrick, *Chicago Schools,* 148–50.

24. Counts, *School and Society in Chicago,* 180–84.

25. Bukowski, *Big Bill Thompson,* 153; Counts, *School and Society in Chicago,* 192–97.

26. Margaret Haley, "The Factory System," *The New Republic* 40 (12 November 1924): 18.

27. "Thursday's dictation—rough draft—platoon, 1923," box 51, folder 4, CTF Papers; *Battleground,* 209–10.

28. Ibid.

29. *Battleground,* 229.

30. Ibid., 211.

31. Herrick, *Chicago Schools,* 150–54; Counts, *School and Society in Chicago,* 115–30.

32. Peter Mortenson to William McAndrew, nd, box 52, folder 5, CTF Papers.

33. *Chicago Tribune,* 3 October 1924.

34. Quoted in Herrick, *Chicago Schools,* 159.

35. William McAndrew, "Arithmetic Outside and Inside," *Chicago Schools Journal* 9 (October 1926): 41–44.

36. Bukowski, *Big Bill Thompson,* 154; Counts, *School and Society in Chicago,* 201–24.

37. Counts, *School and Society in Chicago,* 202–204.

38. Quoted in Herrick, *Chicago Schools,* 160.

39. Quoted in Murphy, "From Artisan to Semi-Professional," 257.

40. *Chicago Daily News*, 7 May 1924.

41. *School Review* 32 (September 1924): 490.

42. *Chicago Tribune*, 10 September 1924.

43. Counts, *School and Society in Chicago*, 227–28.

44. Margaret Haley to Arthur H. Chamberlain, Secretary, California Teachers' Association, 17 March 1914, box 42, folder 3, CTF Papers.

45. "What's Wrong in Our Schools?" reprinted from *The Daily News* in *Margaret Haley's Bulletin*, (31 January 1928): 106.

46. Wrigley, *Class Politics and the Public Schools*, 187–95.

47. *Battleground*, 211.

48. Wattenberg, *On the Educational Front*, 112–13.

49. Stenographic record, 7 July 1922, National Education Association, Department of Classroom Teachers' meeting, box 49, folder 5, CTF Papers.

50. Herrick, *Chicago Schools*, 238.

51. Jennie A. Wilcox, to "Dear friend," 29 July 1928, series 6, box 2, folder 3, Chicago Women's Teachers, Union, AFT Papers, Archives of Labor and Urban Affairs, Walter Reuther Library, Detroit.

52. Florence Curtis Hanson to Amy G. Edmunds, 15 February 1928, box 1, folder correspondence 1928–30, Minneapolis Federation of Teachers Records, 1918–1993, Minnesota Historical Society.

53. Florence Hanson to Mary C. Barker, 23 April 1931, series 1, box 1, folder 2–20, AFT secretary-treasurer office collection, series 1, Florence Curtis Hanson Files, Archives of Labor and Urban Affairs, Walter Reuther Library, Detroit.

54. "Chicago and Los Angeles Women in Verbal Exchange," *The Salt Lake Tribune*, 7 July 1920.

55. Haley Autobiography, 1935, 223, 382–84.

56. *Battleground*, 256.

57. Herrick, *Chicago Schools*, 179–81.

58. Murphy, "Taxation and Social Conflict" 242–60; Herrick, *Chicago Schools*, 184.

59. James A. Meade to Margaret Haley, 9 October 1926, box 18, folder 5, Chicago Teachers' Union Papers, Chicago Historical Society.

60. George Strayer's 1932 report on Chicago schools found that the existing tax system of Chicago and Illinois, where 94 percent of local and state income of schools came from property tax, was the most immediate cause of Chicago's school funding crisis. He recommended a state personal income tax and other modifications in the tax code. George D. Strayer, *Report of the Survey of the Schools of Chicago* (Teachers College, Division of Field Studies of Teachers College, 1932).

61. Herrick, *Chicago Schools*, 186–87.

62. Florence Curtis Hanson to Amy G. Edmunds, 15 February 1928, box 1, folder correspondence 1928–30, Minneapolis Federation of Teachers Records, 1918–1993, Minnesota Historical Society.

63. "Launching Local No. 199," *The American Teacher* 12 (May 1928): 17.

64. Report of Miss Gertrude Powers, Goodrich School, 1930, box 59, folder 4, CTF Papers.

65. Program of the Twelfth Annual Convention of the AFT, 25–29 June, 1928. AFT Convention Proceedings, series 13, box 4, AFT Archives, Archives of Labor and Urban Affairs, Walter Reuther Library, Detroit.

66. "To the Teachers of Chicago," 2 April 1931, box 60, folder 1, CTF Papers; "Answer to Margaret Haley's letter," box 60, folder 1, CTF Papers.

67. George Davis to Helen Orrell, 7 November 1935, series 6, box 23, folder "199 Elementary Teachers of Chicago," AFT Archives, Archives of Labor and Urban Affairs, Walter Reuther Library, Detroit.

68. Flanagan, *Seeing with Their Hearts*, 186–88.

69. "An Open Letter to Doctor Judd from Margaret A. Haley," CTF pamphlet, box 69, folder 4, CTF Papers.

70. Lyons, "The Limits of Professionalism" 4–22.

71. Jennie A. Wilcox to "Dear friend," 29 July 1928; Blount, "Manly Men and Womanly Women" 318–38.

72. *Margaret Haley's Weekly Bulletin*, 2 (25 June 1925).

73. *Margaret Haley's Weekly Bulletin* 2 (14 May 1925), and *Margaret Haley's Weekly Bulletin* 2 (16 April 1925).

74. Haley Autobiography, 1935, 170–71.

75. "Federation Cross-word Puzzle with Variations," box 53, folder 1, CTF Papers.

76. Program for Silver Jubilee Luncheon, Chicago Teachers' Federation, 1925, box 53, folder 3, CTF Papers; Anniversary Luncheon of the Chicago Teachers' Federation, 21 January 1928, box 55, folder 4, CTF Papers.

77. "How to be happy tho married," performed 1 March 1931, box 60, folder 1, CTF Papers.

78. "School Scandels of 1932," 10 June, 1932 box 63, folder 2, CTF Papers.

79. Margaret Haley to Mary McDowell, 18 April 1923, box 51, folder 1, CTF Papers; Margaret Haley, "Dear friend," 31 March 1928, box 55, folder 4, CTF Papers.

80. Margaret Haley, "Events Transpiring June 16–23, 1935," box 68, folder 3, CTF Papers.

81. "Purely Personal," *Utah Educational Review* 14 (September 1920): 8.

82. S. J. Duncan Clark, "Militant Miss Haley: Still Fighting After Thirty Years," *Chicago Daily News*, 17 April 1931. Membership numbers estimated from Minutes of CTF meeting, 19 March 1936 and 15 May 1937, CTF Papers.

83. H. J. Collins to Margaret Haley, 16 March 1930, box 58, folder 2, CTF Papers.

84. Stenographic report of meeting of teachers of elementary schools from Agassiz to Howland, inclusive, 16 August 1933, box 66, folder 1, CTF Papers.

85. Margaret Haley, Western Union Telegram, 25 October 1934, box 68, folder 2, CTF Papers.

86. Margaret Haley dictation, "Reassessment," 1929, box 32, folder 5, CTF Papers.

87. Emma McCredie to Miss Trout, 9 April 1934, box 67, folder 6, CTF Papers.

88. Emma McCredie to Winifred Mathews, 27 April 1934, box 67, folder 6, CTF Papers.

89. Eliza Haley obituary, *Chicago Daily News*, 21 May 1935.

90. The transcribed manuscript, with index, is 846 pages long. Haley Autobiography, 1935.

91. "To the Teachers of the United States," box 68, folder 5, CTF Papers.

92. Margaret Haley probate records, Office of the Circuit Court Clerk of Cook County, Illinois.

93. "Margaret Haley Dies at 73 [sic] of Heart Ailment," *Chicago Daily News*, 8 January 1939.

94. Grace Trout, "Sidelights on Illinois Suffrage History," *Transactions of the Illinois State Historical Society for the Year 1920*, 109; I. T. Greenacre, "Forty Years," *Margaret A. Haley Memorial Booklet* (Chicago, 1939), 9, 14; author conversation with Dr. Peter Richter, 30 June 2003.

95. *Chicago Evening American*, 10 January 1939.

96. "The Good Fight," *The Daily News*, 10 January 1939.

97. Robert C. Moore, "In Memory of Margaret A. Haley," *Margaret A. Haley Memorial Booklet* (Chicago, 1939), 45.

98. Richard Finnegan, *Margaret A. Haley Memorial Booklet*, 17.

99. AFT Convention Proceedings, 1939, box 12, folder 1–7, Archives of Labor and Urban Affairs, Walter Reuther Library, Detroit.

100. Chicago Teachers' Federation collection notes, CTF Papers.

101. *Battleground*, 275–76.

102. Ibid., 276.

CONCLUSION. TEACHER LEADER

1. *Battleground*, 271.

2. Ibid., 272.

3. Ibid., 270–75.

4. Margaret Haley, handwritten note, 3 August 1901, box 36, folder 2, CTF Papers.

5. Christine E. Murray, "Teaching as a Profession: The Rochester Case in Historical Perspective," *Harvard Educational Review* 62 (Winter 1992): 502.

6. Stan Karp, "Money, Schools and Justice," *Rethinking Schools* 18 (Fall 2003): 26–30.

BIBLIOGRAPHIC ESSAY:

WRITING A POLITICAL LIFE

THIS BOOK, THE FIRST FULL BIOGRAPHY of Margaret Haley, centers on her political vision and activities, and it studies her life as a dynamic woman teacher leader. Historians have written pieces of Haley's history, but many of these have been hagiographic portraits of a woman activist, highlighting her most public activities and painting her personality and leadership style in broad generalized strokes. In this study, I have tried to pay as much attention to who Haley was as to what she did, exploring Haley's comprehensive development as an individual, a political leader, an educational activist, and a public intellectual.

My primary resource for this work was the archive of the Chicago Teachers' Federation, housed at the Chicago Historical Society. This substantial collection includes internal correspondence, business and meeting reports, and Federation publications as well as Haley's published articles and transcribed speeches. I also drew on the wealth of resources on the social and educational history of Chicago from other depositories in the region, including the Newberry Library, the Illinois Regional Archives Depository branch collections in De Kalb and Chicago, the Archives of the National Catholic Society of Foresters in Mt. Prospect, Illinois, the Jane Addams Memorial Collection at the University of Illinois-Chicago, the Chicago Roman Catholic Diocese Archives, and the Harold Washington and Carter G. Woodson public libraries in Chicago. The Morris Public Library held an impressive array of resources on the social history of rural northern Illinois and Haley's early life. The American Federation of Teachers collection at the Archives of Labor and Urban Affairs, Walter Reuther Library, in Detroit holds the largest collection of teacher union records in the country. I also drew on sources from libraries and special collections in regions across the country that Haley visited, including the Utah State Historical Society, the Wisconsin

Historical Society, the Minnesota Historical Society, the Schlesinger Library at the Radcliffe Institute for Advanced Study at Harvard University, and the University of Washington.

The challenge facing any biographer who wants to go beyond Haley's political narrative is that she resisted any public understanding of who she was as a person. An enormously active and public woman, Margaret Haley wrote hundreds of pages of political autobiography including in them, as she wrote, "as little of my own personality as is humanely possible."[1] She kept no diary, and she recorded only a few fragmentary stories about her childhood, and literally nothing about a personal life, friends, family, or feelings. Probably Haley's most reflective moment was when she wrote that she was *not* a reflective person. As a political figure, she was highly invested in her public image and her surviving papers represent this: They read as a litany of activities and accomplishments in the halls of government and political organizations. Not only did Haley want to record her activities, but she saw her writings as part of the ongoing education of women teachers in political activism, providing guidance for future organization. For this reason, Haley sat down on five occasions in her professional life to write or dictate various versions of her story. In 1910, on holiday in Massachusetts, she focused on the Chicago tax case; a year and a half later in Seattle, she dictated a more complete version of Federation history. Eighteen years later, in a furious mood over the injustice done to teachers, she dictated an account of Chicago battles over school funding in the 1920s. In 1934, while recovering from an illness in California, the aging Haley recorded some autobiographical notes, and one year later she dictated a rambling, disconnected narrative of her life and work which she planned to publish under the title, *Forty Fighting Years*. But she never found a publisher, and upon her death the manuscript was stored with the Chicago Teachers' Federation, and ultimately donated to the Chicago Historical Society with other Federation papers. In 1982, Robert L. Reid edited and published the manuscript as *Battleground: The Autobiography of Margaret Haley*.[2]

Battleground is Haley's magnus opus, and it is ably edited by Reid, but it is a difficult read. The narrative is a rapid-fire account of campaigns, meeting, arguments, and political triumphs and failures, and reads much as Haley herself lived her life—linking powerful rhetoric about social injustice with minutely detailed accounts of local skirmishes. Haley wrote her autobiography as a public, political statement, and not a personal account. Accordingly, the book is more of a polemic than a sequential account of events, and it offers no coherent narrative of her life and provides no contextual understanding of her activities. My preliminary work as a biographer was to "translate" *Battleground* into a life story that was accessible to readers who were not familiar with turn-of-the-century Chicago politics. Further complicating this work was that Haley described her life by the themes of the major battles in which she was involved and not chronologically. Accordingly, this biography is organized thematically: The first two chapters lay out her early life, while later chapters cover overlapping years. To develop an understanding of her character, I relied on evidence from the myriad archival resources described above, finding clues to her life and character through the accounts of her peers. To develop the historical context of her life, I drew on a range of secondary and primary resources, the most helpful of which are listed in a selected bibliography that follows.

Haley's multiple autobiographies raise complicated methodological questions about memory and authenticity. Although the manuscripts rarely contradict each other, they often provide different emphases and nuances. In her final manuscript, Haley rambled in ways that suggest some senility, although it is also possible that with advanced age, Haley was less circumspect and more honest in her memories. Because of the complications of the different versions, I have tried to validate each citation with a reference from another primary source such as another autobiographical piece, correspondence, or newspaper article. I also qualify some of my references by identifying at what time in her life she recorded an event.

In addition, it was significant in my understanding of Haley as a person that she did write five different versions of her political life. Haley was by all accounts an intense person who was entirely focused on her work to the point of obsession. She was known for her dramatic flair and flamboyance, as well as a powerful ego. In her autobiographical accounts, she often overemphasized her own accomplishments and ignored the work of others with whom she worked, and she sidestepped larger contextual issues in which a political battle was located. Haley's personal style of drilling incessantly into political issues and accentuating her own role offers insights into how she directed her political work, and how she maintained her self-confidence and energy in the face of so many obstacles.

Indeed, Haley's narratives of her political work with the Federation are not only the record of an organization, but her story of her life. By her own account and others, politics *was* her life. Work, she wrote at the end of her life, "has been more than compensation. It has been thrilling joy."[3] Haley's passion for her work exudes from every word she wrote and most contemporary descriptions about her. Haley can thus be seen as a role model for commitment and activism: Knowing the limitations of her own political power as a woman, she recognized the power of the sheer human force of inspiration on the public stage and in the classroom. The corporate giants and political leaders who opposed her knew this about her, and they feared her for it. "They are afraid of one woman," she said in a speech to labor colleagues in 1915. "They are afraid that one woman's spirit may be permitted to animate the souls of the teachers of this city who are sending out the future citizens."[4] For Haley, this was the power of public testimony and political activism, and ultimately, it was the power of organizing and educating citizens.

ENDNOTES

1. Robert L. Reid, ed., Battleground: *The Autobiography of Margaret A. Haley* (Urbana: University of Illinois Press, 1982), 270.

2. Ibid., xxxii–xxxiii.

3. Ibid., 275.

4. Address of Miss Margaret Haley before the Public Ownership League of the Chicago Federation of Labor, 29 August 1915, box 43 folder 3, CTF papers.

SELECTED BIBLIOGRAPHY

"Catherine Goggin." *The Journal of Education* 83 (13 January 1916).

"Chicago Teachers in the Union." *Appeal to Reason* (6 December 1902).

"Margaret A. Haley in Boston." *Journal of Education* 65 (7 November 1901).

"The American Federation of Teachers." *Life and Labor* (June 1916).

Addams, Jane. *Twenty Years at Hull House*. New York: Signet, 1981.

Alexander, Carter. *Some Present Aspects of the Work of Teachers' Voluntary Associations in the United States*. New York: Teachers College Press, 1910.

Allen, Elizabeth A. "Teachers' Pensions—The Story of a Women's Campaign," *The Review of Reviews* 15 (1897).

Baker, Paula. "The Domestication of Politics: Women and American Political Society, 1780–1920." *American Historical Review* 89 (April, 1984).

Barrett, James R. *Work and Community in the Jungle: Chicago's Packinghouse Workers, 1894–1922*. Urbana: University of Illinois Press, 1987.

Bass, Mrs. George. "Mrs. Young and the Chicago Schools." *School and Society* 2 (October 23, 1915).

Blount, Jackie M. "Ella Flagg Young and the Chicago Schools." In *Founding Mothers and Others: Women Educational Leaders during the Progressive Era*, ed. Alan R. Sadovnik and Susan F. Semel. New York: Palgrave, 2002.

———. "Manly Men and Womanly Women: Deviance, Gender Role Polarization, and the Shift in Women's School Employment, 1900–1976." *Harvard Educational Review* 66 (Summer 1996).

———. *Destined to Rule the Schools: Women and the Superintendency, 1873–1995* Albany: State University of New York Press, 1998.

Brown, Corinne S. "Why the Teachers Did It." *The Socialist Spirit* 2 (January 1903).

Buchanan, Frederick S. "Unpacking the NEA: The Role of Utah's Teachers at the 1920 Convention." *Utah Historical Quarterly* 41 (Spring 1973).

Buechler, Steven M. *The Transformation of the Woman Suffrage Movement: The Case of Illinois, 1850–1920.* New Brunswick, NJ: Rutgers University Press, 1986.

Buenker, John D. "Edward F. Dunne: The Limits of Municipal Reform." In *The Mayors: The Chicago Political Tradition*, ed. Paul M. Green and Melvin G. Holli. Carbondale: Southern Illinois University Press, 1987.

Bukowski, Douglas. *Big Bill Thompson, Chicago, and the Politics of Image.* Urbana: University of Illinois Press, 1998.

Candeloro, Dominic. "The Chicago School Board Crisis of 1907." *Journal of Illinois State Historical Society* 68 (November 1975).

Carter, Patricia A. *"Everybody's Paid but the Teacher": The Teaching Profession and the Women's Movement.* New York: Teachers College Press, 2002.

Chenery, William L. "Catherine Goggin." *Life and Labor* (February 1916).

Clark, Hannah B. *The Public Schools of Chicago: A Sociological Study.* Chicago: University of Chicago Press, 1897.

Clark, S. J. Duncan. "Militant Miss Haley: Still Fighting After Thirty Years." *Chicago Daily News*, 17 April 1931.

Collins , Cherry. "Regaining the Past for the Present: The Legacy of the Chicago Teachers' Federation." *History of Education Review* 13 (1984).

Counts, George. *School and Society in Chicago.* New York: Harcourt, 1928.

Creel, George. "Why Chicago's Teachers Unionized." *Harper's Weekly* (19 June 1915).

Cross, Robert D. *The Emergence of Liberal Catholicism in America.* Cambridge: Harvard University Press, 1958.

Cruice, Daniel L., "Direct Legislation in Illinois: A Story of Triumph for Popular Government." *Arena* 31 (June 1904).

Davis, Allen F. *American Heroine: The Life and Legend of Jane Addams.* New York: Oxford University Press, 1973.

Diner, Hasia. *Erin's Daughters in America: Irish Immigrant Women in the Nineteenth Century.* Baltimore: Johns Hopkins University Press, 1983.

Dodge, Chester C. *Reminiscences of a Schoolmaster.* Chicago: Ralph Fletcher Seymour, 1941.

Everett, Marshall. *The Great Chicago Theater Disaster.* Publishers Union of America, 1904.

Flanagan, Maureen A. *Charter Reform in Chicago.* (Carbondale: Southern Illinois University Press, 1987).

———. "Gender and Urban Political Reform: The City Club and the Woman's City Club of Chicago in the Progressive Era." *American Historical Review* 95 (October 1990).

————. *Seeing with Their Hearts: Chicago Women and the Vision of a Good City, 1871–1933*. Princeton, Princeton University Press, 2002.

Flint, Lillian C. "Pensions for Women Teachers." *The Century Magazine* (1901).

Foner, Philip S. *Organized Labor and the Black Worker, 1619–1973*. New York, Praeger: 1974.

Goggin, Catherine. "The Chicago Pension Law." *School Journal* 54 (1 May 1897).

Graebner, William. "Retirement in Education: The Economic and Social Function of the Teachers' Pension." *History of Education Quarterly* 18 (Winter 1978).

Haig, Robert Murray. "A History of the General Property Tax in Illinois." *University of Illinois Bulletin* 11 (June, 1914).

Haley, Margaret. "Why Teachers Should Organize." *Journal of the Addresses and Proceedings of the National Education Association* (1904).

————. "Single Tax Campaign in Seattle." *The Public* 15 (15 March 1912).

————. "The Factory System." *The New Republic* 40 (12 November 1924).

Hard, William. "Chicago's Five Maiden Aunts, " *American Magazine* 62 (September 1906).

————. "Margaret Haley, Rebel." *The Times Magazine* 1 (January 1907).

————. "The Fight for the Schools." *The Times Magazine* 1 (February 1907).

Herrick, Mary J. "Negro Employees of the Chicago Board of Education." PhD diss., University of Chicago, 1931.

————. *The Chicago Schools: A Social and Political History*. Beverly Hills: Sage, 1971.

Hogan, David. *Class and Reform: School and Society in Chicago, 1880-1930*. Philadelphia : University of Pennsylvania Press: 1985.

Holt, Glen E., and Dominic Pacyga, *Chicago: A Historical Guide to the Neighborhoods*. Chicago: Chicago Historical Society, 1979.

Ignatiev, Noel, *How the Irish Became White*. New York: Routledge, 1995.

Johnston, Shepherd. *Historical Sketches of the Public School System of the City of Chicago*. Chicago: Clark and Edwards, 1880.

Kliebard, Herbert M. "Dewey and the Herbartians: The Genesis of a Theory of Curriculum." In Herbert M. Kliebard, *Forging the American Curriculum: Essays in Curriculum Theory and History*. New York: Routledge, 1992.

Kytle Elizabeth. *Home on the Canal*. Cabin John, MD: Seven Locks Press, 1983.

Lagemann, Ellen Condliffe . "Experimenting with Education: John Dewey and Ella Flagg Young at the University of Chicago." *American Journal of Education* 104 (May 1996).

Lazarson, Marvin. "Teachers Organize: What Margaret Haley Lost." *History of Education Quarterly* 24 (Summer 1984).

Lowe, Robert. "The Chicago Teachers' Federation and its Legacy." In *Transforming Teacher Unions: Fighting for Better Schools and Social Justice,* ed. Bob Peterson and Michael Charney. Rethinking Schools: Milwaukee, 1999.

Lyons, John F. "The Limits of Professionalism: The Response of Chicago Schoolteachers to Cuts in Education Expenditures, 1929–1933." *Journal of Illinois History* 1 (Autumn 1998).

McCaffrey, Lawrence J. "The Irish-American Dimension," and Michael F. Funchion, "The Political and Nationalist Dimensions." In *The Irish in Chicago,* eds. Lawrence J. McCaffrey, Ellen Skerrett, Michael F. Funchion, and Charles Fanning. Chicago: University of Illinois Press, 1987.

McGerr, Michael. "Political Style and Women's Power, 1830–1930." *Journal of American History* 77 (December 1990).

McManis, John T. *Ella Flagg Young And a Half-Century of the Chicago Public Schools.* Chicago: A.C. McClurg, and Co., 1916.

Meyerowitz, Joanne J. *Women Adrift: Independent Wage Earners in Chicago, 1880–1930.* Chicago: University of Chicago Press, 1988.

Miller, Donald L. *City of the Century: The Epic of Chicago and the Making of America.* (New York: Simon and Schuster, 1996).

Miller, Kerby A. *Immigrants and Exiles: Ireland and the Irish Exodus to North America.* New York: Oxford University Press, 1985.

Moore, Joel Roscoe. *Taxation of Corporations in Illinois Other Than Railroads Since 1872.* Urbana: University of Illinois Press, 1913.

Munro, William Bennett, ed. *The Initiative, Referendum and Recall.* New York: D. Appleton and Co., 1912.

Murphy, Marjorie. "Progress of the Poverty of Philosophy: Two Generations of Labor Reform Politics: Michael and Margaret Haley." Paper delivered at Knights of Labor Centennial Symposium, Chicago, May 17-19, 1979.

———. "From Artisan to Semi-Professional: White Collar Unionism among Chicago Public School Teachers, 1870–1930." PhD diss., University of California, Davis, 1981.

———. "Taxation and Social Conflict: Teacher Unionism and Public School Finance in Chicago, 1898–1934." *Journal of the Illinois State Historical Society* 74 (1981).

———. "The Aristocracy of Women's Labor in America." *History Workshop* 22 (August 1986).

———. *Blackboard Unions: The AFT and the NEA, 1900–1980.* Ithaca: Cornell University Press, 1990.

Murray, Christine E. "Teaching as a Profession: The Rochester Case in Historical Perspective." *Harvard Educational Review* 62 (Winter 1992).

Nolan, Janet. *Servants of the Poor: Teachers and Mobility in Ireland and Irish America.* Notre Dame: University of Notre Dame Press, 2004.

O'Connor, Paula. "Grade-School Teachers Become Labor Leaders: Margaret Haley, Florence Rood, and Mary Barker of the AFT." *Labor's Heritage* 7 (Fall 1995).

O'Reilly, Mary. "What Organization of the Teachers Means to Labor." *Life and Labor* 5 (November 1915).

Pegram, Thomas R. *Partisans and Progressives: Private Interest and Public Policy in Illinois, 1870–1922.* Urbana: University of Illinois Press, 1992.

Provasnik, Stephen. "Compulsory Schooling, from Idea to Institution: A Case Study of the Development of Compulsory Attendance in Illinois, 1857–1907." PhD diss., University of Chicago, 1999.

Reese, William J. *Power and the Promise of School Reform: Grassroots Movements During the Progressive Era.* Boston: Routledge, 1986.

Reid, Robert L., ed. *Battleground: The Autobiography of Margaret A. Haley.* Urbana: University of Illinois Press, 1982.

Rice, J. M. *The Public School System of the United States.* New York: Arno Press, 1969. Originally published 1893.

Ricker, David Swing. "The School-Teacher Unionized." *Educational Review* 30 (November 1905).

Roberts, Maria Lettiere, and Richard Stamz. *Chicago's Englewood Neighborhood at the Junction.* Chicago: Arcadia, 2002.

Roberts, Sidney I. "The Municipal Voters' League and Chicago's Boodlers." *Journal of Illinois State Historical Society* 2 (Summer 1960).

Roediger, David R. *The Wages of Whiteness: Race and the Making of the American Working Class.* New York: Verso, 1991.

Rousmaniere, Kate. "Good Teachers Are Born, Not Made: Self-Regulation in the Work of Nineteenth-Century American Women Teachers." In *Discipline, Moral Regulation, and Schooling: A Social History,* ed. Kate Rousmaniere, Kari Dehli, and Ning de Coninck-Smith. New York: Garland Press, 1997.

——— "Sixteen Years in a Classroom." In *Silences and Images: The Social History of the Classroom,* ed. Ian Grosvenor, Martin Lawn and Kate Rousmaniere. New York: Peter Lang Publishers, 1999.

———. "Where Haley Stood: Margaret Haley, Teachers' Work, and the Problem of Teacher Identity." In *Telling Women's Lives: Narrative Inquiries in the History of Women's Education,* ed. Kathleen Weiler and Sue Middleton. Philadelphia: Open University Press, 1999.

———. "Margaret Haley and Irish Catholic Identity: The Political Education of an American Teacher Leader." *Vita Scholasticae* (Fall 1999).

————. "From Memory to Curriculum: Teachers and Educational Autobiography." *Teaching Education* (Spring 2000).

————. "Progressive Education and the Teacher: Margaret Haley's Vision." In *Founding Mothers and Others: Women Founders of Progressive Schools and Other Female Educational Leaders*, ed. Alan R. Sadovnik and Susan Semel. New York: St. Martin's Press, 2002.

————, "Being Margaret Haley, Chicago, 1903." *Paedagogica Historica* 39, No. 1/2 (2003).

————, with Kathleen Knight Abowitz. "Margaret Haley as Diva: A Case Study of a Feminist Citizen-Leader." *The Initiative Anthology* www.muohio.edu/InitiativeAnthology/ (2004).

Sanders, James W. *The Education of an Urban Minority: Catholics in Chicago, 1833–1965*. New York: Oxford University Press.

Schiltz, Mary C. "Women on the Chicago Board of Education: A Collective Biography of Three Members in the Early Twentieth Century." *Journal of the Midwest History of Education Society* 21 (1994).

Schneirov, Richard. "Rethinking the Relation of Labor to the Politics of Urban Social Reform in Late Nineteenth-Century America: The Case of Chicago." *International Labor and Working-Class History* 46 (Fall 1994).

Skerrett, Ellen. "The Development of Catholic Identity among Irish Americans in Chicago, 1880–1920." In *From Paddy to Studs: Irish American Communities in the Turn of the Century Era, 1880–1920*, ed. Timothy J. Meagher. New York: Greenwood Press, 1986.

————. "The Irish in Chicago: The Catholic Dimension." In *Catholicism, Chicago Style*, ed. Ellen Skerrett, Edward R. Kantowicz, and Steven M. Avella. Chicago: Loyola University Press, 1993.

Skocpol, Theda. *Protecting Soldiers and Mothers: The Political Origins of Social Policy in the United States*. Cambridge: Harvard University Press, 1992.

Skok, Deborah Ann. "Catholic Ladies Bountiful: Chicago's Catholic Settlement Houses and Day Nurseries, 1892–1930." PhD diss. University of Chicago, 2001.

Smith, Joan K. *Ella Flagg Young: Portrait of a Leader*. Ames, IA: Educational Studies Press, 1979.

Synon, Mary. "Women in Politics Are Soldiers in Second American Revolution." *Chicago Daily Journal* (2 February 1914).

Thomas, John L., *Alternative America: Henry George, Edward Bellamy, Henry Demarest Lloyd and the Adversary Tradition*. Cambridge: Harvard University Press, 1983.

Tostberg, Robert Eugene. "Educational Ferment in Chicago, 1883–1904." PhD diss., University of Wisconsin, 1960.

Tuttle, William M. "Labor Conflict and Racial Violence: The Black Workers in Chicago, 1894–1919." *Labor History* 10 (1969).

Urban, Wayne J. *Why Teachers Organized*. Detroit: Wayne State University Press, 1982.

———. *Gender, Race, and the National Education Association: Professionalism and Its Limitations*. New York: Routledge Falmer, 2000.

Wade, Louise Carroll. *Chicago's Pride: The Stockyards, Packingtown, and Environs in the Nineteenth Century*. Urbana: University of Illinois Press, 1987.

Wattenberg, William W. *On the Educational Front: The Reactions of Teachers' Associations in New York and Chicago*. New York: Columbia University Press, 1936.

Weiner, Lois. "Teachers, Unions, and School Reform: Examining Margaret Haley's Vision." *Educational Foundations* 10 (Summer 1996).

Wesley, Edgar B. *NEA: The First Hundred Years*. New York: Harper and Brothers, 1957.

Wheeler, Adade Mitchel. "Conflict in the Illinois Woman Suffrage Movement of 1913." *Journal of the Illinois State Historical Society* 76 (Summer 1983).

Winship, A. E. "A Woman's Victory for Schools." *Everybody's Magazine* 7 (October 1902).

Woodruff, George W. *Forty Years Ago! A Contribution to the Early History of Joliet and Will County*. Joliet: Joliet Republican Steam Printing, 1874.

Wrigley, Julia. *Class Politics and the Public Schools: Chicago, 1900–1950*. New Brunswick, NJ: Rutgers University Press, 1982.

Young, Ella Flagg. *Isolation in the Schools*. Chicago: University of Chicago Press, 1901.

INDEX